Poppies

A Guide to the Poppy Family
in the Wild and in Cultivation

Poppies

A Guide to the Poppy Family
in the Wild and in Cultivation

Revised Edition

Christopher Grey-Wilson

Timber Press · Portland, Oregon

First published 1993
Reprinted 1995

Revised edition published 2000

Typeset by SX Composing DTP, Rayleigh,
Essex

Printed and bound in Spain by Bookprint, S.L., Barcelona

Published in North America by

Timber Press, Inc.
The Heseltine Building
133 S.W. Second Avenue, Suite 450
Portland, Oregon 97204, U.S.A.

ISBN 0 88192 503 9

A catalog record for this book is available from the Library of Congress

Contents

Illustrations

COLOUR PHOTOGRAPHS

(Unless otherwise stated the photos are by the author)

1. *Macleaya cordata*, the Plumed Poppy, excellent in the herbaceous border but with tiny flowers for a poppy.
2. *Chelidonium majus* 'Flore Pleno', a quite plant for the woodland garden.
3. *Chelidonium majus* var. *laciniatum*, a cultivated form in which both the leaves and petals are dissected.
4. *Chelidonium majus* var. *grandiflorum* is the finest form of the Greater Celandine for gardens.
5. *Hylomecon japonicum* a Japanese woodlander for the spring border.
6. *Stylophorum diphyllum*, the American Celandine Poppy, revels in dappled shade in the garden.
7. *Stylophorum lasiocarpum*, the Chinese Celandine Poppy, easy and prolific in the woodland garden.
8. *Glaucium corniculatum*, the Orange Horned Poppy, probably the finest species in the genus for the garden where, once establish, it will seed around moderately.
9. *Glaucium flavum*, the Yellow Horned Poppy is a denizen of coastal habitats in Western Europe and the Mediterranean region.
10. *Glaucium flavum* var. *fulvum*, photographed in the Greek Peloponnese (Monemvasia), sports a brown spot at the base of each petal.
11. The western Chinese *Dicranostigma franchetiana* is a robust annual that is still rare in cultivation
12. *Dicranostigma lactucoides* inhabits the high dry inner valleys of the central Himalaya and southern Tibet; here photographed in the Marysyandi Valley of Nepal.
13. *Dicranostigma leptopodum*, the smallest species in the genus is relatively new to cultivation.
14. *Eomecon chionanthum* is a patch-forming perennial with decorative scalloped foliage and rather small white flowers.
15. The North American Bloodroot, *Sanguinaria canadensis*, is a plant for a humusy moist soil in dappled shade.

41. *Papaver kerneri*, a small alpine poppy, photographed on high screes of the Hoch Obir in the Italian Dolomites (photo: John Birks).
42. *Papaver lateritium* is a stoloniferous perennial from Turkey, rarely grown in gardens.
43. *Papaver lateritium* 'Fireball' is widely available, being often sold wrongly in garden centres and nurseries as *P. orientalis* 'Fireball'.
44. *Papaver lecoqii*, Babington's Poppy, is occasionally cultivated; it is native primarily to Western Europe including Britain.
45. *Papaver nudicaule* the so-called Iceland Poppy is a native of central and northern Asia.
46. *Papaver nudicaule*; a standard mixture being grown for seed production by Sahin in Zeeland, Holland, with white, yellow and orange predominating.
47. *Papaver oreophilum* is a rare perennial in cultivation, here photographed in the wild north of Mestia in the Georgian Caucasus.
48. *Papaver orientale* one of the prime parents in the evolution of the Oriental Poppies of gardens.
49. *Papaver* Orientalis Group 'Beauty of Livermere'.
50. *Papaver* Orientalis Group 'Cedric Morris', often sold as 'Cedric's Pink'.
51. *Papaver* Orientalis Group 'Curlilocks', one of several cut-petalled cultivars.
52. *Papaver* Orientalis Group 'Garden Glory'
53. *Papaver* Orientalis Group 'Grauwe Witwe'.
54. *Papaver* Orientalis Group 'John III', an excellent modern cultivar.
55. *Papaver* Orientalis Group 'Juliane'.
56. *Papaver* Orientalis Group 'Karine', one of a number of excellent modern German cultivars.
57. *Papaver* Orientalis Group 'Kleine Tanzerin'.
58. *Papaver* Orientalis Group 'Lilac Girl'.
59. *Papaver* Orientalis Group 'Patty's Plum', a unique colour amongst Oriental poppies and a favourite cottage garden flower.
60. *Papaver* Orientalis Group 'Perry's White', an old cultivar dating back to the nineteenth century.
61. *Papaver* Orientalis Group 'Petticoat'.
62. *Papaver* Orientalis Group 'Picotee'.
63. *Papaver* Orientalis Group 'Rosenpokal'.
64. *Papaver* Orientalis Group 'Suleika'.
65. *Papaver* Orientalis Group 'Türkenlouis'.
66. *Papaver* Orientalis Group 'Watermelon'.
67. *Papaver* Orientalis Group, 'Wisley Beacon', growing at the Royal Horticultural Society's garden at Wisley in Surrey.
68. Poppies of the Orientalis Group make fine garden plants, especially for the mixed herbaceous border or with summer flowering bulbs such as *Allium albopilosum*.
69. *Papaver* 'Red Gauntlet', a unique hybrid poppy between a red-flowered member of the Orientalis Group and *P. triniifolia*.

70. The Peacock Poppy, *Papaver pavoninum* has attractively marked flowers and drooping buds with two points.
71. *Papaver radicatum*, a denizen of Arctic tundra, here in the Kongsvoll, Arctic Norway (photo: John Birks).
72. *Papaver rhaeticum*, the common alpine poppy of many parts of the Pyrenees and the southern and western Alps, here on the Rolle Pass in the Dolomites (photo: John Birks)
73. *Papaver rhaeticum* on a high scree in the French Alps.
74. *Papaver rupifragum*, an endemic of cliffs in Andalucia which is rather scarce in cultivation.
75. The vibrant flowers of the Common Poppy, *Papaver rhoeas*, in a field in the Greek Peloponnese.
76. *Papaver rhoeas* relishes disturbed sites; here along a relatively new bypass close to Long Melford in Suffolk.
77. Where left unhindered by herbicides the Common Poppy, *Papaver rhoeas*, can make dense stands on arable land; here a typical British form.
78. *Papaver rhoeas*; a deeply coloured and well-marked form photographed in the Greek Peloponnese.
79. *Papaver rhoeas* 'in the wild' with semi-double blooms; photographed on the Long Melford bypass in Suffolk.
80. Single Shirley poppies come in a range of colours; they are all selections of *Papaver rhoeas*.
81. An attractive modern strain of Shirley poppy grown by Sahin in Holland.
82. A selection of *Papaver rhoeas* on the trial ground of Sahin in Zeeland, Holland, with single flowers, showing the range of colours that is possible.
83. As Pl. 81, but with semidouble flowers predominating.
84. *Papaver rhoeas* 'Mother of Pearl'.
85. *Papaver rhoeas* 'Angel's Choir', a semidouble selection from 'Mother of Pearl'; the reds should be removed from the selection in order to maintain the more pastel shades.
86. The Turkish endemic *Papaver spicatum* (widely known in gardens as *P. heldreichii*) is a noble and eye-catching border perennial.
87. *Papaver triniifolium* is another Turkish endemic that is a monocarpic perennial.
88. *Papaver somniferum*, the Opium Poppy, in a typical single form found in gardens.
89. The attractive bowl-shaped flowers of *Papaver somniferum*.
90. The Opium Poppy, *Papaver somniferum*, bears decorative fruit capsules that are much prized for dried flower arrangements.
91. Field production of *Papaver somniferum* in central France for the pharmaceutical industry and for seed production.
92. As Pl. 90.
93. An unnamed semi-double form of *Papaver somniferum* with near black flowers.
94. *Papaver somniferum* 'Pink Chiffon', a pink selection with semi-double flowers.

95. Double or Peony-flowered forms of *Papaver somniferum* come in a range of bright colours.
96. *Papaver somniferum* Peony-flowered Group 'Black Peony'.
97. *Papaver somniferum* Peony-flowered Group 'Purple Peony'.
98. *Papaver somniferum* Peony-flowered Group 'Crimson Peony'.
99. *Papaver somniferum* Peony-flowered Group 'Crimson and White'.
100. *Papaver somniferum* Peony-flowered Group 'Flemish Antique'.
101. *Papaver somniferum* Peony-flowered Group 'Frosted Salmon'.
102. *Papaver somniferum* Peony-flowered Group 'White Cloud'.
103. *Papaver somniferum* 'Danebrog', a single "Laciniatum" type.
104. *Papaver somniferum* 'Pink Bicton', a double "Laciniatum" type.
105. *Papaver somniferum* 'Swansdown', a semidouble "Laciniatum" type.
106. An unnamed double crimson cut-petalled "Laciniatum' type *of Papaver somniferum.*
107. *Papaver somniferum* 'Hen and Chickens', which is grown primarily for its extraordinary prolific fruit capsules.
108. *Roemeria refracta* photographed in the Andarab Valley in eastern Afghanistan where it replaces the Common Poppy, *Papaver rhoeas*, as a cornfield weed.
109. *Roemeria refracta* on arable land near Tashkent in Kazakstan; note the long narrow seed pods characteristic of the genus.
110. A selected form of *Roemeria refracta* in cultivation.
111. *Cathcartia villosa*, the Woodland Poppy, a native of the monsoon-rich central and eastern Himalaya.
112. *Cathcartia villosa* in cultivation.
113. *Meconopsis bella* in the upper Marsyandi Valley in central Nepal; it is one of the trickiest poppies to cultivate and is very rare in gardens.
114. The Himalayan Blue Poppy, *Meconopsis betonicifolia*, one of the most sought after and freely available members of the genus.
115. *Meconopsis betonicifolia* var. *alba*.
116. The very variable hybrid *Meconopsis* × *sheldonii* is a cross between two blue-flowered species common in cultivation, *M. betonicifolia* and *M. grandis*.
117. A form of *Meconopsis* × *sheldonii* with pale flowers photographed at Branklyn Botanic Garden in Scotland.
118. The Welsh Poppy, *Meconopsis cambrica*, in the wild; photographed in the Val d'Ossoue near Garvarnie in the French Pyrenees.
119. A prolific garden plant, *Meconopsis cambrica* is a coloniser in the garden with a long flowering season.
120. The orange-flowered form of the Welsh Poppy, *Meconopsis cambrica* var. *aurantiaca*.
121. The modern development of the Welsh Poppy, *Meconopsis cambrica*, includes both single and semi-double forms in yellow, orange or red.
122. *Meconopsis delavayi* in the wild; photographed at Wu-to-di north of Lijiang, Yunnan, in the Yulong Shan (Jade Dragon Mountains).
123. As Pl. 120, showing a rather different form in the wild.

124. *Meconopsis delavayi* being cultivated very successfully in a trough in Aberdeen, Scotland (photo: Ian Young).
125. *Meconopsis grandis* in cultivation in the 1980s at Jack Drake's nursery at Inshriach in Scotland.
126. A seedling of *Meconopsis grandis* from a wild collected Sikkimese source.
127. A form of *Meconopsis grandis* in cultivation at Branklyn Botanic Garden in Scotland.
128. Plants of *Meconopsis grandis* derived from GS600; the original collection made by Ludlow and Sherriff in Bhutan more than fifty years ago is no longer in cultivation.
129. *Meconopsis henrici* var. *psilonomma* photographed in the wild above Huang-long-si in NW Sichuan.
130. The true *Meconopsis horridula*, a denizen of high alpine meadows and moraines; photographed above Manang in the upper Marsyandi Valley of central Nepal.
131. *Meconopsis horridula* on the Thorung La in the central Nepalese Himalaya, growing at over 5000 m altitude.
132. *Meconopsis horridula* var. *racemosa* photographed on the Beima Shan in NW Yunnan at about 5200 m.
133. *Meconopsis integrifolia* subsp. *integrifolia* at Huang-long-si in NW Sichuan where it flowers during June and July.
134. *Meconopsis integrifolia* subsp. *integrifolia*, Huang-long-si, NW Yunnan; note the upright goblet-shaped flowers.
135. *Meconopsis integrifolia* subsp. *lijiangensis* on Da-xue-shan (Big Snow Mountain) on the Yunnan/Sichuan border, in June after overnight snow.
136. An unnamed form of *Meconopsis integrifolia* photographed on the Balang Shan in western Sichuan; this form has been called 'Wolong' in cultivation.
137. *Meconopsis lancifolia* in its typical form photographed on the Bemei Shan in NW Yunnan.
138. *Meconopsis lancifolia* on the Da-xue-shan (Big Snow Mountain) in NW Yunnan, where it flowers during June and July.
139. *Meconopsis napaulensis* in cultivation.
140. *Meconopsis napaulensis* in cultivation, showing the characteristic nodding flowers.
141. The young leaf-rosette of *Meconopsis paniculata* photographed on the Phephe La in central Bhutan.
142. An autumn rosette of *Meconopsis paniculata* photographed in the Jaljale Himal in eastern Nepal.
143. *Meconopsis paniculata* showing the giant panicle of nodding yellow flowers.
144. *Meconopsis paniculata* in cultivation.
145. *Meconopsis prattii* photographed near Napa Hai, Zhongdian region, in NW Yunnan; this is the plant that is commonly mistaken for *M. horridula* in gardens.
146. *Meconopsis prattii* near Beta Hai, Zhongdian region, NW Yunnan.

LINE ILLUSTRATIONS IN THE TEXT

Preface to the New Edition

The original edition of *Poppies*, first published in 1993, engendered a great deal of interest and showed above all the importance of this astonishingly attractive and diverse group of plants in our gardens.

It is particularly pleasing to have had the chance to update the original text, adding both new information and some new photographs. The main areas where revisions have taken place are to be found in the genus *Meconopsis* and the genus *Papaver*. In the former, those species not at present in cultivation have been added. This is primarily because, as more expeditions penetrate the remoter regions of Tibet and China, the seed of some are likely to be introduced. In addition, in the light of current research, there has been some extensive revisions of both the *M. horridula* and *M. integrifolia* complexes and the results are presented here as they affect the names of plants currently grown in our gardens. In *Papaver*, the cultivars of the *P. orientalis* complex have been updated, with more complete information provided. This has been made possible by the recent trials of Oriental Poppies at the Royal Horticultural Society Gardens at Wisley in Surrey. Revisions have also been made to the classification of the cultivars and cultivar groups in two other important garden species, *P. somniferum* and *P. rhoeas*, which will be especially useful to gardeners.

Other genera where extra information has been added include *Artomecon*, *Eschscholzia* and *Glaucium*.

Acknowledgements

I am greatly indebted to the following for help and advice in the preparation of this work and, in some instances, for the loan of photographs: Chris Brickell, Dick Brummitt, Phil Cribb and Tony Hall (RBG Kew), James Cobb, Jack Elliott, Sean Hogan, Dave King, Alan Leslie, Brian Mathew, Ron McBeath, John and Hilary Birks, Harold McBride, Linda Jones and Diana Miller (RHS Wisley), Graham Rice, Mache-Parker Sanderson, David Maxwell-Hide, Joe Sharman, Wol and Sue Staines and Ian Young. Very special thanks must go to my good friend in Holland, Kees Sahin, whose prodigious and enviable knowledge of annuals (and poppies in particular), especially their origins and historical development, has been fundamental in the preparation of the cultivar lists included in this work. Finally, to my wife Christine I am endlessly indebted for her fortitude in reading and re-reading the original manuscript.

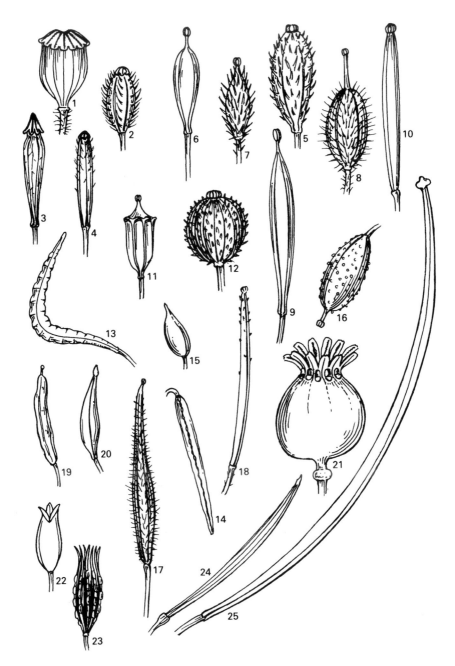

Various poppy fruits: 1. *Papaver rhoeas*, 2. *Papaver hybridum*, 3. *Papaver spicatum*, 4. *Papaver argemone*, 5. *Argemone sanguinea*, 6. *Meconopsis cambrica*, 7. *Meconopsis horridula*, 8. *Meconopsis napaulensis*, 10. *Cathcartia villosa*, 11. *Stylomecon heterophyllum*, 12. *Romneya coulteri*, 13. *Hypecoum imberbe*, 14. *Hypecoum pendulum*, 15. *Bocconia frutescens*, 16. *Stylophorum diphyllum*, 17. *Stylophorum lasiocarpum*, 18. *Roemeria hybrida*, 19. *Chelidonium majus*, 20. *Sanguinaria canadensis*, 21. *Papaver somniferum*, 22. *Platystigma linearis*, 23. *Platystemon californicus*, 24. *Eschscholzia california*, 25. *Glaucium flavum*

Introduction

Poppies are amongst the most-loved and cherished plants in our gardens. Their bold, yet seemingly delicate flowers in a great range of bright colours make them a striking feature in the flower border. What can be more imposing than a bed of Himalayan blue poppies, a drift of red corn poppies, the huge and majestic blooms of the oriental poppies, the brazen colours of the Iceland poppy, or the little pastel blooms of the alpine poppies. Variety is what characterises these plants. Most, in fact, have rather short-lived flowers, but a succession of buds open over a period and thus continue the show for many weeks.

It is therefore somewhat surprising that a book on poppies has not been produced until now, especially as there are so many different species and forms in cultivation. By poppies, I mean not only the true poppies, *Papaver*, but all the members of the poppy family. These include the famous blue poppies, *Meconopsis*; the Mexican or prickly poppies, *Argemone*; the Californian poppies, *Eschscholzia*; the plumed poppies, *Macleaya*; the horned poppies, *Glaucium*; the oriental, alpine, Iceland and annual poppies, *Papaver*; the tree poppies, *Romneya*; and many more besides. With so many different poppies to consider, it has not been possible to include every species in this book. In fact, there are many annual species, especially of *Papaver* itself, that are rare or little known. I have concentrated primarily on the species and forms in cultivation, together with those striking or particularly interesting species, both from a botanical as well as a horticultural point of view, that are not at present in cultivation, but really deserve to be introduced.

Each genus is dealt with separately, although the genera are grouped into their respective subfamilies (p. 29). Apart from general cultivation notes, more specialised cultural requirements are considered under the appropriate genus or species. The species in each genus are dealt with in strict alphabetical order for convenience. I have included important synonyms to avoid confusion or ambiguity and these are also all listed in the index at the end of the book. In addition, botanical authorities are given for all recognised species and synonyms. The authority or author's name (often abbreviated) refers to the botanist who first described the species and gave it its name. For instance *Papaver rhoeas* L., the common corn poppy, was first described by the Swedish botanist Linnaeus (Carl Linné) in 1753. Such matters need not concern the gardener to any great extent, save to recognise the fact that it is important to be able to put an accurate name on a particular plant. How often do we unwittingly purchase a plant from a nursery or garden centre or sow a packet of seeds under one name, only to find that it is already in the garden under quite another name? Just as it is important to know the names of one's friends and associates, so it is equally important to have standardised names for plants. The fact that species names are in Latin should not in any way inhibit their use. The standardisation of plant names throughout the world comes from an agreed set of rules, *The International Code of Botanical Nomenclature*. This technical and demanding book need in no way concern us here; suffice to say that it sets out various rules by which the correct name for a particular species can be ascribed and determined. Of course, for many plants (in fact the majority in our gardens), the names are well established and cause little concern. Name changes, the scourge of horticulturist and gardener alike, are rarely undertaken lightly and without due thought and detailed research. Nor should they be, as repeated 'fiddling' and changing of plant names can only cause concern and ridicule.

It was in fact Linnaeus who established the modern system of naming plants with the publication of his *Species Plantarum* of 1753. Each plant consists of two names, the generic one, such as *Papaver*, and a specific one, such as *rhoeas*. The two brought together give the plant its unique and individual name by which it can be distinguished from all its brethren.

In many ways, cultivar names present far more of a problem. They have much easier names to understand at first glance – 'Goliath', 'Ladybird', 'Midnight' and 'Orange Glow' for instance. Cultivar names are always presented in single parentheses and with a capital letter commencing each word. Modern cultivars are generally easy to trace and readily recognised. This is certainly not true of some of the older names where the correct identity of the plant in question is uncertain, especially where the plant may have become very rare, or indeed may have apparently disappeared from cultivation. In some cases one cannot always be certain what a particular plant found lingering in an old garden is and indeed if it complies fully with a particular cultivar name. In this respect the National Council for the Conservation of Plants and Gardens (the NCCPG) has done sterling work in locating old and rare cultivars. More important is the establishment of national collections of a great range of garden plants, along with active efforts to propagate some of the rarities and make them more available to the gardener. For instance, in Britain there are national collections of both *Meconopsis* and *Papaver* (oriental group).

The availability of plants has been made simple through the annual publication of RHS *The Plant Finder*, which lists in alphabetical order the names of species and cultivars of herbaceous plants, trees and shrubs, ferns, orchids and so on, and which nurseries supply them in Britain and Ireland. *The Plant Finder* does not include annuals and for these (there are many annual poppies of varying genera) one must browse through seed catalogues and lists. Specialist societies such as the Hardy Plant Society, the Royal Horticultural Society, the Alpine Garden Society, the Scottish Rock Garden Club, and similar organisations, produce their own seed lists; these are extremely useful and frequently include rarities not found elsewhere.

The Poppy Family
Papaveraceae

The Poppy family is a relatively small one with some 23 genera and about 250 species in total, distributed primarily in the northern temperate hemisphere, but with representatives in southern Africa as well as South America.

In the main, the family is a fairly homogeneous one and its members are readily recognised. Despite this, however, it is worth reviewing the various features of the genera that, combined, give the family its distinctive character.

THE PLANT

Most of the species are herbs, annual, biennial or perennial, although *Bocconia*, *Dendromecon* and *Romneya* (all American genera) are woody shrubs or subshrubs. When cut, the stems or leaves generally ooze a white, yellow, orange, or sometimes colourless latex; most parts of the plant possess a well-developed system of channels that secrete latex and this is very noticeable in plants such as the Opium Poppy, *Papaver somniferum*. Perennial species may be clump-forming or spread by means of underground stolons. Some species of both *Meconopsis* and *Papaver* are monocarpic perennials, which take a number of years to reach maturity, but, having flowered, they seed and die.

THE STEM

Most species have a well-developed leafy stem, although plants may have all the leaves basal and the flowers borne on leafless scapes, as for instance in *Papaver nudicaule*, the Iceland Poppy, or *Meconopsis quintuplinervia*, the Harebell Poppy. The stem may be simple (unbranched) or branched, usually rounded in sections, but sometimes ridged, smooth or variously adorned with hairs or bristles, or indeed a combination of these various features.

THE LEAVES

The leaves are alternate and without stipules, entire to variously lobed to deeply dissected. They are often aggregated into basal rosettes, which may be persistent or die away during the winter to leave a resting bud. The leaf-surface may be smooth or variously clothed with hairs, bristles or spines, or even pimply or warted.

THE INFLORESCENCE

Flowers may be solitary on basal scapes, borne on branched stems or organised into more formal inflorescences. The typical inflorescence is a raceme or panicle, or it may be a cyme, but rarely a spike. In many of the monocarpic species of *Meconopsis* and *Papaver* the inflorescence may be paniculate in the lower part, but racemose above (i.e. the lower flowers are borne on lateral branches, the upper directly from the main axis of the inflorescence). In *Bocconia* and *Macleaya* the numerous small flowers are borne in diffuse panicles. The inflorescence is terminate, with a flower, often the first to open, terminating the main axis (i.e. at the top). The flowers may be bractless or subtended by a bract, which is often leaflike.

THE FLOWER

Flowers in the Poppy Family are generally large and showy, often brightly coloured, with a relatively simple structure. There are two or three sepals in a single whorl; these closely envelop the flower in bud, but soon fall once the flowers begin to open, so that they are absent from the mature flower in most instances. In *Eschscholzia* the sepals are united into a single hoodlike structure that falls away in one piece. The sepals may be smooth, hairy or bristly. The petals are borne in two whorls (rows) and are most frequently four in total, although six is common in *Argemone* and up to sixteen in the Bloodroot, *Sanguinaria*. The petals are frequently crumpled in bud and have a silky texture, often being very thin and, in some cases, semi-transparent. In many cultivated forms of *Papaver* there are double or semi-double flower forms in which multiple petals occur and these generally wholly or partially replace the stamens. The genera *Bocconia* and *Macleaya* are unique in the family in being petalless and in having small, relatively inconspicuous flowers. There are usually numerous stamens, which form a conspicuous boss in the centre of the cup- or bowl-shaped flowers. In *Hypecoum* and *Pteridophyllum*, sometimes placed in a separate family (p. 29), there are only four stamens. The ovary consists of two or more fused carpels, but usually with a single compartment with intruding placenta that carry the ovules (unfertilised seeds) – the number of these placenta is equal to the number of carpels. The stigmas are equal in number to the number of carpels comprising each ovary; these are sessile or borne on a distinct style or styles.

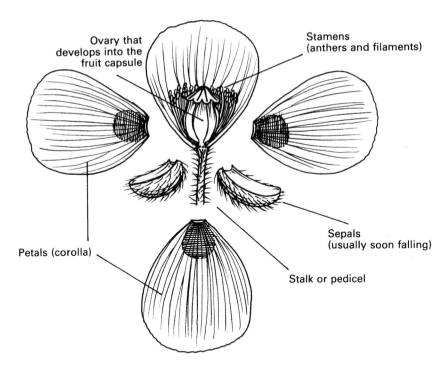

Ovary that develops into the fruit capsule

Stamens (anthers and filaments)

Sepals (usually soon falling)

Petals (corolla)

Stalk or pedicel

Diagram of a typical poppy flower

THE FRUIT

Superficially, the fruit is more variable than any other feature and the characters of the fruit are often very useful diagnostic features for separating the different genera. Most have a capsular fruit that opens by slits or apical pores, but the capsule shape varies from long and linear to elliptical, pear-shaped or globose. Linear capsules may split from the base, as in *Eschscholzia*, or from the top, as in *Glaucium*. Such capsules may dehisce explosively to expel the seed violently, flinging them well away from the parent plant. In the capsule type that dehisce by apical pores (*Papaver* and *Meconopsis*), the dispersal of the seed is passive, the seeds being knocked out by the wind, like pepper from a pepperpot. In some genera there is a distinct style, in others there is no style at all. In *Papaver* the capsule is crowned by a stigmatic disk with radiating stigmatic rays. In *Platystemon* the carpels are more or less free and follicle-like, being united only towards the base. The fruits contain numerous seeds, which often possess an oily endosperm.

In summary, the features that distinguish Papaveraceae are the presence of latex, the two-to-three parted flowers, with sepals and petals in whorls of two or three, the quickly deciduous sepals, the crumpled or wrinkled petals, the large number of stamens and the usually unilocular ovary and capsular fruits.

Cultivation

Although more detailed and specific cultural requirements are included under the different genera, some comments are useful at this point. In general terms it has to be said that the majority of poppies in cultivation are not difficult to grow, with the exception of some species of *Meconopsis*, which demand more specialised conditions if they are to succeed. However, this particular genus has a certain air of exclusiveness that it certainly does not warrant and all who love poppies should certainly be able to grow one or two species, particularly the beautiful Himalayan Blue Poppy, *M. betonicifolia*. Unfortunately, many people in the past have purchased a packet of seeds of this charming and eagerly sought species only to find that nothing germinated or that the resultant seedlings quickly rotted away. However, with care, it can be raised and flowered successfully, even in drier areas and, in any case, plants are often available at good garden centres.

Most poppies will thrive in any average, well-drained garden soil. Nearly all (again with the exception of some species of *Meconopsis*) will grow equally happily in an alkaline, neutral or slightly acid soil, although few will tolerate very acid conditions. With the exception of the Welsh Poppy, *Meconopsis cambrica*, most species of *Meconopsis*, *Cathcartia* and the various forest poppies of the genera *Chelidonium*, *Eomecon*, *Hylomecon*, *Sanguinaria* and *Stylophorum* thrive best in a moist, humus-rich soil – one which has had plenty of organic matter added to it. No poppies like waterlogged soils or heavy clays that retain a lot of moisture during the winter months. Most species in these genera prefer sheltered semi-shaded places in the garden, being particularly effective in the dappled shade of the woodland garden, where deep, leafy, moist soils are greatly to their liking.

Many of the more robust perennial species, as well as the hardy annual types, make fine border plants. The smaller alpine poppies (*Meconopsis* and *Papaver*) are ideal for pockets on the rock garden or scree, or in a large trough or container.

There is some evidence to suggest that the glorious blues of the finest *Meconopsis*, *M. betonicifolia*, *M. grandis* and *M. horridula* for instance, are developed best on acid rather than alkaline soils. Although they will thrive perfectly happily on alkaline soils, the pure blues may well become muddied with pink or purple. To overcome this, special acid beds can be prepared in much the same way as for other acid-loving plants.

Most of the annual poppies, especially species of *Argemone*, *Eschscholzia*, *Hypecoum*, *Papaver* and *Roemeria*, prefer open, sunnier positions in the garden; in deep shade they become drawn, weedy and produce fewer flowers. They are also tolerant of far drier soils and drifts in the flower border can be very effective. Rigorous thinning of the seedlings is essential to allow plants sufficient space in which to develop. Supports, wires or branched-sticks placed around and amongst the young plants of the taller-growing types will provide them with support at maturity and help prevent them being blown over or weighed down by heavy rainfall. Many of the larger annual types such as the Shirley, Iceland and Californian Poppies, *Papaver commutatum* and *Dicranostigma franchetiana* are good fillers for gaps in shrub and herbaceous borders.

Perennial poppies in genera such as *Glaucium*, *Macleaya* and *Papaver* will succeed best in the average flower border. Most will thrive in a sunny position under similar conditions to the annual species and cultivars.

The smaller alpine poppies are low and tufted with solitary flowers borne on leafless stalks. These rather delicate-looking plants prefer very well-drained conditions in full sun and, despite their appearance, they are mostly very hardy and wind-resistant. However, in the wild they are plants of rocky places, screes and moraines, and require very well-drained conditions in our gardens. The rock garden, scree, raised bed or trough is much to their liking, where the gritty coarse compost mimics their native homes in high mountain regions, or Arctic tundra.

The shrubby genera, *Dendromecon* and *Romneya*, are natives of sunny California, where they grow in hot dry habitats. In our gardens they require all the shelter and sun that is possible. In fact romneyas are surprisingly hardy and although cut to the ground during severe winter weather, they can normally be expected to sprout again from below ground during the following spring. Even in my former East Anglian garden, where cold winters with biting east winds were the norm, this exciting shrubby poppy survived and flowered for a number of years. Although often grown in open borders, it is perhaps at its best against a sunny sheltered wall, where it will grow far taller than in more open positions. Beware, however, of its suckering and somewhat invasive tendencies. *Dendromecon*, on the other hand, is much less often seen in gardens because it is a far more tender shrub and needs careful protection during the winter if it is to survive outdoors. If cut back by severe weather, it will not sprout again from below ground level.

PROPAGATION

Most poppies can be grown from seed. In fact, with the annual species, the monocarpic ones and those that tend to be short-lived perennials, seed is the only sure means of maintaining and increasing these plants in cultivation. For these types a regular regime of collecting and storing seed is essential, otherwise the plants will soon be lost.

Seed should be collected the moment it is ripe and quickly dried in a cool place. It can be stored in dry packets or containers in a cool place or refrigerator until required. Seed should be thoroughly cleaned of chaff as this might harbour harmful pests or diseases. Some poppy seeds have a long viability, but others, unfortunately, soon decline or go into a dormancy which appears to be difficult to break without very specialised cultural techniques such as the use of growth hormones. In any event, the longer seed is stored, the poorer will be the resultant germination. For this reason it is often recommended that seed of the rarer types, and especially some of the *Meconopsis*, is sown the moment it is harvested. If this is done early enough in the summer, then the resultant seedlings can be quickly pricked out and good young plants established before the onset of winter.

Seeds of many poppies, particularly *Meconopsis* and some *Papaver* species, require light to germinate and should be only very lightly covered when sown. A very thin layer of silver sand or vermiculite will allow enough light to reach the seeds whilst, at the same time, keeping the vicinity of the seeds sufficiently damp.

Seeds of the hardy annual poppies present few difficulties. It can be direct sown where the plants are to flower; seedlings generally dislike being pricked out or moved. Seed can be sown in the autumn or early spring. I always prefer the latter as the problems of overwintering young seedlings outdoors during very cold or very wet winters are too great. The advantage is that, if the young plants come through the winter satisfactorily, then they will come into bloom long before their spring-sown cousins. Always sow thinly to avoid wasting seed and to limit the rather irksome task of thinning out the seedlings. In some gardens the annual and some of the perennial species seed around freely and there is often no need to sow fresh batches each year, although be prepared for seedlings coming up in the most unlikely places. There are even fortunate individuals (mainly in cooler, moister gardens) who boast of self-sown Blue Poppies!

For most of the perennial types, sowing in the winter or early spring is the norm, despite what I have said. Seed is perhaps best sown in pots or pans using a normal seed compost for the majority of species. *Meconopsis* (except *M. cambrica*) species and seed of the various woodland-loving poppies, such as *Hylomecon* and *Stylophorum*, require a moister peat-based compost, which should never be allowed to dry out, otherwise all will be lost. Again, sow thinly and cover the seeds lightly, topping the pot with a thin layer of fine grit. Pots can be placed in frames or in the glasshouse to await germination. Seedlings of the shade-loving types require shielding from bright sunshine, whereas the alpine species seem to demand it. All seedlings are best pricked out the moment they are large enough to handle. The longer it is left, the more tricky the operation becomes, the more tangled the roots and the greater the likely losses. Seedlings should be carefully protected against the ravages of slugs and marauding insects, but also from damping off, which can sometimes devastate a fine pan of *Meconopsis* seedlings.

Sometimes seed may fail to germinate in the first season, but wait for another year. There is little that can be done about this except to be patient and to avoid the temptation of throwing out the pot thinking that all is dead. During this waiting period the compost should be kept rigorously clear of any alien growth, by hand weeding.

Pots and containers are best watered from below by plunging pots up to their rims in a basin of water. This avoids the problems of washing out the compost or floating all the seeds to one side of the pot. Of course, where large numbers of pots are involved, this procedure is impractical and a watering can with a fine rose attached should suffice.

Seed of perennial cultivars, especially the blousy Oriental Poppies, will seldom come true to type, so be prepared for a mixed and variable batch of progeny. It is always worth a gamble, for one may get an exceptional and unusual form or colour which may be well worth maintaining and propagating. Poor forms and seedlings are best discarded immediately and the temptation to give the plants their parental cultivar name is best avoided at all costs – for obvious reasons, as such practices cause confusion and bring the grower into disrepute. Where several species or cultivars of *Meconopsis* or *Papaver* are grown in close proximity, expect some hybrids to result. Most of these may be extremely fine plants, but to maintain the true species it may be necessary to isolate individual plants and to collect seed only from these, unless of course one prefers the hybrids.

It is a strange fact that amongst growers a plant, however beautiful, immediately takes on a new status once it becomes a success and begins to take over. It becomes less desirable or even a weed and has to be eliminated. In its place other rarer and more difficult plants are sought to fill the void and to challenge the skill of the grower. But many poppies look at their best where they self-sow amongst other flowers in the border.

Perennial poppies can be increased by division, although not those with a tuft of shoot from a single thickened taproot. Certainly, this is a good method for increasing Oriental Poppies and some of the fine forms of *Meconopsis grandis* and *M.* × *sheldonii*. This can be attempted after flowering or in the spring as growth commences. On the whole, though, it is best to establish divisions well before the autumn. Division usually requires the digging up of the parent plant, although suitable slices can sometimes be removed without such an effort. Portions with some attached roots can be cut off (I use a sharp kitchen knife when my wife is not looking!) and the portions planted back in the same bed or potted up. Until established, careful watering and shading will be necessary.

Oriental Poppies can also be readily propagated from root-cuttings and this method is employed commercially in order to get enough stock. Thick fleshy and healthy pieces of root are removed from the parent plant. These are cut into sections 3–4 cm (1⅕–1⅗ in) long and any fine lateral roots removed. The pieces can then be inserted upright (with the original upper end at the top) in pots or frames of silver sand or a sand-peat mixture. The cut end should lie at the surface of the pot. Root cuttings can be treated with a suitable water-based fungicide. Root-cuttings can be taken any time in the spring or summer and generally take four to six weeks before new shoots appear. The cuttings can then be potted on. For the average gardener, this procedure is not generally necessary as ordinary division will supply all the plants one is likely to need.

PESTS AND DISEASES

Most poppies are remarkably free from the attacks of pests and diseases. Slugs and snails may attack seedlings or the emerging shoots in the spring and can be controlled with one of a number of proprietary deterrents available on the market today. Aphids (both greenfly and blackfly –

especially the black bean aphid, *Aphis fabae*) can attack certain species, particularly when they are in bud. Capsid bugs may also sometimes become a problem, especially with young plants. These pests often cause distortion of the flowers or puckering of the leaves. A systemic insecticide provides lasting control or, if like me you distrust such chemicals, then a milder spray such as liquid derris, sprayed at regular intervals will be control enough. Some poppies (of various genera) dislike certain types of systemic sprays, especially if used at a greater strength than the manufacturer advises. Yellowing foliage and distorted growth are indicators of such spray damage. Soil pests such as wireworms (click beetles) or leather jackets (crane-fly maggots) may occasionally attack the base of the plants, but this is rare in my experience. Vine weevils can sometimes prove troublesome, especially with the smaller woodland species.

Fungal infections of seedlings and young plants can prove a serious problem. By the time this has been noticed, many of the young plants may already have succumbed. Young or mature plants of some species, particularly *Meconopsis* and *Papaver*, may suffer from downy mildew (*Peronospora* species), which can be fatal to young seedlings; it is often revealed as yellow blotches on the leaves, with grey mould beneath. Treatment with fungicides can be effective, but many poppy seedlings and young plants are easily damaged by chemical sprays, even when used at the manufacturers' recommended application rate. Better still is to try and control such problems by ensuring that pots and composts are completely sterile in the first instance, that seeds are sown thinly and young plants kept well spaced and with ample ventilation. They must not, of course, become desiccated.

AS CUT FLOWERS

Poppies are often said to make poor cut flowers and this is certainly true of those which are quick to drop their petals. However, a number of different types are sold as cut flowers in Europe. These include the large and flamboyant Oriental Poppies, the Iceland Poppy (*P. nudicaule*) and the Tulip Poppy (*Hunnemania fumariifolia*). Others also make good cut flowers: the Californian Poppies (*Eschscholzia californica*) and the Plumed Poppies (*Macleaya cordata* and *M. microcarpa*). Most poppies 'bleed' badly when cut and soon wilt. This can be overcome by sealing the wounds by burning the ends with a match or lighter, or better still by placing the cut ends into boiling water for a few seconds. This process keeps the stems turgid and upright and prevents wilting. Poppies are best cut just before the buds burst open, for they are great fun to watch unfold, will last longer in a vase and are less likely to get bruised in transit. If cut too immature the buds may fail to open, so the right stage has to be carefully judged.

Classification

Wallace Ray Ernst (1962) outlined the classification of the Poppy Family in his extensive *Comparative Morphology of the Papaveraceae*. In this, the family is divided into four subfamilies based upon critical details of the floral morphology and fruit characteristics. Although this is fairly technical, I have included the main details here for sake of completeness.

1. **Subfamily Chelidonioideae.** A very diverse subfamily with nine genera and some 20–30 species. They mostly possess simple multicellular hairs (but branched in *Bocconia* and *Macleaya*). The ovary consists of two wholly united carpels and the fruit-capsules dehisce into two valves along their entire length, either from the top or from the bottom; the capsules have particularly well-developed dorsal traces (veins). The seeds are often arillate. Genera: *Bocconia, Chelidonium, Dicranostigma, Eomecon, Glaucium, Hylomecon, Macleaya, Sanguinaria, Stylophorum.*

2. **Subfamily Eschscholzioideae.** A smaller and more uniform subfamily with only three genera and about 17 species. The hairs are unicellular. The ovary consists of two wholly fused carpels, as in the previous subfamily, and the fruit-capsules also have well-developed dorsal traces and dehisce violently into two valves from the base to the top. Genera: *Dendromecon, Eschscholzia, Hunnemannia.*

3. **Subfamily Papaveroideae.** The largest subfamily with nine genera and probably in excess of 150 species. Most possess multicellular hairs, often in many rows. The ovary consists of three or more wholly united carpels and the fruit-capsules have poorly developed or no dorsal traces and dehisce by pores or valves, in the latter instance generally from the top downwards. In addition, the ovary and fruit generally have a pronounced stigmatic area, which reaches its most pronounced manifestation in the radiating stigmatic rays seen in the true poppies, *Papaver*. Genera: *Arctomecon, Argemone, Canbya, Cathcartia, Meconopsis, Papaver, Roemeria, Romneya, Stylomecon.*

4. **Subfamily Platystemonoideae.** A small and very distinct subfamily with four genera and 15 species. The hairs are multicellular, often borne in many rows. The ovary consists of a number (often four or more) of carpels held closely together and fused only towards the base, each with its own discrete stigma. The fruit-capsule consists of a bunch of follicles which pull apart at maturity and split along the line of the placenta, not into valves. Genera: *Hesperomecon, Meconella, Platystemon, Platystigma.*

In addition, I have included in this book two further and fairly closely related genera, *Hypecoum* and *Pteridophyllum*. Most authorities have varied in their treatment of these two over the years, some placing them together with *Corydalis, Dicentra* and *Fumaria* into the Papaveraceae, whilst others split off all these genera into a distinct family, the Fumariaceae. However, *Hypecoum* and *Pteridophyllum* have rather intermediate characters between these two families and conform rather unhappily with both and for this reason are sometimes accorded a family of their own, the Hypecoaceae. As if this were not enough, *Pteridophyllum* is also accorded a family of its own, the Pteridophyllaceae, by some authorities. Now, I have put all this in not so much to confuse the reader, but to stress the point that plant families are not always as clear cut as they may often appear to be and that genera do sometimes occur with intermediate characters, or ones that simply do not fit comfortably into a particular family. Both *Hypecoum* and *Pteridophyllum* have small, rather poppy-like flowers with four petals, but there are only four stamens. The fruit is a narrow, two-valved capsule. In both genera the inner petals are somewhat larger than the outer and in the case of *Hypecoum* are generally three-lobed. Although *Hypecoum* has dissected foliage very similar to many members of the Papaveraceae, *Pteridophyllum* stands distinct with its neat, pinnate and rather fernlike, leaves.

RELATED FAMILIES

The most closely related family, as already seen, is the fumitory family, Fumariaceae. Despite obvious similarities in the foliage and fruit characters between the two families, the flowers of the Fumariaceae look very different and are more complex structures all together. The species are annual or perennial herbs, sometimes climbing by leaf-tendrils, and produce a watery sap when cut. The inflorescence is usually racemose and the flowers often nodding or half-nodding. There are two, often tiny and persistent, sepals and four petals. One or both of the outer petals are pouched or spurred at the base and are generally partially united to the smaller inner petals. The six stamens are fused together into two bundles of three, with the filaments extending backwards into the pouched base (bases) of the outer petals, where they secrete nectar. Well-known genera in gardens include the weedy fumitories, *Fumaria*, *Corydalis* and the Dutchman's breeches or bleeding hearts, *Dicentra*.

The cabbage or mustard family, Cruciferae, is also regarded by many authorities to be closely related to the Papaveraceae. The two are not likely to be confused. Members of the Cruciferae generally have rather small flowers with four persistent sepals and four petals, often forming a cross-shape, and six stamens. Many species have more complex hairs, often medifixed or stellate (starry). The ovary consists of two fused carpels, which are often partitioned by a false-septum or membrane. The fruit varies enormously in shape and details, although some come close to the simple linear siliqua-like structures found in certain genera of the Papaveraceae, such as *Chelidonium* and *Dicranostigma*.

DISTRIBUTION

The genus *Papaver*, by far the largest in the family, is distributed primarily in Europe, western and central Asia, with a cluster of closely related species in Arctic regions, northern Asia and Japan; there is a single species in the south-western USA and one in southern Africa. *Glaucium*, *Hypecoum* and *Roemeria* are distributed from Europe to central Asia, whereas *Chelidonium* stretches right across from Europe to Japan.

Exclusively Asiatic genera are *Cathcartia*, *Dicranostigma*, *Eomecon*, *Hylomecon*, *Macleaya*, *Meconopsis* (with one species in western Europe) and *Pteridophyllum*. Interestingly, apart from a few species of *Papaver* and one *Stylophorum*, no other genera are shared in common between Asia and North America.

However, western North America, especially California and the neighbouring territories, are particularly rich in Papaveraceae, with the following genera represented: *Arctomecon*, *Argemone*, *Canbya*, *Dendromecon*, *Eschscholzia*, *Hesperomecon*, *Hunnemannia*, *Meconella*, *Platystemon* and *Stylomecon*. *Sanguinaria* and one species of *Stylophorum* (*S. diphyllum*) are found in the cooler woodlands of North America, away from the west coast; indeed, they are the only members of the Papaveraceae to be found on the eastern side of the continent.

Argemone stretches southwards from the southern United States into Mexico and Central and South America, but *Bocconia* is the only genus exclusively restricted to South America.

Key to Genera

(⋆ exclusively New World genera)

1. Flowers without petals, small and borne in larger terminal panicles . . 2
   Flowers with obvious petals, often large and showy, solitary or in umbels, racemes or panicles 3

2. Leaves palmately-lobed and -veined; plants herbaceous: **Macleaya**
   Leaves pinnately-lobed and -veined; plants shrubby or sub-shrubby: **Bocconia**

3. Leaves mainly opposite or whorled 4
   Leaves alternate or all basal 5

4. Stamens 6–12; carpels mostly 3, united; petals soon deciduous, 3–4 mm, (⅛ in) long: **Meconella⋆**
   Stamens numerous; carpels 6–25, beaded, separating at maturity; petals persistent, 6–20 mm, (¼–⅘ in) long: **Platystemon⋆**

5. Plants shrubby, at least at the base 6
   Plants annual, biennial or perennial, never shrubby 8

6. Plants very prickly, both in leaf and fruit: **Argemone fruitcosa⋆**
   Plants not prickly at all 7

7. Flowers yellow, 5–7.5 cm (2–3 in) across; leaves unlobed,
   entire: *Dendromecon★*
   Flowers white, 10–13 cm (4–5⅕ in) across; leaves lobed: *Romneya★*

8. Leaves cut into numerous linear segments; sap watery 9
   Leaves not as above; sap latex-like, white, yellow or orange usually . 11

9. Petals 3-lobed, the inner pair smaller than the outer; flowers often
   weakly zygomorphic: *Hypecoum*
   Petals entire, generally more or less equal in size; flowers never
   zygomorphic 10

10. Sepals united, hoodlike: *Eschscholzia★*
    Sepals free, not hoodlike: *Hunnemania★*

11. Leaves orbicular, lobed or scalloped; flowers white 12
    Leaves not as above; flowers various colours 13

12. Flowers solitary, scapose; petals 6+; leaves lobed: *Sanguinaria★*
    Flowers in long-stemmed umbels; petals usually 4; leaves
    scalloped: *Eomecon*

13. Leaves pinnately-lobed, frondlike, with broad
    segments: *Pteridophyllum*
    Leaves entire or variously lobed, but never frondlike 14

14. Fruit-capsule 3-valved; leaves all basal: *Platystigma★*
    Fruit-capsule not as above; leaves basal or along stems 15

15. Fruit-capsules linear, siliqua-like, generally splitting lengthwise
    when ripe 16
    Fruit-capsules globose to oblong or elliptical, generally dehiscing
    by pores or slits in the upper third when ripe 22

16. Stem-leaves amplexicaule (clasping), unstalked; flowers yellow
    or orange 17
    Stem-leaves not amplexicaule, generally stalked; flowers yellow,
    orange, red or violet 18

17. Stigma 2-lobed; fruit-capsule without a horny apex: *Dicranostigma*
    Stigma not 2-lobed; fruit-capsule with a horny apex (like a small
    arrowhead):   *Glaucium*

18. Flowers red or violet; fruit-capsule long and linear: *Roemeria*
    Flowers yellow or orange; fruit-capsule short-cylindrical to elliptical
    in outline 19

19. Flowers often solitary; stems unbranched: *Hylomecon*
    Flowers clustered or several on each stem from the upper leaf-axils;
    stems often branched 20

20. Leaves circular in outline, palmately-lobed: *Cathcartia*
    Leaves trifoliate to pinnate 21

21. Flowers rather small, 15–25 mm (⅗–1 in) across, with narrow non-overlapping petals; style very short; bracts absent: ***Chelidonium***
Flowers larger, at least 30 mm (1⅕ in) across, with broader, partly overlapping petals; style obvious; bracts present: ***Stylophorum***

22. Plants tiny, less than 3 cm (1⅕ in) tall; stamens 6–9:   ***Canbya***★
Plants at least 8 cm (3⅕ in) tall; stamens usually numerous 23

23. Plant decidedly spiny or prickly 24
Plants smooth or hairy, sometimes roughly so but not prickly 25

24. Sepals 3, horned; petals white, yellow or golden, occasionally lavender: ***Argemone***★
Sepals 2, not horned; petals usually blue or yellow, occasionally pink, violet or purple: ***Meconopsis***

25. Style absent; ovary topped by stigmatic disc, flat, convex or somewhat concave: ***Papaver***
Style present; ovary not as above 26

26. Annuals with dimorphic leaves; flowers orange-red, rather flat: ***Stylomecon***
Perennials without dimorphic leaves; flowers various colours, but if red, then cup-shaped or lantern-shaped 27

27. Sepals 3; petals 6, white or yellow; plants of semi-desert regions: ***Arctomecon***★
Sepals 2; petals 4–10, white, yellow, blue, purple or red; plants of moist mountains and woodland: ***Meconopsis***

I
Subfamily
Chelidonioideae

The Plumed Poppies
Macleaya

Of all the various members of the poppy family, the genus *Macleaya* is the most unpoppy-like in both leaf and flower. The genus contains only two, rather similar, species that are stout perennials with stiff, erect stems, broad, lobed leaves and large misty panicles of countless tiny flowers.

Macleaya is an Old World genus restricted to China and Japan. The genus is named in honour of Alexander Macleay (1767–1848), one-time secretary of the Linnean Society in London, but later Colonial Secretary for New South Wales. *Macleaya* is readily distinguished by its tall herbaceous stems and alternately arranged palmate leaves with their distinct palmate vein pattern (venation). The large inflorescence is a widely branching panicle with many small flowers which are without petals but there are four small sepals and a cluster of up to 30 stamens. The small, elliptical, somewhat fleshy, fruit-capsule splits from the apex downwards and contains between one and six seeds.

The juice of plumed poppies is orange and will stain the skin, rather like iodine. Indeed, in China the juice is used as an antiseptic treatment for cuts and blisters and may well have other medical uses.

Macleaya was at one time included in the New World genus *Bocconia*, but today most authorities recognise two separate and quite distinct genera. *Bocconia* differs in being a genus of shrub or subshrubs mostly with pinnate leaves, although they may occasionally be unlobed. What is important is the fact that the leaf-veins are pinnately arranged. In addition, the fruit capsule opens from the base upwards and the seeds are adorned with a conspicuous cup-like aril.

The two species of plumed poppies are bold and handsome plants in the garden, fully hardy and thriving on a variety of soils, although preferring a deep moist loam in a sunny position; they dislike very dry soils or exposed positions where the foliage can be easily bruised. Being tall, they are suitable subjects for the back of a deep herbaceous border. However, isolated from other plants and given a border to themselves, a grouping of several plants can be a very attractive feature, the striking leaves a foil to the feathery panicles of flower, which are borne in mid-summer. I have seen them used to good effect in this way as a group planting on the edge of a large lawn. Generally speaking, these are not plants for the small garden, but for large gardens and parks they can provide a trouble-free feature. The stems can be cut down in the late autumn after frost has destroyed the foliage. Then, in the spring, a generous mulch of well-rotted manure or compost will assure vigorous shoots for the following summer. When the clumps get too large and congested, they can be dug up and divided; this can be undertaken in the autumn or the early spring.

Macleayas can also be propagated by the removal of suckers without disturbing the parent plant, or by cuttings. Cuttings can be taken in early summer by cutting up the stem into one node pieces, each with a large leaf attached – discard any damaged leaves or the smaller, upper ones. These pieces can be treated with a suitable hormone rooting agent and then inserted (right way up) into pots filled with a mixture of equal parts peat and sand, and placed in a propagating frame or on a mist bench. Once rooted, the cuttings should be quickly potted on and kept growing by feeding and repotting so that they have time to form a substantial root system by the autumn. Their chances of surviving their first winter are thus greatly improved and the young plants can be planted out the following spring. Plants can also be propagated very successfully from root cuttings taken in the winter; only thick healthy roots should be used and these can be easily prized away from the parent plant. It usually takes two years to get flowering-sized plants from cuttings and for the average garden, where few plants are required, simple division of the parent plant is probably the simplest and quickest method to maintain stock. Seed, which is freely produced, can be sown and will give satisfactory, although slow, results. However, named cultivars should not be increased by this method as the resultant offspring are certain to vary. It is critical when raising any perennials from seed that poor forms (in vigour, foliage details or flower colour) be rogued out and destroyed, otherwise inferior forms will find their way into our gardens.

Macleaya cordata (Willd.)R. Br.   **[Pl. 1]**
(Syn. *Bocconia cordata* Willd.; *B. yedoensis* Carr.)
PLUMED POPPY

A stout, stoloniferous perennial with erect stems 1.5–2.5 m (5–8 ft) tall, forming fairly dense clumps. The large sculptured leaves are alternate, heart-shaped, with rounded and toothed lobes, greyish green above, but paler greyish white beneath and with prominent veining. The tiny flowers are borne in large feathery panicles, the overall colour effect being buff or creamy-white. Each flower has a cluster of 25–30 stamens and the fruit-capsules usually contain four to six seeds at maturity.

M. cordata is a native of eastern China and Japan, where it is a plant of woodlands, gullies and scrub, generally in the mountains and flowering in June and July. It was introduced into cultivation in 1795 as *Bocconia cordata* and featured early in *Curtis's Botanical Magazine* (tab. 1905).

Today the finest form of this species in cultivation is 'Flamingo', which is a handsome and bold cultivar with attractively pink-flushed leaves and flowers of rich pinkish bluff. It, like the straight species, is widely available at nurseries and garden centres.

Macleaya × *kewensis* Turrill

This is a supposed hybrid between *M. cordata* and *M. microcarpa*, little seen in gardens, but with more or less intermediate characters.

Macleaya microcarpa (Maxim.) Fedde
(Syn. *Bocconia microcarpa* Maxim.)

Very similar in both habits and stature to *M. cordata*. It differs primarily in its flowers, which have only 8–12 stamens and in its one-seeded fruit-capsules. The flower panicles are very attractive and have an overall bronzy flush; they appear rather ahead of those of *M. cordata*.

Macleaya microcarpa is a native of China and was introduced into cultivation in 1896. This species is often confused in gardens with its cousin, but the differences in flower and fruit details should serve to distinguish them fairly readily. The finest form in cultivation is the widely available 'Kelways Coral Plume', an especially handsome plant with deep pink flushed flower panicles. 'Coral Plume' has paler flowers.

The Tree Celandines
Bocconia

The genus *Bocconia* is little known in our gardens except as a synonym for the two species of Plumed Poppy, *Macleaya*. The prime reason for this is that the species are plants of the subtropics and tropics of the New World, especially from Mexico and Peru, and are not suitable for temperate gardens. The genus was described by Linnaeus in 1753 and for some years it included both the Old World species, as well as *B. cordata* from China and Japan. In 1826 Robert Brown, recognising differences between the Old and New World species, separated the latter into a new genus, *Macleaya*. *Bocconia* is named after the Sicilian botanist Paolo Bocconi (1633–1703).

Bocconia contains nine species which look superficially similar to *Macleaya*, especially in the character of the inflorescence, but the plants are shrubs or subshrubs, not herbaceous perennials. The main differences are to be found in the leaves, which are entire to pinnate (depending on the species), but with distinctive pinnate veins. Other differences can be seen in the fruit-capsule which, unlike *Macleaya*, opens from the base upwards.

As in *Macleaya*, the latex of *Bocconia* is orange and juicy and is used locally for treating warts and other skin disorders, but also sometimes as a dye plant.

These are excellent and effective plants for subtropical and tropical gardens, although not seen nearly as much as they really deserve. They thrive best in a light, well-drained soil with plenty of moisture during the growing season and ample mulches. An open sunny position is ideal and plants should be given ample space in which to develop.

Plants can be propagated from seed sown in heat in the spring or from cuttings as described under *Macleaya*. Away from tropical and subtropical gardens, they are handsome plants for large glasshouses and conservatories with a minimum temperature of 18°C (65°F).

For *Bocconia cordata* and *B. microcarpa* see under *Macleaya*, p. 36.

Bocconia arborea S. Wats.

A small tree up to 7 m (22 ft) tall with spongy bark. The leaves are pinnately lobed and clustered at the branch tips, the lobes sharply toothed, often downy beneath. The flowers are borne in branched racemes up to 20 cm (8 in) long. This species, the largest in the genus, comes from Central America and flowers in July and August.

Bocconia frutescens L.
(Syn. *B. glauca* Salisb.; *B. sinuatifolia* Stokes)
TREE CELANDINE

An evergreen shrub 1–2 m (3–6 ft) tall with stout, rather stiff, erect stems, softly hairy when young. The leaves are up to 35 cm (14 in) long and pinnately lobed, short-stalked and with a rounded or somewhat truncated base; they are smooth and bluish green above, but paler and somewhat hairy beneath. The greenish flowers are borne in large, diffuse, rather feathery, panicles, each flower with 14–16 stamens usually; as in *Macleaya*, the flowers are small, the sepals only 9–10 mm (⅖ in) long, and petalless. *Bocconia frutescens* is a native of the West Indies and Mexico and has been in cultivation since 1739. It flowers in September and October. This species has become naturalised in Java. I recently saw a thriving plant in cultivation in a garden on the South Island, New Zealand.

Bocconia integrifolia Humb. & Bonpl.
ENTIRE-LEAVED TREE CELANDINE

Very distinct from *B. frutescens*, being a much-branched shrub up to 5 m (17 ft) tall, though often less, the young branches covered in a rather mealy down. The oblong to elliptical leaves have a serrated margin, but are

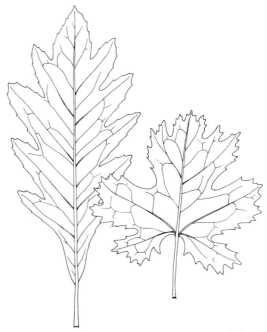

Leaves of *Bocconia frutescens* (left) and *Macleaya microcarpa* (right) showing the basic differences between the two genera

unlobed, green above and with a contrasting white-mealy reverse. The greenish flowers are borne in a rather dense panicle, each flower with about ten stamens.

Bocconia integrifolia has been in cultivation since 1822 and is a native of South America, particularly Bolivia, Colombia and Peru.

The Greater Celandine
Chelidonium

The genus *Chelidonium* is familiar to all those interested in the flora of western Europe, for it is a native widespread in the region. There is only one species in the genus, *C. majus*, often called the Greater Celandine, though quite different to the Lesser Celandine, *Ranunculus ficaria*. The species has a wide distribution from western Europe to Asia. The name *Chelidonium* was used by Dioscoridis, from the Greek *Chelidon*, the swallow; it was said that the plant came into flower with the coming of the swallow, drying up upon its departure in the autumn.

In gardens it is often dismissed as a 'weed' or 'wildling' of little interest. However, this is being wholly unfair to a plant that is extremely useful in dark, damp corners of the garden or for areas left to encourage a wild-flower garden. It is a plant of quiet charm and elegance and I would not be without it somewhere in my own garden. At the same time, the Greater Celandine is one of those plants that needs little attention and is quite happy left to itself. Once established, it has no need for further attention. Some will complain that it seeds around all too freely, but this is a sign of success and it is little trouble to remove excess seedlings or to transplant them to other places where they may be acceptable.

The genus *Coreanomecon* Nakai, described from Korea is a synonym of *Chelidonium*.

Chelidonium majus L.
GREATER CELANDINE, SWALLOW WORT

A tufted perennial herb with pale brittle stems which exude an acrid, saffron-coloured sap when cut; stems branched from close to the base, sparsely hairy, to 60–90 cm (24–36 in) tall in vigorous plants. The leaves are mostly in a loose basal rosette; they are up to 20 cm (8 in) long and once or twice pinnately-lobed, the segments oval, coarsely toothed and generally a rather pale bluish-green; stem leaves similar, but smaller and generally less divided. The small yellow flowers, 18–25 mm (¾–1 in) across, are borne in lax umbel-like clusters just above the foliage; sepals two; petals four, oblong, not overlapping and widely spreading; stamens yellow. The narrow fruit-pods, 3–5 cm (1⅕–2 in) long, are more or less straight and smooth, splitting from the base to the top when ripe by two valves. The seeds are black and shiny with a small white aril at one end; this latter is attractive to ants, who carry the seeds away and so effect dispersal to other areas.

Chelidonium majus is primarily a plant of shady and damp habitats, hedge-rows, woodlands and the bases of rocks, walls or old buildings, generally at rather low altitudes and flowering from May to July, occasionally later. It has so long been associated with humans that its precise natural distribution is uncertain, although it is undoubtedly native to many parts of Europe. However, it has long been cultivated as a medicinal herb and its use goes far back to both the ancient Chinese and Greek civilisations. Like many similar herbs, it was believed to cure a whole range of diverse disorders including warts, gout and scrofula (a kind of tuberculosis). The plant, particularly the bright orange sap, contains a number of potentially harmful alkaloids including chelidonine, protopine, and sanguinarine, so its use could be hazardous to say the least.

Plants are generally rather short-lived in the garden, but there are always seedlings around to replace their parents. The common wild form is rather leggy and, for those who prefer a plant of more distinction, there is a double-flowered form available, 'Flore Pleno' [Pl. 2] or 'Plenum'. Despite its name, this double form has semi-double rather than fully double flowers. There are various forms of it about, some with distinctly larger and darker blooms, and these are well worth seeking out. Most appear to come true from seed.

Another handsome form is var. *laciniatum* [Pl. 3] (*Chelidonium laciniatum*

Miller), which boasts handsome cut foliage with deeply incised segments, more striking than the type. This plant also has the benefit of being more compact overall. The flowers are single, but are noticeably fringed along their margins. Var. *laciniatum* has been known for many years – it was noted first in the Heidelberg garden of the Sprenger apothecaries in 1590 and has been cultivated ever since. Such cut-leaved forms can be found in parts of western Europe as well as western Russia. Crosses between *C. majus* 'Flore Pleno' and var. *laciniatum* produce plants with intermediate leaf characters and semi-double flowers – these are often listed in catalogues as *laciniatum* 'Flore Pleno', though they should not be confused with *C. majus* 'Flore Pleno' or 'Plenum' as it is also listed.

There are also other forms recorded. These include 'Variegatum' with variegated foliage, which was certainly known and shown by J. Salter of the Versailles Nursery in Hammersmith, London, in 1862, but has not apparently been seen since.

Chelidonium majus var. *grandiflorum* (*Chelidonium grandiflorum* DC.) **[Pl. 4]** is similar to the typical plant, but is distinguished, as its name implies, by having larger flowers, up to 3.5 cm (1⅖ in) across, but also in having shorter fruit-capsules and broader bracts. This variety is native to Central Asia to Siberia and north-western China and would certainly be well worth acquiring. However, it does not appear to be in cultivation at the present time, at least not in the West. This large-flowered variety must look very similar to the genus *Stylophorum* (see key on p. 33).

The Forest Poppy
Hylomecon

This delightful little forest-dweller is one of the first poppies to come into flower in the spring. It is an excellent woodland garden plant, but succeeds in any moist, semi-shaded spot in the garden.

As currently understood, the genus *Hylomecon* contains just a single species, *H. japonicum*, although the *Flora USSR* distinguishes the Asiatic mainland plant as a separate species (*H. vernalis*) from the Japanese one. In reality, *H. japonicum* is quite variable in both flower and leaf characters and it would be difficult to uphold two distinct species.

Hylomecon comes close to both *Chelidonium* and *Stylophorum*, differing from both in its unbranched stems. It also differs from *Chelidonium* in having solitary rather than umbellate flowers and in the presence of bracts. In *Stylophorum* the flowers are generally clustered and bear bracts as well as bracteoles. In growth *Hylomecon* is also distinct, forming a slow-spreading clump by means of short rhizomes just beneath the soil surface. In both *Chelidonium* and *Stylophorum* growth radiates upwards from a basal rosette of leaves.

Hylomecon japonicum (Miq.) Prantl & Kündig   **[Pl. 5]**
(syn. *Chelidonium japonicum* Thunb.; *C. uniflorum* Sieb. & Zucc., *Hylomecon vernalis* Maxim; *H. japonica* Bush; *Stylophorum japonicum* Miq.)
FOREST POPPY

A spreading rhizomatous perennial up to 30 cm (12 in) tall, rarely more; stems erect and unbranched, slightly hairy at first. The leaves are pinnate, generally with five leaflets, but sometimes three or seven, the leaflets more or less equal, lanceolate-oblong to almost rhombic, soft, deep green and with a sharply and irregularly toothed margin; basal leaves long-stalked, up to 25 cm (12 in) long, the stem leaves generally only two or three, short-stalked or sessile; bracts present. The erect flower buds are pear-shaped but rather pointed, smooth or, more often, hairy. The bright yellow flowers, 3.5–5 cm (1⅖–2 in) across, are upright and are borne singly on slender stalks, bowl-shaped at first, but becoming rather flat as the petals expand; sepals usually two, soon falling; petals four, very occasionally five or six, rounded; stamens many, yellow, about one-third the length of the petals. The fruit-capsule is a slender, erect, siliqua, 2–8 cm (1–3⅕ in) long, hairless and opening by two valves from just below the apex when ripe.

H. japonicum inhabits leafy soils in moist, shaded woodland in north-eastern China, including Manchuria, Korea and Japan, where it flowers during April and May. It was introduced into cultivation in Europe round about 1870.

In Japan a form with more pointed leaflets and very finely toothed along the margins has been distinguished as var. *subintegra* Fedde. However, it is the coarsely toothed form that is more often seen in gardens.

There is no doubt that this is one of the most charming and colourful poppies for the woodland garden. The species is fully hardy. The flowers generally appear in May and June and, although somewhat fleeting, are produced in quantity on a vigorous plant. The species is sometimes accused of being invasive, but I have never found it to be so and, in any case, plants are fairly shallow-rooted and excess growth can be easily removed.

Hylomecon thrives best in a humus-rich soil and certainly responds to top-dressing of leaf-mould or compost. In drier sunny positions it will linger on, but will rarely thrive or flower well, preferring the dappled shade of trees and shrubs. It is also an excellent little plant for the peat border, though here it may perhaps become invasive.

Plants can be easily propagated from seed, which can be sown outdoors in April. However, division of the parent plant provides a more ready means of increase; divisions can be made in the early spring just before growth commences or, indeed, immediately after flowering. It is as well to mark plants, as they have often disappeared below ground by late summer.

It is pleasant associated with other woodland members of the poppy family such as *Eomecon chionantha*, *Sanguinaria canadensis*, *Meconopsis chelidonifolia*, *Cathcartia villosa* or *Stylophorum diphyllum*. Together, these will provide interesting flowers and foliage from spring to late summer.

The Celandine Poppies
Stylophorum

The genus *Stylophorum*, as currently understood, contains three species, two native to China and one to North America. They are juicy woodlanders with rather bristly stems, with lobed or divided leaves and yellow, four-petalled poppy flowers. They are elegant woodlanders for cool, moist, shaded places in the garden, excelling, as would be expected, in the woodland glade, amongst shrubs or in the peat border. The oblong fruit capsules are bristly or hairy and release their seeds by splitting lengthwise into a number of valves. As the generic name implies, the ovary is endowed with a prominent, rather thick style.

The yellow woodland poppies are much confused in gardens and indeed the closely related Japanese Wood Poppy, *Hylomecon japonicum*, has been placed in the past in both *Stylophorum* and *Chelidonium*. *Stylophorum* differs from *Hylomecon* in having bracteoles and several flowers on a common stem, each flower long-stalked. In *Chelidonium* the stems are freely branched, but without bracts or bracteoles and the flowers are small. In *Hylomecon* the flowers are solitary on unbranched stems and there are bracts present.

In the garden environment all the species in these genera require very similar conditions and are generally relatively easy to cultivate. Their merit is in the coolness of their attractive, yet subtle, foliage and their somewhat fleeting, yellow flowers.

The species of *Stylophorum* can be propagated from seed or *S. diphyllum* by division of the parent plant. Seed can be sown in pots in the early spring under cover, pricking the seedlings out once they have developed their first or second true leaves. They are less temperamental with regard to transplanting in their seedling stage than some poppies, although somewhat brittle. However, they greatly dislike strong sunlight or becoming too dry. An airy, partly shaded frame is ideal for the young plants, which can be put out in the garden in early summer. *S. diphyllum* can be easily divided, either after flowering or in the early spring just before growth commences. Good sized pieces of root will soon re-establish themselves.

Stylophorum diphyllum (Michx.) Nutt.   **[Pl. 6]**
(Syn. *Chelidonium diphyllum* Michx.; *S. petiolatum* Nutt.)
CELANDINE POPPY

This is a tufted perennial, 30–40 cm (12–16 in) tall, with downy stems and leaves. The basal leaves form a lax-rosette from which arise a number of branched stems, leafy in the upper part, but bare below. The leaves are bluish-green, pinnately-lobed, with five to seven oblong, blunt-toothed lobes, each lobe looking rather like a thin oak-leaf. The stem leaves are similar, but shorter stalked, the uppermost much reduced and bractlike. The golden-yellow poppy flowers 3–5 cm (1⅕–2 in) across are borne on slender stalks (pedicels) up to 7 cm (2⅘ in) long, several of these arising together on the stem; petals usually four, rounded, spreading widely to form a shallow bowl-shape. The fruit-capsules are erect at first, but nodding when ripe, oblong to spindle-shaped and beset with spreading hairs, and many-seeded.

Stylophorum diphyllum

S. *diphyllum* is to be found at low altitudes in shaded woodland in eastern North America, relishing cool glades and deep leaf-litter, along with other woodland treasures such as trilliums and cypripediums and bloodroot (*Sanguinaria*). In gardens it has been cultivated since 1854 and is the most satisfactory of the three stylophorums, both in habit and colour. Plants flower between May and July, occasionally throwing a few blooms later in the year.

In favoured gardens it will self-sow, in others it is shy and slow to increase. It is never as invasive as *S. lasiocarpum* or indeed its distant cousin *Chelidonium majus*.

Stylophorum japonicum. See *Hylomecon japonicum* (p. 41).

Stylophorum lasiocarpum (Olivier) Fedde   [Pl. 7]
(Syn. *Chelidonium lasiocarpum* Olivier)
CHINESE CELANDINE POPPY

This interesting Asian species is generally biennial in habit, although plants may sometimes linger into a third or fourth year. It looks rather like an enlarged Greater Celandine, *Chelidonium majus*, reaching up to 45 cm (18 in) tall when in flower. Plants are rather brittle and ooze a reddish sap when cut. The leaves are mostly crowded into a basal rosette, from which arise one or several branched flowering stems with several leaves in the upper half. The leaves are very different from *S. diphyllum*, with a larger sharply lobed and toothed terminal leaflet with several smaller leaflets (up to five pairs) below, decreasing in size down the stalk, green above, but with a whitish bloom beneath; upper leaves similar though short-stalked. The flowers are rather pale yellow, cupped, 3–4 cm (1⅕–1⅗ in) across, several arising together on long slender hairy stalks toward the top of the stems; petals usually four, ovate and somewhat overlapping. The narrow oblong-shaped fruit capsule is covered in soft hairs.

 S. lasiocarpum is a woodland species native to central and eastern China. In gardens it is an easy, accommodating plant, though not often seen. Like its cousins it is a plant for moist, shaded sites and in my garden, at least, seeds around profusely. The resultant seedlings transfer to other quarters without too much difficulty. This plant is rather brittle and the stems and leaves can be easily bruised if it is in too exposed a site. It flowers from May to August, occasionally later.

Stylophorum sutchuenense (Franch.) Fedde
(Syn. *Chelidonium sutchuenense* Franch.)

This is the least known of the three species, but nonetheless attractive. Plants have a similar habit to *S. lasiocarpum*, but generally have a solitary stem that is leafy in the lower part, not bare. The most obvious difference is seen in the distinctive shaggy red hairs that cover the stems and leaves, especially beneath. The yellow flowers, 3–4 cm (1⅕–1⅗ in) across, are borne on slender stalks, 4–5 cm (1⅗–2 in) long, and rise in a cluster from the upper-most leaves. The fruit-capsule is narrowly oval and hairy.

 S. sutchuenense, another woodland species, is native to western China.

The Horned Poppies
Glaucium

The Yellow-Horned Poppy, *Glaucium flavum*, is a familiar coastal plant in parts of Britain and the Mediterranean, as well as in the Atlantic Islands, around the Black Sea and the Caspian, sometimes occurring inland.

This species was well-known to Gerard, who called it *Papaver cornutum flore luteo* or the 'Yellow horned Poppie' in his *Herbal* (1597), and stated that it 'groweth upon the sands and banks of the sea'.

Gerard also attributed the horned poppy with medicinal powers. 'The root of horned Poppie boiled in water unto the consumption of the one halfe, and drunke, provoketh urine, and openeth the stopping of the liver' and 'The juice mixed with meale and honey, ruindisieth old rotten and filthy ulcers'.

The genus *Glaucium* Miller contains some 20 species distributed in Europe, south-western and central Asia. The genus derives its names from the grey or glaucous foliage characteristic of many of the species. As Miller states in the *Gardener's Dictionary*: '[It] is so called from the Greek because the leaves of this plant are sea green colour; it is call'd the Horned Poppy, because it is a species of Poppy, having husks resembling horns.'

Indeed, the fruit characters serve to distinguish *Glaucium* from all other genera in the Papaveraceae. The fruit-capsules are cylindrical, linear, straight or curved and very long, up to 30 cm (12 in) in length, and distinctly capped by a two-lobed stigma. When ripe, the capsule splits into two valves from apex to base, or vice versa, and contains numerous seeds.

Glauciums can be annual, biennial or perennial herbs, often forming a distinctive, though lax, basal rosette of leaves. Most produce yellow sap when cut. Both the branched stems and leaves are usually glaucous, glabrous or hairy, the latter often giving the foliage a typical scurfy or mealy appearance. The upper stem leaves are nearly always unstalked and clasp the stem with a broad base. The solitary flowers are lateral or terminal, often yellow, but also orange or various shades of red; sepals two, soon falling; petals four, somewhat overlapping, sometimes with a pale or dark basal blotch; stamens numerous.

Horned poppies are attractive ornamental species for the garden. In addition, they are sometimes cultivated for the oil extracted from the seeds, which can be used for illumination, soap-making and for various medicinal purposes.

In gardens they are easy plants for a sunny well-drained site. Miller states that 'they delight most in a warm light soil, but will grow in almost any soil, if it be not over-dunged'. Miller lists four sorts:

- *Glaucium flore luteo*, Yellow Horned Poppie (= *Glaucium flavum*)
- *Glaucium flore violacea*, Blue-flower'd Horned Poppie (= *Roemeria violacea*)
- *Glaucium hirsutum, flore Phoenicio*, Hairy Horned Poppie, with a deep scarlet flower (= *Glaucium corniculatum*)
- *Glaucium glabrum, flore Phoenicio*, Smooth Horned Poppie, with deep scarlet flower (= probably *Glaucium grandiflorum*).

Interestingly, these are the commonest species grown in our gardens today, although there are some equally tempting species little known in cultivation or, indeed, not in cultivation at all.

Most horned poppies are rather short-lived in the garden. Grown on rich soils, they tend to form large plants that flower and die. On poorer, drier soils they look more in character and often go on for several years. They have a single thick, rather tough, woody taproot, cannot be divided and absolutely hate disturbance once established. They can, however, be readily raised from seed, although both *G. flavum* and *G. corniculatum* will self-sow in some gardens. Seed can be sown under cover in the early spring, the resultant seedling pricked out when large enough to handle and placed in individual pots in a light airy place in frame or glasshouse. It is a mistake to let seedlings become too large before pricking out, as it is then all too easy to damage the delicate young taproot. Plants can be planted out in mid-summer, certainly before they become pot-bound and starved, so that they can build up a good sized leaf-rosette by the autumn. If they become too pot-bound, plants often remain small and seem incapable of growing to their expected size. Planted in heavy wet soils, they tend, in my experience at least, to rot off during the winter months.

Horned poppies generally dislike being crowded in the flower border. They need space to look their best and to thrive. They look very fine along a gravel path or driveway or against an old wall, where their attractive shape and colouration can provide an interesting contrast to other plantings. Along a beach in southern Greece I once saw some startlingly good, large-flowered forms of *G. flavum* growing with the Sea Stock, *Matthiola sinuata* (all grey and pink) and drifts of *Linum pubescens*, backed by banks of *Lavandula stoechas* and *Cistus salviifolia*; how gorgeous to recreate such a medley in one's own garden.

Key to Cultivated Species

1. Sepals dark grey or blackish, smooth: **G. acutidentatum**
    Sepals grey- or bluish-green, often hairy, scurfy or warted,
    occasionally smooth 2

2. Fruit-capsule splitting from the bottom to the top 3
    Fruit-capsule splitting from the top to the bottom 4

3. Stems with only 1–2 leaves; petals yellow, sometimes with a white
    blotch; biennial or perennial: **G. squamigerum**
    Stems leafy; petals yellow or orange, with a dark basal blotch;
    annual: **G. elegans**

4. Ovary and fruit-capsule white-hairy 5
    Ovary and fruit-capsule smooth to warted, occasionally with a few
    bristles 6

5. Flower buds 2.5–4 cm (1–1⅗ in) long; fruit-stalk longer than the
    subtending leaf; flowers 5–8 cm (2–3¼ in) across: **G. grandiflorum**
    Flower buds 1–2 cm (⅖–⅘ in) long; fruit stalk generally shorter than the

subtending leaf; flowers 3–5 cm (1⅕–2 in) across, occasionally
larger: **G. corniculatum**

6. Fruit-capsule, thin, 2–3 mm (¹⁄₁₂–⅛ in) wide, often slightly constricted
    between the seeds, smooth: **G. leiocarpum**
    Fruit-capsule thicker, 3–5 mm (⅛–⅕ in) wide, not constricted between
    the seeds, bristly, warted or occasionally smooth 7

7. Pedicels long, often more than 10 cm (4 in); fruit-capsule smooth or
    with scattered bristles: **G. fimbrilligerum**
    Pedicels short, rarely more than 10 cm (4 in) long; fruit-capsule
    warted: **G. flavum**

Glaucium acutidentatum Hausskn. & Bornm.

This little-known species has the stature and general appearance of *G. flavum*,
but the basal leaves are more deeply pinnately-lobed; it is biennial or a short-
lived perennial. The sepals are very distinctive and readily separate this
species from the others, being quite smooth and dark grey or blackish in
colour, often with a bluish bloom like a plum. The flowers are an orange-
buff colour, the petals without a basal blotch. The fruit-capsules are erect and
straight, and are quite smooth, without any sign of warts (tubercles).

  An attractive horned poppy endemic to Cappadocia in Turkey, where it
inhabits dry hillslopes and rocky places between 950–980 m (3100–3200 ft)
altitude, flowering from June to September.

Glaucium cappadocicum Boiss

Another Turkish species rarely seen in our gardens. In many ways it is similar
to *G. acutidentatum*, but is a rather smaller plant, 30–50 cm (12–20 in) tall,
apparently always biennial. The leaf-lobes are more noticeably toothed and
the sepals smooth and green. The flowers are yellow, 4–5 cm (1⅗–2 in)
across and are followed by glabrous, curved fruit-capsules, not more than
10 cm (4 in) in length.

  G. cappadocicum grows in similar habitats to *G. acutidentatum* and is endemic
to the region of the Upper Euphrates in Cappadocia, from where the species
gets its name.

Glaucium corniculatum (L.) J.H. Rudolph   [Pl. 8]
(Syn. *Chelidonium corniculatum* L.; *Glaucium grandiflorum* sensu Hayek, non
Boiss. & Huet, *G. phoeniceum* Crantz; *G. rubrum* Smith)
RED HORNED POPPY

This is generally annual, rarely biennial, 7–30 cm (2¾–12 in) tall and with
erect or ascending stems that are covered in rough hairs. The basal leaves, up
to 20 cm (8 in) long, are pinnately-lobed into oblong lobes that are rather
sharply toothed; all the leaves are glaucous and covered in short hairs. The
flowers are relatively small, generally 3–5 cm (1⅕–2 in) across, bright red or

orange in the typical form, each petal with a basal violet blotch, but sometimes with a pale blotch; sepals glabrous or somewhat bristly. The fruit-capsule is generally 10–15 cm, (4–6 in) long, although up to 20 cm (8 in) has been recorded, and is straight or somewhat curved, but characteristically covered in short, often appressed, hairs.

G. corniculatum is native to the Mediterranean Basin and southern Europe, extending to the Atlantic Islands and eastwards to the Caucasus and Iran. It inhabits cultivated, fallow and waste ground or dry hillslopes up to an altitude of 1800 m (5900 ft), flowering from March to June. This is a reasonably common plant in gardens, often found under the name *G. phoeniceum*, a synonym. Its striking blue-grey foliage makes it a useful and decorative plant for a grey or silver border and in many ways the foliage is more appealing than the flowers, which are rather sparsely produced throughout the summer months.

This is Gerard's '*Papaver cornutum flore rubro*' of which he states: '[It] . . . groweth not wilde in England . . . found this red horned poppie in the kingdomes of Aragon and Castile in Spain, and the fields near unto common paths. They grow in my garden very plentifully.'

Botanically *G. corniculatum* is considered to be especially variable in its flower colour. Var. *tricolor* (Bernh. ex Spreng.) Ledeb. (syn. *G. tricolor* Bernh.) is a name given to plants with larger, red or orange flowers in which the basal dark blotch is outlined in white. It comes from the eastern side of the species range, including Cyprus and Turkey. Var. *flaviflorum* DC. has yellow flowers and is also found in the east. This variety can be readily mistaken for *G. flavum* at a glance, but its annual habit and hairy fruit-capsules are good clues to its true identity. Unlike *G. flavum*, it tends to be an inland plant of hills and low mountains. Despite these formal varieties, the variation in flower colour and the presence or absence of petal blotches is by no means clear cut, but this does provide interesting potential for garden 'improvement and selection'.

Glaucium elegans Fisch. & Mey.
(Syn. *G. pumilum* Boiss.; *G. tenue* Regel & Schmalh.)
ANNUAL HORNED POPPY

An annual species up to 30 cm (12 in) tall, though often less, with slender leafy stems that branch from the base. The basal leaves are borne in a small rosette and are pinnately lobed and stalked, whereas the stem leaves are much smaller and irregularly lobed and clasp the stem with unstalked bases. The small flowers are yellow or red, occasionally bicolored, 2–3.5 cm (⅘–1⅖ in) across. The fruit-capsule is very thin, curved or, more often, twisted, generally 6–10 cm (2⅖–4 in) long.

This rather dainty little horned poppy is a native of Central Asia, from the Caucasus to the Tien Shan Mountains, as well as Iran and Afghanistan. It is a plant of rocky slopes, screes and river banks, especially in the lower montane zone, where it can be found in flower from April until June.

G. elegans is an attractive little annual, sometimes seen in cultivation, but certainly worth seeking out if one happens to be an avid collector of the less run-of-the-mill annuals grown in our gardens.

Glaucium fibrilligerum Boiss.
(Syn. *G. fimbrilliferum* B. Fedtsch.; *G. vitellinum* b. Fedtsch.)

A biennial species up to 60 cm (24 in) tall, with rather robust, branching stems. The basal leaves are borne in a large rosette and are pinnately lobed and usually smooth; stem leaves are smaller and half-clasping. The flowers are yellow, with unspotted petals, 4–5 cm (1⅗–2 in) across. The fruit-capsule is somewhat curved, up to 25 cm (10 in) in length and generally sparsely covered in whitish bristles.

This is a plant from Central Asia, being found from the Tien Shan and the Pamir Mountains to Iran and Afghanistan. It is primarily a plant of the lower montane belt, growing along pebbly river beds, on rocky and clay slopes and screes, where it flowers from May to July. Rare in cultivation and best treated as a hardy annual, flowering readily in the first year from seed. It can be reared in pots and planted out, but in favourable positions in the garden it has been known to self-sow.

Glaucium flavum Crantz   [Pl. 9]
(Syn. *G. luteum* Scop.)
YELLOW HORNED POPPY

This familiar species is a robust, rather cabbage-like, glaucous biennial or perennial up to 60 cm (24 in) tall, sometimes taller, with branched, thick stems. The fleshy leaves, up to 30 cm (12 in) long, form a large rosette, the basal stalked and pinnately lobed, with broad oblong, rather undulate lobes, laxly covered in scurfy hairs; stem leaves unstalked and clasping the stem with broad basal lobes. The flowers, 6–9 cm (2⅖–3⅗ in) across are yellow, generally without a dark basal blotch; sepals glaucous and bristly. The fruit-capsule is very long and curved, up to 30 cm (12 in), occasionally longer, hairless, but adorned with small wartlike processes along its entire length.

G. flavum is the most widespread species of horned poppy, being found from southern coastal Britain and the Atlantic Island through the Mediterranean Basin to the shores of the Black Sea and the Transcaucasian region. Typically it is a plant of sandy and pebbly seashores, but it can sometimes be found inland; flowering from May to August, occasionally later.

Theophrastus records that the root 'has the property of purging the belly, and the leaf is used for removing ulcers from sheep's eyes'. Dioscoridis recommends a decoction obtained from the root 'to cure sciaticas, and liver griefs and to help such as piss thick, or cobweb-like matter'.

The Yellow Horned Poppy has been cultivated in gardens for many centuries and in a good form can be a long-lived perennial. In most instances though, it has to be replaced every three or four years.

Yellow is the typical colour, but forms with a dark brown basal blotch to the petals can be found in Greece and Turkey. These latter are handsome plants with very grey foliage and exceptionally large, somewhat frilled flowers; they can be ascribed to var. *fulvum* [Pl. 10]. A form with pure orange flowers also exists; these are probably referable to *G. leiocarpum*.

The horned poppies offer a potential hybridiser some very interesting and variable material. A more long-lived perennial habit and larger red or yellow flowers would certainly attract many gardeners. In gardens G. *flavum* and its close cousin G. *leiocarpum* flower from July to September.

Glaucium grandiflorum Boiss. & Huet.

An attractive species related to G. *corniculatum*, but superior in its larger flowers, 5–8 cm (2–3⅕ in) across, which are dark orange to crimson with a dark violet-black basal blotch to each petal. The plant is 30–50 cm (12–20 in) tall, usually with greener leaves and hairy fruit-capsules 10–15 cm (4–6 in) long; the fruit-stalks are longer than their subtending leaf (shorter in G. *corniculatum*).

G. *grandiflorum* is native to Turkey eastwards to the southern Caucasus, Syria and Iran, and southwards into Sinai, where it is a plant of sandy and stony places. This highly attractive species is rarely seen in our gardens. It certainly merits a wider following and deserves to be reintroduced as seed from the wild.

Glaucium leiocarpum Boiss.
(syn. G. *flavum* var. *leiocarpum* (Boiss.) Stoj. & Stef.; G. *oxylobum* Boiss. & Bukse)
EASTERN HORNED POPPY

This is very similar to G. *flavum*, but a slighter more elegant plant. The flowers can be deep yellow, or occasionally reddish or tawny-yellow and the sepals practically glabrous. The chief differences lie in the fruit-capsules, which are not more than 20 cm (8 in) long (often only 8–12 cm or 3–5 in), smooth or warted only at the apex and often somewhat constricted between the seeds.

G. *leiocarpum* replaces typical G. *flavum* in much of the eastern Mediter-ranean, being found from Crete and the Balkans eastwards to Iran. It inhabits dry stony slopes and seashores, rarely at any altitude.

Occasionally identifiable in cultivation, but so confused with G. *flavum* that its presence is generally overlooked. Some authorities treat it as a variety of G. *flavum*.

Glaucium squamigerum Kar. & Kir.

A little-known perennial or biennial species from the Asian Mountains distinguished by its few, minute stem leaves, small yellow flowers, 2.5–3.5 cm (1–1⅖ in) across, and unusual scaly fruit-capsule. Together with G. *elegans* it is the only other species in this account in which the fruit-capsule splits from the base to the top and not the other way round.

G. *squamigerum* is a Central Asian species and is to be found in the upper montane belt from the Tien Shan to the Pamir in Uzbekistan, Kazakstan and Kirghizia in the Commonwealth of Independent States (CIS). It is a plant of river beds, rocky slopes and screes, sometimes on bare clay soils, and flowering from May until August. Apparently not in cultivation outside the CIS.

The Eastern Horned Poppies *Dicranostigma*

The genus *Dicranostigma* contains three species native to the Himalaya and western China. Superficially they closely resemble the true Horned Poppies, *Glaucium*, but differ in their two-lobed stigmas and shorter, more elliptical-shaped fruit-capsules without the horned apex characteristic of *Glaucium*.

In the garden they are plants for well-drained sunny sites, but with ample moisture during the summer, reflecting the monsoon-soaked terrain from which the species hail. They can be raised quite readily from seed sown either under cover or outdoors. Unlike those of most members of the poppy family, seedlings transplant fairly readily.

Dicranostigma franchetianum (Prain) Fedde **[Pl. 11]**
ANNUAL DICRANOSTIGMA

A grey-green annual, occasionally perennial to 1 m (3 ft) tall, sometimes more, with erect branched, smooth stems. The mealy leaves are mostly basal, oblong in outline, up to 20 cm (8 in) long, pinnately-lobed, the upper lobes larger and more crowded than the lower; upper leaves sparse and smaller. The solitary orange-yellow, half-nodding flowers are cup-shaped, 3–4 cm ($1\frac{1}{5}$–$1\frac{2}{5}$ in) across, often borne in profusion, sepals two, mealy; petals four, oval, scarcely overlapping one another; stamens numerous, yellow with pale filaments. The fruit-capsule is smooth, cylindrical-oblong and tapered, 8–14 cm ($3\frac{1}{5}$ –$5\frac{3}{5}$ in) long.

Dicranostigma franchetianum is a native of south-west China, Sichuan and northern Yunnan, where it inhabits rocky and sandy habitats and river banks in rather open sites, at 2200–4100 m (7200–13,450 ft) altitude, flowering from June to August.

There is a good illustration of this attractive species in *Curtis's Botanical Magazine* (tab. 9409). *D. franchetianum* was formerly more commonly seen in gardens, but it is now relatively rare, although I have seen some fine patches of it in field trials in Holland. Unfortunately, the flowers are short-lived and are of little use for cutting. However, it is a hardy annual plant that produces many flowers throughout the summer and for this reason alone is worth growing. Seed needs to be collected diligently, as I do not know of it self-sowing in the garden. Plants will occasionally survive into the second year or, if sown late, may behave as a biennial. A moist light soil in sun or partial shade suits it well.

Dicranostigma franchetianum

Dicranostigma lactucoides Hook. f. & Th.   **[Pl. 12]**
(Syn. *Stylophorum lactucoides* (Baill.) Hook. f. & Th.)
HIMALAYAN HORNED POPPY

A biennial or short-lived perennial that looks like a small *Glaucium*. Stems branched from close to the base, almost leafless, bristly, up to 40–60 cm (16–24 in) tall. Plants form attractive flattish leaf-rosettes up to 30–40 cm (12–16 in) across. The leaves are oblanceolate in outline, rather fleshy, grey- or bluish-green and somewhat scurfy, pinnately-lobed with the lobes becoming decreasingly smaller towards the short-stalked base; segments rounded to oblong, slightly toothed. The solitary yellow or orange-yellow flowers, 3–4 cm (1⅕–1⅗ in) across, are saucer-shaped; sepals two, scurfy; petals four, elliptical to oval, not overlapping. The fruit-capsule is elliptical-cylindrical and softly-hairy, 4–6 cm (1⅗–2⅖ in) long.

This attractive little species comes from the remoter regions of the Indian and Nepalese Himalayas and southern Tibet (Xizang), at 3200–4500 m (10,500–14,800 ft), where it inhabits high mountain moraines, screes and other rocky places, particularly favouring river banks in very exposed sunny situations, and flowering there from July to September.

Dicranostigma lactucoides has been introduced into cultivation on a number of occasions during the past fifty years, the seeds primarily originating from Nepal. The species is quite hardy in our gardens, but tends to be short-lived. It is certainly resentful of too much winter wet, which causes the base of the plant to rot. This can be overcome by growing plants in an extremely well-drained gritty soil – it makes a fine plant for a large scree garden – and by protecting young plants by a piece of glass during the winter months. I have found it best to sow the seeds under cover, pricking out seedlings whilst they are still very small into individual pots. Young plants can be planted outside in June and will occasionally produce a few flowers in their first season. I have never known it self-sow in my own garden, though others may have been fortunate. Seed is normally produced in quantity, so it is surprising that this species is not more often seen.

Dicranostigma leptopodum (Maxim.) Fedde　　　　　　　　**[Pl. 13]**

This species is very like *D. franchetianum*, but a smaller plant with rather small flowers and very narrow fruit. However, it has to be admitted that these two species are connected by intermediates in the wild, the whole forming a rather complex pattern of variability. Future researchers may well find it impossible to maintain them as distinct species.

A native of Gansu (Kansu) and northern Sichuan provinces, China. Rare in cultivation at the present time but certainly grown by Sahin in Holland.

The Snow Poppy
Eomecon

The name *Eomecon* comes from the Greek *heoros*, eastern, and *mekon*, poppy, for this is a distinctive poppy from eastern China. The genus contains just one species, a woodlander thriving in moist leafy soils in dappled shade, which is grown as much for the simplicity of its elegant white flowers, as for its handsome scalloped leaves.

The leaf shape and the branched flower stems, which are leafless but bear a number of small bracts, serve to distinguish this genus from all other members of the Papaveraceae.

Eomecon chionanthum

Eomecon chionanthum Hance   [Pl. 14]
SNOW POPPY or DAWN POPPY

A rhizomatous perennial with far-reaching underground stolons, oozing orange-red sap when cut. The leaves are basal, heart-shaped to kidney-shaped, with the margin neatly scalloped into a series of short rounded lobes, palmately-veined and carried well above the ground on long stalks, which are rather fleshy, hairless, grey-green with a flush of lilac, but paler beneath, up to 10–15 cm (4–6 in) across, sometimes larger. The flowering scapes, which rise erect to 40 cm (16 in) tall, are branched above into a spreading cyme, each branch with a small scalelike bract at its base. The flowers themselves are white with a central boss of yellow anthers, 3–4 cm (1⅕–1⅗ in) across, with four oval petals that spread widely apart; buds oval with a pointed apex, smooth; sepals two, soon falling when the flowers expand.

Eomecon requires similar conditions in the garden to *Stylophorum* although it behaves quite differently. When well-suited, it runs about underground and there is no telling where the next shoot might arise. Whereas this will undoubtedly annoy the neat-minded gardener, to me this is one of its charms. Suffice to say that it would be unwise to plant the Snow Poppy close to other less vigorous plants for fear of swamping them, and do avoid planting it as I once did on a peat bank – it looked lovely, but little else was left by the time it had occupied the entire bed. Amongst strong herbaceous neighbours or shrubs in a woodland setting it can look most enchanting. The flowers are fleetingly produced during May and June, but after they are gone the handsome leaves, in many ways the best feature of this plant, carry on until browned by the first frosts of autumn.

The Snow Poppy is hardy in all but the coldest districts, provided it is given a reasonably sheltered site. Plants can be propagated from seed, but the more usual method is to lift some of the rhizomes in the summer, when they can be easily identified.

Amongst the gaudier and more brazen races of poppy, this one makes a pleasant and subtler contrast and for that reason it is often dismissed as a 'planter's plant'. This is generally taken to mean that none but the most dedicated gardener would dream of growing it or, indeed, would want to, but this surely would be wholly unjustified.

Bloodroot
Sanguinaria

This North American genus contains a single species that is one of the least poppy-like members of the Papaveraceae. At the same time it is quite one of the loveliest and most sought-after species in the entire family.

The genus gets its name from *sanguis* – blood, a reference to the copious orange-red juice that exudes from most parts of the plant when it is cut; hence the common name of Bloodroot or Red Puccoon.

Sanguinaria canadensis L   **[Pl. 15]**
(Syn. *S. grandiflora* Rosc.; *S. stenopetala* Steud.; *S. vernalis* Salisb.;
S. virginiana Gaertn.)
BLOODROOT

Bloodroot is a herbaceous perennial that dies away completely in the autumn. In the spring (generally in April) the new growth appears: folded leaves with solitary flowers appearing from within the leaf fold. As the flowers fade, the leaves expand gradually to their full extent.

Sanguinaria canadensis

The rootstock consists of a branched, thick, fleshy rhizome, which lies horizontally quite close to the soil surface. The rhizomes give rise to a number of single-leaved buds. The leaves, when expanded, are more or less heart-shaped, with long stalks and a shallowly lobed and scalloped margin, up to 20 cm (8 in) across, bluish-green above and smooth and paler beneath. The solitary white flower arises from within the fold of the leaf and quickly expands to 3.5–4 cm (1⅖–1⅗ in), the two sepals soon fall away; there are eight oblong petals (occasionally 12), the four outer narrower than the four inner; stamens numerous. The fruit consists of a narrow erect capsule borne on a stalk up to 15 cm (6 in) long.

S. canadensis is native to eastern North America, from about North Dakota and Oklahoma eastwards in both Canada and the USA, where it occurs in woodland and on rocky slopes, generally at low altitudes.

Bloodroot is a generally easy garden plant, thriving in a variety of soils but preferring a moist leafy soil, especially if it is on the slightly acid or neutral side. Sun or partial shade will suit it equally well provided that the soil does not dry out severely during the summer. It is undoubtedly a delightful plant for the woodland garden, where its charming anemone-like flowers can enliven a spring glade or peat bank. Even after flowering, the handsome leaves can be a useful feature with other woodlanders.

The wild form, with single flowers, is an elegant little plant and despite the fact that the flowers are over all too soon it is well worth growing. The double-flowered form 'Multiplex' ('Plena') is more often seen in gardens with its fully double flowers with numerous strikingly white petals, which expand to form a globe. Although the purist in me wants to dismiss double freaks from my own garden, I have to admit to a genuine soft spot for this little marvel – the double flowers have poise and an elegance unparalleled in the poppy family and, furthermore, they are considerably longer lasting than its single-flowered counterpart.

In recent times a pretty pale pink form (which perhaps should be given the cultivar name 'Rosea') has emerged, with both the young foliage and the flowers suffused with pink. Although slow-growing, this exciting intro-duction is likely to prove very popular once it becomes more widely available. Pink-flowered cultivars with names 'Amy' and 'Peter Harrison' are also known, but how these all differ I am not sure.

Sanguinaria is generally a rather slow-growing plant in gardens and patience is required until a good-sized clump has built up. Plants creep slowly through the soil and on the whole resent disturbance. An annual top-dressing of bonemeal and leaf-mould is decidedly beneficial, especially as rhizomes can sometimes become exposed at the soil surface. Seed is rarely available and division of the rhizome affords the best means of propagation. When to lift and divide the rhizomes is debatable and authorities are not generally agreed on the best time. Despite this, I and several friends have had success both in the autumn, once the leaves have died down, and in the early spring (March) before growth commences. To avoid lifting a whole prized clump, it is perhaps best to uncover one side and remove pieces of rhizome – as much as is required. The pieces used should be healthy and undamaged, each with a bud or two. These pieces of rhizome should be carefully cleaned of old compost and dead leaf-remains and replanted as quickly as possible in a similar site or in a nursery bed, just covered with a sifted mixture of peat or leaf-mould and sharp grit. The success rate can be very good.

Old established clumps will eventually start to 'go back' and generally lose vigour due to both soil impoverishment and congestion of the rhizomes. Lifting then becomes essential. A fork placed well under the clump and gently lifted will bring up the mass of rhizomes without causing too much damage. This can then be teased apart and the healthy pieces replanted once the site has been enlivened with new compost. Newly planted pieces will often flower, but will take time to build up again into a good clump.

Bloodroot is most effective as a multi-flowered clump. This is how it is seen in its native North American woodlands, where the plant can sometimes blanket the ground in pristine profusion.

In cultivation it is more fickle, delighting in some gardens, but moody and unpredictable in others, and sometimes declining without apparent cause. It is, however, worth every bit of attention to force it to thrive.

II
Subfamily
Eschscholzioideae

The Californian Poppies
Eschscholzia

The Californian Poppy, *Eschscholzia californica*, is well known and has been cultivated in European gardens since 1790. The wild forms have flowers in shades of white, cream, yellow and orange, but in cultivation pink, red, crimson, bronze, apricot, salmon and bicoloured forms exist, as well as those with frilled semi-double flowers. *E. californica* is an easy and adaptable garden flower and has always been a popular summer annual because of its showy blooms produced over a long flowering season. This particular species is the state flower of California, where it can sometimes be found in dazzling numbers in the spring and early summer.

The genus *Eschscholzia* contains in all about ten species, which are restricted to western North America, centred on California. They are primarily plants of dry sandy and stony regions, grassy places, deserts and semi-deserts. The species can be readily recognised by their silky-petalled flowers, finely cut, rather ferny looking foliage and long slender fruit-capsules. However, the most obvious character, and one that clearly separates this from other genera, is the one-piece calyx that abscises at the base and pops off the top of the expanding petals like a tiny pointed cap. This endearing habit was a great source of fascination and amusement to me as a child and to watch the petals unfurl is rather like watching the miracle of the expanding butterfly that has recently emerged from a chrysalis.

The species can be annual or short-lived perennial herbs and when cut ooze a colourless juice. The alternate leaves are generally hairless and ternately divided into numerous fine dissections. The solitary flowers arise on slender leafy or scapose stems and are erect in bud; sepals two, but wholly united to form a smooth cap, which detaches itself in one piece as the flowers open; petals four, occasionally six or eight, folded round each other in bud, often yellow, sometimes white, cream or orange; stamens numerous; ovary cylindrical, dilated at the base to form a funnel-shaped torus, above with a four- to six-lobed stigma, the lobes linear and diverging. The fruit-capsule is linear-cylindrical, ribbed, two-valved, explosive when ripe to expel the seeds, with the two valves usually curling spirally.

The genus is named in honour of Dr J.F. Eschscholz (1793–1831), who was surgeon and naturalist on the Russian expeditions to the Pacific Coast of North America in 1816 and 1824.

In cultivation Californian poppies present few difficulties. They thrive in a wide variety of soils provided they are not waterlogged, though preferring light well-drained ones and full sun. Seed is best sown where the plants are required to flower, taking care not to sow too thickly. This can be undertaken in the autumn (at least with *E. californica*) for a late spring and early summer flowering the following year or, more usually, in the spring (March–April) for flowers that will bloom through the summer and early autumn. They are particularly attractive associated with other annuals such as *Clarkia* and *Godetia* or for a more subtle effect with annual grasses such as *Briza maxima* or *Lagurus ovatus*. For an interesting, if rather gaudy, display try sowing some of the self-colours with *Papaver commutatum* 'Ladybird', *P. pavoninum* or with one of the annual lupins such as *Lupinus varius*. They can look splendid scattered along a wide gravel path or driveway, where they will often self-sow. Dead-heading, the removal of young fruits, will certainly help to prolong the flowering season.

E. californica makes a useful, though not particularly long-lived, cut flower. The buds should be picked just before they burst open. The stems generally hold up well in water.

The named cultivars of *E. californica* would make a very bold bedding display to rival marigolds, salvias and busy-lizzies. However, for some reason they have seldom been used in such a way, probably because, unlike the others, they are not so easily raised in trays or pots for bedding out and generally resent too much disturbance.

The perennial sorts will often overwinter, especially if the weather is mild, to flower early in the following season. If they don't, then they are easy to raise from seed once again or, indeed, they may self-sow themselves.

It is a great pity that *E. californica*, magnificent though it undoubtedly is, should so dominate this genus in cultivation. Several of the other species deserve our attention. Perhaps they will acquire favour when easy annuals (for direct sowing) once more become popular.

Key to Species

1. Flower buds with a rimlike disk immediately beneath   **E. californica**
   Flower buds without a rimlike disk immediately beneath 2

2. Plants scapose with all the leaves at the base of the plant 3
   Plants not scapose, with leafy stems 6

3. Cotyledons bifid; petals yellow, but often with an orange
    base: *E. mexicana*
    Cotyledons entire; petals yellow or orange 4

4. Leaves with few long sub-parallel divisions; flowers pale
    yellow: *E. lobbii*
    Leaves with many short, non-sub-parallel, divisions; flowers bright
    yellow or orange 5

5. Sepal-cap with a long drawn out point; seeds burlike: *E. caespitosa*
    Sepal-cap acute, but not drawn out into a point; seeds
    pitted: *E. glyptosperma*

6. Leaves and sepals hoary with curly white hairs: *E. lemmonii*
    Leaves not as above, usually glabrous 7

7. Flowers small, the petals only 3–8 mm (⅛–⅓ in) long 8
    Flowers larger, the petals 10–30 mm (⅕–1⅖ in) long 9

8. Petals 3–6 mm (⅛–¼ in) long: *E. minutiflora*
    Petals 7–8 mm (⅓ in) long: *E. covillei*

9. Sepals 4–10 mm (⅙–⅖) long; petals 5–15 mm (⅕–⅗ in) long,
    yellow, often with an orange base: *E. ramosa*
    Sepals 10–18 mm (⅖–¾ in) long; petals 10–30 mm (⅖–1⅕ in) long;
    yellow or orange 10

10. Leaves mostly 3-ternate, with blunt segments; flowers yellow or
    orange: *E. caespitosa*
    Leaves mostly 4-ternate, with pointed segments; flowers
    yellow: *E. parishii*

Eschscholzia caespitosa Benth.   [Pl. 24]
TUFTED CALIFORNIAN POPPY

A small annual up to 14–20 cm (5⅗–8 in) tall, with the leaves crowded into
a basal tuft, though sometimes present on short stems, with the erect flower-
scapes greatly exceeding the leaves. The leaves are grey-green and finely
divided into numerous linear blunt lobes, not more than 8–9 mm (⅓ in) long
usually, glabrous or slightly bristly; the leaves vary considerably in length.
The flowers, 30–45 mm (1⅕–1⅘ in) across, open widely and are a pleasant
bright yellow; sepal-cap 10–18 mm (⅖–¾ in) long, long-pointed; petals
rounded, somewhat overlapping. The fruit-capsule is 5–8 cm (2–3⅕ in) long.

   E. *caespitosa* inhabits dry grassy and bushy flats and slopes up to about
1000 m (3300 ft) altitude, growing in sandy places as well as grassland or
chaparral. It is common in California from the South Coast Ranges to Los
Angeles County, where it is generally to be found in flower during April and
May, occasionally later.

   This pretty little annual poppy is occasionally available in the seed trade,
but is certainly listed by some society seed lists. It is a very pleasing plant for

the front of a border in patches or, if you prefer, for edging. The form generally available has been named 'Sundew' and has scented lemon-yellow flowers more subtle than most of the other eschscholzias, but it will flower in abundance right through the summer. It forms multi-flowered tufts and is excellent scattered along a gravel drive.

Various wild varieties of *E. caespitosa* are recognised. Of these, perhaps the most distinct is subsp. *kernensis* Munz, which has leafier stems and larger deep orange flowers and capsules 2.5–4 mm (¹⁄₁₀–¹⁄₄ in) thick. It is native to Kern County and the Tejon Pass region of California, growing on heavy clay soils.

Eschscholzia californica Cham.   **[Pl. 17–19]**
CALIFORNIAN POPPY

This familiar garden poppy is a very variable plant in the wild. It can be an annual or perennial up to 60 cm (24 in) tall, usually glabrous and branched from close to the base. The grey- or blue-green leaves are divided into numerous linear to narrow-oblong, blunt lobes, the basal leaves up to 20 cm (8 in) long, sometimes longer, the stem leaves similar though smaller and short-stalked. The solitary terminal flowers form a wide funnel-shape, 4.5–7 cm (2–3 in) across when fully expanded, the torus unlike that of all other species with two rims, an outer spreading disklike rim and an inner erect transparent one; sepal-cap pointed, 1–4 cm (²⁄₅–1³⁄₅ in) long; petals fan-shaped, satiny, creamy to yellow or orange, rarely white in the wild. The fruit-capsule is 3–8 cm (1¹⁄₅ –3¹⁄₅ in) long.

This species is widespread in California and southern Oregon in both the valleys and foothills up to an altitude of 2000 m (6600 ft), growing in grassy or sandy places (it is common in the western Mojave Desert), rocky areas, along roadsides and embankments or invading areas that have been burnt. It flowers in the wild from February to September, depending on the area and altitude.

E. Californica is very variable in the wild. In California some 50 subspecies have been described in the past, though most of these cannot stand up to close scrutiny and further research is required. Plants are often perennial, but in the south of California and in Baja California an annual form (often called subsp. *peninsularis* (Greene) Munz) predominates. Perennial forms found growing on sand-dunes in California, with rough puberulent leaves and prostrate stems, have been called var. *maritima* (Greene) Jepson (syn. *E. maritima* Greece) **[Pl. 20]**. Another type widespread inland from the Columbia River to southern California has very glaucous foliage and large deep orange flowers in the spring, followed by smaller pale yellow flowers later in the year. This plant is variously called var. *crocea* (Benth.) Jepson or var. *douglasii* (Benth.) Gray (syn. *E. douglasii* Benth.).

This species *sensu lato* is readily identified by the disklike outer rim of the torus, which no other species possesses. In bud this appears as a disk outside and at the base of the calyx and persists into the fruiting stage. Like most Californian poppies, the flowers open in bright weather, but wrap up when it is dull or wet, the petals protecting the stamens within.

E. californica has been long in cultivation and many forms have been bred and selected. From the original yellow, cream and orange introductions have come plants with white, pink, orange, deep red, scarlet, apricot, salmon, bronze, bicolours such as pink or bronze on the outside and cream on the inside, as well as others with semi-double or frilled petals. In many ways, the simple elegance and self colours of the wild type are hard to beat and some of the modern strains are almost offensive to the eye.

Easy to grow and prolific is a descriptive way to sum up the Californian Poppy. They are a great delight in the late spring (from an autumn sowing) and summer and are generally trouble-free, outlasting many annuals in their long flowering season.

They are prolific seeders and seed packets generally contain a very generous helping, although one should not be tempted to sow them too densely as a result.

The two great things that have come from breeders in recent years are the impressive range of colours now found in the Californian poppies and the denser, dwarfer and neater form of many modern cultivars. The prime development of this exquisite poppy came at the beginning of the nineteenth century, when Suttons of Reading introduced dwarf cultivars such as 'Sutton's Flame' and frilled-petal types like 'Sutton's Frilled Pink' and 'Sutton's Gaiety': these interesting cultivars have, alas, sunk into oblivion in the intervening years. The latter cultivar was particularly noteworthy because of its sumptuous frilled bicoloured flowers. But the frilled types, together with a dwarfer habit and an exciting wide range of colours, are present in modern series, especially the Thai Silk Series.

Seedsmen offer various individual colours (generally given cultivar names) of mixtures with single or semi-double, frilled or unfrilled flowers. These are best summarised as follows, although it has to be admitted that there is often some overlap between the series and there appears to be an overlap between some cultivars:

Ballerina Hybrids (often called 'Prima Ballerina'): semi-double selection in a variety of attractive colours.

Double Ballerina Mixed is probably the same

Harlequin Hybrids

Monarch Series

Thai Silk Series

(Unless otherwise stated, cultivars are mostly 20–30 cm (8–12 in) tall)

'Alba': single, creamy-white

'Alba Flore Pleno': semi-double, creamy-white

'Apricot Bush': compact with pale apricot flowers

'Apricot Chiffon': [Pl. 23] semi-double frilled flowers in a warm apricot tone

'Apricot Flambeau': burnished apricot

'Aurantiaca': single, orange

'Caniculata': single with fluted petals in various colours

'Carmine King': single, carmine-red

'Cherry Ripe': cerise-pink

'Chrome Queen': single apricot
'Crimson Carmine': single, carmine-red
'Crocea': single, orange with a paler reverse
'Dalli': semi-double, scarlet with a gold centre
'Dazzler': crimson-scarlet
'Douglasii': single, pure yellow
'Eastern Queen': salmon-apricot, rose-red on the reverse
'Enchantress': semi-double, rose-pink
'Fireflame': single, orange-scarlet
'Flambeau': semi-double, orange-scarlet
'Geisha': single, orange with a red reverse
'Mandarin': single, orange with a reddish reverse
'Mauve Beauty': rose purple
'Mikado': scarlet, compact
'MilkyWhite': single, cream; 45 cm (18 in)
'Orange King': orange
'Orange Queen': orange with a paler reverse
'Purple Gleam': 45 cm (18 in)
'Purple Robe': single, rosy-purple with a white centre
'Purple-Violet': rosy-violet
'Rajah': purple-carmine
'Ramona White': cream with a pink reverse
'Red Chief': 45 cm (18 in)
'Rose Bush': rose-pink; 45 cm (18 in)
'Rose Chiffon': rose-pink with a silvery sheen and a contrasting yellow centre; frilled semi-double flowers
'Rosea': cream flushed pink, with a pale rose reverse
'Sugared Almonds': white flushed pink
'Sulphur Yellow': pale lemon-yellow
'Sunlight': pale lemon-yellow
'Toreador': semi-double, orange with a red reverse

Eschscholzia covillei Greene
(Syn. *E. minutiflora* var. *darwinensis* Jones)

Very similar to *E. minutiflora*, but with somewhat larger flowers, the petals 7–8 mm (⅓ in) long (not 3–6 mm/⅛–¼ in). This plant is restricted to the northern Mojave Desert area of California. It is not, to my knowledge, in cultivation.

Eschscholzia glyptosperma Greene
DESERT POPPY

A small tufted glaucous annual with scapose flowers and leaves crowded into a dense basal tuft. The leaves are much dissected into numerous linear segments; all the leaves are about the same size. The flowers are sharply pointed in bud, not drawn out into a point (apiculum) as in *E. caespitosa*, and are bright yellow 2–4 cm ($\frac{4}{5}$–$1\frac{3}{5}$ in) across usually and borne well above the foliage. The seeds are deeply pitted, unlike those of *E. caespitosa*, which are covered in a rough, meshed network.

E. glyptosperma inhabits the arid regions of the Mojave Desert, extending from California into Utah and Arizona. It grows in sandy and stony places, Creosote Bush scrub and other bushy places, to an altitude of about 1600 m (5200 ft).

This interesting desert species is not in cultivation, but it would be a pretty acquisition, with the general size and constitution of *E. caespitosa* and *E. lobbii*.

Eschscholzia lemmonii Greene

A distinctive plant up to 30 cm (12 in) tall, with branched, somewhat leafy, stems and finely dissected leaves covered with curly white hairs, giving the plant a hoary appearance. The flowers are orange, 3–4 cm ($1\frac{1}{5}$–$1\frac{3}{5}$ in) across, the sepal-cap hoary like the foliage. The fruit-capsule is 3–6 cm (1–$2\frac{2}{5}$ in) long.

This unusual Californian poppy is not cultivated in gardens, though its unusual hoary foliage and orange flowers would certainly be an asset. *E. lemmonii* is restricted in California to the San Carlos Range and the environs of San Luis Obispo County.

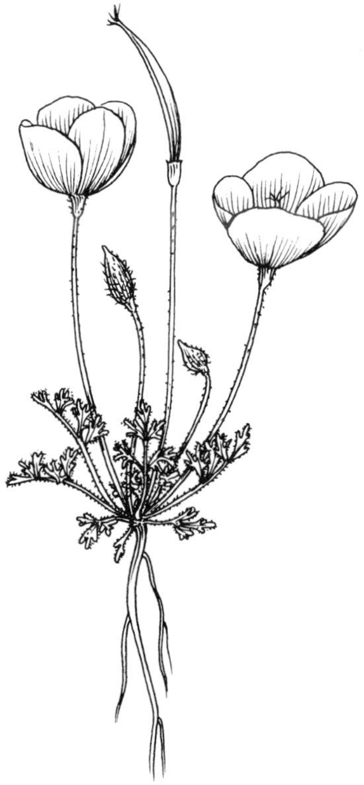

Eschscholzia lemmonii

Eschscholzia lobbii Greene   **[Pl. 26]**
FRYING PANS

This is a small scapose annual with basal tufts of leaves. The leaves are rather distinctive, grey-green, but with comparatively few linear-lanceolate to linear, well-shaped segments. The flowers are pale yellow, like buttercups, 1.5–2.5 cm (⅗–1 in) across, borne well above the foliage or slender glabrous stalks; sepal cap abruptly narrowing to a short pointed apex; petals oval to semi-orbicular. The distinctive seeds are burlike, being adorned with short pointed appendages.

   E. *lobbii* inhabits the gravelly and clay foothills as well as the open valleys of California's North Coast Ranges and the Sacramento Valley, flowering during March and April, but not growing above an altitude of about 650 m (2100 ft).

   This is a very pleasant annual in the garden, to be treated in much the same way as E. *caespitosa*. The two species are much confused, but the few long leaf-divisions of E. *lobbii*, together with its burlike, rather than almost smooth, seeds are sufficient to separate them. E. *lobbii* in fact replaces E. *caespitosa* in the northern part of California.

Eschscholzia mexicana Greene
MEXICAN GOLD

A scapose annual species, with leaves crowded in basal tufts. The leaves are dissected into numerous, narrow, blunt divisions. The flowers, 15–35 mm (⅗–1⅖ in) across are deep yellow, often with an orange base to the petals; in bud the sepals are smooth and abruptly contracted into a short, acute, apical point.

   E. *mexicana* inhabits sandy and gravelly places in Baja California and the Sonora region of Mexico, extending to Colorado, southern Utah and western Texas, where it flowers early in the year, from February to May.

   This species is much confused with E. *caespitosa* and its presence in cultivation is doubtful. In the seedling stage the two species can be readily distinguished; the cotyledons of E. *mexicana* are deeply cleft, those of E. *caespitosa*, and indeed E. *glyptosperma*, are entire. Incidentally, the cotyledons of the well-known E. *californica* are also deeply cleft.

Eschscholzia minutiflora S. Wats.
SMALL-FLOWERED CALIFORNIAN POPPY

A greenish or somewhat greyish annual with leafy, ascending stems. The leaves are finely dissected and thickish, with linear to narrow-oblong lobes. The distinctive small flowers, only 6–10 mm (¼–⅖ in) across are borne on short stalks; buds only 4–6 mm (⅛–¼ in) long, with a short abrupt point. The capsule is 3–5 cm (1⅕–2 in) long.

   A rather weedy species of little garden merit, common in sandy and gravelly places from southern California and Baja California through the

Mojave and Colorado Deserts to Utah, Arizona and the north-western Sonoran Desert, generally at low altitudes, but reaching 1250 m (4100 ft).

The closely related *E. covillei* Greene apparently differs only in its somewhat larger petals, 7–8 mm (⅓ in) long, rather than 3–6 mm (⅛–¼ in). It also has a different chromosome count, n = 12 as opposed to n = 18. This little-known species inhabits the northern regions of the Mojave Desert.

Eschscholzia parishii Greene

A glabrous annual species up to 35 cm (14 in) tall, branched from close to the base. Most of the leaves are crowded at the base of the plant, being finely dissected into numerous linear, acutely-pointed lobes; stem leaves few, scattered and reduced. The flowers are yellow, 2.5–4.5 cm (1–1⅘ in) across and are conspicuous in bud with their long-pointed sepal-cap, 13–16 mm (½–⅔ in) long overall. The fruit-capsule is 5–7 cm (2–3 in) long.

This interesting plant is at once separated from the other species by its sharply pointed, rather than blunt, leaf-segments and the long slender tip to the flowerbuds. It hails from northern Baja California, to California's Mojave Desert and the Colorado Desert, being a plant of dry rocky and stony places, particularly Creosote Bush scrub below 1250 m (4100 ft) altitude.

Not in cultivation.

Eschscholzia ramosa Greene
(syn. *E. elegans* Greene; *E. wrigleyana* Millsp. & Nutt.)

A leafy annual species rather like a large version of *E. minutiflora*, up to 40 cm (16 in) tall, with branched stems. The strongly glaucous, glabrous leaves are finely dissected into numerous linear segments; stem leaves similar to the basal, but short-stalked. The yellow flowers, 15–25 mm (⅗–1 in) across, often have an orange base to the petals; sepal-cap 4–10 mm (⅙–⅖ in), abruptly contracted to a short apical point. The fruit-capsules are 4–7 cm (1⅗–2⅘ in) long.

An attractive species that really should be in cultivation. The flowers are not large, but are produced in abundance and contrast delightfully with the distinctly blue-grey foliage. *E. ramosa* is native to the islands off the Californian Pacific Coast – to Ensenada, Isla Guadalupe and the Channel Islands. It is a plant of rocky and sparsely grassy habitats, flowering from March to May.

The Tulip Poppy
Hunnemannia

This little-known genus with its extraordinary name contains a single species, *H. fumariifolia*. The genus is named in honour of the English botanist and plant explorer John Hunneman, who died in 1839.

Hunnemannia looks very like a Californian poppy, *Eschscholzia*, differing primarily in possessing separate sepals and a broadly lobed stigma.

Hunnemannia fumariifolia Sweet [Pl. 27]
TULIP POPPY

The plant is essentially a perennial with slender, erect stems up to 60 cm (24 in) sometimes taller, which become gradually woody below. The finely divided, ferny leaves, 5–10 cm (2–4 in) long, are thrice ternate with numerous linear, grey-green segments; the leaves are stalked, the stalk (petiole) clearly keeled beneath. The solitary flowers are bright golden-

Hunnemannia fumariifolia

yellow, 5–7 cm (2–2⅖ in) across, broad cups with four rounded, overlapping petals; the two sepals, which are closely united in bud, soon fall away after the flowers begin to open; stamens numerous, rather short and spreading away from the ovary; anthers orange. The linear, siliqua-like fruit-pod is many-seeded and closely resembles that of *Eschscholzia*, splitting from the apex to the base.

H. fumariifolia is native to the highlands of Mexico, where it inhabits rocky and stony habitats and roadsides, mainly at altitudes of 1500–2000 m (4900–6600 ft). It is sometimes called the Mexican Tulip Poppy.

The Tulip Poppy is a choice perennial commonly grown in gardens as a half-hardy annual. Plants flower readily from seed in their first year. They are best sown where they are to flower; thin sowing is essential to get the best from this plant and to avoid excessive thinning at the seedling stage. Plants thrive best in a well-drained, rather light, soil in a sunny position, flowering from July to October from an April sowing. For earlier flowering an autumn sowing is possible in mild districts, although seedlings should be protected from severe weather. Alternatively, seed can be sown under cover during the later winter. Any average seed compost will suffice and to avoid pricking out (not always easy with this species), try sowing two to three seeds in individual pots. A temperature of 10–15°C (50–60°F) is ideal. Plants should be well hardened off before planting out in the late spring. During exceptionally mild winters mature plants may survive in the open, but they cannot be relied upon to do so. In any event, plants are so readily raised from seed that this is not so important.

In California, where *H. fumariifolia* is commonly cultivated, the species has become locally naturalised.

In cultivation, especially large-flowered forms have been selected and these make particularly good 'annual fillers' for the flower border; many annual 'poppies' can be used in this way and it is rather surprising that this is not attempted more often. Colourful annuals of many sorts are invaluable fillers in new herbaceous borders or for a quick display of summer colour in recently constructed gardens. The annual border, a common feature of gardens earlier in the twentieth century, is now alas a rare sight – they have much to recommend them and can provide a very interesting feature in the garden.

H. fumariifolia makes a useful cut flower, picked the moment the blooms open. The blooms are rather longer lasting in water than those of most other poppies. Grown in a well-lit position, it also makes an attractive pot plant indoors, especially for sunny conservatories.

'Sunlite' **[Pl. 28]** is a particularly fine form with sumptuous, more lemony blooms.

The Tree Poppies
Dendromecon

Dendromecon is one of the few truly shrubby members of the poppy family, with woody stems and an evergreen habit; the Latin name literally means tree poppy, from *dendro* tree and *mekon* poppy. If it were only hardier, it would certainly be a very popular shrub in our gardens, with its mass of bright yellow poppy flowers produced during the summer. However, this fine shrub comes from the hot regions of California and although it will survive in a sunny warm position, in more northerly climes it will succumb all too readily to severe winter weather. But this should not deter one from trying it in more favourable gardens.

Most authorities recognise two species in the genus *Dendromecon*, *D. harfordii* and the better known *D. rigida*. However, both species show considerable variability and at least one authority has proposed a more fragmentary revision consisting of some twenty species. The more orthodox interpretation is followed here.

Dendromecon is clearly closely allied to that better known Californian genus, *Romneya*, which can be easily distinguished by its subshrubby habit, far larger white flowers and lobed or toothed leaves; in *Dendromecon* the leaves are always entire.

Of the two species, only *D. rigida* is available in the trade in Britain and seed is sometimes offered in catalogues. It is a plant for a 'hot spot' against a sheltered sunny wall. A deep well-drained loamy soil, with added mortar rubble or a similar aggregate to lighten it further, is essential and during cold winter weather some form of protection may help ensure survival – straw or hessian wrapped around the plant should afford the best protection. In most regions though, a sunny conservatory will certainly afford a more sure means of success. Propagation from cuttings is possible during the summer; cuttings should be of firm, well-ripened, young shoots and consist of two- or three-node pieces. Place them in a sandy compost in moderate heat, but do not expect a high success rate.

Dendromecon harfordii Kell.   [Pl. 29–30]

An evergreen shrub up to 3 m (10 ft) tall, with erect or somewhat arched stems, rather crowded with leaves. The leaves, 3–10 cm (1⅕–4 in) long are elliptical to oval with a blunt, rounded apex. The yellow poppy flowers, 5–7 cm (2–3 in) across, are borne singly on short lateral stalks towards the short tips.

D. harfordii is restricted to the islands of Santa Cruz and Santa Rosa off the coast of California and was first described in 1873. It was introduced into cultivation in the USA as late as 1933, where it is still grown to this day. In Britain it is not in general cultivation; however, it is represented here by var. *rhamnoides* (Greene) Munz (syn. *D. rhamnoides* Greene; *D. arborea* Greene). In this interesting variety the leaves are longer, up to 12.5 cm (5 in), and a paler grey-green with a sharply tapered apex. The leaves are generally less crowded than the type form.

Although this species seems to be somewhat hardier in temperate gardens, it is unfortunately rarely seen outside America. It arrived in cultivation in Britain in 1963, introduced by a former Director of the Royal Horticultural Society's Garden at Wisley, Frank P. Knight. It is a great pity that this plant is not more often seen in our gardens, as it is certainly a finer species than *D. rigida*. In California, at least, it has deservedly found favour in parks and gardens, but then it is quite at home in those sun-drenched environs. I am told by friends in California that it is easy to propagate from seed or cuttings and is a finer garden plant than *D. rigida*, so perhaps more attention should be paid to it in European gardens. It would thrive especially well in those favoured gardens of the Mediterranean region.

Var. *rhamnoides* does not overlap in distribution with the typical plant, var. *harfordii*, being found farther south on the islands of Santa Catalina and Santa Clemente.

Dendromecon rigida Benth.   [Pl. 31]
THE TREE POPPY

An evergreen shrub up to 3 m (10 ft) tall, sometimes more, with slender, woody, branched stems; young stems smooth, grey-green and only slowly becoming woody. Leaves rather leathery, grey-green, narrowly lanceolate to almost elliptical, 2.5–7.5 cm (1–3 in) long, pointed and entire, short-stalked or unstalked. Flowers borne singly and laterally towards the shoot tips on slender stalks, bright yellow, 5–7.5 cm (2–3 cm) across, fragrant; petals four, somewhat overlapping, forming a cup shape, the margin somewhat toothed.

D. rigida is a Californian native and was first discovered there in the wild by the great North American plant explorer David Douglas. However, it was left to William Lobb to introduce it into cultivation in 1854. It is found on the mainland (unlike *D. harfordii*) from Shasta County southwards to northern Baja California.

This fine shrub comes and goes from cultivation in Britain at the whim of the climate. Being tender, it is unlikely to survive for long outdoors unprotected. However, during a succession of mild winters it will thrive well enough and specimens more than 4.5 m (15 ft) tall have been recorded against a hot house wall in the south of England. Its apparent frailty in our gardens should not deter it from being tried, for young plants are vigorous and soon come into flower. The wise gardener will assure its survival by taking cuttings each season for overwintering in a frost-free environment. A shrub in full bloom is a very fine sight.

III
Subfamily
Papaveroideae

The True Poppies
Papaver

The various poppies of the genus *Papaver* have long been favourite plants in our gardens. Their simple yet bold flowers with their satiny petals make them eye-catching features in the flower border. At the same time, their diversity of form, from small annuals to robust perennials, and their enormous range of flower colours, from whites and yellows to oranges, pinks, mauves, purples and reds to almost black, make them suitable subjects for various different aspects in the garden.

The word *Papaver* itself comes from the Latin for the poppy and is said to have been derived from the sound that is made when chewing poppy seeds. Others, however, would claim that the word has the same origin as the Celtic word *papa* (pap) because juice of the poppy (probably *Papaver somniferum*) was given to fractious children to make them sleep – indeed the soporific nature of the poppy was well known to early civilisations.

The genus *Papaver*, the largest in the poppy family, contains some 70 species scattered primarily across the northern hemisphere from sea level to the high mountains. A number of species, such as the annual *P. rhoeas* and *P. dubium*, are almost exclusively associated with arable and cultivated land, others with northern Arctic regions (e.g. *P. radicatum*) or high mountain habitats (e.g. *PP. burseri, rhaeticum*).

The species can be annuals, biennials or perennials with leafy stems or, alternatively, all the leaves may be basal (in which case the flowers are borne on leafless scapes). When cut, the stems generally ooze a white, yellow or orange juice or latex. The leaves vary greatly from one species to another from simple and toothed to variously pinnately lobed, with broad or slender segments; like the stems or scapes, they may be smooth (glabrous), hairy or beset with spreading or appressed bristles. The flowers are usually nodding in bud, becoming erect as the flowers open, this being caused by asymmetric growth of the pedicel, which rectifies itself as the buds mature. Flowers are often solitary, but can also be borne in racemes or panicles. There are two sepals, which fall away quickly as the flowers open and usually four petals (more in some cultivated forms). Numerous stamens surround the ovary. The ovary has no style, but is capped by a stigmatic disk with between four and ten (occasionally more) stigmatic rays. The characteristic fruit-capsule is a 'pepper pot', rounded to oblong or club-shaped, which opens by a ring of pores just below the stigmatic disk; the fine seeds are shaken through the pores by the slightest breeze and scattered over the ground; the number of pores per capsule is the same as the number of stigmatic rays.

Only a handful of poppies are widely grown in gardens. These include the various forms of the opium poppy, *P. somniferum*, some with large double or peony-flowered blooms; the brightly coloured 'Iceland Poppy', *P. nudicaule*; the various races of the common poppy, *P. rhoeas*, including the popular Shirley Poppies; and the large-flowered herbaceous oriental poppies, which have been derived primarily from three Asiatic species, *P. bracteatum*, *P. orientale* and *P. pseudo-orientale*. Of the small perennial species, the most commonly seen in our gardens are the rock garden forms of '*P. alpinum*' (a complex of various alpine poppy species), *P. rupifragum* and *P. lateritium*. However, there are a host of other annual and perennial species well worth seeking out, some being first-rate garden plants, which are mostly unaccountably scarce in gardens.

Cultivation

The annual species are readily grown from seed. In fact, many are the simplest plants to raise in this way. Being far easier than their *Meconopsis* cousins (with the exception of *M. cambrica*), the majority can be sown in the spring where they are to flower. Indeed, most resent disturbance and do not take kindly to being transplanted. In order to get good robust plants, thin sowing is essential, otherwise much laborious thinning will have to take place at the seedling stage.

The taller growing annual types can be supported by suitable 'peasticks', or similar, placed around the groups while they are still young so that the sticks are hidden by the time the plants come into bloom. Most require a well-drained open sunny aspect, although any soil, providing it is neither waterlogged or too acid, will suffice. Few will succeed in dense shade. Most will produce copious seed, which can be collected and stored in a dry container for the following year. Some will self-sow freely, although not all can be relied upon to do so. Named cultivars of *P. somniferum* will undoubtedly hybridise if planted close together so that they must be isolated from one another if 'pure' seed is required. Many of the strains of *P. rhoeas* and *P. radicatum* produce a range of colours, and which will appear from a sowing is a matter of pot luck.

The perennial species can also be grown from seed, which can be sown in pots or directly sown in the border. However, few bother to sow seed of the robust oriental poppies. These can be readily divided or, alternatively, may be propagated from root cuttings (p. 27). Others, such as *P. rupifragum* and *P. spicatum*, are short-lived perennials with a solitary undividable taproot and these must be propagated from seed. In some gardens they may self-sow and young plants can be moved, provided that they are dug up with a good rootball attached – they will generally sulk for a while but, if carefully nurtured, will generally grow well after a few weeks. Spring and early summer are the best time to attempt such moves.

The small perennials of the '*P. alpinum*' complex, as well as the Japanese *P. miyabeanum*, make charming subjects for the alpine or scree garden. Although short-lived, they are very floriferous and can generally be relied upon to self-sow. In any event, seed can be easily collected and resown.

The annual poppies like *P. commutatum*, *P. radicatum* and *P. rhoeas* make striking fillers for gaps in flower borders or indeed for a border devoted to colourful annuals. If space permits, a drift of poppies can be a breathtaking sight that will provide interest over many weeks during the summer. *P. rhoeas*, in its normal red-flower mixtures, is ideal for wild flower meadows or for sowing along road verges or motorways.

The bold forms of oriental poppies with their brazen colours can be eye-catching subjects in the herbaceous border, but they need to be placed with care as their colours can clash with those of neighbouring plants. I once saw an entire border devoted to various oriental poppies – a bold piece of planning to excite the eye and attract the neighbours!

Classification

The species of *Papaver* divide conveniently into a number of sections, of which the bare outlines are presented here, together with typical examples for each.

Section Argemonorhoeades Fedde. Annual herbs, generally hairy or bristly, with the stem leaves not clasping (amplexicaule). Flowers often red, pink or purplish, with the filaments dilated towards the top. Fruit-capsule bristly, at least near the stigmatic disk, which is generally somewhat narrower than the capsule. e.g. *PP. argemone, hybridum, pavoninum*.

Section Carinatae Fedde. Annual herbs, hairy, without clasping stem leaves. Fruit capsules with a disk as wide as the capsule, generally with five to ten keeled rays, which have a deep sinus between each. e.g. *P. macrostomum*.

Section Macrantha Elk (= Oxytona Bernh.). A group of robust, bristly perennials with large flowers, the petals generally red (in the wild species) and 3–9 cm (1¼–3⅝ in) long, four or occasionally six in number; filaments dilated. Fruit capsule often egg-shaped, smooth, with the disk as broad as the capsule and with 7–20 rays, e.g. *PP. bracteatum, orientale, paucifoliatum*.

Section Mecones Bernh. Annual herbs, glaucous and generally hairless, occasionally somewhat bristly, the stem leaves usually clasping and unstalked. Fruit-capsule oblong to rounded, smooth, with a flattish disk as wide as the capsule and 5–18 rays. e.g. *PP. glaucum, somniferum*.

Section Miltantha Bernh. Biennial herbs with bristly stems and leaves and red to orange flowers. Fruit-capsule elliptical to club-shaped with a narrow, pyramidal disk, which has four to seven rays usually. e.g. *PP. armeniacum, caucasicum, triniifolium*.

Section Papaver (= Orthorhoeades Fedde). Annual herbs, occasionally biennials or perennials, generally hairy or bristly, the stem leaves not clasping. Flowers pink, red, orange or purple usually, with linear filaments. Fruit-capsule smooth, with a disk as wide as the capsule, with 4–18 rays; sinuses small. e.g. *PP. commutatum, hybridum, rhoeas.*

Section Pilosa Prantl. (= Pseudo-pilosa M. Pop.). Perennial herbs, usually hairy, with orange flowers which have linear filaments. Fruit capsule oblong to club-shaped with a disk as broad as the capsule and six to seven rays. e.g. *PP. oreophilum, pilosum, spicatum.*

Section Scapiflora Rchb. Plants with basal leaf-tufts, often caespitose, and with solitary scapose flowers. Flowers white, yellow, pink, orange or red, more rarely pink. Fruit-capsule often oblong, sometimes rounded, beset with stiff hairs or bristles, with a disk about as wide as the capsule, mostly with four to eight rays, e.g. *PP. burseri, miyabeanum, nudicaule, radicatum, rhaeticum.*

Key to Species in Cultivation

1. Plants with leafy stems, annuals, biennials or perennials (except *P. monanthum* which has white-bristly sepals and glabrous fruit-capsules) 2
   Plants scapose perennials – all leaves basal; fruit-capsules always hairy . 37

2. Perennials, monocarpic or polycarpic 3
   Annuals, occasionally over-wintering 17

3. Monocarpic plants (dying after flowering in the second or third year); inflorescence paniculate 4
   Polycarpic plants (perennials); flowers solitary or in spikelike racemes 7

4. Leaves 1-pinnate; fruit-capsule 10–15 mm (⅖–⅗ in) long; petals 20–30 mm (⅘–1⅕ in) long 5
   Leaves 2–3-pinnate; fruit-capsule up to 10 mm (⅖ in) long; petals 10–15 mm (⅖–⅗ in) long 6

5. Fruit-capsule hairy: ***P. persicum***
   Fruit-capsule glabrous: ***P. fugax***

6. Leaf-margins revolute; fruit-capsule somewhat beaded (torulose):
                                                        P. armeniacum
   Leaf-margin flat; fruit-capsule smooth: ***P. triniifolium***

7. Flowers relatively small, not more than 6 cm (2⅖ in) across 8
   Flowers large, 6–14 cm (2⅖–5⅗ in) across, sometimes larger 12

8. Flowers born in spikelike racemes 9
   Flowers solitary, not in spikelike racemes 10

9. Fruit-capsules with a rounded base; petals pale brick-red: ***P. spicatum***
   Fruit-capsule with a narrowed (attenuate) base; petals orange-red to deep orange, often with a pale base: ***P. pilosum***

10. Stems unbranched: ***P. lateritium***
    Stems branched close to the base 11

11. Leaves and stems silky-hairy; sepals hairy: **P. atlanticum**
    Leaves and stems subglabrous; sepals glabrous: **P. rupifragum**

12. Petals generally pink or orange-red, unblotched; filaments filiform,
    pale yellow; stigmatic disk with five to nine rays 13
    Petals red, deep orange or pinkish-red (sometimes also pink or
    white in cultivars) often blotched; filaments dilated distally; stigmatic
    disk with 11–18 rays 14

13. Flowers scapose; sepals covered by whitish hairs; fruit-capsule
    12–15 mm (½–⅗ in) long: **P. monanthum**
    Flowers borne on leafy stems; sepals covered by reddish-brown
    hairs; fruit-capsule 15–17 mm (⅗–⅔ in) long: **P. oreophilum**

14. Bracts present immediately beneath the flower 15
    Bracts absent 16

15. Bracts three to five, at least 2 cm (⅘ in) long: **P. bracteatum**
    Bracts two, not more than 1 cm (⅖ in) long: **P. intermedium**

16. Pedicels with appressed hairs; petals four to six: **P. orientale**
    Pedicels with spreading (patent) hairs; petals six: **P. lasiothrix**

17. Fruit-capsules hairy or bristly, usually densely so, but occasionally
    with just a few bristles at the top 18
    Fruit-capsules glabrous 24

18. Flower buds glabrous: **P. apulum**
    Flower buds hairy or bristly 19

19. Flower buds with two large hollow-horns: **P. pavoninum**
    Flower buds without horns 20

20. Fruit-capsules subglobose 21
    Fruit-capsules oblong to elliptical or clavate (club-shaped) 22

21. Petals 2–4 cm (⅘–1⅗ in) long, bright red with a basal black blotch
    edge in white; flowerbuds globose: **P. ocellatum**
    Petals 1.5–2 cm (⅗–⅘ in) long, wine-red or pinkish-red with
    a violet-black basal blotch; flowerbuds oblong: **P. hybridum**

22. Plants decumbent, not more than 15 cm (6 in) tall; petals 10–15 mm
    (⅖–⅗ in) long: **P. minus**
    Plants erect, 20 cm (8 in) or more tall; petals 20–30 mm (⅘–1⅕ in)
    long 23

23. Fruit-capsule 10–15 mm (⅖–⅗ in) long; petals with a large
    dark basal blotch: **P. nigrotinctum**
    Fruit-capsule 15–20 mm (⅗–⅘ in) long; petals unblotched or
    with a small basal blotch: **P. argemone**

24. Fruit-capsule subglobose, with a rounded base 25
    Fruit-capsule oblong to clavate (club-shaped), attenuate at the base . 30

25. Plants glaucous, usually glabrous, sometimes slightly bristly; upper
leaves amplexicaule 26
Plants not glaucous, pubescent to bristly; upper leaves rarely
amplexicaule 27

26. Leaves entire to markedly toothed; fruit-capsule 3 cm (1⅕ in)
long or more: *P. somniferum*
Leaves pinnately-lobed; fruit-capsule to 2 cm (⅘ in) long: *P. glaucum*

27. Leaves pinnate with rounded lobes: *P. chelidoniifolium*
Leaves pinnately-lobed, with narrow, pointed segments 28

28. Petals with a dark blotch above the base (almost in the middle
of the petals); pedicels with appressed hairs: *P. commutatum*
Petals with a dark or pale blotch or zone at the base; pedicels with
spreading (patent) hairs 29

29. Flowers 5–9 cm (2–3⅗ in) across; petals red, often with a dark blotch
at the base, sometimes edged in white: *P. rhoeas*
Flowers 1.5–3 cm (⅗–1⅕ in) across; petals red with a greenish
zone at the base: *P. californicum*

30. Stigmatic disk deciduous, falling away in one piece when the
fruit-capsule is ripe, the rays distinctly keeled: *P. macrostomum*
Stigmatic disk persistent on ripe fruit-capsule, the rays not keeled . . 31

31. Fruit-capsule stipitate (i.e. stalked between the capsule and
the point of attachment of sepals and petals); petals
unblotched: *P. stipitatum*
Fruit-capsule sessile; petals sometimes with a dark basal blotch 32

32. Flowerbuds with two short, nipple-like horns; leaves all
bipinnately-lobed: *P. arenarium*
Flowerbuds without horns; leaves simple pinnately-lobed 33

33. Plants practically glabrous; stem leaves amplexicaule: *P. decaisnei*
Plants bristly or hairy; stem leaves not amplexicaule 34

34. Anthers violet: *P. dubium*
Anthers yellowish or brownish 35

35. Stems appressed-hairy throughout: *P. lecoqii*
Stems with spreading (patent) hairs below 36

36. Stems and leaves hairy: *P. pinnatifidum*
Stems and leaves beset with stout, sharp spines and
bristles: *P. aculeatum*

37. Flowers large, 4–6 cm (1⅗–2⅖ in) across; plants 20 cm (8 in) tall
or more in flower: *P. nudicaule*
Flowers smaller, 4 cm (1⅗ in) or less across, plants rarely more
than 15 cm (6 in) tall in flower, often less 38

38. Fruit-capsule sub-globose, broader than long: **P. miyabeanum**
    Fruit-capsule elliptical, oblong or clavate, clearly longer than broad . 39

39. Flowers small, the petals less than 15 mm (⅗ in) long, yellow,
    orange or red 40
    Flowers larger, the petals at least 15 mm (⅗ in) long, white,
    yellow, pink, rarely orange or red 41

40. Pedicels 4 × the length of the leaves; flowers 1–2 cm (⅖–⅘ in)
    across, with persistent petals: **P. involucratum**
    Pedicels 1–2 × the length of the leaves; flowers 2–3 cm (⅘–1⅕ in)
    across, without persistent petals: **P. suaveolens**

41. Leaf-bases forming a close tunic around neck of plant; lower
    leaf-segments, alternate 42
    Leaf-base not forming a tunic or only a loose one; lower
    leaf-segments opposite 43

42. Flowers white; leaf-segments pointed: **P. sendtneri**
    Flowers yellow rarely orange or red; leaf-segments blunt: **P. rhaeticum★**

43. Flowers yellow or orange, rarely red 44
    Flowers white or pink 48

44. Leaves two- to three-pinnate: **P. kerneri★ & P. nivale**
    Leaves simple-pinnate, rarely two-pinnate 45

45. Leaves glabrous; petals not becoming blue-green
    on drying **P. corona-sancti-stephani**
    Leaves bristly; petals becoming blue-green on drying 46

46. Fruit-capsule widest about the middle, the stigmatic disk usually
    flat or somewhat concave, often with five rays: **P. radicatum**
    Fruit-capsule widest near the top, the stigmatic disk convex, with
    five to eight rays usually 47

47. Stems with white latex when cut, pedicels curved: **P. dahlianum**
    Stems with yellow latex when cut; pedicels straight
    and erect: **P. lapponicum**

48. Scapes decumbent; petals white or pink, often yellowish
    at the base: **P. alboroseum**
    Scapes erect; petals usually white, occasionally pink or red, with a
    yellowish base 49

49. Leaves two- to three-pinnate; petals not drying blue-green: **P. burseri★**
    Leaves simple pinnate; petals becoming blue-green on drying 50

50. Fruit-capsule widest above the middle, the stigmatic disk usually
    flat or somewhat concave, often with five rays: **P. radicatum**
    Fruit-capsule widest near the top, the stigmatic disk convex, with
    five to eight rays usually: **P. dahlianum**

★ *P. alpinum* of cultivation

Papaver aculeatum Thunb.
(Syn. *P. gariepinum* Buch. ex DC.)
SOUTH AFRICAN POPPY

This poppy has the distinction of being the only species native to Africa south of the equator. It is an annual species in the same group as *P. rhoeas* and *P. dubium*, and may reach 30–60 cm (12–24 in) tall, with most of the leaves crowded towards the base of the plant. The whole plant, except for the fruit-capsule, is markedly bristly. The leaves are pinnately-lobed and toothed. The solitary flowers are plain orange with yellow stamens and the smooth fruit-capsule, 18–22 mm (⅔–⅞ in) long, is roughly oval in outline, somewhat narrowed at the base and with a small stigmatic disk with six to eight rays.

P. *aculeatum* is confined primarily to the Drakensberg Mountains of the Transvaal, South Africa and to neighbouring areas of Botswana, up to altitudes of 1850 m (6100 ft). It is rare in cultivation today, although it has been cultivated since about 1825.

Papaver alboroseum Hultén

An interesting little poppy related to *P. radicatum* and differing primarily in its dwarf stature, being rarely more than 10 cm (4 in) tall in flower, with thin, flexuous scapes that are clearly decumbent at the base. The small flowers, only 10–20 mm (⅖–⅘ in) across are white or very pale pink, each petal often with a yellowish basal blotch. The fruit-capsule, 10–15 mm (⅖–⅗ in) long is covered in yellowish or brownish hairs.

P. *alboroseum* is confined to the eastern CIS, Kamschatka region, and Alaska as well as northern British Columbia, where it is to be found growing on gravelly soils and rock outcrops. It is a dainty Iceland-type poppy ideal for screes and raised beds in the garden, where its delicate habit can be best appreciated. It is offered by a number of seed merchants and nurseries and is a real gem to acquire.

The decumbent bases to the flowering scapes and the pale colour of the flowers set this species apart from the other members of the *P. nudicaule* complex.

Papaver alpinum L., nomen ambig.

This much confused name has been widely applied to a number of small alpine poppy species native to the Pyrenees, Alps and the Carpathian Mountains. They are small tufted plants with all the leaves basal and finely dissected. The solitary flowers, often 2–5 cm (⅘–2 in) across, are borne on slender bristly scapes and range in colour from white to yellow, more rarely in shades of orange or red. The fruit-capsules are small, oblong or elliptic in outline and with appressed or spreading bristles.

In the garden they are delightful plants for pockets in the rock garden, raised bed or scree, revelling in gritty, well-drained soils. Although perennial, they are not long-lived, but can generally be relied upon to seed around and excess seedlings can be easily removed. If several of the species are grown in close proximity, they will undoubtedly hybridise, producing a charming range of hybrids often in pastel shades of pink, yellow or orange or pure white. Regular removal of dead flowers will generally ensure a supply of blooms throughout the late spring and summer. Seedlings flower within a few months of germination.

For details of the species involved, see *P. burseri*, *P. kerneri*, *P. rhaeticum*, *P. suaveolens* and *P. sendtneri*. These are generally listed by seed merchants and nurseries as '*P. alpinum*'. Related species from Arctic regions and central Asia include *P. lapponicum*, *P. nudicaule*, *P. radicatum*, *P. miyabeanum* and *P. nivale*.

'Summer Breeze' is a particularly fine selection of floriferous F1 hybrids with bright flowers in shades of red, orange, yellow and white, above mounds of ferny foliage. A white selection is sometimes offered as *P. alpinum* 'Alba', a plant almost indistinguishable from *P. burseri*. They can be grown as half-hardy annuals, or sown direct in the spring, where they are to flower.

Papaver anomalum Fedde
(syn. *P. nudicaule* subsp. *amurense* N. Busch)
A tufted perennial up to 40 cm (16 in) tall, with scapose flowers. Leaves narrow elliptical, pinnately-lobed, the lobes narrow but blunt, untoothed or slightly lobed or dentate, drawn out at the base into a long rather slender petiole. The buds are egg-shaped, the sepals with a few scattered hairs. Scapes slender and erect, usually up to 40 cm (16 in) long, but occasionally to 55 cm (22 in), with rather sparse orange soft bristles. Flowers usually white, occasionally pale yellow or orange, 6–7 cm (2⅖–2⅘ in) across. The fruit capsule is smooth (glabrous), variable in shape from almost oval in outline to club-shaped, up to about 10 mm (⅖ in) across, with a relatively flat disk with generally 8 rays.

Distributed in N and NE China and SE Siberia (Amur, Ussuri). It is a plant of rocky meadows, ridges and river gravels, occasionally being found on cultivated land.

The smooth capsules of *P. anomalum* serve to distinguish it readily from *P. nudicaule* and its allies. It probably finds its closest ally in *P. stubendorfii*, which has small, consistently orange, flowers, small leaves and very slender scapes (see p.97).

P. anomalum was described from a collection made by Ernest Henry Wilson in Hubei province, northern China (under the number 2421). The original plants, and indeed most of those found in the wild, bear white flowers, so that the cultivar name 'Alba' applied to plants grown in gardens, and widely available today in the nursery trade, is superfluous.

It is not entirely clear if the Chinese plants from the Hubei region are the same as the Siberian plants and this requires further research. At the same time, plants found in the Amur region of eastern Siberia, not far from the Chinese frontier, with orange flowers and almost spherical fruit capsules, which are often included here, may in fact belong to another distinct and as yet undescribed species.

P. anomalum is an attractive addition to the flower garden. It is a short-lived perennial, but readily raised from seeds, producing a succession of blooms during the summer months. The flowers are pristine white with a boss of golden stamens in the centre, while the margins of the petals are attractively ruffled.

Papaver apulum Ten.

A Mediterranean poppy very similar to the more widespread *P. argemone*. It can at once be separated by its oval, smooth flower buds and bright scarlet flowers, each petal with a prominent, basal, black blotch. Although the flowers are a similar size and shape to those of *P. argemone*, the fruit-capsule is noticeably smaller, being rarely more than 10 mm (⅖ in) in length and scarcely ribbed.

P. apulum is distributed from southern Italy and Sicily to the Balkan Peninsula, east as far as the Turkish Aegean islands of Ikaria and Ag. Nickolaos, where it grows in grassy and stony places, orchards, olive groves and along roadsides at low altitudes – to 500 m (1650 ft) at the most. It is one of a number of colourful annuals that help to make a tapestry of colour in these Mediterranean regions during the spring – late March to May.

P. apulum is another neglected annual poppy in our gardens. It is quite one of the prettiest and well deserves a little more attention, although it is difficult to find in seed catalogues at the present time.

Papaver arenarium M.–B.
(Syn. *P. dubium* var. *arenarium* Elk.; *P. rhoeas* var. *arenarium*)

The affinities of this species can be readily judged from its synonymy. It can at once be distinguished from *P. rhoeas*, *P. dubium* and their allies by the pair of short horns – about 1–2 mm (1⁄12 in) long – terminating the flowerbuds; these are most easily observed in the young bud stage. As in *P. dubium*, the flower stalks (peduncles) are appressed-hairy and the fruit-capsule oblong in outline, smooth and generally with seven to nine stigmatic rays. The flowers approach the size of those of *P. rhoeas*, being mostly 5–7 cm (2–2⅘ in) across, but are a purple-red rather than scarlet; each petal has a large basal, black blotch.

Fruit of *Papaver arenarium*

The mammil–like apex to the flower buds are a useful diagnostic feature. Similar nipple–like horns occur in *P. pavoninum*, although in that species they are much larger and more pronounced. In addition, the fruit-capsules of *P. pavoninum* are distinctly bristly, rather than smooth.

P. arenarium is a delightful, though unaccountably neglected, garden annual, easy to grow and as charming as any annual poppy. A sunny position and a light sandy soil are its chief requirements. It is occasionally offered in seed catalogues.

Like its cousins, *P. arenarium* is a plant of stony steppes and hillslopes, often at low altitudes but up to 1900 m (6200 ft) in the mountains of northern Iran. It is rarely associated with cultivation and its main area of distribution is from southern Russia and the Caucasus to Iraq and Iran; it is apparently absent from central Asia.

Papaver argemone L.
PRICKLY POPPY

This charming little poppy is one of the commoner poppies seen in Western Europe, being closely related to the rough poppy, *P. hybridum*. It differs primarily in its paler, scarlet or brick-red flowers, the petals widely spreading, rather narrow, rarely overlapping, and with or without a dark basal blotch, and by the oblong fruit-capsule with a few erect bristles; in *P. hybridum* the fruit-capsules are globose and densely beset with curved, straw-coloured bristles.

P. argemone has a wide distribution from Western Europe and North Africa eastwards to Iran, although it is rather rare in old Soviet Central Asia, where *P. hybridum* is far commoner and more widespread. Like *P. hybridum*, it is a plant of cultivated land, fallow fields and stony places, generally at rather low altitudes but up to 2000 m (6500 ft) in the mountains of western Iran.

It is rarely cultivated on purpose in gardens, being less spectacular than some of its showier cousins. However, the more muted, less startling flower colour may be more to some tastes. In some gardens it turns up as a weed and is worth tolerating for its pretty effect amongst other annuals.

Papaver atlanticum (Ball) Cosson   [Pl. 32]
(Syn. *P. rupifragum* subsp. *atlanticum* Ball)
MOROCCAN POPPY

An attractive poppy that is very similar to *P. rupifragum* – indeed, it was at one time placed under that species. It can be distinguished on three counts: the leaves and stems are silky with hairs; the flowers, somewhat larger at 5–6.5 cm (2–2⅖ in) across, are dull orange; and the fruit-capsules are narrowly club-shaped.

Despite such obvious differences, these two pretty little poppies have been much confused in gardens. Of the two, *P. atlanticum* is the commonest; indeed, it is sometimes offered for sale as *P. rupifragum*. The soft orange, tissue–paper blooms are a great delight and, although never produced in great quantity, appear throughout the summer until the first frosts of autumn. Removing the seedheads will promote more flowers and prevent too many unwanted seedlings appearing. There is a semi-double form 'Flore Pleno', perhaps more often seen in gardens than the single form. A very similar strain named 'Double Orange' is offered; this has flowers ranging in colour from brick red to tangerine. These semi-double strains of *P. atlanticum* generally produce some ordinary single-flowered seedlings in their midst and these are best weeded out, saving seed only from the best 'doubles'. *P. atlanticum* is confined in the wild to rock crevices in the mountains of Morocco.

Papaver bracteatum Lindl.
(Syn. *P. orientale* var. *bracteatum* Ledeb.)
'ORIENTAL POPPY'

Few plants in the garden are as spectacular in the vividness of their blooms or indeed for sheer size as the various races of oriental poppy. As explained under *P. orientale* (p. 101), the oriental poppies of gardens have been derived from both that species, *P. bracteatum* and *P. pseudo-orientale* and it is often difficult to assign a particular cultivar to any one. The differences between these closely allied species are outlined under *P. orientale* and to avoid confusion all the oriental cultivars are listed and described under that species.

In the wild *P. bracteatum* is a more robust species than *P. orientale*, making substantial clumps with thick erect, rough bristly stems up to 1.2 m (4 ft), occasionally taller; the lower stem has spreading bristles, whilst on the upper stem they are clearly appressed. The large leaves, up to 45 cm (18 in) long, sometimes larger, are primarily basal, pinnately-lobed, the segments rough, bristly and deeply toothed; the stems are leafy to the top, generally with five or six leaves per stem, the upper two leaves small and pressed close to the base of the flower bud, where there are also, in addition, three to five oval sepal-like bracts. The flowers are very large, cup or bowl-shaped, 10–18 cm (4–7 in) across (but up to 28 cm (11 in) in cultivated forms), blood red to purple-crimson, each of the four to six petals with a prominent, oblong, black basal blotch (longer than broad; the reverse situation is found in *P. orientale*); the stamens have dark filaments and violet or blackish anthers. The large, smooth fruit-capsule, 3–4 cm (1¼–1⅝ in) long, has a flat stigmatic disk often with 14–20 stigmatic rays.

P. bracteatum is endemic to the Caucasus, eastern Turkey (Anatolia) and northern and western Iran, where it is to be found on rocky and scrubby slopes as well as on the neighbouring plains, at altitudes of 1750–2800 m (5750–9200 ft); flowering in the wild from June to July.

The species was described by John Lindley in 1821 from a specimen growing in Chelsea, London. The seed had been sent to Fischer from the Mineralnye Vody region of the Caucasus and specimens in the Fischer Herbarium, under the name *P. orientale*, clearly belong to *P. bracteatum*.

The *Flora of the USSR* (vol. 7) considers *P. bracteatum* to be a relict species isolated geographically from the related *P. intermedium*, which differs in its small, paired, flower bracts. However, other authorities (especially James

Cullen in *Flora Iranica*) consider the species to embrace a large range of variability and to encompass a greater area in the wild, from the Caucasus and eastern Anatolia (Turkey) to northern Iran.

P. pseudo-orientale Medw. (= *P. intermedium* DC.) almost certainly represents a hybrid of ancient origin between *P. bracteatum* and *P. orientale* and the presence of this species has certainly caused some of the confusion in the orientalis-type poppies. However, there is a good deal of evidence that, despite their origins, *P. bracteatum* and *P. intermedium* form a more or less continuous range of variability, one to the other. In such an event it is probably best to consider them to be a single species. Certainly, as far as the garden is concerned, the oriental poppies have complex origins that may well encompass all these various elements originally.

P. orientale and *P. bracteatum* (including *P. pseudo-orientale*) have flower colours in the orange and red range of the spectrum. However, many garden forms have flowers of pink or white. Such colours may have originated from other species introduced into cultivation under the *P. orientale* 'blanket' which are no longer in cultivation, but have been superseded by more robust cultivars. For instance, the Caucasian *P. paucifoliatum* (Trautb.) Fedde, which is closely allied to *P. orientalis* itself, has almost leafless stems and medium-sized flowers of pinkish-red or brick-red, with unblotched petals; native of the extreme north-eastern Turkey and the Caucasus, to an altitude of 2700 m (8850 ft). Some of the almost scapose double oriental poppies are probably derived from this species rather than *P. bracteatum* or *P. orientale*. Another allied species, *P. monanthum* Trautb. (also a Caucasian endemic), has leafless stems and orange-pink flowers, 5–8 cm (2–3⅕ in) across. What is quite certain is that the origins of the oriental poppies are clearly complex and have been confused over time and initially, at least, by a lack of understanding of the wild species involved.

P. monanthum, which is not at present in cultivation, is placed in a separate section (the Pilosa) to *P. orientale* and its allies. This section is distinguished on account of its paler flowers (generally in the pink to pale orange or pinkish-red range), unblotched petals and the slender yellow stamen filaments. Despite this, there are clear transitions between *P. monanthum* and *P. orientale* and the sectional boundaries would not stand up to close scrutiny. Incidentally, *P. monanthum* also shows close affinities with another group of poppies well represented in gardens but restricted to the western Mediterranean region – namely *P. atlanticum* and *P. rupifragum*.

Papaver burseri Crantz
(Syn. *P. alpinum* subsp. *alpinum* sensu Markgraf, non L.)
ALPINE POPPY

A small tufted alpine poppy, almost hairless, with the leaf-bases forming a loose tunic around the base of the plant. The symmetrical leaves are two- to three-pinnately lobed with narrow, lanceolate or linear, pointed segments; the lower leaf-segments are opposite, in contrast to those of the closely related *P. sendtneri*, which are alternate. The single-flowered scapes rise to

20 cm (8 in), though often less, and are appressed-bristly. The cupped flowers, 3–4 cm (1¼ –1½ in) across, are pure white with a generous boss of yellow anthers. The club-shaped, bristly capsule usually has only four stigmatic rays.

This species is a true delight – one of the whitest of poppies. It is the most widely grown of the alpine poppies, though generally hiding under the umbrella of 'P. alpinum' in gardens, which is unfortunate as it is well worth seeking out and by no means difficult to grow. P. alpinum 'Alba' (p. 79) is almost certainly a form of P. burseri.

P. burseri is a native of the northern Alps and the Carpathian Mountains, inhabiting high limestone rocks, screes and moraines between 1200–2000 m (3900–6650 ft).

See also P. kerneri (p. 91) and P. corona-sancti-stephani (p. 86).

Papaver californicum Gray   [Pl. 33]
WESTERN POPPY

A little-cultivated Californian poppy in the same general section as familiar European species like P. rhoeas and P. dubium. P. californicum inhabits the Coast Ranges where it grows on disturbed soils or areas that have been burnt, flowering in the spring during April and May.

Plants are annual with rather erect, smooth or hairy, stems 30–60 cm (12–24 in) tall. The pinnately-divided leaves, up to 8 cm (3⅕ in) long, have narrow, lobed or sharply toothed segments, the lower leaves stalked but the upper sessile. The flowers are small, 1.5–3 cm (⅗–1⅕ in) across, brick-red with a distinctive greenish zone at the base of each petal, borne on appressed-hairy stalks. The smooth capsule is more or less club-shaped, 12–18 mm (½–⅔ in) long, the stigmatic disk with 6–10 rays.

An interesting little poppy occasionally grown in botanic gardens, but seldom seen elsewhere. It is interesting in being one of the few true poppies, Papaver, native to North America. Indeed, it is the only Papaver native to the western United States, where other genera in the family have proliferated – Eschscholzia and Argemone, for instance. The green base to the petals is a useful feature for distinguishing this rather isolated species from its cousins.

Papaver chibinense N. Semen.

This is closely related to P. radicatum and may be only a localised variant of that species, with more finely dissected foliage. It was described from north-west Russia, from the Khibiny mountain area, after which it is named.

Papaver commutatum Fischer & Meyer   [Pl. 34–35]
(Syn. P. rhoeas var. commutatum Elk.; P. strigosum var. commutata Fedde ex Busch)

This handsome species is very closely related to P. rhoeas, being a bristly annual, often branched from close to the base, though rarely more than

50 cm (20 in) tall; the stems are soft with greyish hairs in the lower part, which is especially apparent in young plants. The leaves are soft, greyish-green and with rather blunt segments. If anything, the flowers are an even more intense vivid scarlet, but rather smaller, deeply bowl-shaped, mostly 5–6 cm (2–2½ in) across. The main differences are to be found in the petals, which are broadly oval, rather longer than broad (they are broader than long in *P. rhoeas*) and with a large black blotch (often square) located not at the base of the petal, but almost in the middle. The blotch varies from rounded to square, occasionally waisted in the middle or running almost to the edge of the petal. The stamens have black filaments and the fruit-capsule is also quite smooth, with five to ten stigmatic rays, and has a distinct, though short, stalk.

P. commutatum is native primarily from Turkey eastwards to north-western Iran, the Caucasus and the surrounding regions, as well as isolated localities in Crete. It is essentially a plant of arid steppes, rocky mountain slopes and roadsides, but it also invades cultivated land, particularly arable fields; mainly at an altitude of 800–1800 m (2600–5900 ft); flowering during May and June. In the wild it is said to hybridise on occasions with *P. dubium* where the two species grow in close proximity to one another.

This attractive species is easily distinguished from other similar red poppies by its distinctive petal blotch. Even in fruit, the capsules can be readily differentiated by their short stalk (between the capsule and the point where petals and stamens join the pedicel).

P. commutatum is a fine garden plant generally seen in a form given the name 'Ladybird', which is closely similar to the wild type, though selected for the intensity of its flowers and the especially bold black blotches, which dominate the centres of the petals. In some gardens it will self-sow but, to be sure, it is wise to save some seed each year. It is that startling red that must be placed with care in the garden to avoid clashes with gaudy neighbours. A patch well placed is a certain winner near the front of any border.

P. commutatum finds its closest ally in *P. lacerum* Popov. which hails from Turkey and Armenia. It can be distinguished by its stiffer habit and red or pink petals, which have a basal black blotch. Both also clearly come close to the common poppy, *P. rhoeas*, in which the petals are, however, broader than long and the terminal segments of the leaf-lobes are noticeably longer.

'Flora Europaea' (vol.1:248, 1964) throws some doubt on the validity of this species, more or less equating it with *P. rhoeas* ('Very variable. The following taxa may be worthy of specific distinction'). The two do have a similar growth pattern and flower at the same time, both in the wild and in gardens. However, when seen side by side they are quite clearly distinct. *P. rhoeas* has shallowly bowl-shaped to saucer-shaped flowers, in which the petals are broader than long and are often unblotched or, if they are, then the blotch is right at the base of the petal. In contrast, *P. commutatum* has more substantial petals that are generally longer than broad and with a prominent black blotch suspended above the base of the petal, while the flower shape is a deeper, broader-based bowl. In addition, *P. rhoeas* has noticeably longer and more pointed terminal segments to the leaves. Although the two species bear rather similar seed pods, differences can be noted in the surmounting stigmatic disk.

P. commutatum has become a popular annual poppy in gardens in recent years. Some forms have an attractive silvery picotee edge to the petals and these are being selected out gradually by Sahin in Holland. Overall, it is the intensely deep red petals with their prominent black blotch that make this such an appealing plant to gardeners; the cultivar name 'Ladybird' is highly apt.

This species is wrongly referred to as the Flanders' poppy in some seed catalogues. This is wholly wrong and misleading: the Flanders' poppy is *P. rhoeas*.

Papaver corona-sancti-stephani Zapal.

(Syn. *P. alpinum* L. subsp. *corona-sancti-stephani* (Zapal.) Borza)

This alpine poppy, with its tongue-twisting name, is not in cultivation as far as I am aware, although it is listed by Llanbrook Alpine Nursery near Clinton, Shropshire. However, it is another delight in the '*P. alpinum*' complex, coming closest to *P. burseri* and *P. kerneri*; being distinguished by its less divided hairless leaves, only one- or two-pinnate, and more rounded fruit-capsules, only 7–10 mm (⅓–⅖ in) long. The small flowers are yellow, 18–26 mm (¾–1 in) across. It is a native of the eastern and southern Carpathian Mountains of Romania.

P. pyrenaicum subsp. *degenii* Urum. from south-western Bulgaria, with rather smaller flowers in yellow or orange, is probably only a variant of *P. corona-sancti-stephani* and is sometimes listed by nurseries as *P. degenii*. I have grown plants of the latter for a number of years on a raised scree bed, where they seed around with abundant regularity. The small flowers with rather narrow petals vary in colour from pale yellow to orange, salmon and white. They are probably better referred to the '*P. alpinum*' complex, as I am very doubtful whether they are the true *degenii*. Despite this, they are a joy to have about and always attract the attention of visitors to the garden, who often carry away a seedpod to try for themselves.

The plant described as *P. alpinum* subsp. *tatricum* A. Nyárády from the western Carpathian Mountains may be little more than a localised variant of *P. corona-sancti-stephani*, differing in its white flowers, more lanceolate leaf-segments and rather larger fruit capsules, usually 10–11 mm (⅜ in) long.

Papaver dahlianum Nordh.

(Syn. *P. radicatum* subsp. *brachyphyllum* Tolm. & subsp. *polare* Tolm.)

A little-known species most closely related to *P. lapponicum*, but with white latex when the stems are cut and more dissected leaves. The scapes are often decumbent and the yellow or white flowers relatively small, 3–4.5 cm (1⅕–4⅘ in) across.

P. dahlianum is restricted to Arctic Norway and the neighbouring part of Russia. Seed is rarely offered.

Papaver dubium L.   [Pl. 36–37]
(Syn. *P. modestum* Jordan; *P. obtusifolium* Desf.)
LONG-HEADED POPPY

A poppy of the *P. rhoeas* persuasion, but in every way more modest. The pinnately dissected leaves often have a somewhat greyish-green appearance and when cut, like the stem, exude a prominent white latex. The pedicels have distinctly appressed rather than spreading bristles. The flowers are paler and smaller, generally being pale scarlet or pinkish-red, 2.5–5 cm (1–2 in) across. The petals are often wider than long, with or without a basal dark blotch. The smooth fruit-capsule is decidedly oblong to club-shaped in outline and up to 2 cm (1 in) long, with generally five to nine stigmatic rays.

P. dubium is equally widely distributed as *P. rhoeas*, occurring from Europe and north Africa, eastwards into western Asia to Iran and the Caucasus, and southwards to Ethiopia, where it is a plant of cultivated and waste land, rather bare stony slopes and roadsides.

It is rarely grown in gardens, though often turning up in some as a weed. However, it is worth growing, if only for the more subtle hue of its flowers, less brazen than many red poppies and perhaps more easy to place in the flower border. It is an example of a common plant being ignored through familiarity.

In Cyprus, parts of Turkey and Syria a similar, though more prostrate, plant with rather smaller, pale scarlet or orange-red flowers is distinguished as *P. postii* Fedde. The fruit-capsule is only 6–8 mm (¼–⅔ in) long when mature and bears only five or six stigmatic rays. *P. postii* is primarily a plant of rocky places and screes in the mountains, above 450 m (1500 ft).

Papaver dubium subsp. albiflorum (Besser) Grey-Wilson, stat. nov.
(Syn. *P. albiflorum* (Besser) Pacz.)

This is readily distinguished by its white or pale pink flowers, with unblotched petals. It is primarily restricted to south-eastern Europe.

Papaver fauriei (Fedde) Tatew. & Miyabe
(Syn. *P. alpinum* var. *microcarpum* sensu Kawak.; *P. nudicaule* sensu Makino, non L.; *P. n.* L. subsp. *xanthopetalum* Fedde var. *fauriei* Fedde)

A charming little alpine poppy that is restricted to the gravelly slopes of Mt Rishiri (1721 m/5646 ft), on Rishiri island, which lies off Japan to the north-west of Hokkaido. It is a rare species, which has been much confused in the past with another Japanese species, *P. miyabeanum*.

Both species are dainty little poppies of the general appearance and stature of the *Papaver 'alpinum'* complex, forming small tufts of leaves and producing a succession of small scapose flowers during the summer months. *P. fauriei* produces primarily bipinnately lobed leaves in which the lobes are more or less wedge-shaped, while *P. miyabeanum* has pinnately lobed leaves with rounded tips to the lobes. In addition, the flowers of *P. fauriei* are a rather clear yellow, 1.5–2.5 cm (⅗–1 in) across, whereas those of *P. miyabeanum* are larger (mostly 3–5 cm/1⅕–2 in) across and a greenish-yellow. Furthermore, Eckenwalder (1989) in his 'Classification of Arctic and Alpine Poppies' shows that *P. fauriei* is a hexaploid species, whereas *P. miyabeanum* is an octoploid.

The species was named by Friedrich Fedde in 1936 in honour of the French missionary Urbain Faurie, who was a significant collector of Japanese plants during the nineteenth century.

P. fauriei is rare in cultivation and any plant found under the name generally proves to be the relatively widely grown *P. miyabeanum*. Both species thrive in the garden in a well-drained gritty soil such as a scree garden or raised bed. Although they are generally not long-lived, they produce seed in plenty and, under the right conditions, will self-sow. Seed can also be gathered and planted in the spring. Plants dislike being transplanted, like those of most annual or short-lived poppies.

Papaver fugax Poir.   [Pl. 38]
(Syn. *P. caucasicum* M.–B.; *P. floribundum* Desf.)

An interesting western Asian species related to *P. triniifolium* and, like that species, a biennial. It differs primarily in its angled lower stems, simply dissected (one-pinnately lobed) leaves, one pyramidal, paniculate inflorescence and rather larger pink or pale red flowers, each petal with a pale yellow base. The stamens are yellow and the grey-green fruit-capsules smooth, oblong-club-shaped, 10–15 mm (⅖–⅗ in) long, the stigmatic disk usually with only four to six rays.

P. fugax is a plant of dry rocky slopes and screes, 1700–3100 m (5600–10,200 ft) altitude, in eastern Turkey (Anatolia), the Caucasus, northern and north-western Iran, as well as northern Iraq.

This is another species apparently lost to cultivation. It is very variable and authorities are not generally agreed on the circumscription of the species or indeed its relationship to its allies. For instance, intermediates between it and *P. persicum* occur in the wild, particularly in Iraq. These are generally given the name *P. partuschianum*, although it is not clear whether this represents a hybrid between two distinct species or indeed intermediates linking two extremes of a single variable species. Such problems are scarcely likely to hinder the horticulturist and gardener, as none of these plants are in cultivation at the present time. *P. persicum* in fact represents an altogether more bristly version of *P. fugax*, the leaves, flowerbuds and fruit-capsules being furnished with yellowish or brownish bristles.

All these 'species' are well worth growing and if seed becomes available, they should certainly be given a try. All will undoubtedly require a hot sunny site and an acutely drained light soil. Plants under the names of *P. caucasicum* and *P. persicum* have certainly been cultivated in the past and there was then no question as to their hardiness.

It seems a pity that such plants should be lost to cultivation purely from neglect or from not being more widely distributed in the first instance.

Today, when such efforts are still being made to bring new species into cultivation and to reintroduce those lost, it seems extremely important that a real effort must be made to maintain those species already in cultivation, otherwise the whole exercise becomes rather pointless, especially as so many desirable plants are becoming increasingly rare in the wild. Annuals and biennials have always presented a challenge to the cultivator. Many are not too difficult to grow, but because they are transitory, seed needs to be collected on a regular basis to ensure that they remain in cultivation. Changes in fashion in recent years, especially in the growing of such subjects, has unfortunately relegated many to the scarce or rare category in our gardens. I was fortunate in seeing this interesting species in the wild in NW Georgia (Caucasus Mountains in 1998) growing in river gravels. Unfortunately it was only just in flower and no seed was available.

Papaver glaucum Boiss. & Hausskn. [Pl. 39]
TULIP POPPY

This charming, but little grown, species is closely related to the opium poppy, *P. somniferum*, but it is a slighter plant not more than 45 cm (18 in) tall and with distinctly more deeply lobed leaves. The flowers, 6–10 cm (2½–4 in) across, are borne on bristly stalks and are deep scarlet, each petal having a black blotch at its base. The small fruit-capsule is globose and quite smooth, not more than 2 cm (¾ in) long.

P. *glaucum* is native to Anatolian Turkey, Iran, Syria and Iran, where it inhabits rocky and waste land, olive groves and vineyards, mountain slopes and sandy places, generally at an altitude of between 700–1800 m (2300–5900 ft), flowering in May and June.

A neglected annual in gardens, well worth acquiring if it can be found. It tends not to self-sow with any vigour, so it is wise to collect some seed each year for sowing the following spring.

Papaver hybridum L. [Pl. 40]
ROUGH POPPY

This widespread European and Asian Poppy is one of the common 'red poppies' of the region, although it is in fact rather rare in Britain, being confined to scattered localities in the south and east of the country.

The species is an annual up to 30 cm (12 in) tall, occasionally taller, the bristle-haired stems generally branched from the base, ascending to erect. The bristly leaves are bipinnately lobed, the lanceolate to oval segments toothed or further lobed, the lower leaves stalked, the upper sessile, smaller and less lobed. The solitary flowers are borne on slender, appressed-hairy, rather flexuous stalks, the somewhat bristly flower buds without apical horns. The flowers, 20–30 mm (⅘–1⅕ in) across, are crimson or rose-red, the petals with a conspicuous black or violet basal blotch; stamens relatively few in number with black or violet filaments and blue pollen. The globose to broadly oblong fruit-capsule, 10–14 mm (⅖–⅗ in) long is ribbed and covered with rows of spreading to recurved, straw-coloured bristles; the stigmatic disk has four to nine rays.

P. hybridum is found from western Europe eastwards to Pakistan and central Asia, where it is a plant of cultivated, fallow and waste ground, stony and sandy steppes, generally at low altitudes, occasionally to 800 m (2600 ft) in the lower mountains.

The broad, short fruit-capsules and the lack of horns on the flower buds serve to distinguish this species from its closest allies *P. pavoninum* and *P. argemone*. In addition, the flowers are generally rather smaller.

P. hybridum is seldom cultivated in gardens, although sometimes occurring there as a weed. Its prickly fruits are useful for small dried arrangements in the house.

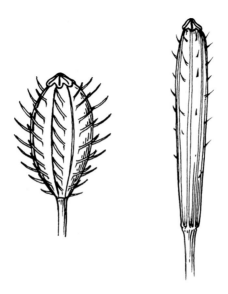

Fruits of *Papaver hybridum* (left) and *P. argemone* (right)

Papaver involucratum M. Pop.

Another little poppy of the *P. radicatum* persuasion, but scarcely known in cultivation. In general stature it is about the height of *P. radicatum,* but is at once distinguished by its very small flowers, only 15–20 mm (⅗–⅘ in) across, which are orange-red, each petal with a yellow basal zone. These are borne on long slender, hairy scapes held well above the leaf tuft. As in *P. radicatum*, the dried petals persist around the developing fruit-capsule.

P. involucratum has a very restricted distribution, being endemic to the western Pamir Alai in the southern CIS (Tadzikistan), where it is apparently confined to indurated moraines at 2800–3300 m (9200–10,800 ft). It may also possibly be found across the border in the Afghan Pamir, in the mountains of the Wakhan Corridor.

Papaver kerneri Hayek   [Pl. 41]

A small alpine poppy of the *P. burseri* persuasion, but readily distinguished on account of its yellow, rather than white, flowers. The fruit-capsule usually has five stigmatic rays.

A native of the south-eastern Alps of Austria, Italy and the neighbouring regions of Yugoslavia, where it inhabits high mountain rocks, screes and moraines.

Occasionally offered in seed lists, but by no means common in cultivation.

Papaver kluanense D. Löve

A delightful little sulphur-yellow poppy of the *P. radicatum* complex endemic to the Canadian rockies, where it inhabits rocky places, particularly screes. In the wild it is seldom more than 9 cm (3½ in) tall, though in cultivation it can be rather taller. I am not sure how it differs from *P. radicatum* and its brethren, so have not included it in the key to species. That said, this is a charming little plant which, like its cousins, tends to be short-lived in cultivation, so seed needs to be resown at regular intervals. A well-drained scree or sheltered raised bed suits it best. Seed is sometimes offered by specialist alpine societies.

Papaver laestadianum (Nordh.) Nordh.

This species with its tongue-twisting name is closely allied to *P. radicatum*. It is distinguished by its more finely dissected leaves which have a distinctive yellowish-bristly indumentum, and in the pedicels that are curved at the base rather than straight. In addition, the fruit capsules are more or less cylindrical rather than elliptical in general outline, with a stigmatic disk of about the same width; in *P. radicatum* the disk is distinctly narrower than the capsule.

An interesting species, but apparently not in cultivation. It is native to Arctic Norway and Sweden.

Papaver laevigatum Bieb.

Similar to *P. dubium*, but an almost glabrous plant with smaller flowers, the petals not more than 15 mm (⅗ in) long, while the fruit capsule has a somewhat convex rather than flat disk.

This species is not in cultivation. It hails from Bulgaria and Turkey, as well as the areas further north, particularly the Crimea and the southern Ukraine.

Papaver lapponicum (A. Tolm.) Nordh.
(Syn. *P. radicatum* subsp. *lapponicum* A. Tolm.)

A tufted perennial closely related to *P. radicatum*, but its stems and flowerbuds are grey-brown rather than blackish- or reddish-brown hairy; this gives them an overall grey appearance. Plants are densely tufted and produce yellow latex. The leaves, 5–12 cm (2–5 in) long, are covered in whitish hairs. The flowers are relatively small, 25–35 mm (1–1⅖ in) across, the petals generally falling off as the fruits develop. The fruit-capsule is usually more slender than those of *P. radicatum*, being only 4–7 mm (⅙–⅓ in) wide (not 7–10 mm/⅓–⅖ in) and widest in the upper part; the stigmatic disk has five to eight rays.

P. *lapponicum* is restricted to Arctic Norway and western Siberia, where it is a plant of stony tundra, screes and moraines. It is occasionally offered in seed lists, but is scarcely as good a plant in gardens as '*P. alpinum*'. However, *P. lapponicum* has probably been used in the breeding of the modern Iceland poppy strains, together with *P. nudicaule* and *P. radicatum*.

In Arctic Siberia similar but stockier plants, seldom more than 15 cm (6 in) tall are distinguished as *P. pulvinatum*. In addition, plants with very narrow, linear, leaf-segments and elegant, tapered fruit-capsules, also from Arctic Siberia (Yenisei region), are called *P. angustifolium*.

Papaver lasiothrix Fedde

This little-known species is probably not in cultivation at the present time or is very rare. It is closely related to *P. orientale*, from which it differs in having blood-red flowers with consistently six petals, only 4–5 cm (1⅗–2 in) long (not 4.5–9 cm (1⅘–3½ in) in the wild form). In addition, the bristles on the flower stems (peduncles) are spreading rather than appressed. The flower may occasionally have two small bracts immediately beneath.

P. *lasiothrix* is found in the wild up to 1450 m (4750 ft) in meadows and along woodland margins, occasionally on rocky slopes, in Turkey (Lazistan to Cappodocia), the Caucasus and northern and north-western Iran.

Papaver lateritium C. Koch   [Pl. 42]
ARMENIAN POPPY

A tufted stoloniferous perennial with mostly basal leaves and many slender, hairy stems reaching up to 50 cm (20 in) tall, though often less. The leaves are lanceolate, coarsely toothed to pinnately-lobed, stalked, hairy like the stems. The solitary flowers are a bright brick-red, sometimes apricot, 4.5–6 cm (1⅘–2 in) across, with orange-yellow anthers; the sepals are covered in long yellowish hairs. The smooth fruit-capsule is club-shaped, the broadest part below the stigmatic disk.

P. *lateritium* is a native of the mountains of Turkish Armenia (Lazistan), where it inhabits rocky places, cliff crevices and screes at an altitude of 1200–3000 m (3900–9850 ft); flowering in July and August.

This is another good garden poppy fairly closely related to the western Mediterranean *P. atlanticum* and *P. rupifragum*. Unlike those species, it is a long-lived perennial, readily raised from seed and, in favoured gardens at least, sowing itself around once established. Unlike its cousins, *P. lateritium* is more seasonal in flowering, with most blooms appearing during May and June. It is perfectly hardy, to at least −15°C (5°F).

The relationship of these poppies to *P. orientalis* and its allies is not properly understood and it is not clear whether or not these species all hybridise readily in cultivation. *P. lateritium* is very close to the Caucasian *P. oreophilum* and *P. monanthum*. This latter species does (as explained on p. 139) form an interconnecting series with *P. orientale* and its allies, despite the fact that some

Papaver lateritium

botanists place them in different sections of the genus.

P. lateritium has become naturalised in several localities in Britain, perhaps elsewhere in southern Europe.

The exact status of 'Fireball' **[Pl. 43]** (= × *hybridum* 'Flore Pleno', 'Nanum Flore Pleno', 'Nana Plena'), a charming little poppy, is unclear, although current thinking would have it as a form of *P. lateritium*, or at least to have that species in its parentage. In literature it is often classed as a form of *P. orientale*, although that is clearly wrong. This is a small plant with mostly basal, bristly leaves and slender bristly stems 20–30 cm (8–12 in) tall, carrying double, orange-scarlet flowers, each 3–4 cm (1¼–1½ in) across and with numerous rather narrow uneven petals. This dainty poppy is perfectly hardy; a nomadic plant that seldom stays where planted for long, but soon pops up elsewhere because of its wandering underground runners.

Because of its stature, this is a plant for the front of the border, but its bright colour is not always easy to place sympathetically – perhaps it should be isolated amongst grey- or silvery-leaved plants in the herbaceous border. Unfortunately, it does not stay in bloom for very long and does not repeat flower in my experience. In cultivation there are at least two forms of 'Fireball' available, one more robust and almost twice the height of the other and with rather larger flowers, but both the same fiery colour. Like *P. lateritium*, it is a long-lived perennial in the garden.

Papaver lecoqii Lamotte [Pl. 44]
BABINGTON'S POPPY

Very similar to *P. dubium*, but flowers more orange-yellow and with yellow anthers. In addition, the leaves are more deeply dissected and less glaucous-looking. An interesting feature of this plant is that the latex produced from a cut surface quickly turns yellow on exposure to air; in *P. dubium* it remains white.

A native of western and south-western Europe from Britain and Belgium southwards to Spain, Portugal and Corsica. It is also found in a few localities in Greece. *P. lecoqii* is a plant of cultivated, fallow and waste land like its close cousins, being sometimes found along roadsides where it flowers from May to July, occasionally later. Rarely cultivated but worth acquiring.

Papaver macrostomum Boiss. et Huet
(Syn. *P. dalechianum* Fedde; *P. divergens* Fedde; *P. floribundum* Ledeb.; *P. kurdistanicum* Fedde)

A spectacular Asian poppy with large flowers of deep purple or red. *P. macrostomum* is a softly bristly annual 20–60 cm (8–24 in) tall, generally branching close to the base. The leaves are pinnately lobed, or at least deeply incised with long, lanceolate, sharply toothed, pointed segments, each terminating in a bristle, otherwise virtually hairless. The solitary flowers are borne on long and flexuous, appressed-bristly stems, the hairy, oval buds relatively large, to 20 mm (⅘ in) long. The flowers, 4–5 cm (1⅗–2 in) across, occasionally larger, are purple or deep rose-red, each of the wide overlapping petals with a black oblong, squarish or kidney-shaped, basal black blotch; stamens with slender black filaments and black anthers. The fruit-capsule is very distinctive, smooth and bluish-green, oblong-club-shaped, 10–20 mm (⅖–⅘ in) long, with the stigmatic disk falling away to open the capsule when it is ripe; the disk has five to ten distinctly keeled rays with wide sinuses between the lobes.

This striking and distinctive poppy is native from Anatolian Turkey eastwards to the Caucasus, Syria, Iran and Afghanistan, as well as occurring in southern Russia. Like so many annual poppies, *P. macrostomum* inhabits cultivated and fallow land, roadsides and waste land, but it can also be found on stony steppes and hillslopes, at an altitude of 1300–2000 m (4250–6550 ft); flowering from late May until July.

Fruit capsule of *Papaver macrostomum*

The distinctive feature of the ripe fruit-capsule serves to distinguish it from the other annual red poppies. It is primarily for this feature that *P. macrostomum* occupies its own section, the Carinatae, within the genus.

P. macrostomum is occasionally seen in cultivation, primarily in botanic gardens. However, it is a very fine and colourful annual and certainly deserves to be more widely known. Like its cousins, it requires an open sunny site, thriving best in light, well-drained, soils.

P. piptostigma Biernert ex Fedde and *P. tubuliferum* Fedde, both endemic to Kurdistan (north-eastern Iraq and north-western Iran), are probably only forms of *P. macrostomum* but are little known.

Papaver maeoticum Klokov

This interesting Ukrainian species fits into the *P. dubium* group, coming closest to *P. stipitatum* in the details of its fruit capsules, although the stigmatic disk has 6–8 rays instead of the usual 5 found in those of *P. stipitatum*. However, the feature that readily distinguishes this species from all others is the two-blotched petals: the red petals bear a small basal purplish black spot with a larger, rather square, blotch above, giving them a unique appearance.

Unfortunately, this exciting plant does not appear to be in cultivation. In the wild it is restricted to the south-eastern Ukraine in the Zhdanov region.

Papaver minus (Boiv.) Meikle
(Syn. *Closterandra minor* Boiv.; *Papaver belangeri* Boiss.)

A small poppy very closely related to *P. argemone* with which it is frequently confused. It differs primarily in its decumbent habit, crimson or purplish, funnel-shaped flowers with erect petals, each 10–25 mm (⅖–1 in) long and with a dark blotch at the base. The oval fruit-capsule has generally a few erect bristles close to the top.

P. *minus*, which is more widely known than *P. belangeri*, is native to the eastern Mediterranean region and western Asia eastwards to Iran and the Caucasus. It is a plant primarily of cultivated and fallow fields to an altitude of 1500 m (4900 ft). It is probably not in cultivation.

Papaver miyabeanum Tatew. & Miyabe
(syn. *P. nudicaule* Matsum., non L., *P. nudicaule* L. subsp. *xanthopetalum* Fedde var. *fauriei* sensu Tatew., non Fedde; *P. n.* subsp. × var. *shimshirense* Miyabe & Tatew.)
JAPANESE POPPY

Another delightful little poppy in the *P. nudicaule* – *P. radicatum* association. P. *miyabeanum* is seldom more than 7.5–10 cm (3–4 in) tall and forms quite dense tufts of rough greyish, pinnately-lobed leaves. The bristly scapes bear solitary pale yellow poppies, 3–4 cm (1⅕–1⅗ in) across with similarly coloured or somewhat darker stamens. The fruit-capsule is almost globose, with appressed bristles and a broad stigmatic disk with six to nine rays.

This dainty poppy has been in cultivation only for a few years, yet it is quite widely available. It is without doubt one of the finest poppies for the scree or rock garden. Plants are short-lived and resent winter moisture, often rotting off at ground level. However, it is easy to collect some seed each year and sow afresh in the spring. I find that, although the parent plants invariably succumb to the vagaries of the winter, seedlings often appear spontaneously the following year so that I have never needed to sow fresh seed to maintain stock.

P. *miyabeanum* comes from the Kurile Islands, to the north of Japan. The name has been much abused in literature, appearing variously as P. *moyabeanum*, P. *myabeanum*, P. *myerbeanum*, P. *moyabenum* var. *tokwokri*, P. *takedaki* var. *myerbeanum* . . . I could go on. The plant was in fact named by Dr Misao Tatewaki in honour of Dr Kingo Miyabe (1860–1951), a well-known Japanese botanist and author of the *Flora of the Kurile Islands*, so the correct name and spelling of the plants is *Papaver miyabeanum* Tatewaki.

Papaver nigrotinctum Fedde

A little-known Greek species closely related to *P. argemone*, but a smaller plant, not more than 20 cm (8 in) tall, with numerous ascending stems and bipinnately dissected leaves, and broad, scarcely overlapping red petals and a large basal, black blotch. The fruit-capsule is narrower than that of P. *argemone*, not more than 15 mm (⅗ in) long.

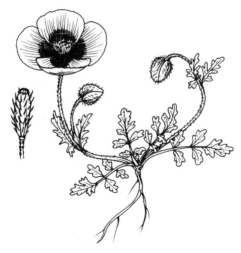

Papaver nigrotinctum

This interesting species is restricted to the Aegean region, to Korinthos and the Cyclades, where it grows on stony ground and in sandy or waste places at low altitudes, flowering there during April and May.

P. nigrotinctum is generally believed to be of hybrid origin between *P. argemone* and *P. apulum* and reveals more or less intermediate characters between these two species. It differs from *P. apulum* primarily by its hairy and rounded, rather than smooth and oval, flowerbuds. Although it has been in cultivation from time to time, it does not appear to be so at present, although it may exist in collections at botanic gardens.

Papaver nivale A. Tolm.

A small poppy restricted to eastern Siberia at relatively low altitudes of 914–977 m (3000–3200 ft). Unlike the other scapose poppies of the CIS, *P. nivale* has two-pinnately divided, rather than simple pinnate, leaves. This and its other characteristics put it closer to the European '*P. alpinum*' complex, being perhaps closest to *P. rhaeticum* in its bright yellow flowers, 3–4 cm (1⅕–1⅗ in) across. The darkly bristly fruit-capsule are smaller, not more than 10 mm (⅖ in) long.

A little-known species, but clearly with the charm and elegance of its '*P. alpinum*' cousins. It has not, to my knowledge, been recorded in cultivation, but should present few problems should seed ever become available.

Papaver nudicaule L. [Pl. 45–46]
'ICELAND POPPY'

This name conjures up as much confusion in horticulture as does the related *P. alpinum*. *P. nudicaule* is commonly called the Iceland poppy. However, it does not come from Iceland; indeed, it is restricted to Asia. But this species is related to a whole group of closely allied species that form a complicated network of variability, which can leave the poor gardener wholly distracted. The species concerned have a wide distribution across many of the cold regions of the northern hemisphere, stretching southwards into Asia, Afghanistan and the western Himalaya. Of these, a number of elements can be clearly recognised amongst wild populations, including *P. nudicaule* itself; *P. alboroseum*, which is restricted to the Kamschatka region; *P. involucratum* centred on the mountains of southern central Asia, particularly the Pamir Alai; *P. lapponicum*, which is to be found in Arctic Europe and the neigh-bouring parts of Russia; and *P. radicatum*, which perhaps has the widest distribution of all, encompassing as it does much of Arctic Europe and North America, Greenland, Iceland and western Russia and Siberia.

This latter species is almost certainly the true Iceland poppy. In cultivation *P. nudicaule* has been crossed with its cousins and selected to produce a sturdy race of rather gaudy poppies commonly called Iceland poppies and generally found in catalogues and lists under the name *Papaver nudicaule*.

True *P. nudicaule* is a relatively tall plant with solitary-flowered, rather bristly, scapes up to 50 cm (20 in) tall, though often only 30–40 cm (12–16 in). The basal leaf-tufts are covered with greyish hairs, the leaves pinnate with oblong or lanceolate segments. The flower buds are quite large, being 1–2 cm (⅖–⅘ in) in diameter, the sepals with greyish or brownish hairs. The flowers are yellow, broadly cup-shaped and mostly 4–6 cm (1⅗–2⅖ in) across. The fruit-capsules are narrowly club-shaped to oblong and covered in appressed whitish or reddish-brown bristles.

P. nudicaule is distributed in Asia from Siberia to Mongolia, southwards into the mountains of central Asia as far as Afghanistan. In these remote regions it is primarily a plant of mountain screes and moraines, steppes and river gravels, at altitudes up to 4600 m (15,100 ft).

Although it has been noted that *P. nudicaule* is commonly listed in catalogues and plant lists, the wild species is seldom seen in cultivation, but rather a complex derived from various species which hybridise readily – for more details, see under *P. radicatum* (p. 123).

The following are sometimes listed as varieties of *P. nudicaule*, but are considered by some to be distinct species in their own right, often with a very limited distribution (see, for instance, *Flora of the USSR* Vol. 7: 456–494).

var. croceum (Syn. *P. alpinum* var. *croceum* Ledeb.; *P. croceum* Ledeb.; *P. nudicaule* subsp. *commune* var. *rubro-aurantiacum* N. Busch)

Differs in having bright orange or red flowers, the buds with rusty-brown hairs and the leaf segments often toothed.

Native to scattered localities in Siberia, the mountains of central Asia, the western Himalayas and Mongolia.

var. microcarpum (Syn. *P. Alpinum* var. *microcarpum* Ledeb.; *P. microcarpum* DC.)

A small plant up to 20 cm (8 in) tall, though often less. Flowers small, 20–30 mm (⅘–1⅕ in) across, orange to orange-red, the petals falling off as the fruit develops.

Restricted to Kamchatka, where it may intergrade with *P. alboroseum*.

var. *rubro-aurantiacum* Fisch. ex DC. (Syn. *P. rubro-aurantiacum* Fisch. ex Steud.)

Distinct on account of its grey leaves and the flower buds, which are silky with whitish hairs. Flowers orange or orange-red, 35–40 mm (1⅜–1½ in).

Restricted to eastern Siberia (Dauria) and Mongolia.

The Iceland poppies, as known today in gardens, have strong scapes up to 60 cm (24 in) tall and carry large flowers, up to 17.5 cm (7 in) across, in a range of brash colours – orange, red, yellow, apricot, pink, salmon, cream and white shades predominating. They often have more than the normal ration of four petals and semi-double forms are not uncommon. The first flowers to open on each plant are the largest.

These bright poppies are good garden plants, excellent in summer bedding displays, and will flower over a long season. They can be raised from seed in much the same way as many hardy and half-hardy bedding plants. Sow thinly in pots to avoid the problem of damping off and prick out seedlings when they have developed one good leaf. Alternatively, sow directly where the plants are to flower, thinning seedlings out to 15–20 cm (6–8 in) in order to get good strong plants. They are often sold in pots at garden centres where individual colours can be selected, but it is far better to buy seed if more than just a few plants are wanted. Although perennial, these tufted plants often rot off during wet winters, so annual sowings are perhaps the best way of maintaining it in the garden.

The Iceland poppies also make excellent cut flowers and these are commonly seen for sale in bunches in both Holland and Germany. Commercially, they are grown in light airy glasshouses or polythene tunnels. They are normally sown successively from early spring until the summer in rows some 25–30 cm (10–12 in) apart for summer and autumn harvesting. Alternatively, midsummer sowing will produce a saleable crop of flowers early the following year, though modest heat is required during the winter for such production or indeed for producing pot-grown plants early in the season. The wide range of bright colours and the 'crepe de chine' petals make them popular cut flowers in some countries. For cutting, they are best gathered whilst the sepals are still attached but after the buds have taken on an upright position – just before the petals burst out. The cut stems ends should be sealed in hot water or burnt to improve the lasting quality of the blooms.

Various seed strains of Iceland poppy are sold by seed merchants and are invariably listed under *P. nudicaule*. Although some are very distinct, others reveal a remarkable degree of overlap.

'Aurora Borealis': a fine strain with exceptionally large flowers in the full range of colours.

'Ballerina Mixture': a bright and cheerful mixture of sturdy plants up to 30 cm (12 in) tall, with yellow, orange, red and white shades prevailing.

'Champagne Bubbles': up to 40 cm (16 in) tall; large flowers in various shades.

'Garden Gnome' ('Gartenzwerg'): a dwarf strain only 30 cm (12 in) tall, neat and compact, with flowers in a range of reds, pinks, yellow, orange and white.

'Hamlet': another large-flowered race, in shades of orange and red mainly.

'Kelmscott Giant': up to 80 cm (32 in) tall with flowers in pastel shades.

'Matador': large flowers 10–12 cm (4–4¾ in) across of the deepest, brightest scarlet.

'Meadow Pastels': 60–70 cm tall (24–28 in) tall, this is a fine mixture of single poppies in shades of white, cream, yellow, orange, red, pink, rose, and includes some bicolors. They are robust plants, flowering over a long season from a spring sowing. The flowers are borne on stiff stems and are said to cut well. Although many plants in this mixture have pastel-coloured flowers, others are more vibrant, especially the red and orange shades.

'Oregon Rainbows': a strain developed for the cut-flower market in the USA, with sturdy stems with blooms often 18 cm (7¼ in) across, single or semi-double, in the full range of colours, including also bicoloured forms and picotées with pale or darker margins.

'Pacino': dwarf form with pale yellow flowers.

'Red Sails': 60–75 cm (24–30 in) tall, this interesting recent cultivar produces 12.5 cm (5 in) orange-scarlet flowers on sturdy stems that are good for cutting. The brightness of the petals contrast with their pale whitish base and the central boss of yellow stamens.

'San Remo': another large flowered mixture with mostly single flowers in a wide range of the usual colours.

'Sea Shanty': a fine selection 40–60 cm (16–24 in) tall with good-sized flowers of scarlet-red contrasting with the boss of yellow stamens in the centre of the flower. The flowers are borne on strong stiff stems which makes them highly suitable for cutting.

'Unwins Giant Coonara': bright flowers in yellow, orange and red, 50 cm (20 in).

'Wonder Hybrids': another good colourful dwarf mixture, sometimes available, and including whites.

'Wonderland Mixed': a good dwarf selection to 25 cm (10 in), producing relatively large 10 cm (4 in) flowers in a wide range of colours. Useful as a pot plant or for spring bedding displays.

'Wonderland Yellow': a selection from the above, with perfectly formed, somewhat frilled, saucer-shaped flowers of pure, clear yellow.

In addition, several companies offer a general or special mixture of Iceland poppies, both single- and double-flowered.

Papaver occelatum Woron.

This poppy is sometimes regarded as a synonym of *P. pavoninum*, but differs primarily in its hornless sepals and in the stamen filaments, which are clearly thickened towards the anther end. The flowers are very pretty, being a pure red, the petals with a basal black arc often with a red area or ocellus inside, like a large bright eye. The fruit-capsule is adorned with thin spreading bristles.

P. ocellatum is native to Central Asia, from the Caucasus to the Tien Shan, including northern Iran, where it inhabits sandy and clay steppes, fields and roadsides, flowering from April to July. It is probably not in cultivation at the present time, but confusion with *P. pavoninum* may mean that it is still being grown somewhere under the wrong name.

Papaver oreophilum Rupr. [Pl. 47]
(Syn. *P. lateritium* var. *minus* Boiss.)

This interesting Caucasian poppy looks like a dwarf *P. orientale*, being generally only 10–20 cm (4–8 in) tall. The leaves are mostly basal, narrow lanceolate and pinnately lobed into sharply toothed segments, often terminating in a weak bristle; most of the leaves, except for the uppermost, are stalked. The solitary flowers, 6–10 cm (2½–4 in) across, are borne on long peduncles, the oval flower buds covered in soft reddish-brown hairs; the four petals are bright orange-red without a dark basal blotch; stamens with yellow filaments and anthers. The smooth fruit-capsule is 15–17 mm (⅝ in) long, greyish-green, the stigmatic disk usually with five to seven rays.

P. oreophilum is endemic to the Caucasus, where it inhabits alpine meadow, rocks and stony slopes at altitudes of 1700–2500 m (5600–8200 ft).

This interesting species is occasionally cultivated in gardens, although it is not generally available in trade. In many ways it is a half-way species between *P. orientale* and *P. lateritium*, being clearly more closely associated with the latter from which it differs in its larger flowers and broader fruit-capsule.

Papaver orientale L. [Pl. 48]
(Syn. *P. pollakii* A. Kerner)
ORIENTAL POPPY

Much confusion has surrounded this name, in both botanical and horticultural circles. In gardens, the oriental poppies are in fact primarily a mixture of three distinct, though closely allied species, *P. orientale*, *P. bracteatum* and *P. pseudo-orientale*. If this is not confusing enough, most plant catalogues fail to distinguish between them, grouping all the cultivars under *P. orientalis* or under a general heading of oriental poppies. Perhaps this is of little concern to the gardener, but, from a botanical perspective at least, it is necessary to distinguish these entities most clearly.

The main confusion stems from the fact that not only do these species look alike, but they inhabit the same geographical region in the wild – broadly, western Asia from Anatolian Turkey to Iran and the Caucasus; although they grow in the same general region, they appear to be mostly isolated from one another.

P. orientale differs from *P. bracteatum* in being a slighter plant, rarely more than 90 cm (36 in) tall, often less, with slender stems 2–3 mm (to ⅛ in) in diameter. The flowers, somewhat smaller, are without bracts immediately

Fruit of *Papaver orientale*

below (at the top of the pedicels and pressed close to the base of the calyx) and the petals have a rounded or squarish black blotch just above their base, or no blotch at all. In contrast, *P. bracteatum* is a more robust plant, up to 1.2 m (4 ft) tall, sometimes taller, the stem stouter, 3–5 mm (⅛–⅕ in) diameter. The large flowers have three to five ovals, sepal-like bracts immediately below the sepals; in addition, there may also be one or two small leaves. The petals have a prominent oblong, basal, black blotch. For *P. pseudo-orientale* see p. 83.

The oriental poppy (in its widest sense) was certainly known to Miller and in his *Gardener's Dictionary* he recorded '*Papaver Orientale hirsutissimum, flore magno* – Very Rough Oriental Poppy with large flower' and stated: 'The Oriental Poppy is an abiding Plant, which produces a large single flower in May, which make a beautiful appearance. This may be propagated from Seeds, or by parting their roots. The best time to transplant them is at the beginning of March; this must have a light soil and a warm situation.'

P. orientale is a tough, tufted perennial with the new leaves appearing in the autumn and generally with a stoloniferous habit. The bristly stems rise to 50–90 cm (20–36 in) and are generally unbranched, leafy in the lower two-thirds – usually with three to six leaves per stem. The large bristly leaves, up to 30 cm (12 in) long, are oblong to lanceolate in outline, but deeply pinnately-lobed, each lobe toothed and terminating in a large bristle; the basal and lower leaves are clearly stalked, while the upper are smaller and unstalked. The large showy flowers are bright orange or orange-red, broadly cup-shaped, 10–16 cm (4–6⅖ in) across (rather larger in cultivated specimens), the four to six petals with a violet-black blotch just above the base, or sometimes unblotched; the numerous stamens have dark filaments, which are dilated towards the top, and violet anthers. The smooth, globose fruit-capsule, 2–3 cm (⅘–1⅕ in) long, has a flat stigmatic disk with 10–16 rays, occasionally fewer.

P. orientale is native to the Anatolian region of Turkey, the Caucasus and northern and north-western Iran, where it is primarily a plant of meadows, stony slopes, open forest glades, especially in the subalpine zone at altitudes of 1950–2800 m (6400–9200 ft) where it flowers during May-July.

P. orientale was first described by Linnaeus, who cited it as 'in oriente'. It was subsequently discovered by the seventeenth-century French botanist J.P. de Tournefort near Erzurum in eastern Anatolia and described in his *Relation d'un voyage au Levant*. It was first grown in Britain early in the eighteenth century by the royal gardener and nurseryman George London.

It is undoubtedly a very fine garden plant and for those who desire a less brash and more delicate oriental poppy, this is the one to select, rather than the more robust, overbearing races of *P. bracteatum*. Some may find its stoloniferous and invading habit (at least in some forms) annoying, though it does afford a ready and time-saving means of propagation. In my experience, these stolons are best removed and replanted in the autumn as the new leaves begin to emerge, for this allows the new plants time to build up sufficiently for a good display of flowers the following summer.

The oriental poppies are the most accommodating garden plants, vigorous and free-flowering and succeeding on light or heavy garden soils, indeed virtually any soil, provided it is not waterlogged. Their boldness and brashness of colour make them often difficult to place satisfactorily in the border, but when well placed, they will make a spectacular feature. They are so bold that they will often swamp associated plants in the herbaceous border by sheer size and colour, so it is perhaps best to plant later flowering perennials in their immediate vicinity – michaelmas daisies, red hot pokers (*Kniphofia*) or rudbeckias, for instance. If the oriental poppies have an irritating habit, it is that once having flowered the plants immediately begin to die down and turn brown. This ugly mass of stems and leaves can soon be cleared away, but it does leave a nasty void in the border, so planting later flowering subjects close by is a good means of filling such gaps.

Propagation is simple. For most gardeners, who need just one or two extra plants, lifting and dividing the clumps in the late summer is probably the best method. The various cultivars grow in rather different ways; some sucker freely, whilst others remain as a discreet dense clump. The former can be propagated simply by carefully digging up suckers while leaving the parent clump intact. With the latter, the whole clump needs to be lifted and prized apart with a couple of forks placed back to back. A careful slicing up with a spade does not, in my experience, cause significant damage and mutilated pieces will soon sprout anew. Most oriental poppies start into growth again in the early autumn, the leaves remaining small until the following spring, when they rapidly expand.

Commercially, the oriental poppies are propagated by root cuttings. The thick fleshy roots are ideal for this purpose. Healthy roots can be chopped into 3–4 cm (1⅕–1⅗ in) long pieces and placed upright in a peat/sharp-sand mixture in pots or a gently heated propagating frame. The cuttings should be placed topside up and just covered. They will soon sprout new leaves. This habit of growing from pieces of root can be irritating in the border, for the slightest piece left in when clearing a piece of ground will sprout anew. Despite this, these flamboyant plants, so characteristic of the cottage garden, deserve a place in every garden.

Oriental poppies can be grown from seed and some seed merchants offer several varieties or a mixture. Many of the resultant seedlings are fine plants, but can be expected to vary in colour from plant to plant and this offers great scope for further selection and hybridisation. Indeed, new colours are constantly coming on to the market. Seed can be sown in pots or sown directly into the soil where they are to flower, either in drills or scattered – spring is the best time. Young plants should be finally set apart at about 40–50 cm (16–20 in) and will flower in the second or third year from seed. Plants are best moved or divided in the autumn.

Many of the strong-stemmed oriental poppies make spectacular cut flowers and are quite commonly sold in the summer flower markets of Holland, Germany and elsewhere. They are best cut just before the sepals split apart to reveal the petals. The cut ends of the stems should be sealed by burning them or placing them for a short while in boiling water; this prevents them wilting.

Although many 'oriental poppy' cultivars are available today, this was not always so. At the turn of the twentieth century only the wild red form existed in gardens. Their development is due primarily to the nurseryman Amos Perry, of Enfield near London. In 1906 he discovered a pink-flowered one amongst a batch of red-flowered seedlings and named it after his wife; 'Mrs Perry' is a fine cultivar still much grown today. In 1913 he received an irate letter from a customer complaining that his pink and red border had been ruined by a single white poppy – another chance seedling that Amos Perry had sent out unflowered. Perry managed to exchange this non-conformist poppy for a few Montbretia corms and named it 'Perry's White', which is still one of the finest white 'oriental poppies' today. Perry's Hardy Plant Farm began to select and specialise in this 'gorgeous group of plants'. Among the finest selected were 'E.A. Bowles', 'May Queen', 'Indian Chief', 'Mrs Stobart' and 'Peter Pan', besides the two already mentioned.

What is unclear is the part played by *P. orientalis* in the breeding of *P. bracteatum* hybrids because few have been produced by a deliberate and systematic programme of hybridisation. To avoid confusion, all the oriental poppy cultivars are listed here whether or not they have bracts below the flower buds. All flower in the period from mid-May to early July.

Today, more than 80 cultivars are listed, and many are widely available at nurseries and garden centres. Horticulturists have tried to group these into *P. bracteatum* and *P. orientale* cultivars on the presence or absence of bracts beneath the flowers, but this really is not practical and is, in general, a futile exercise, especially as some cultivars can bear bracts or not on adjacent flowers on the same plant. They are much better listed as the Oriental Group.

Trials of Oriental poppies at the Royal Horticultural Society Gardens at Wisley from 1996 to 1998 produced some interesting results. Foremost, it revealed the confused state in the naming of cultivars; quite a few entries in the trial were wrongly named and some entries (there were three plants in each) proved to be mixed collections, sometimes with two different cultivars, and on several occasions three. Although the presence of bracts below the flowers is usually indicative of a particular cultivar, the size and number can vary a lot. Some cultivars have consistently large and leaflike bracts, whereas others have small sepal-like, undivided bracts. Others can have a range of bracts bunched together between these two extremes, while several cultivars produced bracted as well as bractless flowers. The presence of a blotch at the base of the petal is also a useful diagnostic character, but this feature can be inconsistent. The blotch can fade away as the flowers age in some cultivars, whereas in others early flowers can be boldly blotched while later flowers on the same plant can be weakly blotched. On occasions, late flowers can be unblotched altogether or with the weakest hint of a blotch.

Another factor which was observed (and which is often commented upon by gardeners) is the presence of malformed buds or buds held at an odd angle on the elongating stems. This can affect almost any cultivar, but the earlier flowering ones are particularly prone. A cultivar which is affected one season will not necessarily be afflicted in the next. The reason for this is unclear, but it may be weather-related. It has been suggested, for instance, that a spell of cold frosty weather during the early developmental stage of the young shoots may be the cause of the problem. The leaves of the majority of cultivars arise in the autumn and early winter, although stem elongation does not occur until the following spring, but the bud primordia are initiated at a very early stage in development of the stem.

In the Wisley trials a number of the new German cultivars ('Karine' for instance) did extremely well and a number were awarded the AGM (Award of Garden Merit). These mark a break from the extremely tall old British cultivars with large blooms and stems that need careful staking if the plants are to remain upright in bloom. They stem from the nursery of Hélène Countess von Stein-Zeppelin (Gräfin von Zeppelin).

ORIENTALIS GROUP

Availability: all cultivars currently in cultivation are indicated with an asterisk (*). The majority of these will be found in the current edition of *The RHS Plant Finder*, but some cultivars are available only in Continental Europe or the USA. There is little accurate information available on some of the more obscure cultivars or those no longer in cultivation. Those marked 'originally a seed strain' are still sometimes seed-raised and most seedlings come close to the parents, if not identical with them. However, to be sure of getting the correct cultivar, it is wise to select plants that have been vegetatively propagated from the mother plant.

'**Abu Hasan**'*: flowers single, orange-pink with a whitish centre, white outside, the petals pleated and overlapping, with a small dark blotch at the base, the margins shallowly toothed (fringed); buds large, rounded to egg-shaped, with a few prominent leaflike bracts; 70–80 cm (28–32 in).

'**Aglaja**' AGM* (probably the same as 'Aglaya'): flowers single, bright salmon-pink, the petals widely overlapping, ruffled and slightly pleated, with a faint (blurred) reddish blotch or flush at the base; buds egg-shaped and rather twisted, with a ruff of large leaflike bracts; 70–80 cm (28–32 in) with thick sturdy stems which sometimes produce a secondary bloom. Similar in stature to 'Derwisch', but the flowers are noticeably pinker.

'**Aladin**'*: flowers single, luminous (shiny) orange-red, whitish outside, the petals thick, overlapping and wavy (frilled), with a large black blotch at the base; buds oblong with a slight twist, with a ruff of slightly recurved, undivided bracts; 90–100 cm (36–40 in), with long stiff stems.

'Allegro'★: flowers single, rather papery, bright orange-red, the petals with a bold basal black blotch; 60–70 cm (24–28 in).

'Allegro Vivace': flowers single, glowing orange-red, the fairly smooth petals without a basal blotch; buds egg-shaped, without bracts; 85–95 cm (34–38 in). Reared from the same seed strain as 'Allegro'; it would be a brave person to say exactly what the difference between the two is, as the presence or absence of a basal black blotch cannot be relied upon in this seed strain. Both are frequently listed without any qualification.

'Ali Baba'★: very similar to 'Aladin', but flowers orange, not whitish on the outside and petals unblotched, reddish towards the base; 80–100 cm (32–40 in) with long stiff stems.

'Arwide'★: flowers single, luminous salmon-pink, white on the outside and towards the centre inside, the petals overlapping and somewhat ruffled, with a basal blotch made up of close dark lines; buds egg-shaped with many prominent leaflike bracts; 80–100 cm (32–40 in), with very long stout flower stems.

'Aslahan'★: flowers single, salmon-pink, the petals overlapping and somewhat frilled, with a pale basal blotch that quickly fades; 80–100 cm (32–40 in). Late flowering.

'Atrosanguineus'★: a tall old cultivar with stiff stems and medium-sized dark red flowers, the petals with a basal black blotch; 95-105 cm (38-42 in).

'Avebury Crimson'★: flowers neat and weather resistant, single, rich crimson-red, with overlapping petals which have a prominent oblong basal black blotch; buds egg-shaped, with a ruff of large and prominent leaflike bracts; 80–100 cm (32–40 in), with sturdy stems and neat foliage.

'Barr's White': seems to be very similar to 'Perry's White', but the former no longer seems to be in cultivation.

'Beauty of Livermere' AGM★: **[Pl. 49]** a fine old variety formerly very popular in gardens, but now unfortunately often muddled with other large red-flowered cultivars and for that reason sometimes listed under the Goliath Group: the differences between 'Beauty of Livermere' and 'Goliath' are very clear as far as colour goes. Flowers single, especially large, deep lustrous crimson-scarlet, the petals with a prominent large basal black blotch; buds oblong, with large and conspicuous leaflike bracts; 90–110 cm (36–44 in), with sturdy stems and grey-green foliage. Late flowering. Many plants sold under this name prove to be incorrect.

'Beauty Queen'★: flowers single, rather delicate in appearance, brownish, flushed with apricot or orange, the petals thin and rather crumpled; buds egg-shaped, without bracts; 75–100 cm (30–40 in), with thin stems.

'Big Jim'★: flowers deep raspberry-pink, otherwise rather similar to 'Beauty of Livermere'; 85–95 cm (34–38 in).

'Black and White' AGM★: flowers single, pure white, the petals overlapping and somewhat ruffled, with a prominent black blotch just above the base, which shows through to the outside; buds oblong with a pointed apex, usually with one or two medium-sized bracts; 70–80 cm (28–32 in), with sturdy stems, floriferous. The whitest Oriental cultivar. Sometimes confused with 'Perry's White', which has pink-tinged flowers with a paler purplish blotch (reddish on the outside) and broader more rounded buds.

'Blackberry Queen'★: really like an improved version of 'Patty's Plum' with purplish-lilac flowers; 70–80 cm (28–32 in). Extremely handsome and well worth adding to a collection: why plants like this have not received the AGM accolade, it is difficult to say and gardeners should not be put off acquiring them just because they fail to have one.

'Blickfang': brilliant red flowers; 75–80 cm (30–32 in).

'Blue Moon'★: flowers single, particularly large, up to 25 cm (10 in) across, mauve-pink with a greyish flush, the petals somewhat pleated, overlapping, with a very large and prominent black blotch at the base, veined with maroon on the outside; buds rounded, with a few large leaflike bracts; 100–110 cm (40–44 in), with rather ungainly stems and large leaves that tend to sprawl. Flowers are the largest of any Oriental poppy, 20–25 cm (8–10 in) across.

'Blush Queen': flowers single, blush-pink or flesh-pink, the petals with a purple basal blotch.

'Bobs': flowers large, brilliant scarlet.

'Bonfire'★: sometimes listed as 'Bonfire Red', this cultivar has large and dark orange-scarlet flowers with a crinkled (ruffled) margin; the petals are unblotched.

'Border Beauty': apparently very similar to 'May Queen', but the flowers possibly larger and redder.

'Brilliant'★: flowers single, large, scarlet-red, the petals somewhat frilled, with a bold basal black blotch; 75–90 cm (30–36 in). Very similar to 'Beauty of Livermere'; this is a seed-raised cultivar, said to come true to type.

'Burgundy'★: flowers single, pale orange, the petals slightly ruffled, without a basal blotch; 70–85 cm (28–34 in), with rather washy yellow-green leaves and runners; capsules tend to bend downwards. A silly and confusing name for a plant with orange flowers.

'Carmen'★: flowers single, neat bowl-shaped, reddish-orange, the petals slightly pleated, with a black blotch that does not quite reach the base; buds rounded, with subtending prominent leaflike bracts; 70–85 cm (28–34 in).

'Carmine'★: very similar to 'Carmen', but petals with a neat blotch that reaches the base, and buds without bracts.

'Carneum'★: a seed strain with salmon-pink flowers; not as fine as many of the other cultivars in this colour range.

'Carnival'★: flowers single, orange-red, the petals stiff (thick) and squarish, pale at the margins, overlapping, pleated, with a very large basal black blotch; buds egg-shaped, with several uneven leaflike bracts. 75–85 cm (30–34 in). Similar in shape and substance to 'Petticoat', but later flowering.

'Carousel': flowers single, bright luminous orange, the petals with a neat black blotch at the base; buds oblong, with several medium leaflike bracts. 70–85 cm (28–34 in).

'Catharina': flowers large, single, bright salmon-pink, the petals overlapping and rather crumpled, with an often rather indistinct reddish-purple basal blotch; buds egg-shaped, with several large leaflike bracts; 75–85 cm (30–34 in).

'Catherine'★: flowers orange-red, the petals with a small basal black blotch; 80–90 cm (32–36 in).

'Cavalier': flowers medium size, dark red, the petals with a prominent basal black blotch.

'Cedar Hill'★: flowers pink borne on a rather dwarf plant; 50 cm (20 in).

'Cedric Morris' ('Cedric's Pink') AGM★ **[Pl. 50].** A very popular cultivar with large, single, soft pink flowers with a hint of grey, the petals overlapping, frilled and somewhat pleated, with a large basal black blotch; buds oval to egg-shaped, with a few large leafy bracts; 70–90 cm (28–36 in), suckering, with strong stems that, nevertheless, often tend to sprawl unless staked. The flowers tend to fade and yellow somewhat with age: Cedric Morris himself described it as a 'dirty pink knicker colour'. Often sold under the name 'Cedric's Pink'.

'Charming'★: flowers single, pale pink, the petals somewhat crumpled and with an ill-defined basal blotch in the form of streaks; 65–75 cm (26–30 in). Similar in colour to 'Karine', but a larger plant. The original 'Charming', dating back to 1916, was quite different, with orange-scarlet flowers and buds with a ruff of leafy bracts, which makes the modern 'Charming' an invalid name, if indeed it is correctly identified in the first instance.

'China Boy'★: rather similar to 'Picotee', but with larger flowers, single, white with a broad uneven orange margin, the petals thick and somewhat ruffled, purplish at the base, but not blotched; buds egg-shaped, with several medium-sized leaflike bracts; 75–90 cm (30–36 in).

'Choir Boy'★: a delightful large poppy with pure white, attractively ruffled petals, each with a large and prominent oblong black basal blotch, surrounding a boss of yellowish stamens. It is sold as both plants and seed, although it is not entirely clear if the seed strain comes true to type or reveals awkward variation. If unsure, seek plants from a reputable source.

'Clara Curtis': likened to a dwarf 'Perry's White', the petals with a conspicuous chocolate-brown basal blotch. A cultivar dating back to 1915.

'Colonel Bowles': a sturdy cultivar dating back to 1916 with extra large single flowers of brilliant crimson, the petals with a bold reddish-black blotch at the base.

'Coral Reef': flowers single, vivid coral-pink, with attractively ruffled, overlapping petals, each sporting a small purple-black blotch at the base. Buds oblong with one or two short leafy bracts beneath. 60–75 cm (24–30 in). A recent Thompson and Morgan introduction said to be a unique colour amongst Oriental poppies; however, the colour is not far removed from that of various other modern cultivars such as 'Aglaja' and 'Kleine Tänzerin'. A seed strain said to come true to type.

'Corinna': flowers single, lustrous pale salmon-pink, the petals thick and overlapping, giving the flower a semi-double appearance, with a small red blotch at the base; buds large and oblong, with a ruff of large leafy bracts; 75–90 cm (30–36 in), with stout leafy stems.

'Countess of Stair': a tall poppy with medium-sized flowers of bright salmon-rose.

'Crimped Beauty': **[Pl. 51]** flowers of orange-scarlet with crumpled petals.

'Curlilocks'★: flowers single, bright orange-red, the petals deeply serrated with cuts up to about 2 cm (¾ in) deep along the margin, with a prominent basal black blotch; buds egg-shaped with a ruff of medium leaflike bracts; 70–80 cm (28–32 in).

'Darkness': an old cultivar that is no longer available; flowers deep maroon.

'Delicata': a cultivar from 1907, with large flowers of a delicate rose-white, merging to pure white at the petal margin and with a basal black blotch.

'Degas': flowers rich salmon-pink, the petals widely overlapping and ruffled, with a small and rather indistinct crimson basal blotch.

'Derwisch'★: flowers single, bright orange-salmon-red, the petals pleated and with a small basal black blotch that soon fades; buds oblong and twisted, with a prominent ruff of large leaflike bracts; 75–90 cm (30–36 in), with stout very leafy stems, late flowering. A von Zeppelin introduction (Hélène Countess von Stein-Zeppelin: the nursery is called Gräfin von Zeppelin).

'Double Delight': an early flowering seed strain with orange-scarlet, semi-double flowers; 70–80 cm (28–32 in).

'Double Flame': flowers semi-double, very large, bright flame-orange; 50–70 cm (20–28 in).

'Doubloon'★: flowers semi-double, bright orange-red; 75–90 cm (30–36 in) tall. A rare cultivar that is now available from several nurseries.

'Duke of Teck': flowers brilliant deep crimson-scarlet.

'Dwarf Allegro'★: flowers single, large (15 cm/6 in), vivid-scarlet flowers, the petals with a basal black blotch; a compact bushy plant not more than 50 cm (20 in) tall. Doubtfully distinct from 'Allegro'; this is a seed strain that reveals some variability.

'E.A.Bowles': a cultivar from 1920, with medium-sized apricot flowers with ruffled petals. The flowers are said to fade to shell-pink.

'Edna Perry': flowers semi-double, large, rose-salmon, the petals with a fringed margin and a large basal black blotch. Dates from 1912.

'Effendi' AGM★: flowers single, very large, bright salmon-pink, the petals somewhat pleated, frilled and overlapping, reddish at the base but with an uneven blotch above the base; buds narrow-oblong and slightly twisted, with a ruff of large leafy bracts; 70–85 cm (28–34 in), with stout leafy stems and runners.

'Elam Pink'★: sumptuous flowers of mid blush-pink, the petals somewhat ruffled and with a medium-sized black blotch at the base; buds egg-shaped with one or two small leafy bracts a little below; 70–80 cm (28–32 in).

'Enchantress': see 'Wunderkind'.

'Enfield Beauty': a late-flowering cultivar from the early part of the twentieth century, with salmon-maroon single flowers.

'Enfield Belle': with similar origins to the preceding cultivar, bearing flowers of pale salmon-pink.

'Eskimo Pie'★: another tall new cultivar with large well-proportioned dazzling white flowers, the petals with a pronounced black base. Nice, but scarcely distinguishable from some of the older white cultivars such as 'Black and White' or 'Perry's White'; 75–87 cm (30–35 in).

'Ethel Swete': an old cultivar with large flowers of cherry-pink (sometimes described as salmon-rose), the petals with a toothed margin and a basal black blotch.

'Fatima'★: flowers single, white with a salmon-pink edge (the pink sometimes flushing well into the centre of the petals), the petals frilled and overlapping, with a reddish-purple blotch at the base; buds egg-shaped, with a dense ruff of medium leafy bracts; 60–75 cm (24–30 in), with stout leafy stems and with the flowers held only just clear of the foliage.

'Feurriese'★: flowers fire-red; 75–85 cm (30–34 in).

'Feuerzwerg'★: an interesting new dwarf cultivar with intensely red flowers appearing as early as late May; 30–37 cm (12–15 in).

'Fiesta'★: another new introduction, this robust cultivar sports flowers of bright apricot-salmon, the petals pleasantly ruffled; 75–87 cm (30–35 in).

'Fire King': large flowers of deep scarlet, the petals with a black blotch at the base.

'Flamenco'★: glossy orange-red flowers; 70–80 cm (28–32 in).

'Flore Pleno': see *P. lateritium* 'Fireball'.

'Forncett Banner'★: flowers single, rather small and red, the petals fringed (finely cut) along the upper edge, with a deep red flush at the base, but without a blotch; buds oblong with a few small spiky bracts, not ruffed; 70–80 cm (28–32 in). 'Türkenlouis' is very similar, but has larger, more scarlet flowers, with petals that are more deeply fringed along most of the margin. 'Curlilocks' has smaller flowers but even more deeply cut petals which are clearly black-blotched at the base.

'Forncett Post'★: flowers single and very symmetrical, crimson, the petals somewhat pleated at the top and with a large basal black blotch; buds egg-shaped, with a large ruff of persistent leafy bracts; 65–75 cm (26–30 in), with stout stems ands rather neat compact foliage. Not dissimilar to 'Avebury Crimson', but with rather less vivid, neat and not so floppy, weather-resistant flowers, borne on a rather more compact plant.

'Forncett Summer'★: flowers single, bright salmon-pink, the petals overlapping and with a deeply cut margin and a small basal black blotch; buds oblong, with a few medium leafy bracts. Very similar to 'Forncettt Banner', but flowers pink rather than red.

'Fringed Beauty': flowers medium-sized, orange-scarlet, with deeply fringed petals.

'Garden Glory'★: [Pl. 52] flowers single, large, orange-pink with a pale red flush, the petals markedly overlapping, frilled and with a fringed margin of blunt narrow lobes, unblotched but reddening towards the base; buds round, large, with a small tight ruff of small leafy bracts; 75–90 cm (30–36 in), with thick sturdy stems. Similar to 'Prinz Eugen', but a larger plant with bigger flowers.

'Gibson's Salmon': flowers salmon-pink, the petals with a prominent basal black blotch.

'Glowing Embers'★: flowers single, glowing lustrous scarlet-red, the petals thick and pleated, with a large black blotch at the base; buds oblong, slightly twisted and with a ruff of large leafy bracts; 80–100 cm (32–40 in) with stiff, sturdy stems, with the foliage up amongst the flowers.

'Glowing Rose'★: flowers deep rose-pink; 65–75 cm (26–30 in).

'Goldschmidt': flowers very large, rich deep crimson, with a large basal black blotch to each petal.

'Goliath'★: often confused with 'Beauty of Livermere', but quite distinct when the two are seen side by side; flowers orange-scarlet with a large black blotch at the base of each petal. A large and vigorous plant 100–120 cm (40–48 in), with immense flowers up to 20 cm across. It is widely grown in gardens, but beware, many plants sold under the name are incorrect.

'Graue Witwe'★: [Pl. 53] flowers single, white flushed with the palest grey-pink, but eventually becoming white, the petals flushed with a small, variable (sometimes rather indistinct, a blush rather than a clear blotch), dark purple or maroon blotch above the base, overlapping; buds egg-shaped, with medium leafy bracts; 70–85 cm (28–34 in), with upright stems, very floriferous. Not unlike 'Perry's White', but the flowers with a slight pink cast, especially when they are fresh.

'Halima'★: flowers salmon-pink, the petals with a prominent basal red blotch; sturdy stems up to 60 cm (24 in).

'Harvest Moon'★: flowers semi-double, deep orange at first, but gradually fading, the petals strongly ruffled, overlapping, not blotched; buds egg-shaped with a few or none, medium leafy bracts; 90–110 cm (36–44 in). One of the boldest Oriental poppies.

'Helen Elizabeth'★: see 'Turkish Delight'

'Helen Ellis'★: see 'Turkish Delight'.

'Henri Cayeux': supposedly an improved form of 'Hewitt's Old Rose'.

'Hewitt's Old Rose'★: large old-rose blooms. An old cultivar.

'Hula Hula'★: flowers pink, the petals with a basal black blotch and a deeply cut margin; 70–80 cm (24–28 in).

'Ida Brailsford': flowers pale apricot shading to shell-pink.

'Immaculata'; medium-sized flowers of bright scarlet, unblotched.

'Indian Chief'★: flowers single, large and of great substance, deep mahogany-red.

'Iris Perry': small flowered cultivar with tulip-shaped flowers of bright salmon; said to be excellent for cutting.

'Jeannie Mawson': flowers very large, salmon-rose.

'John III' AGM★: [Pl. 54] flowers single, neat and bowl-shaped, lustrous pinkish-red with a flush of orange, with overlapping pleated petals that are unblotched; buds egg-shaped, with a small ruff of scalelike undivided bracts; 60–70 cm (24–28 in). A delightful recent Zeppelin cultivar which is similar in size and substance to the popular 'Karine', from the same 'stable', but with redder flowers.

'John Metcalf'★: flowers single, pale orange with a whitish unblotched centre, the petals somewhat pleated; buds rounded to egg-shaped, with a prominent ruff of large leafy bracts; 60–75 cm (24–30 in), with sturdy leafy stems.

'Juliane'★: [Pl. 55] flowers single and held clear of the foliage, delicate pale pink, the petals thick, overlapping and pleated, unblotched but flushed with red at the base; buds large and egg-shaped with a few small bracts; sturdy stems, 70–85 cm (28–34 in).

'Karine' AGM★: **[Pl. 56]** flowers single and bowl-shaped, a charming shell-pink, the petals overlapping, slightly pleated and unblotched but with a reddish purple basal zone; buds egg-shaped with a somewhat pointed apex, without bracts; 60–70 cm (24–28 in) with sturdy erect stems. An excellent modern German, self-supporting, weather-resistant cultivar, originating at the von Zeppelin nursery.

'King George'★: essentially similar to 'Curlilocks', but the petals more deeply serrated, the margins cut to about 3 cm (1⅕ in) depth (2 cm or ⅘ in in 'Curlilocks'); 80–90 cm (32–36 in).

'Khedive' AGM★: flowers single, large and held above the foliage, salmon-pink with a flush of orange, with a whitish centre, fading gradually, the petals broad and overlapping and frilled to give the flower a semi-double appearance, with a small purple blotch at the base; buds fat and rounded, with a prominent ruff of medium leafy bracts; 60–75 cm (24–30 in), with sturdy stems. Another fine von Zeppelin introduction.

'Kleine Tänzerin'★: **[Pl. 57]** flowers single, rather small, bowl-shaped, with dark pink flowers, the petals overlapping and frilled, with a distinct dark purple blotch towards the base; buds egg-shaped, with a few small bracts; 60–75 cm (24–30 in), with stiff very leafy stems and underground runners. Similar in colour to 'Mrs Perry', but with smaller flowers and a small ruff of bracts.

'Kollebloem'★: flowers single, large, dark red-black (deep blood-red), the petals with a prominent basal black blotch; buds egg-shaped, with a few large leafy bracts; 85–100 cm (34–40 in), with stiff rough-bristly stems and leaves. Fairly close to 'Avebury Crimson', but with larger and even deeper flowers. Both cultivars belong to the 'Beauty of Livermere' group, but this cultivar is generally distinguished by its rather brighter red flowers and softly bristly leaves and stems.

'Ladybird'★: flowers single, substantial, vermillion-red with a hint of orange, the petals ruffled and overlapping, with a prominent large basal black blotch; buds plump egg-shaped, with a few large leafy bracts; 70–80 cm (28–32 in). A von Zeppelin introduction with a rather sprawling habit and large blowsy blooms, probably the largest of any Oriental poppy; early flowering. Often misidentified as 'Goliath'. Not to be confused with the annual poppy under the same cultivar name: see *Papaver commutatum* 'Ladybird'.

'Lady Fermour Hesketh': flowers salmon, the petals with a dark basal blotch. An old cultivar from 1916; possibly the same as 'Lady Haskett'.

'Lady Haskett': a dwarf cultivar with salmon-pink flowers, the petals with a prominent basal crimson blotch.

'Lady Moore' ('Lady Frederick Moore') AGM★: flowers single, opening widely into a saucer shape, clear salmon-pink, the somewhat ruffled petals with a prominent black basal blotch; buds egg-shaped, without bracts; 70–85 cm (28–34 in). A fine cultivar distributed originally from Glasnevin Botanic Garden, Dublin. Rather similar to 'Karine', but the flowers more salmon and borne on taller stems with grey, less frizzled foliage.

'Lady Roscoe'★: flowers single, apricot-rose, the petals pleated, with a prominent purple-black basal blotch; buds rounded to egg-shaped, without bracts; 80–95 cm (32–38 in). A delightful cultivar with nicely formed flowers.

'Lambada'★: flowers bright red with a white centre; 60–70 cm (24–28 in).

'Lauren's Lilac'★: a new cultivar making a very robust plant with flowers of mauve-purple with a ruff of small leaflike bracts, the petals somewhat ruffled and with a black basal blotch; 87-100 cm (35-40 in). A good cultivar for those who like older cultivars such as 'Patty's Plum' or 'Raspberry Queen'.

'Leuchtfeuer' AGM★: flowers single, lustrous reddish-pink with a flush of orange, the petals long and widely overlapping, somewhat ruffled, with a small oblong, purplish-black basal blotch; buds oblong, with a few medium to large leafy bracts or none; 70–80 cm (28–32 in), the stems with neat, rather attractive silvery-grey leaves.

'Lilac Girl'★ ('Lavender Girl'): [**Pl. 58**] flowers single, large, pale lilac-purple, fading in strong sunshine, the petals pleated and overlapping; buds egg-shaped, with a few large leafy bracts; 80–100 cm (32–40 in), with very leafy stems.

'Lighthouse' AGM★: flowers single, large and rather floppy, pale salmon-pink, fading with age, the petals frilled and slightly pleated, with a large shiny red basal blotch; buds oblong to egg-shaped with a few medium to small leafy bracts; 80–95 cm (32–38 in). The pale whitish-green ovary and rays are distinctive, forming a pale eye to the flower. It is doubtful if the plant given an AGM at the Wisley trials in 1997 is in fact the true 'Lighthouse' and as a consequence, the award is probably best rejected.

'Little Prince': small flowers of rich scarlet; good for cutting.

'Lord Lambourne': flowers large, single, orange-scarlet; 70–90 cm (28–36 in). Said to be an improved form of 'King George'. Probably no longer in existence.

'Lovely': flowers deep scarlet.

'Magnificence': flowers very large and brilliant scarlet, borne on extremely sturdy stems.

'Mahony': an old cultivar that is now no longer available; flowers single, deep maroon.

'Mahony Amelioré': flowers rich mahogany-purple.

'Maiden's Blush': flowers very soft blush-pink; 75–85 cm (30–34 in).

'Marcus Perry'★: flowers single, satiny orange-scarlet, the petals overlapping and somewhat ruffled, with a dark blotch at the base; buds large and rounded, with a ruff of large leafy bracts; 70–80 cm (28–32 in), with stiff, self-supporting stems.

'Master Richard'★: flowers rose-pink, the petals with a finely serrated margin; 70–80 cm (28–32 in).

'May Queen'★: very similar to 'Olympia', but flowers opening less flat and with somewhat quilled petals, paler and orange-red; other details the same. 'Harvest Moon' is sometimes mistaken for this cultivar; however, the flowers are more orange and regular, although semi-double, and the buds often bear one or two small bracts; 65–75 cm (26–30 in).

'May Sadler'★: an old cultivar from the 1920s with deeply fringed flowers of pale salmon-rose.

'**Midnight**'★: flowers single, large, orange-pink; 70–80 cm (28–32 in) with stiff leafy stems.

'**Mrs H.G. Stobart**' ('Mrs George Stobart')★: flowers single, large, cerise, the petals with a large black blotch at the base.

'**Mrs Marrow's Plum**'★: same as 'Patty's Plum'.

'**Mrs Perry**' AGM★: flowers single, rich salmon-pink, the petals broad and overlapping, somewhat pleated, with a prominent oblong purple basal blotch which gradually fades; buds oblong, with several small to large leafy bracts or smaller scalelike bracts; 80–100 cm (32–40 in), with tall stems that are leafless towards the top. A fine old and popular cultivar.

'**Nancy**': flowers single, crimson-red, the petals overlapping and ruffled, with a basal black blotch; buds rounded, with variable bracts, some small, recurved and scalelike, others larger, spreading and leaflike; 75–85 cm (30–34 in), with rather crumpled deep green foliage.

'**Nanum Flore Pleno**': see *P. lateritium* 'Fireball'.

'**Olympia**'★: flowers semi-double, orange-scarlet that open out widely to a saucer shape, the petals rather flat but somewhat ruffled, without a basal blotch; buds oval, without bracts; 65–75 cm (26–30 in), with thin, rather flexuous stems that are leafless above; markedly stoloniferous. Probably the most double of any Oriental poppy, although a fully double type does not exist. Originally from a seed strain.

'**Olympic Flame**'★: flowers semi-double, orange-scarlet; 85–95 cm (34–38 in). One of the earliest cultivars to flower. Originally from a seed strain.

'**Orangeade**'★: flowers bright orange; one of many rather indistinguishable cultivars in this particular colour range.

'**Orange Glow**'★: flowers brightest orange, borne on stems about 100 cm (40 in) tall.

'**Oriana**'★: flowers single, orange, forming a bowl shape, the petals somewhat overlapping and crumpled, with a purple-mauve basal blotch; buds narrow egg-shaped, with a few large leafy bracts; 75–85 cm (30–34 in), with rather thin, often sprawling, stems.

'**Pale Face**'★: flowers single, very pale pink, fading to an almost white centre, the petals overlapping and somewhat ruffled, with a basal blotch; buds egg-shaped, without bracts; 75–85 cm (30–34 in), with dark green leaves.

'**Patty's Plum**' (Mrs Marrow's Plum')★: [**Pl. 59**] flowers single, purple, burnishing and fading with age, the petals overlapping and somewhat pleated, with a basal black blotch; buds oblong and sometimes pointed, with a few large leafy bracts; 70–85 cm (28–34 in), the stiff stems leafless just below the flowers.

'**Perry's Blush**': a sturdy plant with large white flowers flushed with rose. Dates from 1913.

'**Perry's Favourite**': flowers single, tulip-shaped, rosy-salmon, the petals with a bold crimson blotch at the base. A cultivar dating back to 1916 and said to have been derived from 'Princess Ena'.

'**Perry's Pigmy**': a dwarf plant with single, cup-shaped flowers in rich salmon, the petals with a dark chocolate-crimson basal blotch. Dates from 1915.

'Perry's Unique': small, single flowers of brilliant scarlet, with deeply lacerated petal margins and a bold black mark at the base of each. Very similar to 'Curlilocks' and dating from 1915.

'Perry's White'⋆: [Pl. 60] flowers single, white with the faintest of pink flushes, the petals overlapping and somewhat ruffled, with an un-distinguished purple (reddish on the exterior of the flower) blotch or zone at the base, which soon begins to fade; buds egg-shaped to oval, with several small leafy bracts or scales, sometimes bractless; 85–95 cm (34–38 in) tall with sturdy, erect, leafy stems. The original 'Perry's White' was said to be pure white with a bold crimson blotch at the base of each petal. Plants circulating under the name today do not seem to conform to this description and it may be that the original plant has been long lost to cultivation. Those going under the name today may well be selected seedlings of the original!

'Peter Pan'⋆: almost indistinguishable from 'Olympia' and perhaps one and the same cultivar. Both are Perry's introductions dating back to the late 1930s.

'Petticoat'⋆: [Pl. 61] flowers single, salmon-pink, opening widely, the petals strongly frilled and pleated, with a whitish margin, with a small purplish-black broken basal blotch; buds egg-shaped, with several small to medium leafy bracts; 70–80 cm (28–32 in), with stiff, erect stems. A von Zeppelin introduction.

'Picotee'⋆: [Pl. 62] flowers single, white in the centre, widely and unevenly banded towards the margin with salmon-orange, the petals broadly over-lapping and somewhat frilled and pleated, without a blotch; buds egg-shaped and rather pointed, with a ruff of medium-sized leafy bracts; 65–80 cm (26–32 in), with the flowers held on rather thin stems above the foliage. A very distinctive cultivar, but not a true picotee; the amount of colour towards the petal margins varies a lot from flower to flower, often on the same plant, and this may be partly weather-related. Despite this, there appear to be several different clones of 'Picotee' in existence. 'Pinnacle' is probably the same or a somewhat improved form.

'Pink Beauty': flowers single, tulip-shaped, rich pink.

'Pink Lassie': flowers large, single, clear pale salmon-pink, the petals over-lapping and rather smooth, with a large reddish-purple basal blotch and unusual pale purple anthers; buds narrow-oblong and twisted, with several large leafy bracts; 80–100 cm (32–40 in). Fairly similar to 'Lady Moore', which is rather deeper coloured and with a prominent black blotch at the base of each petal.

'Pink Panda'⋆: another new cultivar, with robust stems and rather over-sized flowers of blush pink, the petals ruffled and with a basal black blotch; 80-90 cm (32-36 in).

'Pinnacle'⋆: white flowers with a salmon-orange margin: see also under 'Picotee'.

Pizzicato Group⋆: a relatively dwarf selection of seed-raised Oriental poppies 50–60 cm (20–24 in) tall, but with large flowers often fully 15 cm (6 in) across, sometimes more. The flowers range in colour from red and scarlet to orange, salmon, mauve, pink and white, generally marked with a dark blotch at the base of each petal. A seed strain.

'**Polka**'★: flowers orange-red merging to a white centre; 70–80 cm (28–32 in).

'**Prince of Orange**'★: flowers glowing orange borne on a sturdy plant: 80–90 cm (32–36 in).

'**Princess Ena**': flowers single, tulip-shaped, pale orange-salmon, with a dark blotch at the base of each petal. Dating from 1907 and named after the then Queen of Spain.

'**Prinz Eugen**'★: very similar to 'Garden Glory' and difficult to separate, but the stems are perhaps stiffer and not quite as long; 70–80 cm (28–32 in).

'**Prinzessin Victoria Louise**' ('Princess Victoria Louise')★: flowers very large, single, salmon-pink, the petals thick and slightly pleated with a distinct purplish-black basal blotch; buds egg-shaped, with a few small bracts; 70–90 cm (28–36 in), with strong stiff stems. Originally a seed strain.

'**Private Gerald Perry**': large semi-double flowers of apricot-pink, opening widely. This cultivar dates back to 1915 and is no longer available.

'**Prospero**'★: very similar to 'Oriana', but perhaps taller; 80–90 cm (32–36 in).

'**Queen Alexandra**'★: an old cultivar dated 1906, with extra large luminous salmon-scarlet flowers that have a large, deep, glistening crimson-black blotch at the base of each petal. Distinctive, but only occasionally available today.

'**Raspberry Queen**'★: flowers a lovely raspberry pink with darker streaks; 80 cm (32 in).

'**Raspberry Ruffles**'★: a new introduction with raspberry-pink flowers, the ruffled petals in a double row; 80–90 cm (32–36 in), not blotched at the base. Similar to 'Raspberry Queen' but perhaps rather duller in bloom, without the 'mascara'. This is a seedling from that old favourite 'Cedric's Pink'.

'**Redizelle**'★: flowers single, deep scarlet and glossy, the petals fairly smooth, with a bold black basal blotch and masses of purple anthers; buds narrow-oblong and twisted, with several medium leafy bracts; 80–90 cm (32–36 in). Later flowering than most cultivars.

'**Rembrandt**'★: flowers single, deep red, the petals overlapping, with a rather indistinct basal blotch; 75–85 cm (30–34 in). Originally a seed strain.

'**Rosenpokal**'★: [Pl. 63] flowers single, pink, the petals with a small purplish-black basal blotch; buds egg-shaped, with a few medium leafy bracts; 75–100 cm (30–40 in), with rather lanky stems, but free-flowering.

'**Reggie Perry**': a small-flowered cultivar that dates back to the First World War years, with tulip-shaped flowers of salmon-rose that have a deep maroon-black blotch at the base of each petal.

'**Rose Queen**'★: an old cultivar thought at one time to be lost to cultivation but now resurrected; flowers rose-pink; 80–90 cm (32–36 in).

'**Royal Chocolate Distinction**'★: flowers medium sized, of an unusual red overcast with deep brown; 70–80 cm (28–32 in).

'**Royal Prince**': flowers large and brilliant scarlet and lustrous, with a prominent black blotch at the base of each petal.

'**Royal Scarlet**': a free-flowering cultivar with large deep scarlet flowers with a dark blotch at the base of each petal.

'Royal Wedding'★: flowers pure white, the petals with a black basal blotch; 75–85 cm (30–34 in). Originally from a seed strain; the offspring can vary.

'Ruby Perry': another cultivar from the First World War era, with small salmon-apricot flowers; a dwarf plant.

'Salmon Beauty': flowers large and wide-opening, a delicate shade of salmon-rose.

'Salmon Glow'★: flowers semi-double, large, salmon-orange with a silvery sheen, the petals very frilled, with a small basal black blotch; 85–95 cm (34–38 in).

'Salmon Perfection': flowers a rich salmon-scarlet, with a black blotch at the base of each petal.

'Salmon Queen': dating from 1916, this cultivar has rich rose-salmon flowers flushed with apricot.

'Salome'★: flowers large, single, pink, the petals slightly pleated, reddish towards the base but without a blotch; buds egg-shaped, without bracts; 90–110 cm (36–44 in). Early flowering.

'Scarlet King'★: flowers large, scarlet-red; 80–90 cm (32–36 in).

'Showgirl' AGM★: flowers single, orange-pink with a hint of salmon, fading with age, the petals somewhat pleated and white-margined, widely overlapping, with a purplish basal blotch that soon fades; buds egg-shaped, with a few medium leafy bracts; 75–90 cm (30–36 in), with thin stems. The flowers fade almost to white on ageing. Similar to 'Petticoat', but the flowers are a redder pink and the petals less markedly pleated.

'Sindbad' (sometimes spelled 'Sinbad')★: flowers single, orange-red, the petals somewhat frilled, paler, almost whitish towards the red-flushed base but without a blotch; buds egg-shaped, with a few small bracts cupped around the base of the bud; sturdy stems, 85–105 cm (34–42 in).

'Silberblick': an unusual cultivar with rich orange-scarlet flowers and a contrasting boss of white anthers.

'Silver Queen': flowers medium-sized, white with a flush of pink, with a chocolate centre, but the petals unblotched.

'Snow Goose'★: another new cultivar. The flowers are pure white, the ruffled petals in two rows and with a basal black blotch; 80–90 cm (32–36 in).

'Spätzünder'★: flowers single, brilliant glossy orange-red, the petals widely overlapping, pleated and with a cut margin, with a large and distinct basal black blotch; buds large, egg-shaped, with several large leafy bracts; 60–75 cm (24–30 in), with sturdy erect stems. A late-flowering cultivar.

'Springtime'★: flowers pale salmon merging into white in the centre; 70–80 cm (28–32 in).

'Sturmfackel' ('Stormtorch')★: Very similar to 'Turkish Delight', but flowers more orange; 70–80 cm (28–32 in).

'Suleika'★: [Pl. 64] flowers single, orange-vermilion with a paler or whitish margin, the petals widely overlapping, pleated, purplish towards the base but without a blotch; buds egg-shaped, somewhat twisted, with a few medium leafy bracts, which later wrap around the developing fruit-capsule; 75–90 cm (30–36 in). A von Zeppelin introduction.

'**Sultana**'★: flowers single, small, cerise-rose, redder on the outside and towards the base, the petals somewhat crumpled and frilled, with an indistinct blackish-purple basal blotch; buds narrow-oblong, with one or two bracts, or bractless; 65–75 cm (26–30 in), with thin erect stems and rather pale foliage. Very similar to 'Watermelon', but the flowers often bractless and the plants much shorter. In addition, differences can be seen in the fruit capsule which bears a rather flat disk with a small knob in the middle, while in 'Sultana' the disk is domed and with a distinctive well in the centre.

'**Sungold**': flowers single, bright orange-red, the petals overlapping, somewhat frilled, without a basal blotch; buds egg-shaped, without bracts; 90–100 cm (36–40 in) with tall rather floppy stems.

'**Surprise**': flowers single, bright vermillion-red, the petals thick and pleated, with a rounded basal black blotch; buds narrow-oblong, twisted, with a few small bracts; 75–90 cm (30–36 in).

'**The Cardinal**': bold, 15 cm (6 in) flowers of deep cardinal-red, each slightly frilled petal with a small squarish black blotch near the base. Plant about 100 cm (40 in) tall. A seed strain sold by Plants of Distinction in the UK. It is not clear if the seedlings come 100% true to type or not.

'**Thora Perry**': an outstanding dwarf cultivar (only 40 cm/16 in tall), with small snow-white flowers set above neat grey foliage on slender stems. A Perry introduction dating back to 1922 and sadly no longer available.

'**Tulip**': an old cultivar from 1913 which is no longer available and which had distinctive long-tapered flowerbuds and single, deep red, tulip-shaped flowers; said to be the colour of *Tulipa gesneriana*.

'**Türkenlouis**'★: [**Pl. 65**] flowers single, large, deep scarlet-orange, the petals deeply fringed with obtuse lobes, blotched blackish-red at the base; buds egg-shaped, with a few medium leafy bracts; 70–80 cm (28–32 in). The name is often mistranslated as "Turkish Delight", which is quite a different cultivar. Similar to 'Curlilocks' at a glance, but the absence of blotches and the blunter petal lacerations are distinctive.

'**Türkenlouis Rose**': similar to the proceeding, but the flowers are rose-red, the petals perhaps slightly less deeply fringed, but with a similar rather small blotch towards the base.

'**Turkish Delight**' ('Helen Ellis', 'Helen Elizabeth') AGM★. Flowers single, bowl-shaped, soft salmon-pink, the petals somewhat ruffled, without a basal blotch; buds egg-shaped, without bracts; 60–75 cm (24–30 in), with stiff, erect stems, forming a neat bushy plant.

'**Tutu**'★: flowers semi-double, orange-red; 65–75 cm (26–30 in).

'**Victoria Dreyfuss**': flowers single, vivid orange-red, the petals pleated, with a large purple-black basal blotch; buds rounded to egg-shaped, without bracts; 90–110 cm (36–44 in), with lanky stems, the flowers held well above the foliage.

'**Water Babies**'★: a new American cultivar; flowers a subtle mixture of pale pink shades; 70–80 cm (28–32 in).

'**Waterloo**': an old cultivar which is no longer available; the plants had rather grey, woolly-looking leaves and flowers of deep crimson suffused with purple.

'**Watermelon**'*: [**Pl. 66**] flowers single, bowl-shaped, pale pinkish-purple, the petals somewhat ruffled, with a large basal black blotch; buds rounded or egg-shaped, with a ruff of small undivided sepal-like bracts at the base; 80–100 cm (32–40 in), with stiff stems and the flowers held well above the foliage. One of the most unusual Oriental poppies; the flowers' colour has been described as "bubble gum pink" or a mixture of "stewed blackcurrants and cream".

'**Wild Salmon**'*: large frilly salmon-pink flowers, the petals with a small darkish blotch near the base; 85–100 cm (34–40 in). A seed strain.

'**Witchery**': very similar to 'Graue Witwe', but the flowers pinker and with a more prominent basal crimson-black blotch, and the petals, if anything, rather less ruffled.

'**White King**'*: plants going around under this name seem to be indistinguishable from 'Black and White'.

'**White Knight**'*: comments as for 'White King'.

'**Wisley Beacon**'*: [**Pl. 67**] a fine cultivar grown unnamed at the Royal Horticultural Society's garden at Wisley for a number of years and now named. The flowers are substantial and beautifully cupped, glowing orange, the petals slightly ruffled and with a neat basal black blotch; 60-70 cm (24-28 in). One of the finest orange-flowered Oriental Poppies and certainly one of the more distinctive.

'**Wunderkind**'('Enchantress')*: flowers single, bright raspberry-pink, the petals somewhat frilled, with a prominent black basal blotch; buds plump and rounded, with a few large leafy bracts; 65–80 cm (26–32 in). A fine Continental cultivar which is somewhat similar to 'Sultana', but the leaves are less divided and with a distinctive wide midrib.

Other Oriental poppy cultivars exist, although their status is unclear: most are sold by a single nursery and often prove not to be indistinct from existing and well-established cultivars. For reference, they are listed here, but they should be purchased with caution: 'Diana', 'Garden Gnome', 'Goldie', 'Grenadier', Humphrey Bennett', 'Lady Haig', 'Pink Chiffon', 'Prince of Orange', 'Saffron', 'Snow Queen', 'Tom Tit', and 'Wild Salmon'.

In addition, selections are offered as seed and called 'Border Vars Mixed'. 'New Hybrids' is a fine large-flowered mixture with blooms in shades of white, pink, salmon, orange, scarlet, crimson and mahogany tinted with gold or violet, mostly with dark centres and some with picotée edges. A delightful mixture, but which colours will appear is a matter of pot luck.

ORIENTAL HYBRID
'**Red Gauntlet**': [**Pl. 69**] flowers single, 12.5 cm (5 in) across, bright orange, with 4 petals that spread widely apart; buds narrow-oblong, bristly, without bracts, borne on slender stalks well above the foliage; 75–85 cm (30–34 in). This is an intriguing plant which arose as a chance cross between an Oriental poppy and the Turkish endemic *Papaver triniifolia*. It is especially interesting as it represents the first such cross and is also a hybrid between a long-lived perennial species and a monocarpic one. In many ways, the

character of the hybrid, which is quite variable, is midway between the parents; the neat grey, neatly dissected, stiffly bristly leaves are clearly inherited from the monocarpic parent, as are the 4-petalled flowers, while the solitary flowers and colour are inherited from the Oriental poppy parent; in fact, unlike the Oriental poppies, 'Red Gauntlet' often bears branched stems with up to 30 flowers. The stems are thin, yet fairly stiff and carry the flowers well above the foliage on stems up to 70 cm (28 in) tall, appearing in June and early July. The overall effect is both elegant and pleasing and opens up the interesting prospect of a whole new range of garden hybrids involving the Orientalis Group. On the face of it, this would seem an improbable hybrid in the first instance. The plants have proved to be fully hardy and properly perennial in nature. This exciting and unexpected hybrid turned up in the garden of David Maxwell-Hide, who gardens in East Molesey in Surrey, and I am deeply grateful to him for supplying me with some live plants. It flowers towards the end of the Oriental poppy season. This appears to be a sterile hybrid; although fruits are set they do not contain viable seed.

Papaver paucifoliatum (Trautv.) Fedde.
(See also general remarks under *P. bracteatum*, p. 82)

This species, which looks like a small and daintier version of *P. orientale*, has practically leafless stems and smaller flowers. In gardens it tends to make a spreading patch and is ideal where the more robust 'oriental' types would be out of place.

   This species is restricted to subalpine meadows in the Caucasus Mountains. It is sometimes listed as *P. orientale* var. *paucifoliatum* Trautv. and indeed it was first described as such. In gardens it is best considered a variety of that species.

Papaver pavoninum Schrenk   [Pl. 70]
PEACOCK POPPY

This is another of those exciting scarlet poppies that can cause a mass display of colour in the early summer. In the steppes and hill country of Uzbekistan and Kazakhstan where I have seen it, blankets and ribbons of scarlet stretch across the landscape, a gaudy profusion reminiscent of the poppy fields of western Europe. In the wild, *P. pavoninum* often grows in association with *Roemeria refracta* and at a glance the two can readily be confused. However, examination of the fruits soon reveals the difference, those of the latter long and linear, of the former broad and bristly.

   P. pavoninum is an annual, generally 20–30 cm (8–12 in) tall, though occasionally taller in deeper and moister soils. The erect stems are generally branched close to the ground and are beset with stiff bristles. The basal leaves are long-stalked and bipinnately lobed, with oblong to oval, sharply toothed, segments, each lobe ending in a short bristle; the stem leaves are similar although often less dissected and short-stalked or sessile. The flower buds are oval in outline, bristly and terminating in a characteristic pair of hollow horns. The flowers, 3.5–5.5 cm (1⅖–2⅕ in) across are scarlet, each petal with

Papaver pavoninum flowerbud and fruit

a basal black blotch, which is sometimes outlined by a thin white line; the black or dark violet anthers produce blue pollen. The fruit-capsule is oval in outline, 5–10 mm (⅕–⅖ in) long, ribbed and with semi-spreading pale bristles, the stigmatic disk with four to eight (occasionally up to 11) rays.

P. pavoninum has a wide distribution in central Asia, from northern Iran to Pakistan and northwards through the Tienshan and Altai from Turkmenistan to Kazakhstan. In these regions it is a plant of cultivated land, stony steppes, foothills and dry mountain slopes at altitudes of 500–2600 m (1650–8500 ft), though mostly at the lower altitudinal range.

This species is closely related to *P. hybridum* and *P. argemone*; they all belong to section Argemonorhoedes, which is characterised by fruit-capsules that are covered in stiff bristles and capped by a narrow stigmatic disk. Within this section, *P. pavoninum* is at once distinguished by the two conspicuous hollow horns which terminate the sepals and by the uniformly linear stamen filaments; in the other related species the filaments are distinctly thickened towards the top.

P. ocellatum is sometimes regarded as a variant of *P. pavoninum* in which the sepal horns are virtually obsolete.

In gardens *P. pavoninum* is sometimes confused with *P. commutatum*. They look superficially alike in flower, but the hornless flower buds and smooth fruit-capsules of the latter are 'giveaway' identification features.

P. pavoninum is an easy and floriferous garden plant, best sown in the early spring where it is to flower. It will sometimes self-sow in the garden, but cannot always be relied upon to do so, and it is wise to collect some seed each summer for the following year. Some forms in cultivation have a violet, or violet and black, basal blotch to each petal, rather than plain black.

Papaver pilosum Sibth. & Sm.

This Turkish poppy is very closely related to *P. spicatum*, differing primarily in its fruit-capsules, which are broader and with a rounded rather than tapered base and capped by a more or less flat (not pyramidal) stigmatic disk. The flowers range in colour from orange-red to deep orange or lurid scarlet, the petals often with a pale, whitish, basal blotch. The flower buds are almost spherical, rather than oval as in *P. spicatum*.

Fruit of *Papaver pilosum*

P. pilosum is restricted to the provinces of Bithynia and Galatia, where it is a plant of rocky mountain habitats; flowering in July and August. The related *P. apokrinomenon* Fedde, from Phrygia in Turkey, is generally regarded as being rather intermediate between *P. spicatum* and *P. pilosum* and may show that these elements are in fact extremes of a single variable species – this requires further investigation.

Occasionally seen in cultivation, but by no means common. Treat as for *P. spicatum*.

Papaver pinnatifidum Moris.
MEDITERRANEAN POPPY

Very similar to *P. dubium*, but differing mainly in the stems, which have spreading hairs in the lower part of the plant, and also in the yellow, rather than violet anthers. In addition, the fruit-capsule is more club-shaped and has a somewhat tapered base and a slightly convex, rather than flat stigmatic disk, with six to eight rays.

P. pinnatifidum is a native of the Mediterranean region from Spain and north-west Africa, eastwards to Greece, as well as Portugal. It is also found in the Canary Islands and the Azores, where it may also be native rather than introduced. It flowers from April to June. It is not in cultivation at the present time.

Papaver postii Fedde

A small, spreading to decumbent, slightly bristly annual, not more than 20 cm (8 in) tall, often only 6–10 cm (2⅖–4 in). The leaves are deeply pinnately-lobed, 2–8 cm (⅘–3⅕ in) long, with narrow, pointed segments, sometimes slightly toothed, mostly in a basal rosette. Flowers solitary on slender stalks (pedicels), orange-red to pale scarlet, 2–3.5 cm (⅘–1⅖ in) across, the petals without a dark basal blotch; stamens with yellow or brownish anthers and violet-purple filaments. The fruit-capsule is smooth or somewhat ribbed, top-shaped or broadly club-shaped, 6–8 mm (¼–⅓ in) long, with a flat disk with five to seven stigmatic rays.

This small poppy inhabits rocky places, hill and mountain slopes and screes, up to an altitude of 800 m (2600 ft), sometimes being found along roadsides, where it flowers from April to June. *P. postii* is native to Turkey, Cyprus and Syria.

P. postii is related to *P. rhoeas* and *P. dubium*, being readily distinguished by its spreading to decumbent habit and small flowers, the petals never more than 2 cm (⅘ in) long. As far as I am aware, it is not in cultivation.

Papaver pseudo-orientale – see under *P. bracteatum*, p.83.

Papaver radicatum Rötbb.   **[Pl. 71]**
ARCTIC POPPY

This widespread Arctic species is closely related to *P. nudicaule*, being a tufted perennial, but it is a small plant, seldom over 25 cm (10 in) tall in flower. The stems and leaves, like those of *P. nudicaule*, exude a yellow, occasionally white, latex when cut. The leaves, 3–6 cm (1⅕–2⅖ in) long, are pinnately-lobed with small oblong to lanceolate, pointed segments and are clothed in darkish hairs. The slender scape and sepals are covered in dark brown or blackish hairs. The flowers are usually dark yellow, 2.5–4 cm (1–1⅗ in) across, more rarely pinkish or white, the petals often withering and persisting around the developing fruit. The fruit-capsule is oval to rounded in outline, 10–17 mm (⅜–¾ in) long and covered in dense, appressed or spreading, reddish-brown bristles; there are generally five stigmatic rays.

P. radicatum is a plant of moraines and screes, river gravels and stony steppes, from North America to Greenland, Iceland, Arctic Europe and Arctic Russia, where it sometimes forms large scattered colonies from near sea level to 1850 m (6050 ft) in the mountains of Scandinavia.

This is undoubtedly a very variable species with many local forms and races – no less than 14 subspecies have been described from Europe alone, mostly restricted to small areas in the mountains of Scandinavia.

Seed of the wild type is sometimes available in cultivation. However, it is as a contributor to the garden forms of the Iceland poppy that it is perhaps best known. These vigorous, often gaudy, large-flowered poppies have an obscure origin that involves a number of closely related species which, though often isolated from one another in the wild, freely hybridise with one another in cultivation.

Other names in the 'P. radicatum complex' that occasionally turn up in seed lists include *P. alaskanum* Hultén, *P. macounii* Greene, *P. nigro-flavum* Hultén and *P. walpolei* Porsikil. However, it must be emphasised that although many of these entities can be separated geographically, their overall characters show considerable overlap and a wide-based research programme in both the Old and the New World is needed to ascertain whether or not any of these 'minor species' can be properly maintained. In cultivation they are often very difficult to separate, generally hybridise freely and tend to be short-lived. All are colourful and pretty little poppies that are well worth growing.

Fruit of *Papaver rhaeticum*

Papaver rhaeticum Leresche   **[Pl. 72–73]**
(Syn. *P. alpinum* subsp. *rhaeticum* (Leresche) Hayek; *P. pyrenaicum* subsp. *rhaeticum* (Leresche) Fedde)
RHAETIAN POPPY

A charming little alpine poppy confined to high mountain rocks, moraines and screes in the Pyrenees, south-western and eastern Alps as far as Yugoslavia, at altitudes of 1500–3050 m (4900–10,000 ft); a plant generally found on limestone.

P. *rhaeticum* is a small tufted, bristly perennial with the leaf bases forming a compact tunic around the base of the plant. The leaves are one- or two-pinnately divided, with short blunt lobes; the lower leaf-segments are alternate. The scapes, up to 20 cm (8 in) tall, have appressed bristles and bear solitary yellow (rarely red) flowers, 4–5 cm (1⅗–2 in) across. The oblong fruit-capsule, up to 14 mm (⅝ in) long, has five to seven stigmatic rays.

One of the finest members of the '*P. alpina*' group sometimes offered in seed exchanges and catalogues. Not difficult to grow, but short-lived in gardens.

See also the closely related *P. sendtneri* (p. 130). Both species were formerly grown in gardens as *P. pyrenaicum* and occasionally are still found under that name.

Papaver rhoeas L.   **[Pl. 75–78]**
COMMON POPPY, CORN POPPY, FLANDER'S POPPY

This is undoubtedly the most familiar of the poppies and probably the 'flowers of the field' mentioned in the Bible. It is the red that stains the arable lands of Europe and western Asia, reddens the motorway verges and roadside embankments. Yet this familiar plant has become drastically reduced in many areas in recent years due to modern farming practises, particularly the widespread use of herbicides.

It is the poppy of Flanders fields and its blooms have come to symbolise the dead of the two World Wars – the crimson petals, the drops of precious blood spilt in battle. Despite this, early peoples looked upon the plant as a symbol of rebirth, for the plants sprang up like magic in the spring after the harshness of the winter, to bring new life to the soil; literally rebirth to the land. On cultivated land, especially in corn fields, the red poppies must have been a widespread, conspicuous and familiar sight throughout much of central and southern Europe, as well as western Asia, and it had certainly reached north-western Europe and the British Isles with the arrival of arable crops, probably during Roman times, or earlier.

The fragility of the poppy, scattering its scarlet petals on the ground after just a day or two, reminds us of the transience of life and our own fragility. Early European colonisers transported the seeds of these poppies inadvertently with their crop seeds (wheat, rye and barley in particular) wherever they travelled in the temperate world; it must have been a cheerful reminder of home during the harsh colonising years.

P. rhoeas, like a number of related species, is almost exclusively associated with cultivated habits, particularly where land has been recently disturbed; seeds can persist in the soil for many years without germinating and it is often quite remarkable how huge colonies of *P. rhoeas* spring up on land shortly after it has been ploughed or otherwise disturbed. This effect will last as long as regular annual disturbance is repeated.

It is wrong to think that all the red poppies seen in the wild are *P. rhoeas*,

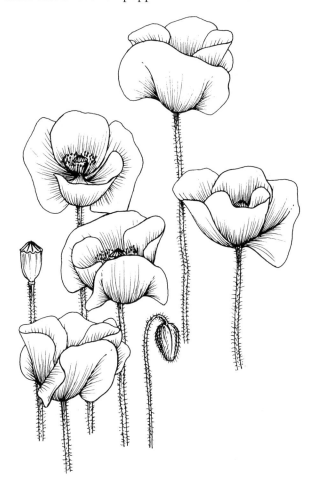

Papaver rhoeas

for there are a number of similar looking species that are generally readily distinguished in fruit. In Europe *P. argemone*, *P. dubium* and *P. hybridum* are also widespread red poppies of cultivated, especially arable, land and in parts of the Mediterranean region *P. apulum* and *P. nigrotinctum* add to the confusion. In western Asia *P. arenarium*, *P. commutatum* and *P. pavoninum* are equally widespread. In parts of central Asia, especially the southern CIS (Tadjikistan to Kazakstan and Uzbekistan), Iran and Afghanistan, *Roemeria refracta* can be easily mistaken for *P. rhoeas*. However, its telltale linear pods, quite unlike those of any true *Papaver*, make it easy to distinguish.

P. rhoeas is a very variable annual, 25–90 cm (10–36 in) tall, with bristly stems and leaves. The stem is usually branched and leafy, but in depauperate specimens growing on poor thin soil, they may be unbranched. The leaves are once or twice pinnately-lobed into narrow, toothed segments, the lower leaves stalked, but the upper generally sessile. The buds are bristly, nodding at first, but becoming erect as the petals emerge. The solitary, erect flowers open to a broad bowl shape, 6–9 cm (2⅖–3⅗ in) across and are usually rich scarlet, although paler shades often occur amongst large populations. The broad rounded, overlapping petals often, though not always, have a basal black blotch, which is sometimes edged with white. The stamens bear purplish filaments and characteristically blue anthers. The fruit-capsule is quite distinct in being almost rounded, smooth and capped by 8–12 stigmatic rays, occasionally more.

P. rhoeas is widespread in Europe and North Africa eastwards into western and central Asia, where it is primarily a plant of cultivated and disturbed land from sea level to the hills and lower mountains, rarely above an altitude of 1800 m (5900 ft).

This splendid plant, often considered a weed in gardens, has been cultivated for many centuries and presents no problem to the cultivator. Indeed, once sown, germinates readily and sets abundant seed, which will appear year after year without fail.

P. rhoeas is an ingredient of many wild flower mixtures. In fact, it is an

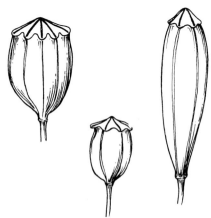

Comparison of the fruits of *Papaver rhoeas* (left), *P. dubium* (right) and *P. commutatum* (centre)

essential ingredient for those trying to establish an annual wild flower meadow, along with other notable arable 'weeds' such as the Corn Marigold, *Chrysanthemum segetum*, and the Cornflower, *Centaurea cyanus*. In Britain and northern Europe many seeds sold are of the southern European form of the species: these can be readily distinguished by their often larger, much more intensely scarlet, or more or less crimson flowers which are usually well-blotched, with a white halo surrounding the black of the blotch. These southern types find their way into the seed mixtures of unscrupulous dealers and although admittedly very fine plants, they are not correct for those wishing to develop a genuine annual wild flower meadow in Britain and elsewhere in the north and west of Europe. Furthermore, these southern poppies are finding their way from sown waysides and cultivated fields (in Britain and elsewhere) into the countryside in general and are polluting the native stock of the species, which is a pity.

The common scarlet forms are as delightful as any, but in the wild occasional colour variants can be found – those with pale red or orange flowers, or red edged with white, or purely pink petals are not infrequent, as are others with fully or semi-double flowers [Pl. 79]. A particularly fine strain in gardens are the famous single-flowered Shirley Poppies [Pl. 80–83], developed from a wild selection by the Rev. W. Wilkes, vicar of Shirley near Croydon in Surrey. He told how 'in the summer of (I think) 1879 or 1880 I noticed in a wilderness corner of my garden, among a patch of field poppies, one bloom with a narrow white edge'. After he had subsequently carefully selected from this, eliminating those with black blotches on the petals, he raised a race with a 'wonderfully light, bright, tissue paper-like appearance'. These varied in colour from palest pinks to deep reds, lilacs and mauves, with varying degrees of white around the edge of the petals and they became known as Shirley Poppies.

Shirley Poppies

The true Shirley Poppy has single flowers in a number of colours from white to pink, orange to red, with no hint of a black blotch at the base of the petals, and with pale stamens. The finest Shirley Poppies are perhaps the picotée types, the petals edged with a paler or darker colour. Modern strains of Shirley Poppies often contain double and semi-doubles, but these scarcely have the elegance and charm of the singles. The mixture of doubles and singles once found favour as the 'Reverend Wilkes Strain', though these poppies are not nearly so popular as they once were, due in large measure to the decline of the annual border in our gardens. However, one does not need an annual border to enjoy these delights: simply scatter the seed about in the early spring in any vacant patch in a border; thin sowing and ample thinning produce the best results. Some strains of Shirley Poppy have too many plain red forms. Rogueing out these the moment they come into bloom will tilt the balance in favour of the paler shades for future generations of poppies and ensure a pleasant balance of colours. Today most seed merchants supply selected mixtures of single- or double-flowered Shirley Poppies.

'American Legion': an attractive selection of the common poppy with bright scarlet flowers in which each petal has a basal white blotch instead of the usual black, providing a startling contrast to the centre of the flower.

'Angel's Choir': [Pl. 85] developed by Thompson and Morgan at Ipswich, also in Suffolk, from 'Mother of Pearl', this is another super selection in a similar range of colours, but the flowers are semi-double. In fact, 'Mother of Pearl' often produces a certain percentage of semi-double types and 'Angel's Choir' is a simple refinement. The literature calls the flowers double, but this is certainly not the case and most flowers retain almost a full compliment of stamens. The range of colours is primarily soft and pastel, as in 'Mother of Pearl', with pale pinks, grey, mauve and soft apricot shades dominating. However, unlike 'Mother of Pearl', deep shades, reds and oranges, as well as some brazen picotees have crept into the mixture, even as sold by Thompson and Morgan. This is a pity as these brighter colours can be readily acquired in singles and semi-double types in various different mixtures of Shirley poppies sold by dealers. In the garden it is best to weed out the deeper and brighter colours in favour of the more subtle shades in order to give a delightful soft tone to the flower garden. If this is not done, the deeper shades will soon begin to dominate future generations. 'Angel's Choir' perhaps lacks the grace and refinement of 'Mother of Pearl', but the flowers do last longer and the cultivar is certain to prove a popular addition to the range of annual poppies grown in the garden. 'English Poppies', a mixture of subtle pastel shades and semi-double flowers, sold by Plants of Distinction of Needham Market in Suffolk is similar, if not identical, to 'Angel's Choir' and may well share the same origins.

'Mother of Pearl': [Pl. 84] this plant is irritatingly known under various other names including, 'Angel's Wings', 'Cedric Morris', 'Fairy Wings' and 'Valerie Finnis' and probably others; enough to confuse even the most die-hard gardener. In fact, it was the late Sir Cedric Morris, painter and gardener, in his garden by Hadleigh in Suffolk, who selected out, and presumably named, 'Mother of Pearl', retaining only those plants with pale, misty or smoky colours, especially greys and pinks, as well as some with delightful flecking and paler or darker margins. Such seed mixtures often throw red and orange plants in the garden and these have to be rigorously rogued out if the subtle tones of 'Mother of Pearl' are to be retained. This is quite one of the loveliest and subtle poppy mixtures grown in our gardens. Unfortunately, to add to the confusion, some Shirley poppy mixes sold also turn out to be predominantly 'Mother of Pearl'.

Thompson and Morgan of Ipswich have recently (see their 2000 seed catalogue) issued a 'new' cultivar under the name 'Cedric Morris', described as 'a delightful mixture of exquisite soft and pastel shades, ideal for that wonderful "natural look" in the garden'. The accompanying picture shows a mixture of soft mauve, pink and greyish shades, with the petals subtly flecked, which is exactly how 'Mother of Pearl' should look. This might be a refined selection of 'Mother of Pearl', but it is certainly no more than that. Unfortunately, it was also Thompson and Morgan who applied the name 'Fairy Wings' to 'Mother of Pearl', creating even more confusion. Under the former name, it can be found in their 2000 catalogue, although the accompanying picture shows some dark rose shades that were never intended for the cultivar and should have been rogued out of the seed mixture.

This is as it may be, but 'Mother of Pearl' is undoubtedly a very lovely poppy and well deserves to be cherished in the garden. One can't help thinking that the late Cedric Morris would take great delight in the confusion caused by his cultivar; one can almost hear him chuckling with delight in the heavens.

In addition, Kees Sahin in Holland is developing some exciting modern strains of Shirley Poppy, both single and semi-double types, in a range of bright and pastel shades. This is something to look forward to and to relish.

'Flamenco': Yet another development for the 'Mother of Pearl' type with flowers in shades of pink (some too bright for 'Mother of Pearl'!) and generally with a broad white or whitish margin. The flowers are almost single, generally with 5-8 petals.

Searching back through old seed catalogues from the turn of the century, one will see other forms of *P. rhoeas*, including a dwarf form with double flowers in a variety of colours and so-called 'Japanese Pompon' varieties. Sadly, these are no longer with us today. Forms with lacerated petals are sometimes seen, though these are rather rare today.

Although these various strains of the corn poppy are considered to be of relatively recent origin, similar plants were certainly known to John Miller and are graphically described in the third edition of his *Gardener's Dictionary* of 1768. Miller describes *Papaver erraticum majus* as the red poppy or corn rose and states: 'The Red Poppy, or Corn Rose, is never propagate in the garden, but is very common upon chalky dry soils in almost every part of England, where the Plants come up amongst the Corn, and are very troublesome. The Flowers of this kind are brought into Markets for Medicinal use. There are many varieties of this Plant with double Flowers, which are cultivated in the Flower Garden, but especially the Dwarf Sort, of which there are some with very double Flowers, which are beautifully edged with white.' Miller goes on to list the various sorts:

'Great Wild Poppy, whose flowers-leaves are variegated'
'Double Wild Poppy, commonly called the Dwarf Poppy'
'Wild Poppy, with a double Vermilion-colour'd flower'
'Wild Poppy, with a double fiery Flower'
'Wild Poppy with a double purple Flower and white Bottom'
'Lesser Wild Poppy or Dwarf Poppy' (this may refer in fact to *P. dubium*)

Seed of all the types available today can be sown in the autumn or spring and seedlings should not be closer than 15–20 cm (6–8 in) if good strong plants are desired.

Apart from its horticultural merits, *P. rhoeas* has a number of economic uses. The dried flowers ('*Flores rhoeades*') were formerly used in medicine; they contain rhoeadine and tiny quantities of morphine, often used as a soporific drug. The petal pigment, anthocyanidin, is sometimes used as a colour dye in some medicines, syrups and wines.

Ancient preserved flowers of this species found in tombs dating back to 1100 BC are housed in the famous Cairo Museum and show that, even in former times, this poppy was held in high esteem by man.

Papaver rupifragum Boiss. & Reut. [Pl. 74]
SPANISH POPPY

This perennial species and the closely related *P. atlanticum*, which comes from Morocco, are delightful and accommodating garden poppies, long-lived and often seeding around freely once established.

P. rupifragum has a slender branched taproot and a basal tuft of sparsely bristly leaves; these are oblong to elliptical in outline, pinnately-lobed and with toothed segments and a slender stalk. Many sparsely branched stems (up to 50 cm/20 in tall) arise from the leaf-rosettes and are sparsely leafy below, the slender stalks hairless or somewhat bristly, carrying solitary flowers, 35–45 mm (1⅖–1⅘ in) across, the crimped petals a clear brick-red. The sepals are smooth and the stamens have orange-yellow anthers. The fruit-capsule is smooth, oblong-club-shaped, up to 2.5 cm (1 in) long and slightly ribbed.

This dainty perennial poppy inhabits limestone cliff crevices and mountain rocks in southern Spain (Andalucia) in the region of Serrania de Ronda. Despite its very restricted distribution in the wild, it has proved an easy garden plant. Semi-double flowered forms 'Flore Pleno' are equally common in gardens, as are those with the normal 4-petalled flowers.

The closely allied *P. atlanticum* can be distinguished by somewhat larger dull orange flowers and hairier leaves and stems. Both species are readily raised from seed. Young plants can be moved without ill effect, but I have found that mature plants resent disturbance and, although they don't die, they sulk, without properly flowering and never ever regaining their full vigour.

P. rupifragum is a plant for the front of the border, where it will flower throughout the summer. Although sometimes recommended for the rock garden and scree, its invasive seeding habit really does preclude it from such a position unless one enjoys weeding amongst the gravel.

Papaver sendtneri Kerner ex Hayek
(Syn. *P. alpinum* subsp. *sendtneri* (Kerner ex Hayek) Schinz & Keller; *P. pyrenaicum* subsp. *sendtneri* (Kerner & Hayek) Fedde)

This species is very closely related to *P. rhaeticum* and is generally separated by its more pointed (acute) leaf-segments and somewhat smaller white flowers. The fruit-capsule usually has only five stigmatic rays.

P. sendtneri is a plant of moraines and screes, at altitudes of 2000–2700 m (6550–8850 ft), in the central and eastern Alps.

It is rarely offered in seed catalogues or, if it is, it is generally masked under the '*P. alpinum*' aggregate. All the members of this complex are well worth cultivating – jolly little poppies ideal for the small garden and with a long flowering season.

Papaver somniferum L. **[Pl. 88–92]**

OPIUM POPPY

This widely cultivated plant is familiar in many gardens where, once sown, it often comes up without fail year after year, never failing to surprise and delight in its subtle variations of flower shape and colour.

It is almost certain that the opium poppy was first cultivated for seed in Neolithic times and that it was gradually spread by humans throughout western and northern Europe from the eastern Mediterranean Basin. At the same time, it spread eastwards to India. The oldest known reference to this poppy is to be found in Mesopotamia in the *Assyrian Herbal* of 2000 BC, although its use almost certainly goes back as far as the Sumerians, 5000 BC. In ancient Egypt the narcotic properties of the opium poppy were well known and it was employed as a sleep-inducing medicine.

In ancient Greece various gods were directly associated with the sleep-inducing properties of opium – the god of dreams and the god of death, for instance; indeed the word *opium* is of Greek origin. The Greeks prepared an extract from the stems, leaves and fruit-capsules called *meconium*. This was drunk as a pain killer and thought to have first originated in the town of Mekon, near modern-day Corinth, round about 800 BC. Hippocrates, the Greek physician (460–370 BC), referred to this drink as 'poppy-wine' and noted carefully its effects. The Greeks also learnt how to extract opium resin from the unripe fruit by making incisions along the capsule, a method well known to Theophrastus (300 BC). The Roman physician Galen was also enthusiastic about the use of opium.

Although the Greeks are generally credited with discovering both how to extract opium by incision of the capsule and the medicinal uses of opium, it is the Arabs who appear to have disseminated this knowledge to various parts of the world. Certainly, by the seventh century AD the cultivation of opium was common throughout the Arab empire and its narcotic and medicinal uses well established. The Arabs referred to the opium poppy as *Abou-el-noum*, 'father of sleep'.

By about AD 1000 the growing of opium was widespread in Europe and Asia. The earliest record of it in India dates from about this period.

In China at this time, *P. somniferum* was regarded more as a food and ornamental plant. By the fifteenth century it was widely grown in most provinces of China. However, opium was primarily imported into the country from India during the eighteenth century, where its widespread use as a narcotic drug had long been established. Britain found a highly lucrative trade in opium, which was grown in British India and exported to China in exchange for gold and silver. This in turn was used to buy tea and silks for import into Europe. This dangerous trade was controlled by the British East India Company who employed local traders (called country traders) licensed by the Company to smuggle opium along the Chinese coast, passing the proceeds in turn to the East India Company.

By the middle of the following century opium addiction had become rife in China and the Chinese government banned the use and import of opium.

This, in turn, led to dire conflict within China, culminating in the Opium Wars fought against the British, the first of which lasted from 1839 to 1842. In 1860 China was forced to finally agree to the import of the drug, but in turn charged a tax on it. In 1917 voluntary restrictions finally finished off this heinous trade.

The fact is that for many centuries opium was the only effective painkiller and its dangers as an addictive drug were not generally realised in the West until the beginning of the present century.

Today opium, the source of heroin, is still a major narcotic drug widely grown in the Third World and smuggled into many of the better-off countries. Much comes from the area of northern Burma (Myanmar), Thailand and south-western China known as the Golden Triangle. In this region the opium poppy is grown as a cash crop after the main crop of maize. The collection and refinement of opium takes place in numerous small factories along the Burma–Thai border and the revenue is used by local insurgents to fight their wars. The resultant heroin finds its way to Europe and America and today it is one of the major sources of drug abuse and addiction. Yet the opium poppy is, at the same time, of immense use in medicine, especially for its sleep-inducing and pain-killing properties.

In fact, opium resin contains a complex mixture of alkaloids (over 20 have been isolated) that include codeine, morphine, narceine, narcotine, papaverine and thebaine, all of which are of significant use in the pharmaceutical industry. These are extracted from the latex present primarily in the fruit-capsule and in the upper stem. Many different varieties of opium poppy are grown for medicine and differ primarily in the ratio and quantities of different alkaloids. Medicinal drugs based on opium are analgesic, sedative and anti-spasmodic, as well as soporific, and are also used in the treatment of various stomach disorders.

Crude opium is gathered for the narcotic trade by lancing the semi-mature capsule with a series of longitudinal grooves using a special implement for the purpose. Latex, which is contained in specialised tissue (articulate lactiferous vessels) close to the surface, exudes along these grooves to accumulate at the base of the capsule. Within twenty-four hours it solidifies and can then be collected. This brown gum is rolled into balls and stored – it will keep for a long time – and is converted to heroin by a process of 'cooking' and the addition of various chemical catalysts.

P. somniferum is also widely grown for its seeds (which contain no appreciable levels of harmful alkaloids). These are edible and can be used as a condiment on bread, salads and so on. They also have importance as a source of oil used for a variety of purposes – cooking oil, paint, soap and illumination. It is also used to make an important oil cake, (prepared as a mash from the whole plant) that forms a wholesome food for cattle, etc.

Other species of *Papaver* also contain appreciable quantities of useful pharmaceutical alkaloids – *P. bracteatum* and *P. orientale*, for instance, are sometimes grown on a commercial scale for such purposes.

Despite its sinister attributes, the opium poppy is a delightful garden plant, existing in a range of different and exciting forms. The plant was well known to Gerard (1597) who states: 'The leaves of White Poppie are long, broad, smooth, longer than the leaves of Lettuce . . . There are divers varieties of Double Poppies of both these kindes, and their colours are commonly either white, red, dark purple, scarlet, or mixt of some of these. They differ from the former only in the doubleness of their flowers.' Gerard also records the use of this poppy: 'The oile which is pressed out of it is pleasant and dilightfull to be eaten, and is taken with bread or any other waies in meat, without a sense of cooling . . . A greater force is in the knobs or heads, which doe specially prevaile to moove sleepe, and to stay and represse distillations or rheums, and come neere in force to opium, but more gentle. Opium, or the condensed juice of Poppie heads is strongest of all: Meconium (which is the juice of the heads and leaves) is weaker. Both of them any waies taken either inwardly, or outwardly applied to the head, provoke sleepe. Opium somewhat plentifully taken does also bring death, as Pliny truely writeth.'

John Miller (1768) refers to the opium poppy as *Papaver hortence, semine nigro* – garden poppy, with black seeds. Of it he states: 'The Black Poppy grows wild in divers Parts of England: The Seeds of this kind are sold to feed birds, by the name of Maw Seed. Of this sort there are a vast Numbers of Varieties, some of which produce exceedingly large Double Flowers of various colours, and beautifully strip'd: but there are apt to vary from seed; therefore you should never save the Seed of any but such as are very double, and well colour'd, from which you may always expect to have good sorte produced.'

P. somniferum is an erect, generally unbranched, hairless, leafy annual, up to 1 m (3 ft) tall, sometimes more. The bluish- or greyish-green leaves are rather fleshy, oblong in outline but pinnately lobed and rather undulate along the margin, the lower short-stalked, but the upper unstalked and clasping the stem with broad bases. The large cup-shaped, erect flowers are 5–12 cm (2–5 in) across in wild forms (up to 18 cm/7in in cultivated forms), white to pink or purple, often with a dark blotch at the base of each petal; the flowers are borne on long stalks, drooping at the tip in bud. The petals are broad, rounded and partly overlapping and the yellow or cream anthers are borne on pale filaments. The smooth fruit-capsule, up to 9 cm (3⅗ in) long, is globose or egg-shaped with a deeply lobed stigmatic disk that has 5–12 rays, sometimes more.

P. somniferum is probably native to the Mediterranean Basin, but it is widely naturalised in many temperate regions of the world and its precise natural distribution is uncertain. Plants are usually found growing on cultivated or waste land, orchards, olive groves, disturbed places or on rocky hillslopes, generally at low altitudes.

This species is extremely variable and a number of subspecies have been described in the past. Of these, the most important is subsp. *setigerum* (DC.) Corb. (syn. *P. setigerum* DC.), which is a slighter plant, rarely more than 60 cm (24 in) tall, the leaves with bristly midribs and veins, with each lobe terminating in a characteristic bristle. The flowers are pale purple and the fruit-capsule not more than 6 cm (2⅖ in) long, often less. Taxonomists often believe this to be the wild ancestor of the opium poppy and native to the west and central Mediterranean region, but widely naturalised further east.

In gardens the opium poppy presents few problems, except that it will often seed around in profusion. Seedlings should be ruthlessly thinned if they are to produce good strong plants. The ordinary single-flowered forms grown in gardens have a range of colours, though pinks, purple and reds predominate, the petals sometimes with a delightful gradation of colour reminiscent of shot-silk. Poor-coloured forms should be rogued out the moment they come into flower, otherwise after only a few years poor pinks and dirty purple will begin to dominate.

It is, however, the double-flowered or peony-flowered types that have found greatest favour in gardens, so named because of their resemblance to the double flowers of the peony. In these some, or indeed most, of the stamens are replaced by a close mass of petals filling the entire centre of the flower and obscuring the ovary. A wide range of colours are available, from white and cream, to pink, purple, red, lilac and almost black. These are listed by seed merchants variously as peony (paeonia)-flowered, peony series or 'paeoniflorum' and are sold most often as a mixture of different colours.

All these plants are vigorous, sometimes reaching 1.5 m (5 ft) tall, so they require plenty of space to develop. They are certainly an arresting sight in full flower – dare one say that some are almost too gaudy for the average garden? The doubles have a distinct advantage over the single-flowered forms in that their blooms last far longer, although heavy rain can bow their voluminous heads. All of them have a pleasing, though somewhat heady fragrance, much loved by bees.

The stiff-stemmed seed heads are a joy for dried decorations and are best gathered when matured, but before they become too discoloured. They can be hung in bunches, upside down, in a warm airy room to dry. The seeds can be collected for use on breads, buns and so on. A large-fruited form sold in the trade as 'Giganteum' or 'Gigantic Podded Mixed' has the largest fruits and is ideal for drying and painting.

Another, rather eccentric form is 'Hen and Chickens' in which the main fruit-capsule is surrounded by a halo of small pods; a novelty much enjoyed by some flower arrangers and a real curiosity in the mixed flower border.

Most of the double-flowered forms are good as a cut flower – bruising or burning the cut end of the stems will generally prevent them wilting in water; choose recently opened blooms for the best effect. Successive sowings from March to June will ensure a supply of blooms throughout the summer. Like all the annual poppies, sow them where they are to flower as they hate disturbance and will sulk or die if moved.

CULTIVARS

Peony-flowered types ('Paeoniflorum') Sometimes spelled paeonia or paeony, these have fully double flowers with a mass of petals, like balls of crumpled tissue paper. The petals are ruffled but do not have deeply cut or lacerated margins like some other cultivars – 'Swansdown', for instance. In the majority there is a very reduced number of stamens in the centre of the flower, but enough pollen is produced to ensure pollination and seed set.

Most, but not all, those listed below come true to type, or with an acceptable amount of variation. The peony-flowered types are generally listed simply by colour; all are about 75-90 cm (30-36 in) tall:

'Black Peony': [Pl. 96] the flowers are intensely dark and satiny, more a deep maroon-purple than black, but exceptional. The flowers, especially the latter blooms, are not as full and as frilled as some of the other peony-flowered types.

'Crimson Peony': [Pl. 98] flowers very full, deep satiny crimson; there is a similar unnamed cut-petal version of this [Pl. 106].

'Pink Peony': very full, frilly, globose flowers of soft pink.

'Purple Peony': [Pl. 97] flowers large and very full, globose, soft purple.

'Salmon Peony': very full, frilly, globose flowers of soft salmon-rose. Very similar in most respects to 'Frosted Salmon', but the flowers paler and less rosy.

'Scarlet Peony': flowers very full and frilly, forming an almost complete ball and a startling bright scarlet.

'White Peony': this name, sometimes seen in literature, probably equates with 'Swansdown'.

'Yellow Peony': see 'White Cloud' below.

In addition, some companies, such as Thompson and Morgan, sell packets of mixed seed, generally as 'Peony-flowered Mixed'. One selection has been named 'Summer Fruits', see below.

Other peony-flowered types ('Paeoniflorum')

'Black Beauty': large, frilly flowers of such intense, deep purple-maroon as to appear black in most lights. Seems to be indistinguishable from 'Black Peony', the prior name.

'Burnt Orange': flowers more of a scarlet-orange than the burnt orange alluded to in the cultivar name, but nonetheless a fine cultivar with semi-double blooms; the outer four petals are large and unruffled, but the inner ones numerous and very frilled. These are followed (as in most cultivars) by attractive fruit-capsules that are good for drying.

'Crimson and White': [Pl. 99] fully double flowers packed with frilly crimson petals with an attractive sheen, the lowermost four petals with a large oval basal white blotch which is only seen from below.

'Flemish Antique': [Pl. 100] large fully double, flowers with very ruffled white petals that are streaked with crimson-pink or maroon, especially towards the petal tips. The amount of crimson in the petals varies a lot from plant to plant and deepens somewhat as the flowers mature. In some the flowers are very dark, the petals white only in the centre and towards the base.

'Frosted Salmon': [Pl. 101] flowers very full and frilled with numerous petals, giving the flower a globular appearance, the petals deep salmon-rose but paler towards the margins to give an attractive 'frosted' appearance.

'Pink Chiffon': delicate pink semi-double blooms, the centre of the bloom partly filled with rather uneven smaller petals; not a true peony-flowered type, but nonetheless a very pretty plant.

'**Summer Fruits**': peony-flowered types in a range of 'fruit colours', especially pink, rose, deep crimson and creamy-white. This is the same as the Formula Mixture produced by Sahin in Holland, which contains some thirteen colours.

'**White Cloud**': [Pl. 102] a peony-flowered type with more or less fully double, frilly, pure white flowers with a hint of cream, generally with just a few stamens in the centre. The whole effect is like a ballet dancer's very full tutu. Sometimes sold under the incorrect name of 'Swansdown', see below. It also appears to be indistinguishable from the seed strain sold as 'Yellow Peony', a wholly misleading epithet as the flowers are in no way yellow; indeed, it would be difficult to class them as cream.

Cut-petal types ('Laciniatum'): sometimes referred to as Carnation-flowered Series. These bear single, semi-double or fully double flowers with deeply fringed or lacerated petal margins.

'**Aigrette**': large, almost fully double, frilly blooms, recalling the peony-flowered types but with deeply cut petals, almost ostrich-feather-like. The colour range includes pink, crimson, deep rose, salmon and white. The flowers, which are produced in abundance, are long-lasting and are followed by large decorative fruit-capsules.

'**Crimson Feathers**': flowers lustrous crimson, very ruffled and with the bright green ovary revealed in the centre; petals deeply and finely lacerated.

'**Danebrog**' (= 'Danish Flag'): [Pl. 103] a very striking bicolour with single large flowers that are blood-red with a large rounded basal white blotch to each petal and a deeply cut margin. A striking and unusual cultivar. Also sold as 'Danebrog Laced'.

'**Danebrog Laced**': see under 'Danebrog'.

'**Lilac Time**': flowers very full and ruffled with very few stamens, the petals a delicate lilac, deeply cut into numerous narrow ribbon-like segments.

'**Pink Bicton**': [Pl. 104] large, almost fully double flowers with finely and deeply cut petal margins. The flowers open almost crimson, but soon fade to an attractive deep rose-red.

'**Rose Feathers**': very similar to 'Crimson Feathers', but the flowers a deep rose-pink.

'**Swansdown**': [Pl. 105] large semi-double, rather shaggy, white flowers with a hint of cream, the petals with deeply lacerated margins. The flowers retain quite a few stamens in the centre. Sometimes sold as 'White Cloud', which is a peony-flowered type (see above). A beautiful and rather graceful cultivar that is well worth acquiring.

A good seed mixture incorporating most of the above colours is sold by Sahin in Holland as 'Formula Mixture' and also by Plant of Distinction in the UK as 'Laciniatum Mixed', with flowers in shades of pink, salmon, white and crimson.

Single-flowered, with uncut margins

'**Queen's Poppy**': an attractive cultivar with single, cupped flowers of royal-pink (or perhaps cherry-pink), each petal with a large white oval basal blotch, giving the centre of the flower a cross effect. An elegant plant with simple uncluttered flowers.

Fruit

Most of the opium poppies can be grown for their fruits, but the single-flowered types really produce the best pods for drying. The size of the fruit capsules differs from plant to plant, although the first flower out tends to produce the largest pod. When fully mature, the fruits can be cut, just before they start to brown in the garden, and hung in bunches, upside down to dry in a airy dry place. Any leaves can be stripped off at the same time.

Likewise, the seed of all the types is edible, although the single types also produce a greater number of pods and seeds.

'**Hen and Chickens**' (also known as 'Monstrosa' and 'Prolifera'): **[Pl. 107]** in this extraordinary cultivar the main pod is surrounded by a basal ring of smaller, rather uneven little pods, all borne on a common stiff stem. This novelty is much enjoyed by some flower arrangers, although not all. It is a real curiosity in the flower garden and is bound to engender comment one way or another. The flowers are a rather dull and unappealing lilac.

Some cultivars of *P. somniferum* have indehiscent fruit capsules. To extract the seeds, the mature capsules have to be broken apart by hand.

Papaver spicatum Boiss.   **[Pl. 86]**
(Syn. *P. heldreichii* Boiss.; *P. pannosum* Schwarz)
SPICATE POPPY

This fine Turkish species is one of the most handsome and distinctive poppies grown in our gardens. Its specific name aptly describes its slender, spikelike racemes of flowers held close to the main axis of the inflorescence.

Plants are perennial with a long, thick, generally forked taproot that produces a large tuft of leaves at the top, which more or less dies away each autumn. The leaves are pale green and softly white-hairy, oblong to elliptical, up to 20 cm (8 in) long and coarsely toothed; the basal and lower leaves are stalked, the upper stem leaves smaller and generally sessile. The erect branched inflorescence rises to 60 cm (24 in), although often less; each branch has a slender raceme carrying a succession of pale brick-red flowers, each 3–4.5 cm (1⅕–1⅘ in) across and held close to the stem, often facing sideways. The uppermost flowers are usually sessile. The stamens have pale filaments and pale orange-yellow anthers. The smooth fruit-capsule is small, 10–15 mm (⅖–⅗ in) long, narrowly oblong (tapered below) and smooth, the stigmatic disk pyramidal with four to six rays.

P. spicatum is native to the Taurus Mountains in western and southern Turkey, where it is endemic to the limestone mountain screes and rocks of

Lydia and Lycia, as well as adjacent Iscaurian and Pisidian, usually at altitudes of 600–1400 m (1950–4600 ft); flowering during June and July.

This distinctive poppy makes a fine addition to the front of the herbaceous border, where its rather pale flowers are a relief from the brilliant blooms of so many other poppies. This is certainly one of my favourite poppies, a dignified plant whose erect habit can provide interesting contrast in the border. Although never a profuse bloomer, the flowers are borne over quite a long season, each branch with one or two blooms open at a time. In gardens it is not always easy to please, sulking in some and prone to rotting off during the winter months in others. However, when properly established it is certainly long-lived and there are even gardens where it will, on occasions, self-sow.

P. spicatum needs a light, well-drained soil in the full sun. Plants greatly resent disturbance and once planted should be left well alone. In fact, they normally set copious seed and it is little effort to raise a new stock. I have found that it is far wiser to plant out new plants in the spring, for this ensures they get a quick start, although they are unlikely to flower in most instances until the following year. Seed is best sown in the spring under glass and the seedlings pricked out into individual pots as soon as they have produced their first true leaf.

P. spicatum is available from a number of different nurseries and seed is occasionally listed in catalogues, generally under the name *P. heldreichii*.

Papaver stipitatum Fedde

Another of the *P. dubium* group, *P. stipitatum* is readily distinguished by its short-stalked fruit capsules; the stalk or carpophore (the area at the base of the capsule but above the lace of insertion of the flower parts) is at least 1 mm (¹⁄₁₆ in) long. In this respect the species comes close to *P. tenuissimum*, but it is altogether a larger plant 30–60 cm (12–24 in) tall with capsules 12–15 mm (³⁄₈–⁵⁄₈ in) long, although in both the pedicels are appressed hairy and the petals unblotched.

Papaver stipitatum is restricted to the Greek Aegean (Skopelos).

Fruit of *Papaver spicatum*

Papaver strigosum (Boenn.) Schur

Described as long ago as 1877, this poppy is found in much of Europe and western Asia, where *P. rhoeas* is likely to be seen. In fact, it is often dismissed as only a form of that species, distinguished by having rather purplish flowers with unblotched petals. In addition, the stems bear appressed rather than spreading bristly hairs.

Papaver tenuissimum Fedde

Rather similar to *P. dubium*, but with unblotched petals and a smaller capsule (not more than 10 mm or ⅖ in long at maturity) that is distinctly stalked at the base (above the point where the flower parts are inserted).

Papaver tenuissimum is a small plant, rarely exceeding 25 cm (10 in) in height, and is restricted to central Greece.

Papaver triniifolium Boiss [Pl. 87]

Another rarely cultivated species, but an intriguing one in that it is one of the few biennial species in the genus. In this respect and in the character of its handsome first year leaf-rosettes, it is perhaps more reminiscent of several of the species of *Meconopsis*. However, once seen, the typical *Papaver* fruit-capsules leave one in no doubt as to which genus it truly belongs. Reginald Farrer wrote of it being in 'the group of monocarpic or biennial poppies . . . the most beautiful we have . . . (in foliage at least), is *P. triniifolium*, which comes, like all the others, from the hills of Asia Minor. Here the silver-glaucous leaves are cut and cut again into the finest silver fringe work . . . The resulting pyramid of bloom seems hardly a worthy conclusion to so much beauty, for the flowers are small, pale coloured . . . in utmost haste to shed their petals'.

P. *triniifolium* forms a rather dense spreading, grey-green leaf-rosette in the first season; this is up to 30 cm (12 in) across in vigorous specimens. The narrow, stalked, somewhat bristly leaves are lanceolate in outline, but pinnately-lobed, up to 20 cm (8 in) long, the segments rather distant and further lobed or toothed into narrow oval or elliptical divisions, each terminating in a bristle-tip. In the second season a central, leafy stem rises to 40 cm (16 in) with spreading glabrous branches bearing a succession of flowers. The flowers are small, 2.5–4 cm (1–1⅗ in) across and pale red or scarlet. The fruit-capsule, 8–12 mm (⅓–½ in) long, is smooth and greyish-green, the stigmatic disk with four to six rays.

This is a pretty little species, not spectacular like some, but worth growing, if only for its handsome, first-year leaf-rosettes. Indeed, some gardeners think it is more interesting in its rosette form than when it is in flower, although I would not support this view. *P. triniifolium* is hardy, the leaf-rosette persisting through the winter months. Because it is biennial (occasionally not flowering until the third year), seed needs to be collected regularly to ensure a supply of new young plants – I have not known it self-sow in my own garden but, in any event, it is readily raised from seed sown in pots in a cold frame early in the year. Pricked out as soon as they are large enough to handle, the seedlings grow away rapidly and can be planted out by mid-summer. This is an ideal plant for the rock or scree garden, planted close to a path, where its subtle beauty can be best appreciated.

Plants prefer a moist, though well-drained, light soil, but do not seem to be affected by winter wet, provided these conditions are met. This is probably a reflection of its native home in Turkey, where most rain falls during the winter months. Strangely enough, unlike some of the rosette-forming species of *Meconopsis*, slugs do not appear to like *P. triniifolium* and the rosettes survive the winter unchewed. In the garden it usually comes into flower during May.

P. triniifolium is native to eastern Turkey and north-western Iran, being found from southern Cappadocia to the Pontic Ranges. It was first described by Boissier from material collected by Balansa in the so-called subalpine region of Mesmeneu Dağ, part of the Ala Dağ Range in Cappadocia. *P. triniifolium* inhabits limestone rocks and screes at altitudes of 2600–3400 m (8500–11,150 ft).

Plants are occasionally offered in the horticultural trade, though it is probably easier to obtain seed from specialist seed merchants or society seedlists. Plants are self-fertile and a single plant can be expected to produce copious good seed.

The closely related *P. armeniacum* (L.) DC. (syn. *Argemone armeniaca* L.; *Papaver roopianum* (Bordz.) Sosn.) can be easily distinguished by its numerous stems, which arise from the basal leaf-rosette and by the racemose rather than paniculate inflorescence. In addition, the flowers are smaller and orange-red, the petals not more than 15 mm (⅗ in) long.

Papaver tumidulum Klokov

An interesting, but relatively little known species of the *P. rhoeas* association, in which the scarlet petals bear one (sometimes two) particularly large black spots and a larger fruit capsule measuring 12–20 mm (½–¾ in) in length and only half as broad. In the wild it is restricted to the Ukraine and it is doubtful whether it is in cultivation.

INTERESTING SPECIES NO LONGER IN CULTIVATION
[not in key]

Papaver belangeri Boiss.

See *P. minus* (p. 96).

Papaver bornmuelleri Fedde

This species is endemic to the Kermanshah region of Iran and the neighbouring area of Iraqi Kurdistan. It probably finds its closest ally in *P. macrostomum*, but can be distinguished by having sparsely bristly fruit-capsules. A generally smaller plant with purple flowers.

Papaver chelidonifolium Boiss. & Buhse

This is a delicate species restricted to the Caucasus and northern Iran, where it is to be found in cultivated and bare fields, in scrub or on stony slopes. It is an annual with slender, rather membranous, pinnate leaves, one to three pairs of small lateral lobes and a large terminal lobe, often three-lobed; the upper leaves are generally smaller and more dissected, the flowers are pale red, 2–3 cm (⅘–1⅕ in) across; the oval petals have a dark, almost black, basal blotch. The fruit-capsules are smooth and small, only 6–7 mm (¼ in) long and more or less club-shaped, with five to seven stigmatic rays.

Papaver cylindricum Cullen

A close relation of *P. fugax* (p. 88), being distinguished primarily in fruit. The fruit-capsule is smaller and narrower, 8–15 × 3–5 mm (not 14–16 × 4–8 mm) (⅓–⅗ × ⅛–⅕ in, not ⅗–⅔ × ⅙–⅓ in) and with a decidedly more conical stigmatic disk.

P. *cylindricum* is restricted to Iraqi and Iranian Kurdistan at an altitude of 1400–1800 m (4600–5900 ft).

Papaver gorgoneum Coutinho

This is the only species of *Papaver* endemic to the Cape Verde Islands. It comes closest to *P. pinnatifidum* Moris. Both species have red flowers with pale yellow anthers. The main difference is to be seen in the fruit-capsule, which in the former is more or less cylindrical, but clearly contracted at the base, whereas in the latter the capsule is more club-shaped.

Papaver hookeri Bak. ex Hook. f.

A plant from the western Himalaya scarcely distinguishable from *P. rhoeas*. The flowers are pale pink to bright crimson-red, the petals with a basal black blotch.

Papaver monanthum Trautb.

See *P. bracteatum* (p. 83).

Papaver nordhagenianum Löve

A Scandinavian variant of *P. radicatum* up to 35 cm (14 in) tall and bearing numerous yellow flowers.

Papaver paucifoliatum (Trautb.) Fedde.

See *P. bracteatum* (p. 83).

Papaver persicum Lindl.

See *P. fugax* (p. 88).

Papaver pseudocanescens Popov

Like *P. radicatum*, but with broader leaf-lobes and flowers with more numerous stamens. A native of Siberia and Mongolia.

Papaver pygmaeum

A tiny poppy of the *P. radicatum* persuasion endemic to the American Rockies, where it is only found on the high moraines and screes of the Glacier National Park region. Not in cultivation.

The Long-fruited Poppies
Roemeria

The genus *Roemeria* contains three or four species native to the eastern Mediterranean, western and central Asia, with one species, *R. hybrida*, extending west into the western Mediterranean and southern Europe.

Although the species look superficially very similar to the true poppies, *Papaver*, the genus is more closely allied to *Chelidonium* and *Glaucium* in its long, parallel-sided fruit-capsules which, when ripe, split from apex to base into two, occasionally four, similar valves.

The genus is named in honour of Johann Jakob Roemer (1763–1819) who was Professor of Botany at Zurich.

All the species are rather slender annuals with yellow sap and finely divided, pinnately-lobed leaves.

Roemeria hybrida (L.) DC.
(Syn. *Chelidonium hybridum* L.; *violaceum* Lam.; *Glaucium violaceum* (Lam.) Juss.; *Roemeria violacea* Medicus)
VIOLET HORNED POPPY, WIND ROSE

A rather distinctive poppy with violet-coloured flowers. Although confined primarily to the Mediterranean region and the drier parts of Asia, this plant was at one time well-naturalised in East Anglia in the UK, where it was a weed of arable land, particularly wheat fields. However, in recent times it has become very scarce there due to modern farming practices.

The plant was well known to Gerard. In his *Herbal* of 1633 he lists it as '*Papaver cornutum flore-violaceo* (Violet coloured horned Poppie)' and commented: 'There is another sort of horned Poppie altogether less than the last described [*Glaucium flavum*], having tender leaves, cut into fine little parcels: the flower is likewise lesser, of a blue-purple colour like the double violets.'

R. hybrida is a hairy annual 10–50 cm (4–20 in) tall, generally with branched stems. The alternate leaves, up to 20 cm (8 in) long, are two- or three-pinnately divided, glabrous or somewhat bristly, the segments narrow and bristle-tipped; the upper leaves are smaller and sessile, the lower clearly stalked. The solitary flowers, 5–7 cm (2–2⅖ in) across, are borne on long slender stalks and are lilac, violet or purplish-red with a dark basal blotch to each petal; sepals two, hairy, soon falling; petals four, roundish with a broad wedge-shaped base; stamens numerous, with violet-filiform filaments. The fruit-capsule is narrowly cylindrical, 4–8 cm (1⅗–3⅕ in) long, straight or curved and bristly in the upper part; when ripe it opens by three or four valves.

R. hybrida has a wide distribution, from the Iberian Peninsula and northwest Africa eastwards to Turkey, Iran and the neighbouring regions of central Asia. It is primarily a plant of cultivated, waste and fallow land from sea level to 1500 m (4900 ft), sometimes higher; flowers March to May.

This is an attractive poppy for a light well-drained soil in full sun. Seed should be sown in the early spring where the plants are to flower. It is well worth selecting out the better violet-coloured forms from the wishy-washy lilac flowers or the muddier purplish-reds. In gardens, plants will generally flower from late June to August or early September; they normally set abundant seed and sometimes self-sow, especially on lighter soil. Although very striking in its best coloured forms, the flowers are fleeting beauties, opening at dawn but their petals generally fall by midday. For this reason, it is often overlooked on arable land.

Roemeria orientalis Boiss.

This plant has been much confused with *P. hybrida*, but differs in its squatter habit, short and broader leaf-segments, smaller flowers and shorter, thicker fruit-capsules, covered with bristles. This species, which is not in cultivation, grows in the drier desert regions of Egypt and Sinai, north-eastwards through southern Iran to the regions of the Aral Sea. The relationship between these two species requires further investigation.

Roemeria refracta (Stev.) DC. [Pl. 108–110]

(syn. *Glaucium refractum* Stev. ex DC.; *Roemeria bicolor* Regel; *R. rhoeadiflora* Boiss.)

ASIAN CORN POPPY

If the true poppies (*Papaver*) did not exist, then this splendid species would surely rate very highly in our gardens. As it is, its effect in flower is so similar to that of *Papaver rhoeas* or *P. pavoninum* that it is sadly much neglected.

Roemeria hybrida

The plains around Samarkand and Taskent in Soviet Central Asia, where I have seen it, are stained with the deep scarlet of *R. refracta* during April and May – a sight as unforgettable as the poppy fields of western Europe.

Plants grow 40–50 cm (16–20 in) tall and are branched from close to the base; stems hairy or rather bristly. The leaves are two- or three-pinnately-lobed, with elliptical or oblong, slightly bristly segments, the lower leaves stalked, but the upper sessile usually. The solitary, long-stalked flowers, 4–7 cm (1⅗–2⅘ in) across, are pendent in bud, but become erect as they open; sepals two, bristly, petals four, bright red to scarlet with a large black basal blotch, which is often outlined with white, half-spreading to form a deep cup-shape; stamens numerous, with black filaments, which are somewhat dilated at the top, and yellowish-brown anthers. The fruit-capsule is linear–cylindrical, to 10 cm (4 in) long, smooth or bristly.

R. refracta is native to an area stretching from Armenia to Iran, Afghanistan and western Pakistan, to Kazakstan and Kirghizystan, where it is a plant of cultivated, fallow and waste ground and the foothills and lower mountain slopes, flowering there during April and May.

Seed of this species is sometimes offered and should certainly be tried. Cultivation is the same as for *R. hybrida* or indeed any annual *Papaver*.

The colour of the flowers ranges from an orange-red to scarlet, those of the deepest scarlet hues being the most splendid of all. I would dearly love to see plants with 'violet or near blue flowers' reported in *The Plantsman* (Sept. 1991), but suspect this is a wholly erroneous report; petals of a number of red poppies often dry purplish and violet and this may have been the basis of such a record.

In the wild, populations are quite variable. Var. *albomarginata* is a name given to flowers in which the black basal blotch is outlined in white, whereas var. *setosa* applies to those plants with bristly fruits. However, I have observed large populations of these plants in the Samarkand area, in northern Afghanistan, as well as in western and eastern Iran, and can record that all these manifestations can be found quite readily within the same population. Of course, in cultivation the white ring is a most attractive feature of the flower; a similar ring is found in forms of both *P. rhoeas* and *P. pavoninum*.

The Woodland Poppy
Cathcartia

The genus *Cathcartia* was described in 1851 by William Jackson Hooker, based on a single species *C. villosa*, which had been discovered in Sikkim by his son, Joseph Dalton Hooker, in 1849.

In 1934 George Taylor transferred the species to *Meconopsis* and most people have since followed Taylor's conclusion. However, the presence of rounded, palmately lobed and veined leaves, a sessile stigma and a slender fruit-capsule that splits almost to the base are so distinctive compared to the other members of *Meconopsis* that it would seem far better to place the species in a distinct genus. The *Flora of Bhutan* (1(2), 1984) followed this line, which I wholly agree with.

Cathcartia smithiana Hand.-Mazz.
(Syn. *Meconopsis smithiana* (Hand.-Mazz.) G. Tayl.)

A herbaceous perennial with the stock covered in the persistent leaf-bases, and rusty-brown bristles. The stems are erect and unbranched, generally 60–90 cm (24–36 in) tall and sparsely bristly. The leaves are alternate and rather sparsely scattered along the stem, the lamina trifoliate, up to 11.5 cm (4⅗ in) long and just over half as wide, the surface covered in sparse bristles, the lower leaves being stalked while the upper are unstalked or practically so; terminal leaflet larger than the others and pinnately lobed, while the lateral leaflets are often bipinnately lobed. The 2–4, nodding or half-nodding, yellow flowers are borne on each stem, from the axil of the uppermost leaves, and are about 3.8 cm (1½ in) across; petals rounded and somewhat notched at the apex. The ovary is covered in rusty-brown bristles and bears a 5-lobed stigma. The mature fruit is unknown.

C. smithiana is a little known species restricted in the wild to the north-eastern part of Upper Burma (Myanmar) and the neighbouring regions of north-western Yunnan, at altitudes of 3050–3660 m (10,000–12,000 ft). It is a denizen of damp woodland and the upper forest fringes and the lower alpine meadows. It was first discovered in north-western Yunnan in 1916 by Handel-Mazetti and named by him in honour of Sir William Wright Smith, the then Regius Keeper of the Royal Botanic Garden, Edinburgh. It was subsequently collected on the Burmese side of the border by Reginald Farrer, but since then nothing has been seen of it to my knowledge, despite the fact that it was said to be locally abundant on 'stony alpine meadows'.

C. smithiana is very closely related to *C. villosa*. The prime differences are to be seen in the trifoliate rather than undivided (although lobed) leaves, the rather smaller flowers and in the densely bristly rather than glabrous ovary. It would be an attractive plant to have in cultivation and, like its cousin, it would undoubtedly make a fine addition to the woodland garden, revelling in a deep moist humusy soil in dappled shade.

Cathcartia villosa Hook. f. ex Hook.   [Pl. 111–112]
(Syn. *Meconopsis villosa* (Hook. f. ex Hook.) G. Taylor)
HIMALAYAN WOODLAND POPPY

Another rather modest species, but handsome enough in foliage and flower to make it acceptable for the woodland garden. Indeed, *C. villosa* deserves to be more widely grown in gardens, for it is not a difficult species to cultivate.

The species is an herbaceous perennial with leafy stems and a rather short rootstock covered in persistent leaf-bases and reddish bristles. The long-stalked, bristly basal leaves are oval or rounded in outline and partly cut into three to five lobed segments. The upper leaves are similar in size and shape, but short-stalked. The slender bristly stems rise to about 60 cm (24 in) and each bears one to five semi-nodding flowers, borne on slender stalks from the upper leaf-axils. The flowers are yellow, 4–5 cm (1⅗–2 in) across, with four rounded, somewhat overlapping petals and a central boss of golden or yellow stamens – the anthers become brown on ageing. The fruit-capsule is almost cylindrical, up to 8.5 cm (3⅖ in) long, and smooth and, rather unusually, it splits for more than a half of its length into four to seven valves.

C. villosa is a native of the Himalayas from the Mt. Everest region of Nepal eastwards to Bhutan, at altitudes of 2900–4480 m (9500–14,700 ft). It is a plant of woodland glades and banks, of stream margins and rock crevices. I have observed it on several occasions in both the upper reaches of the Arun and Tamur valleys in east Nepal. There it often forms large patchy colonies in woodland where sunlight filters on occasion, and in areas subjected to heavy summer monsoon rains.

This species was discovered by Joseph Dalton Hooker in 1849 in Sikkim. Seed sent home by Hooker flowered at the Royal Botanic Gardens, Kew, two years later.

C. villosa is one of my personal favourites. It can in no way be considered brash, but the attractive and rather distinctive leaves and handsome flowers make it a charmer for the woodland garden or for a semi-shaded place amongst shrubs. It is a species that requires a moist soil and will tolerate an almost totally shaded position, provided that it is not too dry. A few central leaves always remain at ground level during the winter to mark the position of the plants.

Seed is generally produced in quantity, but tends to germinate rather sparingly in my experience. Furthermore, seedlings should be pricked out with care as losses can be expected if they are roughly handled. Young plants seem to resent too much disturbance and once planted out are best left to their own devices. Established plants generally flower in their second season and will go on for many years. Large plants can be divided in the spring, but I would rather leave them alone and grow new plants from seed than risk loosing mature plants. An annual top-dressing of well-rotted compost or leaf-mould, placed around the plants is highly beneficial.

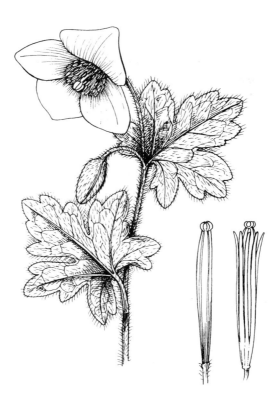

Cathcartia villosa

The Blue Poppies
Meconopsis

Of all the varied members of the poppy family, none has created such excitement and intrigue as the famous blue poppies. No other genus in the Papaveraceae has plants with blue flowers and, for this alone, they have long stolen the hearts of gardeners.

One can perhaps judge the feeling of disbelief when the first blue poppies were reported from the wild and the general astonishment when the first unfurled its translucent petals in cultivation. The most famous of the blue poppies is undoubtedly *Meconopsis betonicifolia*, which first flowered in cultivation in 1924 under the name *M. baileyi*. Seldom has a plant gained such popularity so rapidly in cultivation and today, despite the fact that this glorious species has been in our gardens for more than 60 years, it is as popular as ever. However, this was by no means the first of the blue poppies to be introduced into cultivation: *M. wallichii* first flowered in 1852, *M. grandis* in 1895, *M. horridula* in 1904, *M. latifolia* in 1908 and *M. quintuplinervia* in 1914–15. Of these, *M. grandis* closely rivals *M. betonicifolia* for the size and blueness of its flowers, as well as ease of cultivation.

It is wrong to think of *Meconopsis* as containing only blue-flowered species, for those with yellow, violet, purple, red and occasionally white flowers are well represented. The genus in fact contains some 43 species, all but one being natives of the Himalayas and western China. The exception is the Welsh Poppy, *M. cambrica*, which is confined to western Ireland and Wales, southwards through western France to northern Spain.

The genus was established by L.A.G. Viguier, Montpellier, in 1814, based upon Linnaeus's *Papaver cambricum*, which was transferred to the new genus. *Meconopsis* was distinguished from the closely similar *Papaver* primarily by the presence of a short style and the absence of a sessile stigmatic disk on top of the ovary. While these features serve to distinguish the majority of subsequent species of *Meconopsis* from *Papaver*, several species in the former genus have no appreciable style but, at the same time, do not possess any sign of a disk. Thus the two largest genera in the poppy family are distinguished by very fine details. However, species do not always conform to generic boundaries as simply as the taxonomist would wish. In *Meconopsis* two species, *M. discigera* and *M. torquata*, bear fruits with a short style as well as a well-developed (but non-stigmatic) disk. This disk is generally regarded by taxonomists as a derived character with no direct relationship to *Papaver*. Curiously, in most of the regions inhabited by *Meconopsis* there are few species of *Papaver* – they are concentrated primarily in Europe and western Asia with species also represented in North America, Africa and Australia. In gardens the two genera are unlikely to be muddled, even at a casual glance.

The Mexican Poppies or prickly poppies, *Argemone*, confined to the New

World, are also very closely related to *Meconopsis*. They can be readily distinguished by their very prickly stems and leaves, and the presence of three sepals, rather than two, per flower, each adorned with a 'horn' at the apex.

The main problem facing the taxonomist and horticulturist with *Meconopsis* is the position of *M. cambrica* itself and the delimitation of the individual species.

It is indeed curious to have *M. cambrica* restricted to western Europe, whilst the rest of the species occur a great distance away to the east. There are features of habit, pollen and seed structure, as well as cytology in *M. cambrica* that are rather at variance with other members of the genus, though none of these are obvious without a detailed study (see Ernst, 1962). There are, as a result, good reasons perhaps to separate this species from the others and give it a genus to itself. Herein lies a tricky dilemma for the taxonomist, for *Meconopsis* is based upon *M. cambrica* and if the genus has to be split, then all the other species would have to move to a new genus; as no existing name is available, one would need to be created. To do so would be to excite the wrath of the horticultural world and serve no great purpose except to gain the perpetrator, however well-intentioned, a certain degree of notoriety.

Amongst the species there are those that are readily recognised and easily defined. However, as in many similarly sized genera, some of the species show a good deal of variation and even some overlap in their overall characters as seen in the wild and this can serve to blur specific boundaries. This is most prominent between species like *M. napaulensis* and *M. paniculata* and within species such as *M. grandis* and *M. horridula*, where there is a great deal of variation between populations or, indeed, sometimes within a single population.

In cultivation the problem is often of a different nature for, in many instances, only a few forms represent most species rather than the whole span of possible variations. The problem in certain groups has been the propensity towards hybridisation (especially between *M. napaulensis*, *M. paniculata* and *M. regia*) so that the species identities become blurred, or worse, lost altogether.

The first serious studies of *Meconopsis* were undertaken by David Prain, whose paper of 1896, published in the *Journal of the Asiatic Society of Bengal*, was the first detailed study of the genus. This was followed by a more comprehensive account in the *Annals of Botany* in 1906. Prain made a further revision in 1915 when he recognised some 43 species within *Meconopsis* (in *Bulletin of Miscellaneous Information Kew* – now *The Kew Bulletin*). Frank Kingdon-Ward, who had observed many species in their native habitats, proposed various amendments to Prain's classification, which he published in the *Gardener's Chronicle* during 1926. However, the most comprehensive and far-reaching study was George Taylor's monograph *The Genus Meconopsis*, which was first published in 1934 and has remained the devotee's bible on the subject ever since. The only other significant work on the genus is James L.S. Cobb's *Meconopsis*, published by Christopher Helm in 1989. Whereas this work can in no way be described as a monograph of the genus and adds little to our understanding of the taxonomy and botany of the species, it is at the same time, the most comprehensive and useful work on the cultivation of this beautiful group of plants.

Meconopsis are perennials, some being long-lived and flowering year after year, whilst others are monocarpic, dying once they have flowered and seeded. The long-lived perennial species may form a taproot crowded by a tuft of shoots or the rootstock may be more diverse, plants spreading by means of a branching, generally slender underground rhizome giving rise to shoots at interval and resulting in a spreading patch. The monocarpic species generally form a solitary rosette of leaves, which can in some reach 60 cm (24 in) or more across. The leaf-rosettes may be permanent or they may wither down to a resistant central bud in the autumn. Stems, when present, bear few to many alternate leaves, the uppermost sometimes arranged in a whorl. Monocarpic species may flower in their second season or take a number of years to reach flowering size.

Leaves are very variable within the genus and range from simple undivided and untoothed types to those that are deeply cut into a number of lobes or divided into separate leaflets. Many species ooze a yellowish sap when cut. The leaves can be smooth or variously adorned with simple or branched hairs or bristles.

Flowers are borne on simple (leafless) scapes, in racemes or in more complex terminal panicles forming a stout inflorescence. The sepals are generally two (very occasionally three or four) and soon fall once the buds open. There are most commonly four petals per flower, but there may be as many as ten, especially in cultivated plants. There are numerous stamens, which have slender stalks (filaments). Fruit-capsules vary in shape from globose to oblong to narrowly cylindrical and may be smooth, hairy or bristly, dehiscing by means of valves in the upper part, these sometimes splitting almost to the base of the capsule. Mature capsules, which are nearly always erect, bear numerous seeds.

Cultivation

Meconopsis species range from those that can be considered easy to grow to those that are difficult or indeed have proved almost impossible over the years. They are often regarded as connoisseur's plants and as such they have attracted an aura of exclusivity they do not altogether warrant.

These are beautiful plants and one sight of a border with patches of blue, red, pink or yellow *Meconopsis* is enough to send any keen gardeners scurrying home to try and grow some for themselves. With the exception of the Welsh Poppy, *M. cambrica*, which can be readily grown in most temperate gardens, provided the soil is not too dry, the remainder, which are exclusively Asian in origin, need more careful treatment.

To understand the cultural requirements of *Meconopsis*, it is wise to examine their habitat conditions in the wild. The species are all to be found in mountain regions, particularly the Himalayas and the mountains of western China. They are plants of woodland, scrub, alpine meadows, screes, moraines or cliffs, often, though not exclusively, growing on acid or neutral soils. In these regions most of the precipitation falls as monsoon rain during the summer months, whilst during the winter any precipitation will normally be as snow. This means that during the winter months, when temperatures can drop well below freezing, plants are often protected beneath a blanket of snow and will be dormant as well as relatively dry. In the spring, as the snow melts and the temperatures increase, the plants come into growth. In the early summer (late May and June) the monsoon rains arrive and they persist right through the peak growing and flowering season, only easing off in the autumn, when plants are in seed and beginning to die down or cease growing for the year. The season of highest temperatures therefore coincides with maximum rainfall. In our gardens such conditions can rarely be found and the situation is often reversed with the winters being mild and wet and with a great reduction in rainfall in the summer period. This is why in northern Britain and in north-west North America (the region around Vancouver and Seattle, for instance), where the winters are more reliably cold and there is a good deal of rainfall during the summer, meconopsis thrive far better than elsewhere – the conditions are more akin to their native habitats.

However, this should not put anyone off attempting to grow at least one or two species in their gardens. Walk round a large garden such as the Royal Botanic Gardens at Kew, the Saville Gardens at Windsor, or indeed a host of southern gardens in the early summer and you are almost certain to find several different species in bloom. In such places more care needs to be taken over their culture, with plenty of rich humus added to the soil and liberal mulches provided during the summer to keep the moisture level high around the base of the plants.

For those growing *Meconopsis* for the first time, there are several species and their cultivars that can be considered reasonably easy to grow – *M. betonicifolia*, *M. cambrica*, *M. chelidonifolia*, *M. dhwojii*, *M. grandis*, *M. napaulensis*, *M. paniculata*, *M. quintuplinervia* and *M. regia* fit into this category. Of course, there is an inherent danger in listing 'easy species', for in some gardens one or several may prove to be difficult for one reason or another.

Soil preparation is important. Before planting, the area should be deeply dug and ample humus (compost or well-rotted manure) dug into the soil. The ideal site is a sheltered one, preferably not in a frost pocket, with dappled shade, where the sunlight can filter through surrounding trees or shrubs. An open, windy site with unshielded sunlight is wholly unsuitable, as is a soil that at any time becomes waterlogged.

Plants are best placed in their permanent positions in the spring or early summer so that they have plenty of time to become established before the winter arrives. A generous mulch (compost, bark chippings, straw or similar) placed closely around the plants will keep the soil moist and cooler throughout the summer.

Monocarpic species such as *M. napaulensis*, *M. paniculata* and *M. regia* will produce huge evergreen rosettes if well grown and these can be quite a feature in themselves. They, like most of the other species, are greedy feeders and will 'consume' as much humus and manure as can be supplied. For these species, which extend up to 2 m (6 ft) tall in flower, a sheltered site is essential, otherwise plants can be easily blown over or the handsome foliage bruised.

There is no doubt that these plants look best in groups, rather than as isolated individuals in the border and, where space allows, a drift can be a most arresting sight.

For the less-hardy types (see under individual species), some form of protection in the spring will help prevent frost damage to emerging shoots and buds. For those that may be prone to rotting in winter (especially in mild wet areas), a frame light, cloche or other cover will help ward off excessive moisture. At the same time, care needs to be taken that the plants do not become too dry, otherwise they may wither from drought.

The more difficult and rarer species require more specialist treatment, unless you are fortunate enough to be in a very favourable region for their culture. The construction of special humus-rich screes with integral irrigation, peat beds and misted benches has been advocated; indeed, some have found these a highly successful way of growing some of the gems in the genus. For those who want to try some of these difficult poppies, I can do no better than to refer them to James L.S. Cobb's excellent book *Meconopsis*, which deals with their individual cultural requirements in great detail.

Plants can be purchased from a number of different sources, especially of the easier species and cultivars. However, for those wishing to build up a good stock of plants, seed provides the readiest and cheapest means of acquiring plants. Seed should be as fresh as possible. Spring sowing is perhaps easiest, although some advocate an autumn sowing, especially for species such as *M. punicea*, which requires a cold winter before it will germinate. One problem of autumn sowing is that if the seeds germinate quickly, the tiny seedlings then have to be nurtured through the winter months. It is important to remember that meconopsis seed will deteriorate if left unsown for too long and some loss of viability must be expected. If collecting home-grown seed, this can, if it is ready in time, be sown the moment it is ripe and this will give just enough time before the winter to build up strong little plants that will have a fair chance of coming through the winter, especially if they are confined to a protective frame or glasshouse.

The ideal compost for seed sowing is a moist organic compost; I scarcely dare say today that a good peat-based compost is ideal for the purpose, but until really proven alternatives come along I have no alternative but to advocate their use in such instances. James Cobb recommends a '50 per cent soil-less compost or plain moss peat (sedge peat forms a hopeless skin on composts and should be avoided), 30 per cent sphagnum and 20 per cent coarse grit or expanded rock granules'.

Seed should be sown very thinly to help avoid overcrowded seedlings, which would invite problems with damping off. The seeds require light to germinate so that a very thin covering is all that is required – fine sharp grit is ideal for the purpose. Pots should be well watered from below and placed in a sheltered frame away from too strong sunlight. Seed sown in the late winter can be boosted into germination by placing the pots over a soil-warming cable or in a propagator with a range of 10–20°C (50–68°F) night to day. At all stages, before and after germination, it is disastrous to allow the compost to dry out and this will result only in failure.

Seedlings should be pricked out as soon as they are large enough to handle and will only suffer if they are allowed to linger on in the original pot and become congested. Seedlings should be grown on as fast as possible, although different species vary a good deal in vigour, especially in their first season. The most vigorous types, such as *M. betonicifolia*, *M. napaulensis* and *M. paniculata*, should be constantly potted on to build up large plants in the shortest possible time. In this way, the more vigorous species may be large enough to plant out by mid-summer. If not, they should be overwintered in an airy frame and kept moist, although not excessively so.

Collecting home-produced seed is an enjoyable pastime. If enough is gathered, then there is plenty to hand on to other gardeners or to send to seed exchanges. Meconopsis seed, like all poppy seed, should be gathered the moment the capsules begin to split, otherwise much valuable seed may be wasted. The best way is to detach the fruit-capsules and tip the contents into dry envelopes. Seed should be thoroughly dried in a cool room and any debris (chaff) removed. Care should be taken to mark the name of the plant on the packets, otherwise awful confusion results and you will not be popular around the seed exchanges! Sealed dried packets can be placed in air-tight plastic containers and placed in a refrigerator until the seed is required. Commercially, seed can be stored in special cabinets in a seed bank, where the conditions can be carefully controlled. Under ideal conditions, seed can be kept for a number of years in this way. For most of us, however, careful cleaning and storage is all we can do and, with meconopsis at least, ensuring that seed is sown reasonably quickly after harvesting.

Some species can be relied upon to produce a good annual harvest of seed, others are more tricky. During hot dry weather, developing fruit may abort and no seed results, which is very unfortunate where the monocarpic species are concerned. During such periods, it is as well to nurture plants and try to keep up the moisture content of the soil to ensure at least some seed set.

Perennial species such as the various forms of *M. grandis*, *M. chelidonifolia* and *M. quintuplinervia* can also be propagated by division of the parent plant. This can be undertaken in the spring as growth commences or, preferably, the moment the plants finish flowering. With the former species, the easiest method is to dig up the parent plant and to slice it up carefully into one or two shoot portions. With the latter two species, which have a more spreading habit, it may be necessary only to remove the outer shoots by digging around the outside and leaving the main plant intact. Divisions should be kept moist and shaded for some weeks until it is clear that they are growing successfully.

Meconopsis suffer from few pests. Slugs and snails may attack soft young shoots or buds as they emerge in the spring and these can be easily guarded against. Aphids may sometimes infest the young leaves or inflorescences, though this is not a major problem – some systemic pesticides harm meconopsis, so an organic cure is preferable.

Various fungal diseases attack *Meconopsis*, causing damping off of seedlings, root rots or worst of all, crown rot (possibly bacterial in origin). Where any of these are suspected, then a regular spray with a systematic fungicide (used strictly at the manufacturer's instructions) may alleviate the problem. Crown rot in established plants may indicate stresses in the plants caused by adverse soil conditions, such as waterlogging. Damaged plants are best removed and burnt.

Classification

George Taylor recognised two subgenera and a number of sections in his *An Account of the genus Meconopsis* (1934). With a few modifications, this has remained the basis of classification ever since. The most significant difference has been the removal of two species, *M. villosa* and *M. smithiana*, to their former genus *Cathcartia*.

Subgenus Dioscogyne G. Tayl. This subgenus is characterised by the presence of a flat disk surmounting the ovary and from the centre of which arises the short style. Contains only two species, *MM. discigera, torquata*.

Subgenus Eumeconopsis (Prain) Fedde. Characterised by the absence of a disk. Most species bear a distinct style; occasionally, no style is present, but then the stigmatic lobes do not radiate outwards over a disk as in *Papaver*. Contains three main sections:

1. Section Cambricae (Prain) Fedde. Perennial herbs with leafy stems and a tufted, non-bristly base. Flowering stems several from each tuft; flowers yellow or orange, 4-petalled. *M. cambrica* (the only species).

2. Section Eucathcartia (Prain) G. Tayl. Perennial herbs with a tufted and bristly base. Flowers yellow, four-petalled, borne on a solitary flowering stem. *MM. chelidonifolia, oliverana*.

3. Section Polychaetia Prain. Monocarpic or polycarpic perennials – if the latter, then flowers never yellow.

> **Subsection Eupolychaetia G. Tayl.** Monocarpic perennials with a persistent leaf-rosette during the winter months.

> **Series Superbae Kingdon-Ward.** Leaf-margin finely serrated, not lobed, with a dense silky pubescence. *MM. regia, superba*.

> **Series Robustae Prain.** Leaves deeply lobed, generally bristly. *MM. dhwojii, gracilipes, longipetiolata, napaulensis, paniculata, wallichii*.

> **Subsection Cumminsia (Prain) G. Tayl.** Monocarpic or polycarpic perennials without a persistent winter rosette of leaves.

> **Series Simplicifoliae G. Tayl.** Species tend to be polycarpic, with dense, bristly, leaf-rosettes. Flowers borne on leafless scapes. *MM. punicea, simplicifolia, quintuplinervia*.

> **Series Grandes Prain.** Species monocarpic to polycarpic, with dense leaf tufts and leafy stems with the uppermost leaves in a whorl below the flowers. *MM. betonicifolia, grandis, integrifolia*.

> **Series Primulinae Prain.** Monocarpic perennials with a basal leaf tuft

and stems with a few alternate leaves; flowers solitary or several. *M. primulina* – not in cultivation.

Series Delavayanae G. Tayl. Small, tufted, polycarpic perennials with few entire leaves and a branched rootstock. Flowers solitary and scapose. *M. delavayi* (the only species).

Series Aculeatae Prain. Large series of monocarpic perennials with a solitary taproot and basal rosette of leaves. Flowers borne in a well-defined leafy inflorescence or scapose (some then borne from the same leaf-rosette). *MM. aculeata, forrestii, henrici, horridula, lancifolia, latifolia, prattii, rudis speciosa.*

Series Bellae Prain. Small, tufted, polycarpic perennials with finely divided leaves and solitary scapose flowers; pedicels arching over in fruit. Fruit capsule pear-shaped. *M. bella* (the only species).

Since the first edition of this book, significant work has been done on the taxonomy of the genus. This has been aided to a great extent by a number of expeditions into the heartland of *Meconopsis*, not least to south and western China and southern and south-eastern Tibet. I have personally been able to observe different species in north-western Yunnan, in western and north-western Sichuan and also in the extreme south of Gansu and have been able to compare these sightings with those made in the Himalaya (particularly Nepal) on previous journeys. In addition, seed has been introduced from these areas by a number of different expeditions and several species have been re-introduced into cultivation as a result.

The two prime groups of *Meconopsis* in need of reconsideration are the yellow-flowered species centred on *M. integrifolia* and the blue-flowered group based on the bristly-leaved *M. horridula*. In his monograph of 1934, George Taylor takes a very wide view of the species circumscription, including within each a whole range of rather disparate elements in the view that the 'species' were infinitely variable and highly polymorphic. However, current research does not support this view, and this has been backed up by a great deal more herbarium material being collected since Taylor wrote his monograph of the genus, and by more detailed field observations by the present author and others. For further elaboration, see under *M. horridula* and *M. integrifolia*.

Key to Species

(* rare in cultivation)
1. Leaves in a false whorl where the flowers arise (plants occasionally with one or two basal scapose flowers in addition) 2
   Leaves not as above; stems leafy or flowers all scapose 5

2. Flowers yellow, plants monocarpic 3
   Flowers blue, purple or reddish, occasionally white; plants perennial, occasionally monocarpic 4

3. Leaves with 3 main veins from the base to the apex; flowers erect
   to semi-erect, without a style (rarely up to 4 mm or ⅙ in long), but
   with a broad stigma: . . . . **M. integrifolia**
   Leaves with one main vein from the base to the apex; flowers
   nodding to half-nodding, with a distinctive style up to
   11 mm (⅖ in) long: **M. pseudointegrifolia**

4. Basal leaves with a truncated or somewhat heart-shaped base;
   fruit-capsule oblong, densely bristly: **M. betonicifolia**
   Basal leaves with a narrowed, wedge-shaped base; fruit-capsule
   narrow-elliptical, glabrous to somewhat bristly: **M. grandis**

5. Ovary and fruit-capsule with a broad disk at the top – below
   the short style: **M. discigera**★
   Ovary and fruit-capsule without a disk 6

6. Flowers solitary, scapose – all the leaves basal 7
   Flowers borne in distinct racemes or panicles; bracts often present . . 14

7. Leaves dissected, occasionally subentire, but then some leaves
   with at least several lateral lobes; fruit capsule pear-shaped, borne
   on a curved stalk: **M. bella**★
   Leaves entire, never with lateral lobes; fruit capsule oblong to
   almost globose, borne on an erect stem 8

8. Flowers deep crimson, nodding; petals elliptical, 6–10 cm
   (2⅖–4 in) in length: **M. punicea**
   Flowers blue to violet-purple, lavender or pink, nodding to
   erect; petals oval to almost rounded, 3–5 cm (1⅕–2 in) in length . . . 9

9. Plants very bristly in all parts except for the petals, the bristles
   stiff and prickly to the touch: **M. horridula**, in part
   Plants not as above 10

10. Petals 5 or more; flowers semi-erect to half-nodding; plants
    monocarpic to perennial (polycarpic) 11
    Petals usually 4; flowers fully nodding; plants perennial (polycarpic)   13

11. Stamen filaments markedly dilated towards the base: **M. henrici**★
    Stamen filaments not dilated towards the base 12

12. Flowers pink; anthers yellow or brownish: **M. sherriffii**★
    Flowers blue; anthers blue: **M. simplicifolia**★

13. Flowers pale lavender-blue; plants spreading, with persistent,
    bristly leaf-bases: **M. quintuplinervia**
    Flowers violet-blue; plants tufted, not creeping, the leaf-bases
    neither bristly not persistent: **M. delavayi**★

14. Plants perennial (polycarpic); flowers yellow, orange or red 15
    Plants monocarpic (dying after flowering and seeding); flowers
    yellow, pink, red or blue, occasionally white 16

15. Leaves oblong, pinnately divided to the midrib; plant scarcely hairy, the tufted base without bristles; flowers yellow, orange or red (sometimes semi-double or double):   **M. cambrica**
Leaves rounded in outline, three- to five-lobed; plants densely hairy with a tufted bristly base; flowers always yellow (never semi-double or double):   **M. chelidonifolia**

16. Plants deciduous, the leaf-rosettes dying away to a resistant bud in the late autumn 17
Plants evergreen, with a large leafy rosette present throughout the winter 25

17. Leaves deeply pinnately dissected, cut to the midrib 18
Leaves not dissected to deeply toothed, often with an undulate margin; if lobed, never cut for more than one third of the way to the midrib 19

18. Ovary and fruit armed with a stout style and reddish-brown bristles: **M. speciosa**★
Ovary and fruit armed with a slender style and straw-coloured bristles: **M. aculeata**

19. Flowers pale blue, generally with 4 petals; leaves broadly oval, coarsely toothed; leaf-bristles without a dark base: **M. latifolia**
Flowers deep blue to mauve, lavender-blue or wine-red, generally with 5–8 petals; leaves elliptical to narrow-oblong, generally more or less untoothed; leaf-bristles often with a dark base 20

20. Inflorescence without bracts 21
Inflorescence with bracts (at least to the lower flowers) 23

21. Flowers pale blue, borne only on the upper part of the inflorescence; fruit-capsule narrow-cylindrical, without a style: **M. forrestii**★
Flowers mid to deep blue, violet-pink or purplish, borne from the base to the top of the inflorescence; fruit capsule elliptical, with a style . . 22

22. Leaves densely bristly, the bristle with a dark, often blackish, base: **M. horridula**★ in part
Leaves sparsely bristle, the bristles without a dark base: **M. lancifolia**★ in part

23. Tall plant as much as 1.2 m (4 ft) tall, generally 30–70 cm; leaf bristles without a dark base; scapose flowers never present:
            M. prattii (*M. horridula* of gardens)
Dwarf plants, rarely more than 25 cm (10 in) tall, often much smaller; leaf bristles with a dark base; scapose flowers often found at the base of the inflorescence 24

24. Leaves blue-green (often markedly glaucous) with rather sparse bristles; anthers cream or white: **M. rudis**★

Leaves deep green, sometimes flushed with purple, usually densely
bristly; anthers yellow to orange: *M. horridula★* in part

25. Leaves unlobed, with a finely toothed margin; flowers yellow
    or white; stigma deep purple-black 26
    Leaves shallowly lobed to deeply pinnately dissected; flowers
    yellow, blue, red or purple; stigma greenish or whitish, occasionally
    pale purple 27

26. Flowers yellow; leaves covered in gold hairs: *M. regia★*
    Flowers white; leaves covered in greyish hairs: *M. superba★*

27. Flowers blue, red or purple 28
    Flowers yellow, occasionally white 29

28. Leaves deeply pinnately dissected, the lower segments distant along
    the slender stalk (rachis); flowers pale- to mid-sky blue   *M. wallichii*
    Leaves shallowly lobed, never cut all the way to the midrib; flowers
    pink or red   *M. napaulensis*

29. Leaves shallowly pinnately lobed, sometimes the lower lobes deeply
    separated, almost to the midrib; stigma pale purple: *M. paniculata*
    Leaves deeply pinnately lobed with rather distant division and a
    slender rachis; stigma, pale green or whitish: 30

30. Leaves densely bristly, the bristles with a purple-black base: *M. dhwojii*
    Leaves sparsely bristly, the bristles pale: *M. gracilipes★*

Meconopsis aculeata Royle

This species is closely related to *M. horridula* and *M. prattii*, from which it can
at once be differentiated because of its dissected leaves.

Like *M. horridula*, plants are monocarpic, the leaves withering away to a
resting bud in the autumn prior to flowering – generally in the second or
third year. The leaves, up to 30 cm (12 in) long, are pinnately-lobed and with
a stalk often equalling the blade in length; the initial lobes are further lobed
or toothed, both surfaces with a sparse covering of pale straw-coloured
spines. The upper stem leaves are usually unstalked. The flowers, 4.5–6 cm
(2–2⅖ in) across, are borne in a bristly raceme up to 60 cm (24 in) high, and
varying in colour from pinkish- to purplish-blue. There are usually four
rounded petals and a central boss of golden stamens. The stigma varies in
colour from green to purple. The fruit-capsule is oblong to almost globose,
densely spiny and splitting by four to six valves close to the styled apex.

M. aculeata hails from the western Himalayas (eastern Afghanistan through
Kashmir to Kumaon in India). It inhabits rocky meadows, screes and boggy
ground, particularly along stream margins, at altitudes from 2500–4375 m
(8200–14,400 ft).

This species has been in cultivation since 1864, when it first flowered at
the Royal Botanic Gardens at Kew. It is undoubtedly an attractive plant with
much grace and appealing silky flowers. It is perhaps less tolerant of winter

wet than its cousin *M. prattii* and it may be advisable to protect plants by a
cloche or frame light during this vulnerable period of the year.

Some forms in cultivation, with less dissected leaves, may be hybrids with
M. horridula (Cobb, 1989) or *M. prattii* (*M. horridula* of gardens), but recent
seed introductions from Kashmir by Chris Chadwell and others have introduced authenticated wild material once more into our gardens and perhaps
some interesting variation may turn up.

Although generally taprooted, plants like those of several other monocarpic species in the genus may sometimes produce a more spreading and
fibrous root-system.

There is a very charming white-flowered form in cultivation, with contrasting purple anthers and stigma. Being monocarpic, such forms are often
difficult to establish in cultivation for any length of time.

Meconopsis argemonantha Prain

A species known only from a few fragments collected by Colonel Bailey in
south-eastern Tibet early in the twentieth century. It appears to be most
closely allied to *M. primulina*. The leaves are narrowly oblong to almost
elliptic and up to 8.5 cm (3⅖ in) long, the lamina pinnately lobed towards
the base and sparsely bristly, green above but glaucous beneath. The solitary
white flowers, about 5 cm (2 in) across, are borne on slightly bristly stalks that
are at least 8.7 cm (3½ in) long; petals 6–8, oblong, with a rounded apex;
anthers yellow; ovary with a style up to 10 mm (⅖ in) long.

This interesting and tantalising species is known only from a single locality
in south-eastern Tibet, close to Mirpak in the Tawang District at an altitude
of about 4210 m (13,800 ft). The white flowers make it a very distinctive plant.

Meconopsis bella Prain   **[Pl. 113]**

This is perhaps the most tantalising and prettiest little blue poppy of all.
Tantalising in that, despite numerous introductions from the wild over the
years, *M. bella* has proved a fickle and temperamental plant in cultivation. It
can be likened to an alpine poppy (*Papaver alpinum*) in overall dimensions.

M. bella is a small perennial with a slender, carrot-like taproot, covered by
the persistent leaf bases. The leaves, which in the wild die away during the
winter, are all basal, and variously pinnately lobed or unlobed, with a long
stalk, hairless or with a few scattered bristles. The solitary flowers are borne
in succession and arise on slender, slightly bristly scapes up to 12 cm (5 in)
long. The cupped flowers range from clear pale blue to pink or purplish-blue
and are 4–5.5 cm (1⅗–2⅕ in) across, with a central boss of golden anthers
borne on filaments coloured like the petals. There are four, occasionally five
or six, rounded, partly overlapping petals. The fruit-capsule is narrow, pear-
shaped and smooth, splitting by four to seven valves close to the top, and
borne on a curving stalk.

This is another Himalayan species found from central Nepal eastwards
through Sikkim to Bhutan at altitudes of 3750–5150 m (12,300–

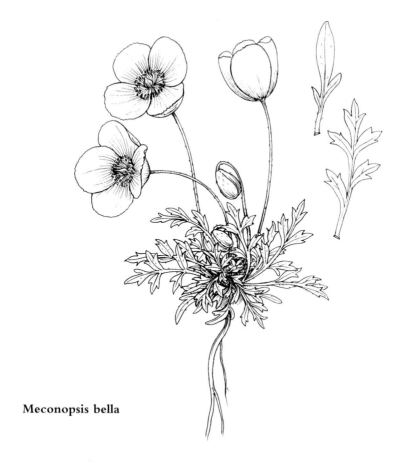

Meconopsis bella

16,900 ft). In these high remote regions it inhabits damp, shaded cliff habitats or sloping meadows or banks with a low scrub of dwarf rhododendrons and other woody plants.

Most who have seen it in the wild describe it as a plant confined to deep, mossy, cliff crevices where its long taproot penetrates deep into the rocks. However, I have twice seen scattered colonies of it in the wild and never in that type of habitat, but on sloping meadows where it nestled beneath dwarf shrubs in moist, shaded places, with the flowers poking through low, ground-hugging branches. The fragile flowers, translucent and watery, were a pale to deep lavender-blue of the utmost beauty and refinement. In fact, the picture in James Cobb's *Meconopsis* shows *M. bella* growing in just such a habitat.

The degree of dissection of the leaves is very variable and whereas some plants may have markedly dissected leaves, others are undissected or with few lobes. George Taylor (1934 Monograph) was unaware of forms with undissected leaves. It seems to me that this requires further investigation, for plants from central Nepal (particularly the Marsyandi Valley) are of this type whereas those from the eastern Himalayas have finely dissected leaves in all the recorded samples.

1. *Macleaya cordata*, the Plumed Poppy, excellent in the herbaceous border but with tiny flowers for a poppy.

2. *Chelidonium majus* 'Flore Pleno', a quiet plant for the woodland garden.

3. *Chelidonium majus* var. laciniatum, a cultivated form in which both the leaves and petals are dissected.

4. *Chelidonium majus* var. grandiflorum is the finest form of the Greater Celandine for gardens.

6. *Stylophorum diphyllum*, the American Celandiner Poppy, revels in dappled shade in the garden.

5. *Hylomecon japonicum*, a Japanese woodlander for the spring border.

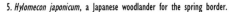

7. *Stylophorum lasiocarpum*, the Chinese Celandine Poppy, easy and prolific in the woodland garden.

8. *Glaucium corniculatum*, the Orange Horned Poppy, probably the finest species in the genus for the garden where, once establish, it will seed around moderately.

9. *Glaucium flavum*, the Yellow Horned Poppy is a denizen of coastal habitats in Western Europe and the Mediterranean region.

10. *Glaucium flavum* var. *fulvum*, photographed in the Greek Peloponnese (Monemvasia), sports a brown spot at the base of each petal.

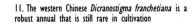

11. The western Chinese *Dicranostigma franchetiana* is a robust annual that is still rare in cultivation

12. *Dicranostigma lactucoides* var. *maritima* in cultivation.

13. *Dicranostigma leptopodum*, the smallest species in the genus, is relatively new to cultivation.

14. *Eomecon chionanthum* is a patch-forming perennial with decorative scalloped foliage and rather small white flowers.

15. The North American Bloodroot, *Sanguinaria canadensis*, is a plant for a humusy moist soil in dappled shade.

16. *Sanguinaria canadensis* 'Multiplex', the finest form of the Bloodroot for gardens, and the most readily available.

17. *Eschscholtzia californica* in Snell Valley, Napa County, California (photo: Mache-Parker Sanderson).

18. *Eschscholtzia californica*, Riverside County, California (photo: Sean Hogan).

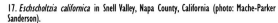

19. The Californian Poppy, *Eschscholtzia californica*, in cultivation.

20. *Eschscholtzia californica* var. maritima in cultivation.

21. *Eschscholtzia californica*; typical mixed colours of garden forms.

22. The vibrant colours of modern strains of Californian poppies on trial by Sahin in Holland.

23. *Eschscholtzia californica* 'Apricot Chiffon' a compact modern cultivar with frilled blooms.

24. *Eschscholtzia caespitosa*, a small annual occasionally seen in gardens is restricted to California in the wild.

25. *Eschscholtzia caespitosa* 'Sundew' is a modern selection with creamy-yellow blooms.

26. *Eschscholtzia lobbii*, a fine small Californian poppy for the front of the flower border, known in California as 'Frying Pans'.

27. The Mexican Tulip Poppy, *Hunnemannia fumarifolia*, is one of the finest annual poppies, yet surprisingly rarely seen in gardens.

28. *Hunnemannia fumarifolia* 'Sunlite', a modern selection with sumptuous cupped blooms (photo: Kees Sahin).

29. *Dendromecon harfordii*, a Californian endemic, is an excellent evergreen shrub for a warm, sunny, sheltered site (photo: Sean Hogan).

30. *Dendromecon harfordii* (photo: Sean Hogan).

31. *Dendromecon rigida*, commoner in cultivation than *D. harfordii*, but a generally less desirable garden plant.

32. The Moroccan *Papaver atlanticum* is common in gardens but is much confused with the Spanish *P. rupifragum* in cultivation.

33. *Papaver californicum*, the only true poppy (*Papaver*) found in California; scarcely known in cultivation.

34. *Papaver commutatum* is often sold under the cultivar name 'Ladybird', despite the fact that plant in gardens does not vary from its wild counterpart; here mixed with *P. rhoeas*.

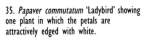

35. *Papaver commutatum* 'Ladybird' showing one plant in which the petals are attractively edged with white.

36. *Papaver dubium* amongst other ephemeral annuals south of Monemvasia in the Greek Peloponnese.

37. *Papaver dubium* showing the dusky centre to the bloom characteristic of the Mediterranean form.

38. *Papaver fugax*, a monocarpic or biennial species from the Caucasus Mountains, here photographed in a dry valley near Kasbegi, northern Georgia.

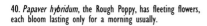

39. *Papaver glaucum*, a close relative of the Opium Poppy, but rarely seen in gardens.

40. *Papaver hybridum*, the Rough Poppy, has fleeting flowers, each bloom lasting only for a morning usually.

41. *Papaver kerneri*, a small alpine poppy, photographed on high screes of the Hoch Obir in the Italian Dolomites (photo: John Birks).

42. *Papaver lateritium* is a stoloniferous perennial from Turkey, rarely grown in gardens.

43. *Papaver lateritium* 'Fireball' is widely available, often being sold wrongly in garden centres and nurseries as *P. orientalis* 'Fireball'.

44. *Papaver lecoqii*, Babington's Poppy, is occasionally cultivated; it is native primarily to Western Europe, including Britain.

45. *Papaver nudicaule*, the so-called Iceland Poppy, is a native of central and northern Asia.

46. *Papaver nudicaule*; a standard mixture being grown for seed production by Sahin in Zeeland, Holland, with white, yellow and orange predominating.

47. *Papaver oreophilum* a rare perennial in cultivation, here photographed in the wild north of Mestia in the Georgian Caucasus.

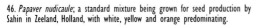

48. *Papaver orientale* one of the prime parents in the evolution of the Oriental Poppies of gardens.

49. *Papaver* Orientalis Group 'Beauty of Livermere'.

50. *Papaver* Orientalis Group 'Cedric Morris', often sold as 'Cedric's Pink'.

51. *Papaver* Orientalis Group 'Curlilocks' one of several cut-petalled cultivars.

52. *Papaver* Orientalis Group 'Garden Glory'

53. *Papaver* Orientalis Group 'Grauwe Witwe'.

54. *Papaver* Orientalis Group 'John III', an excellent modern cultivar.

55. *Papaver* Orientalis Group 'Juliane'.

56. *Papaver* Orientalis Group 'Karine', one of a number of excellent modern German cultivars.

57. *Papaver* Orientalis Group 'Kleine Tanzerin'.

59. *Papaver* Orientalis Group 'Patty's Plum' a unique colour amongst Oriental poppies and a favourite cottage garden flower.

58. *Papaver* Orientalis Group 'Lilac Girl'.

60. *Papaver* Orientalis Group 'Perry's White' an old cultivar dating back to the nineteenth century.

61. *Papaver* Orientalis Group 'Petticoat'.

62. *Papaver* Orientalis Group 'Picotee'.

63. *Papaver* Orientalis Group 'Rosenpokal'.

64. *Papaver* Orientalis Group 'Suleika'.

65. *Papaver* Orientalis Group 'Türkenlouis'.

66. *Papaver* Orientalis Group 'Watermelon'.

67. *Papaver* Orientalis Group 'Wisley Beacon' at the Royal Horticultural Society's garden at Wisley in Surrey.

68. Papavers of the Orientalis Group make fine garden plants, especially for the mixed herbaceous border or with summer flowering bulbs such as *Allium albopilosum*.

69. *Papaver* 'Red Gauntlet', a unique hybrid poppy between a red-flowered member of the Orientalis Group and *P. triniifolia*.

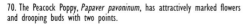

70. The Peacock Poppy, *Papaver pavoninum*, has attractively marked flowers and drooping buds with two points.

71. *Papaver* radicatum, a denizen of Arctic tundra, here in the Kongsvoll, Arctic Norway (photo: John Birks).

72. *Papaver rhaeticum*, the common alpine poppy of many parts of the Pyrenees and the southern and western Alps, here on the Rolle Pass in the Dolomites (photo: John Birks)

73. *Papaver rhaeticum* on a high scree in the French Alps.

74. *Papaver rupifragum*, an endemic of cliffs in Andalucia, which is rather scarce in cultivation.

75. The vibrant flowers of the Common Poppy, *Papaver rhoeas*, in a field in the Greek Peloponnese.

76. *Papaver rhoeas* relishes disturbed sites; here along a relatively new bypass close to Long Melford in Suffolk.

77. Where left unhindered by herbicides, the Common Poppy, *Papaver rhoeas*, can make dense stands on arable land; here a typical British form.

78. *Papaver rhoeas*; a deeply coloured and well-marked form photographed in the Greek Peloponnese.

79. *Papaver rhoeas* 'in the wild' with semi-double blooms; photographed on the Long Melford bypass in Suffolk.

80. Single Shirley poppies come in a range of colours; they are all selections of *Papaver rhoeas*.

81. An attractive modern strain of Shirley poppy grown by Sahin in Holland.

82. A selection of *Papaver rhoeas* on the trial ground of Sahin in Holland, with single flowers, showing the range of colours that is possible.

83. As Pl. 82, but with semidouble flowers predominating.

84. *Papaver rhoeas* 'Mother of Pearl'.

85. *Papaver rhoeas* 'Angel's Choir', a semidouble selection from 'Mother of Pearl'; the reds should be removed from the selection in order to maintain the more pastel shades.

86. The Turkish endemic *Papaver spicatum* (widely known in gardens as *P. heldreichii*) is a noble and eye-catching border perennial.

87. *Papaver triniifolium* is another Turkish endemic that is a monocarpic perennial.

88. *Papaver somniferum*, the Opium Poppy, in a typical single form found in gardens.

89. The attractive bowl-shaped flowers of *Papaver somniferum*.

90. The Opium Poppy, *Papaver somniferum*, bears decorative fruit capsules that are much prized for dried flower arrangements.

91. Field production of *Papaver somniferum* in central France for the pharmaceutical industry and for seed production.

92. Commercial production of *Papaver somniferum*.

93. An unnamed semi-double form of *Papaver somniferum* with near black flowers.

94. *Papaver somniferum* 'Pink Chiffon', a pink selection with semi-double flowers

95. Double or Peony-flowered forms of *Papaver somniferum* come in a range of bright colours.

96. *Papaver somniferum* Peony-flowered Group 'Black Peony'.

97. *Papaver somniferum* Peony-flowered Group 'Purple Peony'.

98. *Papaver somniferum* Peony-flowered Group 'Crimson Peony'.

99. *Papaver* somniferum Peony-flowered Group 'Crimson and White'.

100. *Papaver somniferum* Peony-flowered Group 'Flemish Antique'.

101. *Papaver somniferum* Peony-flowered Group 'Frosted Salmon'.

102. *Papaver somniferum* Peony-flowered Group 'White Cloud'.

103. *Papaver somniferum* 'Danebrog', a single "Laciniatum" type.

104. *Papaver somniferum* 'Pink Bicton', a double "Laciniatum" type.

105. *Papaver somniferum* 'Swansdown', a semidouble "Laciniatum" type.

106. An unnamed double crimson cut-petalled "Laciniatum' type of *Papaver somniferum*.

107. *Papaver somniferum* 'Hen and Chickens' which is grown primarily for its extraordinary prolific fruit capsules.

108. *Roemeria refracta* photographed in the Andarab Valley in eastern Afghanistan where it replaces the Common Poppy, *Papaver rhoeas*, as a cornfield weed.

109. *Roemeria refracta* on arable land near Tashkent in Kazakstan; note the long narrow seed pods characteristic of the genus.

110. A selected form of *Roemeria refracta* in cultivation.

111. *Cathcartia villosa*, the Woodland Poppy, a native of the monsoon-rich central and eastern Himalaya.

112. *Cathcartia villosa* in cultivation.

113. *Meconopsis bella* in the upper Marsyandi Valley in central Nepal; it is one of the trickiest poppies to cultivate and is very rare in gardens.

114. The Himalayan Blue Poppy, *Meconopsis betonicifolia*, one of the most sought after and freely available members of the genus.

115. *Meconopsis betonicifolia* var. *alba*.

116. The very variable hybrid *Meconopsis* x *sheldonii* is a cross between two blue-flowered species common in cultivation, *M. betonicifolia* and *M. grandis*.

117. A form of *Meconopsis* x *sheldonii* with pale flowers photographed at Branklyn Botanic Garden in Scotland.

118. The Welsh Poppy, *Meconopsis cambrica*, in the wild; photographed in the Val d'Ossoue near Garvarnie in the French Pyrenees.

119. A prolific garden plant, *Meconopsis cambrica* is a coloniser in the garden with a long flowering season.

120. The orange-flowered form of the Welsh Poppy, *Meconopsis cambrica* var. *aurantiaca*.

121. The modern development of the Welsh Poppy, *Meconopsis cambrica*, includes both single and semi-double forms in yellow, orange or red.

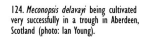

122. *Meconopsis delavayi* in the wild; photographed at Wu-to-di north of Lijiang, Yunnan, in the Yulong Shan (Jade Dragon Mountains).

123. As Pl. 120, showing a rather different form in the wild.

124. *Meconopsis delavayi* being cultivated very successfully in a trough in Aberdeen, Scotland (photo: Ian Young).

125. *Meconopsis grandis* in cultivation in the 1980s at Jack Drake's nursery at Inshriach in Scotland.

126. A seedling of *Meconopsis grandis* from a wild collected Sikkimese source.

127. A form of *Meconopsis grandis* in cultivation at Branklyn Botanic Garden in Scotland.

128. Plants of *Meconopsis grandis* derived from GS600; the original collection made by Ludlow and Sherriff in Bhutan more than fifty years ago is no longer in cultivation.

129. *Meconopsis henrici* photographed in the wild above Huang-long-si in NW Sichuan.

130. The true *Meconopsis horridula*, a denizen of high alpine meadows and moraines; photographed above Manang in the upper Marsyandi Valley of central Nepal.

131. *Meconopsis horridula* on the Thorung La in the central Nepalese Himalaya, growing at over 5000 m altitude.

132. *Meconopsis horridula* var. *racemosa* photographed on the Beima Shan in NW Yunnan at about 5200 m.

133. *Meconopsis integrifolia* subsp. *integrifolia* at Huang-long-si in NW Sichuan where it flowers during June and July.

134. *Meconopsis integrifolia* subsp. *integrifolia*, Huang-long-si, NW Yunnan; note the upright goblet-shaped flowers.

135. *Meconopsis integrifolia* subsp. *lijiangensis* on Da-xue-shan (Big Snow Mountain) on the Yunnan/Sichuan border, in June after overnight snow.

136. An unnamed form of *Meconopsis integrifolia* photographed on the Balang Shan in western Sichuan; this form has been called 'Wolong' in cultivation.

137. *Meconopsis lancifolia* in its typical form photographed on the Bemei Shan in NW Yunnan.

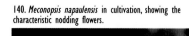
140. *Meconopsis napaulensis* in cultivation, showing the characteristic nodding flowers.

138. *Meconopsis lancifolia* on the Da-xue-shan (Big Snow Mountain) in NW Yunnan where it flowers during June and July.

139. *Meconopsis napaulensis* in cultivation.

141. The young leaf-rosette of *Meconopsis paniculata* photographed on the Phephe La in central Bhutan.

142. An autumn rosette of *Meconopsis paniculata* photographed in the Jaljale Himal in eastern Nepal.

146. *Meconopsis prattii* near Beta Hai, Zhongdian region, NW Yunnan.

143. *Meconopsis paniculata* showing the giant panicle of nodding yellow flowers.

144. *Meconopsis paniculata* in cultivation.

145. *Meconopsis prattii* photographed near Napa Hai, Zhongdian region, in NW Yunnan; this is the plant that is commonly mistaken for *M. horridula* in gardens.

147. *Meconopsis pseudointegrifolia* in its typical form growing on the Mekong/Yangtse Divide (near Da-cai-ba); note the wide nodding flowers and protruding style.

148. *Meconopsis pseudointegrifolia* subsp. *pseudointegrifolia* photographed at Tianchi Lake, Zhongdian region, NW Yunnan

149. *Meconopsis punicea* photographed at Jui-zhai-gou in NW Sichuan where it flowers during June and July.

150. *Meconospis punicea* with its drooping scarlet flowers; photographed at Jui-zhai-gou, NW Sichuan.

151. *Meconopsis quintuplinervia*, the Harebell Poppy, photographed at Jui-zhai-gou in NW Yunnan.

152. The leaf-rosette of *Meconopsis rudis* photographed on the high screes of the upper Gang-ho-ba, Lijiang, NW Yunnan.

153. *Meconopsis rudis* a denizen of high rocky places; photographed at Wu-to-di, Yulong Shan, near Lijiang, NW Yunnan.

154. *Meconopsis rudis* flowering in July in the upper Gang-ho-ba, Yulong Shan, near Lijiang, NW Yunnan.

155. *Meconopsis wallichii* photographed west of Taplejung in eastern Nepal, where it flowers from late June until August.

156. A selected form of *Meconopsis wallichii* growing at the Logan Botanic Garden in Scotland.

157. A new and undescribed species of blue poppy, *Meconopsis*, photographed near Jui-zhai-gou, NW Sichuan where it inhabits high alpine meadows.

158. As Pl. 155; note the black petal base, a unique feature in the genus *Meconopsis*.

159. *Argemone mexicana*, the Mexican Poppy, a widespread and pernicious weed in some parts of the world but, nonetheless, a fine garden plant (photo: Kees Sahin).

160. *Argemone munita* photographed in the wild in Kerr County, California (photo: Sean Hogan).

161. *Argemone munita* photographed in the wild in California (photo: Mache-Parker Sanderson).

162. *Argemone ochroleuca* in cultivation.

163. *Argemone platyceras* in cultivation where it is often sold under the erroneous name of *A. Albus*.

164. *Argemone platyceras* in a selected form called 'Silver Charm' (photo: Kees Sahin).

165. *Argemone polyanthemos* in cultivation (photo: Kees Sahin).

166. *Arctomecon californica* photographed in the wild (photo: David King).

167. *Arctomecon californica* in the wild in California; note the characteristic dark ovary (photo; David King).

168. One of the smallest known poppies, *Arctomecon humilis* is very restricted in the wild, being found in a single site in Utah (photo: David King).

169. The extraordinary leaf-rosette of the rare and little known *Arctomecon merriamii*, photographed in the wild in California (photo: David King).

170. As Pl. 169; the white flowers appear in May (photo: David King).

171. The annual *Stylomecon heterophylla* in cultivation.

172. *Stylomecon heterophylla* 'White Satin', a rare and little-known white selection.

173. *Romneya trichocalyx* in cultivation.

175. *Romneya* x *hybrida* 'White Cloud'.

174. *Romneya trichocalyx* in cultivation, showing the sumptuous blooms.

176. *Platystemon californicus* in Bear Valley, Coluso County, California (photo: Mache-Parker Sanderson).

177. *Platystemon californicus* in Bear Valley, Coluso County, California (photo: Sean Hogan).

178. *Platystemon californicus* in cultivation in Holland, showing the typical cream-coloured flowers.

179. A selection of *Platystemon californicus* with yellow petals, grown by Sahin in Holland.

180. The empheral annual *Meconella californica* fills some valleys in the wild in California; it is scarcely known in cultivation (photo: Mache-Parker Sanderson).

181. *Hypecoum trilobum*, a weed of arable land and waysides; photographed near Samarkand in Uzbekistan.

182. *Hypecoum imberbe* showing the typical lobed petals; photographed in Northern Cyprus.

Whatever their source, *M. bella* has proved very difficult – a great pity, as this is a real gem of a plant. The first seed sent to Britain were dispatched by King in 1888 (the year of its discovery) from Sikkim. Since then there have been several collections, but few have resulted in flowering plants. According to accounts, seeds germinate reasonably well, but it is difficult to get large enough plants by the autumn that will survive the winter. Older plants are prey to severe frosts and the expanding shoots vulnerable to the ravages of slugs. Plants are slow-growing and often take four or more years to come into flower.

Such treasures as *M. bella* are bound to attract the grower who thrives on the challenge of growing to perfection a plant considered by many to be almost impossible to grow. The horticultural world is full of such challenging plants and, in most instances, someone will eventually master the cultivation of each. As far as *M. bella* is concerned, I can do no better than refer readers to James Cobb's detailed analysis of its cultivation as outlined in his book *Meconopsis*. I have never tried growing this charmer myself and leave it to those who have the time, patience and necessary skills.

Meconopsis betonicifolia Franch.   [Pl. 114]
(Syn. *Cathcartia betonicifolia (Franch.) Prain;* Meconopsis baileyi Prain; *M. betonicifolia* var. *baileyi* (Prain) Edwards)
HIMALAYAN BLUE POPPY

A perennial, sometimes monocarpic, with erect stems reaching to 1.6 m (5 ft). The leaves are oblong, up to 15 cm (6 in) long, coarsely toothed and with a distinctive truncated or somewhat heart-shaped base, the basal and lower stem leaves stalked, the upper half-clasping the stem, the upper three to four often in a close whorl (at least on the main stem) where the flower stalks arise; all leaves covered by a scattering of rusty-coloured bristles. The flowers are sky blue to rose-lavender, 7.5–10 cm (3–4 in) across, nodding to facing sideways, few, mostly on the upper half of the plant, each borne on long bristly stalks up to 15 cm (6 in) long, though often less. The broad oval to almost rounded petals are most often four in number, but sometimes five or six, often somewhat frilled or wavy and spreading widely apart to expose the prominent boss of golden-yellow anthers terminating white filaments. The oblong capsule splits by four to seven valves in the upper third and is densely bristly.

M. betonicifolia is native to the eastern Himalayas, from south-eastern Tibet (Xizang) and Upper Burma (Myanmar), northwards to north-western Yunnan, where it inhabits woodland, ravines and moist alpine meadows and stream margins or scrub, at an altitude of between 3120 and 4000 m (10,200–13,100 ft).

This, the commonest of the blue poppies grown in gardens, is a superb plant and worth every possible attention. Its discovery is credited to the French missionary and collector Père Delavay, who found it in north-western Yunnan in 1886. Fragmentary specimens collected by Colonel Bailey from the neighbouring region of south-eastern Tibet were described by Prain in 1915 as *M. baileyi*. Prain did not connect his specimens with

Franchet's *M. betonicifolia*. In the summer of 1924 Frank Kingdon-Ward, one of the most intrepid of plant-hunters, collected further and far more complete material, at the same time introducing the species into cultivation under the name *M. baileyi*. It was only later that Otto Stapf and then George Taylor realised the affinity of *M. betonicifolia* and *M. baileyi* and the fact that they represented in all probability geographical variants of a single species. The main difference is in the far more densely bristly fruit-capsule of plants from south-eastern Tibet – it is this form that is in cultivation today.

Established names often take many years to disappear and despite the fact that the correct name for this poppy is *M. betonicifolia*, it can still be found in some catalogues as *M. baileyi* or Bailey's Blue Poppy.

The species is unlikely to be confused in gardens with any other, except perhaps *M. grandis*. The leaves of the latter are generally larger with a distinctly tapered base and the flowers rather more substantial, the petals more cupped and less frilled. Furthermore, the fruit-capsules of *M. grandis* are long and slimmer, with or without bristles, but never as densely so as in *M. betonicifolia*.

The main confusion in gardens between these two closely allied species lies in the fact that many plants sold as *M. grandis* are, in fact, *M. betonicifolia*. If unsure, simply check the leaf-bases of plants – if they are tapered they are probably *M. grandis*, if somewhat heart-shaped or truncated, *M. betonicifolia*. In reality the latter sets copious seed in an average year, whereas the former rarely sets much in cultivation, so seedlings of *M. grandis* are always more scarce.

M. betonicifolia varies in cultivation from a biennial to a perennial. Even when perennial, it seldom survives for more than four or five years in my experience. However, it is so easy from seed, or relatively easy, that it is usually simple to ensure a supply of plants. The leaves die away completely in the late autumn, so it is wise to mark the position of plants with care lest they be dug up by mistake. One of the joys of this species is to watch the new shoots arise, rusty-haired and fresh, sometimes flushed with purple, in the spring.

In the best forms the flowers are a clear sky blue, sometimes with the merest hint of lavender. Other forms are a darker blue tinged with purple. However, there is little doubt that plants grown on acid soils produce the best blue flowers, but, despite this, it is well worth seeking out a good coloured strain in the first instance.

It used to be said that this lovely species could be grown only in the cooler, moister parts of Britain, but provided there is ample moisture in the soil and some shade from fierce sun, this simply is not so. In my former Suffolk garden in a region of Britain becoming notorious for its summer droughts, I grew *M. betonicifolia* satisfactorily, not in large patches as they can in the north and west of the country, but in more modest groups. Soil preparation requires more care with plenty of added leaf-mould and compost as well as diligent watering during dry summer periods. I prefer to plant them in a semi-shaded position, where the dappled light sets them off against other woodlands novelties. The only disadvantage is that, even with much care and attention, little seed is set when the air is very dry and the plump seed pods sometimes prove to be quite empty. However, one sight of the first blue petals bursting from the flowerbuds makes every effort worthwhile.

When selecting plants from a nursery, pick healthy, vigorous-looking plants, particularly those with several side shoots – these are more likely to prove to be properly perennial. Weakly plants and those with a single shoot at the end of the growing season are likely to prove to be monocarpic and although they will flower well enough, they will almost certainly die after fruiting.

Seed sown in very early spring probably ensures the best means of increase. Avoid sowing too thickly, as the delicate seedlings are notorious for damping off at this vulnerable stage. Prick out as soon as they are large enough to handle and grow on as fast as possible to help ensure vigorous plants more likely to be perennial. Plant out in late summer to allow them enough time to become established before they enter winter dormancy. Seed or divisions from known polycarpic (fully perennial) forms are more likely to be long-lasting in the garden.

Seed can be sown in the late summer and autumn from freshly gathered seeds. This certainly gives a good germination, but seedlings then need to be overwintered in a glasshouse or frame and unless you are very skilled, some losses must be expected.

There are various forms of *M. betonicifolia* available: 'Branklyn'† and Harlow Carr Strain are both fine blue selections; var. *alba* **[Pl. 115]** has white flowers which are attractive in their own right, but scarcely with the beauty of the best blues, though this is a plant worth having in a collection. Lilac-coloured forms of *M. betonicifolia* were noted by George Taylor and there is a colour photograph of one such plant in his 1934 monograph. Today there are several lilac forms in existence, although only one can be described as very attractive. This interesting and rather beautiful deep lilac form was obtained by James Cobb from Les Newby and is likely to be a good introduction, especially as the plants are very fertile and come 100% true to type from seed. The name 'Hensol Lilac' has been proposed for this cultivar; the plant originated at Hensol.

Meconopsis × *sheldonii* G. Taylor (*M. betonicifolia* × *M. grandis*) **[Pl. 117]**
This name encompasses all the hybrids between *M. betonicifolia*, a species generally regarded as a biennial or short-lived perennial in gardens, and the more substantial, clump-forming, long-lived perennial *M. grandis*. The result is a series of exciting hybrids which together have produced some of the very finest perennial blue poppies that we grow in our gardens. Unfortunately, many of these are sterile or produce very little seed, although the fairly recent cultivar 'Lingholm' is fully fertile and this has made possible the mass production of plants for the gardening market. However, most of the other cultivars are generally rather scarce and often difficult to obtain, being slow to increase by vegetative means.

The original cross was made by W.G. Sheldon at Oxted in Surrey in 1934 and later described by George Taylor. The same cross was undertaken several times subsequently by different growers. The fact that various different forms of the hybrid are grown is a reflection of which species was used as the seed parent and, perhaps more importantly, which form of the species was employed. This applies particularly to *M. grandis* which exists in cultivation in various colour forms (see under *M. grandis*).

Unfortunately, *M. × sheldonii* presents a rather complex picture. Straight crosses between *M. betonicifolia* and *M. grandis* tend to produce sterile offspring. However, the hybrids can be back-crossed on purpose or inadvertently to one or other parent, particularly the latter. The result is fertile hybrids: both 'Lingholm' and 'Kingsbarn Hybrids' are presumably of such origin. This picture is further complicated by the genes of other species, especially those of *M. integrifolia* and *M. pseudointegrifolia* that have adulterated the × *sheldonii* gene pool. Most of these have turned up spontaneously and often the parent 'species' can only be guessed at, for few records of deliberate crosses have been kept. It is not surprising, knowing the fecundity of *Meconopsis,* that when several species are grown side by side in the garden hybrids should turn up fairly regularly. Clearly, a lot more could be done with a thorough and systematic approach to *Meconopsis* hybridisation in the garden, especially amongst the blue poppies. Apart from telling us a great deal about the species relationship, it would undoubtedly pave the way for some exciting new hybrids for the garden.

Crewdson Hybrids These plants clearly have *M. × sheldonii* in 'their blood', but it has been suggested that *M. integrifolia* has also been involved in their evolution, which, if true, means that they should not be classed under the former. They were originally raised after the Second World War by a great grower of *Meconopsis*, Cicely Crewdson. The plant looks very like *M. × sheldonii,* except that the flowers are somewhat smaller and a deeper blue, rather than a blue-green, while the petals are rather narrower and less overlapping. 'Miss Jebb' (often written 'Mrs Jebb') is almost certainly a selection from the Crewdson Hybrids. It was named by Henry and Margaret Taylor of Invergowrie by Dundee after Miss Jebb who gardened Brooklands near Castle Douglas in Northern Ireland. 'Miss Jebb' has become inextricably linked with Crewdson Hybrids, although it is clearly a selection from it, and the name cannot properly be regarded as a synonym. The plant is quite stately, with long, parallel-sided leaves that are flushed with purple along the margin, while the flowers are very rounded in outline and face sideways. Be that as it may, two forms of Crewdson Hybrids are in circulation: the true plant is apparently sterile, while the imposter (which is also an excellent garden plant) is fully fertile. All the plants in this association appear to be fertile. It has been suggested that 'Miss Jebb' (or 'Mrs Jebb's Variety') be changed to *Meconopsis × hybrida* 'Cicely Crewdson', but this would be rather confusing, especially if, as seems almost certain, the plant in question was a selection from Crewdson Hybrids in the first instance. Clearly, if this is a

† Sometimes regarded as a form of *M. × sheldonii*. It should not be confused with *M. grandis* 'Branklyn' (see p. 178).

M. integrifolia × *M.* × *sheldonii* cross, the epithet *hybrida* would not be inappropriate, but this superposition has also yet to be substantiated. Whatever the name turns out to be, these are all very attractive and excellent garden plants, when given the moist, humusy soil that they thrive in.

'Aberchalder Form'. A rare cultivar with rounded, rather pale blue flowers.

Kingsbarn Hybrids. Fine plants of the *M.* × *sheldonii* persuasion, raised from a rare fertile plant of the latter. They are vigorous hybrids, which lend themselves to vegetative propagation. The flowers vary quite a lot in colour, from mid to deep blues and lavender. I have not seen any plants under this name and they do not appear to be available at the present time. In any case, they must be fairly close to 'Lingholm', which has certainly superseded all other cultivars, perhaps with the exception of 'Slieve Donard'. Kingsbarn Hybrids probably arose as a result of a backcross between *M.* × *sheldonii* and either *M. betonicifolia* or *M. grandis* to produce highly fertile offspring.

'Miss Dickson'. This white-flowered cultivar is a rare and lovely plant, often listed under *M.* × *sheldonii*, but it is likely that it is simply a white form of *M. grandis*. Albino forms of *M. grandis* do turn up in cultivation from time to time, but they are difficult to maintain for long. Unfortunately, plants sold as *M. grandis* 'Alba' generally turn out to be *M. betonicifolia* var. *alba*, which is nice but scarcely as exciting as a white *grandis*. Attempts to produce a white *M.* × *sheldonii* by crossing *M. betonicifolia* 'Alba' with *M. grandis*, undertaken by James Cobb and others, have so far failed. One might expect a certain number of white-flowered plants to turn up in second-generation seedlings if seed can somehow be procured from the first.

'Ormswell'. A cultivar of *M.* × *sheldonii* from a cross made by Alec Curle of Edinburgh, plants of which were subsequently given to Edrom Nursery, where they were named 'Ormswell'. This cultivar, which is rarely available, looks very similar to the original raising of *M.* × *sheldonii*.

'Slieve Donard'. This fine and exciting plant originated in Scotland, but found its way to the Slieve Donard Nursery in County Down, Northern Ireland, where it was named and from where it was widely distributed. It was initially called *M. grandis* 'Prain's Variety', an invalid name later changed to 'Slieve Donard'. This robust, clump-forming perennial, makes large tufts of ascending elliptical leaves that are quite pointed. The large, well-formed flowers are a delightful clear blue and are held well above the foliage, opening to a broad saucer shape and projecting slightly downwards from the vertical.

'Lingholm' (syn. 'Blue Ice', 'Correnie'). This is a fully fertile form of *M.* × *sheldonii* that turned up in the 1970s. It arose as a fertile pod set on a plant of *M.* × *sheldonii* that was noted by Mike Smith, the head gardener at Lingholm in the Lake District. It has since proved to be very popular. 'Lingholm' has proved to be an allopolyploid; the doubling of the chromosomes no doubt explains the sudden fertility characteristic of this cultivar, but is rare in *M.* × *sheldonii* as a whole. Unfortunately, the plant has already acquired several

names, apart from being distributed by several nurseries as simple *M.* ×
sheldonii. The fact that several forms exist in cultivation is hardly surprising, as
seedlings of 'Lingholm', which are now being raised by a number of growers,
produce quite a bit of variation. It is quite easy to see how the identity of even
a new cultivar can be lost simply by being diluted by its own offspring. The
true plant, as first seen, is remarkable for its large, rich blue flowers which,
when flattened, can measure as much as 15 cm (6 in) in diameter. The leaves
tend to lean to one side as they grow, which is a useful diagnostic character
and on occasion they can be Y-shaped, perhaps a result of the fusion of two
blades for part of their length. Most fertile manifestations of *M.* × *sheldonii* turn
out to be 'Lingholm'. However, as the offspring is variable, there is every
danger that unscrupulous growers will apply a plethora of new names to
different forms. The answer surely is to call the whole lot Lingholm Group
and then to pick out the very best and give them cultivar names. Clearly, only
those that can be adequately propagated (vegetatively or from seed) should be
named. There is absolutely no point in applying a new cultivar name to a
plant, however beautiful, that cannot be readily propagated. Indeed, it is a
complete waste of time if seed-raised progeny is very variable, for that will
cause only doubt and confusion in the long run. After all, if gardeners buy a
plant under a particular name, they want to ensure that is what they are
getting, not a plant that 'only somewhat resembles' it.

Other hybrids include:

M. × *auriculata* (*M. aculeata* × *M. betonicifolia*) – not in cultivation today.
M. × *coxiana* (*M. betonicifolia* × *M. violacea*) – not in cultivation today.
M. × *musgravei* (*M. betonicifolia* × *M. superba*) – apparently fertile, but not in
cultivation today. It would be a very fine plant!
M. × *sarsonii* (*M. betonicifolia* × *M. integrifolia*). A fine, fertile hybrid which can
be properly perennial or monocarpic. Plants bear glorious clear sulphur-
yellow flowers in the best forms. The character of the plant and leaves most
closely resembles *M. betonicifolia* and it can be propagated in a similar way.
The similar-looking *M.* × *beamishii* (*M. betonicifolia* × *M. grandis*) can be
distinguished by its tapered leaf-bases and generally five to eight (not four)
petals per flower.

   Interestingly, poppy hybrids involving blue and yellow parents invariably
give offspring that have cream flowers. For example, *M.* × *finlayorum*
(*M. integrifolia* (yellow) × *M. quintuplinervia* (lavender-blue)) bears ivory-
coloured offspring, while *M.* × *beamishii* (*M. integrifolia* (yellow) × *M. grandis*
(blue)) has cream-coloured flowers.

Meconopsis cambrica (L.) Vig.   **[Pl. 118–119]**
(Syn. *Papaver cambricum* L.; *P. luteum* Lam.; *Argemone cambrica* (L.) Desportes;
Cerastites cambrica (L.) Gray; *Stylophorum cambricum* (L.) Spreng.)
WELSH POPPY

This widely grown, easy and readily available species is familiar in many gardens, where it is often dismissed as weedy and unruly. However, to my mind, it is a real charmer, easy and free-flowering, with a good deal of elegance and poise. If it does seed around rather too freely, does this matter from a plant that is so willing to put on a show from spring until the first frosts of autumn? A shady path lined with Welsh poppies or a woodland glade where the flowers glow amongst the dappled shade is a sight worth seeing in any garden.

Plants are fully perennial, forming lax basal tufts of rather pale green leaves. These are up to 20 cm (8 in) long and variously divided into a number of lobed divisions, hairless or somewhat hairy. The flowering stems are branched and carry several leaves in the lower part, the flowers carried aloft on slender stalks up to 60 cm (24 in) tall, often less. The flowers are yellow in the ordinary form, 5–6.5 cm (2–2⅗ in) across and more or less erect, each with four broad petals. The narrow-oval fruit capsule has a distinctive short style, is completely smooth and opens by four to seven valves in the upper quarter.

M. cambrica is a native of western Europe, inhabiting damp and shaded rocky, wooded and grassy places in western Ireland, Wales, south-west England, western France and north-west Spain. It usually grows below an altitude of 600 m (2000 ft) and is widely naturalised in other parts of these regions.

The Welsh poppy has been cultivated for many centuries and the wood engraving in Parkinson (1640), under the name *Argemone Cambro-Britanica lutea,* is the earliest known drawing of the species.

M. cambrica holds an isolated position in the genus, both geographically and taxonomically (see p. 149).

The Welsh Poppy is a sheer delight in the garden and I would not be without it. Few perennial poppies are easier to cultivate and so productive of flower. From late spring until the frosts of autumn, it produces its blooms in glorious succession, uninhibited by the weather, only pausing to flower during long hot dry summer periods. Once the first crop of bloom has passed, then the whole plant can be sheered off; it will soon burst into growth once more and repeat its floral display.

Yes, I know it can be a weed in some gardens, seeding around with profusion, but its success as a garden plant cannot be denied. It is such a shame that this gem is relegated in some books to the wild garden, being described as a wildling (whatever that is supposed to mean), as if it does not deserve a place in the 'real garden' amongst supposedly choicer plants. Of course, if this were a rare plant from distant China, it would be described as a novelty and everyone would be after it and it would soon be endangered in the wild. As it is, there are few British native plants that are so good and colourful in our gardens, except perhaps for the primrose and the bluebell (both also prolific seeders!).

Apart from *Papaver atlanticum,* I do not know of another poppy that has such a long flowering season.

The species gets both its scientific and common names after Cambria or Wales, although the plant is not specific to Wales in the British Isles, for it is also found in the south-west of England. In addition, it has become naturalised in various places, especially in the Lake District.

These species present little problems in cultivation. Seed and plants are readily available. As they come so easily from seed, there is no need to resort to vegetative propagation, unless to preserve a particularly fine form. They include:

var. *aurantiaca* – a form with orange flowers. **[Pl. 120]**
'Flore Pleno Aurantiaca' – the orange counterpart of 'Flore Pleno'.
'Flore Pleno' – a form with semi-double yellow flowers.
'Frances Perry' – an unusual single-flowered variant with deep orange-crimson flowers which, for some reason, is seldom seen in gardens.
'Muriel Brown' - semi-double red flowers.
'Rubra' – this almost certainly equates with 'Francis Perry'.

In my own garden I grow all the cultivars. Hybrids between the double or semi-double 'Aurantiaca' and the single orange-crimson 'Francis Perry' have produced an exciting range of plants, including those with semi-double orange, semi-double yellow and semi-double crimson flowers, some with pale whitish streaks on the narrower inner petals, as well as the same range of colours in single flowers. The 'double' types vary from those with a rather loose petal arrangement to those more akin to a pompon flower. The 'double types' (especially the reds) tend to produce rather smaller plants. In fact, fully double-flowered forms do not exist in my experience and all, however double, bear some fertile stamens in the centre of the flower.

All these different forms will self-sow readily in gardens, especially in moist shaded areas. In dry gardens they can be more difficult to establish initially. It is wise to keep them away from rock and scree gardens to prevent them becoming a problem from seeding around.

Meconopsis chelidonifolia Bur. & Franch.

This is one of the more modest species in the genus, but one that has a quiet charm all of its own. It has been likened, as its name infers, to the Greater Celandine, *Chelidonium majus*, and although larger in all its parts, it does bear a superficial resemblance to that species.

M. chelidonifolia is a perennial with a branching root-system and perennating by means of lateral buds that slowly form a spreading mat. The leaves, which are rather pale green, are pinnately cut into a number of broad, lobed segments, bristly on both surfaces; the upper leaves tend to be trifoliate or trilobed, whilst the basal have generally withered by flowering time. The slender branched stems rise to 90 cm (36 in), sometimes more, and are erect and arched, with the flowers borne on very slender stalks from the upper leaf-axils. The flowers are clear yellow, rather small, 2.5–3.5 cm (1–1⅖ in) across, and generally half-nodding. There are four rounded, somewhat overlapping petals. The fruit-capsule is elliptical in outline, smooth or somewhat bristly, and splitting by five or six valves close to the apex.

This dainty species inhabits mountain thickets in western Sichuan at an altitude of 1875–2800 m (6150–9200 ft).

It was first collected by Faber on Mt. Omei (Emei Shan) in 1887, though it was not described until 1891. Seed was introduced to Britain by Ernest Henry Wilson, who probably collected it close to Tatsien-lu (now Kangding), an area of great interest to plant collectors in the earlier part of the twentieth century.

M. chelidonifolia (often misspelled '*chelonidifolia*') has never been very popular in cultivation. Admittedly, it has none of the brashness of some of its cousins, but, at the same time, this is a species with a delicate charm and its little dancing flowers enliven a woodland setting. Indeed, this is a species for the woodland glade, in a damp, humusy pocket. It has few demands, although is best if the slender stems are allowed to grow through the branches of low shrubs, otherwise they tend, in my experience, to fall over.

Vegetative buds are produced at the upper leaf-axils, a feature this species shares in common only with one other − *M. lyrata*. These can be detached and can be easily grown on to produce new plants. Division of the parent plant in early spring is another means of increase, but seed is rarely produced in cultivation and plants are considered to be self-sterile.

Meconopsis delavayi (Franch.) Franch. ex Prain　　　**[Pl. 122–124]**
(Syn. *Cathcartia delavayi* Franch.)

In a genus of big and bold species with flamboyant blooms, it is pleasant to be able to observe some of the smaller, but equally attractive, members. *M. delavayi* certainly fits into this latter category. The species is a perennial, with a rootstock that is branched above, each short branch terminating in a small leaf-cluster that dies away during the winter months to leave a resting bud. The leaves are bluish-green, quite thick, elliptical or diamond-shaped, untoothed and abruptly narrowed below into a short stalk, not more than 15 cm (6 in) in length overall, generally less, with scattered bristles on both surfaces. The solitary flowers are a deep violet-purple and nod on leafless scapes up to 25 cm (10 in) tall. There are generally four somewhat over-lapping petals, oval to rounded, making the flower 4–6 cm (1⅗–2⅖ in) across when fully opened; anthers orange, hidden beneath the 'umbrella' of petals. The fruit-capsule is narrow, oblong, smooth, and opens at the apex by three to five short valves.

M. delavayi has a very limited distribution in the wild, being restricted to north-western Yunnan, primarily to the eastern-flanks of the limestone Lijiang (Lichiang) mountains, at altitudes between 3100 and 4375 m (10,200–14,350 ft). In this region it inhabits mainly sloping wet meadows, but can also sometimes be found on damp limestone screes.

This little gem of a species was first discovered in 1884 by Père Delavay, who did most of the early collecting, and made many new discoveries, in the Lijiang mountains of north-western Yunnan. Delavay collected little live material and it was left to George Forrest a few years later collecting on behalf of the Royal Botanic Garden, Edinburgh. However, *M. delavayi* has never proved easy in cultivation and has always been very rare. Yet one person, R.D. Trotter of Brin House, Inverness, a fine and skilled plantsman, mastered its cultivation at one time, discovering that broken pieces of root inserted upright in a sand bed will eventually produce both roots and shoots. This is best undertaken in spring using a propagator or, at least, a little bottom heat. Despite this discovery, this much cherished species has remained relatively rare in cultivation.

M. delavayi is undoubtedly one of the true alpine gems in the genus. Today there is more live material in circulation than previously, due to importations of seed from the wild in the past twenty years. It has been found that plants do particularly well in a trough filled with plenty of gritty compost and lots of rock fragments. The taproots can also be sandwiched between two slanting rocks. Ian and Margaret Young grow this plant to perfection in their Aberdeen garden, the plants thriving in the Scottish climate. Their secret is to sow the seed in early January and not to prick it out until the second year, when the young plants will have produced a firm taproot. As growth commences in the second year, the plants are then separated out and potted on or placed directly outdoors; they grow theirs in shaded troughs containing a coarse gritty compost. Plants will generally flower in their third year and will carry on happily for six years or more. The Youngs' plants come from several different collections. No doubt, the cross-fertilisation between the different collections helps to keep the vigour in the stock. Plants can be rather taller in cultivation than in the wild, with the fruiting stems as much as 37 cm (15 in) tall. Some cultivated plants reveal a little toothing in the middle part of the leaf-blade, although this has never been noted in the wild.

M. delavayi is a dainty delight to see in the wild; it created a feeling of great excitement when I travelled in the Lijiang region, an area so remote in the days of Delavay and Forrest, but now reasonably accessible. In the company of two fine plantsmen, Tony Schilling and Ron McBeath, I climbed over these mountain slopes for several weeks in the spring of 1987. High above the Lijiang Valley are steep, almost inaccessible mountain slopes covered with fir and rhododendron that give way in places on the eastern flanks to steep grassy meadows interspersed by scree. These meadows are full of treasures: corydalis, lilies, globe-flowers and primulas. Amongst all the joys we found scattered colonies of *M. delavayi*. Many plants bore one or two flowers, though up to eight were counted. The colour ranges from pale violet-blue to violet-purple, the flowers nodding harebell-like or with the petals spreading widely apart to reveal the stamens beneath. The joy and excitement of seeing such a splendid little beauty so perfect in the wild can never be matched in cultivation. Long may it thrive on those distant slopes.

Meconopsis dhwojii G. Taylor

An attractive monocarpic species with an evergreen rosette of long-stalked, pinnately-lobed leaves. The leaves, up to 30 cm (12 in) long, have rather distant lobes and are covered in bristles that have a distinctive purplish-black base; the upper stem leaves are similar, but smaller and short-stalked. The flowering stem, which can reach 1 m (3 ft) tall, is erect and branched in the upper two thirds, the lower branches bearing several flowers, but the uppermost with a solitary bloom. The flowers are a soft pale yellow and cupped, often half-nodding and 4–5 cm (1½ in) across, with four rounded petals. The anthers are orange-yellow and the stigma greenish or yellowish. The fruit-capsule is more or less elliptical in outline, covered in dense spreading bristles and splitting by five or six valves just below the styled apex.

M. *dhwojii* was discovered in eastern Nepal by Lall Dhwoj, an officer in the Royal Nepal Army. It is recorded to grow at altitudes of 3850–5625 m (12,600–18,450 ft), although the upper altitudinal limits seem far too high to me for this type of species.

In cultivation *M. dhwojii* first flowered in 1932 and it has been in cultivation ever since. Plants are particularly pleasing in flower, with both some lower and upper flowers opening simultaneously. The evergreen leaf-rosettes are very distinctive and are unlikely to be confused with any other species; they generally come into bloom in their second or third seasons from seed.

There seems to be no great difficulty with this species in cultivation. It comes readily from seed and grows away quite quickly if pricked out at an early stage and kept well fed and watered. Like its brethren, it thrives in a rich humusy soil and has thrived with me on several occasions in a peat border, although in my Suffolk garden I cannot boast those more robust and splendid specimens one sees in northern gardens. However, it does seem to over-winter with ease and comes into flower in early summer, apparently unhindered by late spring frosts. *M. dhwojii* finds its closest ally in *M. gracilipes*, which is restricted to an area of central Nepal to the west. It differs primarily in the coarser, less finely cut, foliage without purple blotches at the base of the spines. However, despite this, the two species are very closely related and further research may show them to be extremes of the same species. Both species hybridise in gardens with *M. napaulensis*.

M. × *ramsdeniorum* (*M. dhwojii* × *M. nepaulensis*) is a poor thing, with yellow or pink flowers of little merit, and fortunately sterile. Why such hybrids are continuously named is a mystery to me; let us leave well alone and name only the very best and those proven in gardens. Many such hybrids disappear as quickly as they first appeared. To avoid such horrors in the garden, the answer is not to grow species close together that hybridise freely. One can always grow a few plants in isolation simply to produce pure seed and then the species will not be threatened by hybrid progeny.

M. *dhwojii* is a fine species and worth a place in any garden. Being undoubtedly easier and hardier than some, it well deserves a wider following.

Meconopsis discigera Prain

This species is at once distinguished from all other species of *Meconopsis* in cultivation by the disk-like process surmounting the ovary and fruit-capsules. It is a rather slow-growing monocarpic perennial with a long thickened taproot and a dense basal rosette of leaves, the lower of which gradually wither but persist so that the live rosette sits on top of a felted mat of dried leaves; each leaf is up to 18 cm (7 in) long, oblong to wedge-shaped, often with a three-lobed apex, although sometimes entire, the surface, particularly the petiole and midrib, densely covered in golden bristles. The bracts are similar to the leaves, but smaller and usually entire. The rather stout flowering stem rises to about 40 cm (16 in), occasionally taller, and is both grooved and bristly and carries up to 20 flowers in a narrow raceme. The flowers vary considerably in colour, including yellow, pale to mid-blue, purple, crimson, red and whitish, each 6–8 cm (2⅖–3 in) across, and with their short stalks running down the stem (decurrent) in a distinctive manner; petals four; stamens with rather dark filaments and yellow anthers. The fruit-capsule, 3–4 cm (1⅕–1⅗ in) long, is oblong, ribbed and bristly and with a distinctive lobed stylar disk at the apex; this disk overlaps the top of the ovary and has a toothed margin; when ripe, the capsule splits just below the stylar disk by 6–10 short valves.

M. discigera is a native of the high Himalayas from central Nepal to southern Tibet (Xizang), Sikkim and Bhutan, being a plant of rocky places, cliffs, screes and moraines at an altitude of between 3500 and 4100 m (11,500–13,450 ft); flowering from June to August. *M. discigera* holds a rather isolated position within the genus. The only other species with a disk-like process on top of the ovary is the little known *M. torquata*, which comes from an area of Tibet close to Lhasa. It differs primarily by its narrower leaves, in the petals being hairy on the outer surface and in the absence of a style.

M. discigera cannot be regarded as being in any way easy in cultivation. Over the years seed has been introduced on many occasions, although few have succeeded in flowering well and many plants fail even to get to the flowering stage. The handsome leaf-rosette gradually increases in size (a mature rosette may be 20 cm (8 in) across). As the lower leaves die, they persist, so that after several years they form a dense mat at the base of the plant, a very characteristic feature of the plant in the wild. I have seen it on several occasions in the Nepalese Himalayas and it always seems to inhabit

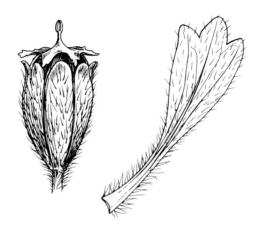

Leaf and fruit capsule of *Meconopsis discigera*

the bleakest and most inhospitable places where most *Meconopsis* would never dream of growing. This is almost certainly why it is so difficult to grow. Such plants are like a magnet to growers and as long as seed is available, there will be those who will want to attempt to raise them. The successful cultivation of such species is not just to rear them from seed to flowering, but to maintain them in cultivation thereafter. Monocarpic species such as *M. discigera* provide a special challenge, for unless viable seed is set all is lost.

In the autumn the rosette dies back to a large resting bud and in cultivation this is very prone to rotting during the winter. It is clear that plants must be protected from excessive moisture in the autumn and winter, but, at the same time, allowed plenty of moisture during the growing season. A very well-drained soil is an absolutely essential ingredient. After all, the species is basically a plant of high screes and moraines. However, getting the conditions just right in cultivation is a tricky balancing act that will test the most skilled of growers.

Meconopsis florindae Kingdon-Ward

A rare and little known species allied to *M. lyrata* and known only from a single locality in south-eastern Tibet (Tra La), where it was discovered in 1924 by Frank Kingdon-Ward. It is a woodland species with distinguishing pale yellow flowers, found at an altitude of 3350–3960 m (11,000–13,000 ft).

Apart from the obvious difference in flower colour, *M. florindae* has more numerous stamens than *M. lyrata*, shorter and broader fruit capsules and a yellow rather than green stigma. The former usually has 5–7-petalled flowers about 3 cm (1⅕ in) across, while in the latter 4 is more the norm and the flowers are somewhat larger.

In both species the flowers are semi-pendulous, up to 6 being borne from the axils of the upper stems leaves (bracts). This would undoubtedly be an interesting species to cultivate, if seed can ever be obtained.

Meconopsis forrestii Prain

Another species related to *M. horridula*. It can be easily identified by its racemose inflorescence (never with accompanying basal scapes) and the pale blue flowers concentrated on the upper half of the stem. In addition, the fruit-capsules are narrower, almost cylindrical and with scarcely any style. The flowers are rather small, being rarely more than 4 cm (1⅗ in) across. The long narrow fruits are perhaps the most useful diagnostic feature of this species.

M. forrestii has been introduced into cultivation on a number of occasions. Seed was certainly collected by Forrest, Rock and more recently by the Sino-British Lijiang Expedition (SBLE). Plants are said to inhabit alpine meadowland, but in the only situation that I have seen it in the wild (in the Lijiang Mountains of north-western Yunnan) it inhabited a coarse, rather moist scree. The altitudinal range of the species is 3050–4400 m (10,000–14,400 ft). Besides north-western Yunnan, *M. forrestii* also occurs in south-western Sichuan.

Early introductions failed to produce flowering plants and it is to be hoped that more recent seed collections will prove more successful.

Unfortunately, quite a few of the seed collections made recently in the wild have proved to be misidentified and I still wait with eager anticipation to see the genuine plant in cultivation.

The original collections were made by George Forrest in 1914 and although the seed germinated well, no plants reached maturity. It was subsequently collected by Schneider, Handel-Mazzetti and Joseph Rock in the vicinity of Lijiang.

Meconopsis georgei G. Tayl.

This relatively little known species was discovered during the final expedition of George Forrest in 1931. The plant was named in his honour by George Taylor (it is commonly thought to commemorate the latter, but this is not so!). Subsequently, following Forrest's death near Tengueh in Yunnan, several of his native collectors collected specimens and sent them to Britain. Joseph Rock also collected it in the wild. The species is confined to north-western Yunnan in the vicinity of the Mekong-Yangtse Divide (Forrest found it in the Fu-chuan Shan) at an altitude of 3660–4420 m (12,000–14,500 ft.). Although seed was sent home by Forrest's native collectors, the species does not appear to have succeeded in cultivation.

M. georgei is a monocarpic tap-rooted species up to 32.5 cm (13 in) tall in flower. The leaves are aggregated towards the base of the plant and are oblong, narrowed gradually below into slender stalk, with an entire or somewhat wavy margin, glabrous or with a scattering of sharp bristles on both surfaces, green above but glaucous beneath. Up to 10 yellow flowers are borne in an inflorescence, with the lowermost flowers arising from the axils of the uppermost leaves, while the upper flowers are bractless. The sharply-bristly flower stalks (pedicels) are long, those of the lowermost flowers being up to 20 cm (8 in) in length. The flowers are 6–7.5 cm (2⅖–3 in) across and bear 5–8 rather rounded petals; stamens numerous with orange-yellow anthers, browning on ageing. The narrow-oblong fruit capsules are covered in sharp spreading bristles and spit close to the top into 3–5 valves.

This interesting species is closely linked to *M. horridula* and its allies, being immediately distinguished from them by its distinctive yellow flowers.

Meconopsis gracilipes G. Tayl.

This pretty monocarpic species is closely related to *M. dhwojii* (see under that species for general remarks). The beautiful yellow, half-nodding, cup-shaped flowers are perfectly formed. A rare plant in cultivation, flowering in three to four years from seed usually. *M. gracilipes* is endemic to the Khorlak region of central Nepal.

Meconopsis grandis Prain   **[Pl. 125–127]**

A stout, tufted perennial rising up to 60 cm (24 in) in flower, occasionally more; stems stiff and erect, usually bristly. The leaves vary from lanceolate to elliptical or oblong and are irregularly toothed along the margin, sometimes rather obscurely so, with the base of the leaf-blade tapering into the petiole; the upper leaves are unstalked, generally smaller, but more coarsely toothed; all leaves covered by scattered rusty-coloured bristles, the upper three to five leaves aggregated into a whorl where the flower stalks arise. Flowers rich blue, purple or wine-purple or occasionally pinkish-purple, 8–12 cm (3–5 in) across, borne on slender, bristly stalks 12–15 cm (5–6 in) long, but elongating to twice or three times that length in fruit, mostly borne on the upper half of the plant, but occasionally solitary from a basal scape. The almost rounded to broadly oval petals are commonly four in number, occasionally more, and form a wide cup-shape, the individual petals scarcely frilled. The yellow anthers are borne on the ends of whitish filaments. The narrow-oblong capsule may be smooth or somewhat bristly and dehisces by four to six valves in the upper quarter.

All the eulogies poured on to *M. betonicifolia* could well be used on *M. grandis*. In many ways this is the blue poppy *par excellence*. The intense blues of the finest forms, the substance and poise of the cupped flowers and the perennial nature of this stunning plant are enough to assure it a place in our gardens. That it is not so often seen in our gardens is perhaps due to frequent confusion in the trade with *M. betonicifolia* and the fact that the best forms seldom set seed in cultivation. This apart though, *M. grandis* is fairly easy to propagate from side shoots or careful divisions. If the resultant plants are a little costly to purchase, does it matter for such a superb poppy?

M. grandis was first discovered in the Jongri district of Sikkim in the eastern Himalayas in the 1880s. Since then its distribution has been extended to cover Nepal, east of Mt. Everest, and parts of south-eastern Tibet (Xizang), as well as Bhutan. In these regions it is a plant of open woodland, alpine thickets, rocky stream margins and yak pastures at altitudes of 3120–5300 m (10,200–17,400 ft).

Its introduction into cultivation is generally attributed to David Prain and it first flowered at the Edinburgh Botanic Garden in 1895. Since then *M. grandis* has been re-collected in the wild on a number of occasions; notably by Ludlow and Sherriff in Bhutan and south-eastern Tibet and by various collectors, in more recent times, in eastern Nepal. I have seen it on several occasions in Nepal at altitude and nearly always close to, or in association with, yak pasturage, where it can form substantial colonies.

M. grandis is quite variable in the wild. In Nepal, for instance, the fruit-capsules can be longer, narrower and often smooth, whereas elsewhere they are shorter and often bristly. Flower colour also varies from the eastern forms, which appear to be the best blues, to those in the west, particularly Nepal, which can be a less pleasing and decidedly inferior wine-purple.

This species is closely allied to *M. betonicifolia* and the differences between these two species is outlined on p. 162. Like *M. betonicifolia*, plants die down

Flower, leaf and fruit of *Meconopsis grandis* **(left) and** *M. betonicifolia* **(right)**

in the late autumn, leaving withered leaves on the soil surface. The thick leaf buds that arise in the spring vary from pale green to purple and are densely beset with pale straw- or rust-coloured hairs. The blueness of the flowers is quite breathtaking in the finest forms, but, as with other blue poppies, the precise colour can be greatly affected by soil alkalinity, even when all other conditions suit the plants. More alkalinity turns the best blues more pinkish or purple; the more acid the soil, the better the blue.

Plants thrive best in good rich, moist, humusy soil and are unable to tolerate too much dry hot weather. Even so, I have always managed to grow one or two forms in my dry Suffolk garden in a carefully prepared bed, though they do not increase as vigorously as in other more favoured northern gardens. Nonetheless, I have managed to propagate several plants simply by shaving off side shoots with a sharp kitchen knife without having to resort to disturbing the parent plant; with care, such shoots will come away with some root attached and if carefully nurtured in a shaded frame will quickly become established.

Plants are very hardy and there is no need for winter protection, except possibly in early spring, when severe frost may threaten the newly emerged shoots.

As with *M. betonicifolia*, weak seedlings may throw all their effort into flowering in the second season and die quickly afterwards. Removal of the flowering stem (often a single-flowered scape in small plants) may sometimes force the plant into producing several side shoots for future years, but this is a bit of a gamble and does not always work, unfortunately.

It is wise to check named forms with some care, as they are sometimes not what they purport to be. In any case, if plants are raised from seed (some forms set some seed!), they are unlikely to be exactly like their parents. Divisions of the finest forms is therefore the best means of assuring a succession of good plants. Some seedlings may well prove to be hybrids with *M. betonicifolia*, *M. × sheldonii* (p. 163).

Cultivars include:

'Alba': a fine white form, but rare in cultivation and generally difficult to acquire.

'Betty Sherriff's Dream Poppy': one of the very best forms of *M. grandis*, with deep blue, half-nodding flowers borne on strong elegant, dark stems. The discovery of this plant is well worth relating. It concerns the wife of George Sherriff (of Ludlow and Sherriff fame). I can do no better than quote from the account in the book *A Quest of Flowers* (1975) by Harold R. Fletcher, a former Reguis Keeper of the Royal Botanic Garden, Edinburgh: 'Their collecting at Shurigbe (in Bhutan) began auspiciously – and in somewhat surprising circumstances. During the night of 25 May, Betty Sherriff dreamt that her husband walked into her tent, stood beside her campbed and gave her instructions for collecting on the following day. She was to seek out below the camp a small track leading to the Me La; to follow the track for about three miles until it bifurcated; to take the right hand fork and walk some 300 yards to a large rock mass. On the far side of the rock she would see a poppy she hadn't found before. As Sherriff left the tent he turned, shook a finger at her and said: "Be sure you go." The next morning at their usual time 5.00 a.m. breakfast, when she told Hicks and Tsongpen the substance of her dream, they were both sceptical and urged her to keep to their original plant . . . But the dream and the shaking finger had been so vivid and the instructions so clear and positive, that she determined to leave the rest of the party to seek her dream poppy. She had no problems; she found the track easily; she found the mass of rock easily and behind it she found a glorious blue meconopsis which she hadn't collected before, a form of *Meconopsis grandis*. Hicks at first unbelieving, returned to the spot the next day and took several photographs'.

In the autumn Hicks in fact returned to collect seed. In cultivation this gem became known in Scottish gardens as 'Betty's Dream Poppy'.

'Branklyn': originally a selection made from GS600, with exceptionally large, good blue flowers. It is doubtful whether plants now under this name are the same as those originally selected at Branklyn Gardens by Perth, Scotland. Distinct from *M. betonicifolia* 'Branklyn' (see p. 163).

GS600: [Pl. 128] a selection from a collection of George Sherriff, this is a fine blue poppy of exceptional quality that was certainly in circulation in the 1950s and 1960s. However, plants doing the rounds under that number today are fine plants, but they are sterile and they should not be regarded as GS600, which in reality has probably been lost to cultivation. The imposter is almost certainly of hybrid origin, having arisen as a cross between GS600 and another blue poppy (possibly *M. betonicifolia* or one of the manifestations of *M.* × *sheldonii*).

'Keillour Crimson': plants originally from a Nepalese collection, with dark purple flowers, scarcely the eye-catcher of the blue forms. Rarely available.

'Miss Jebbs': a dwarf variant with deep blue flowers. Occasionally available.

'Nepal Form': vigorous plants with bluish-purple flowers. Occasionally sets seed, but plants are generally available in the trade.

'Prain's Form': (sometimes called 'Keillour Crimson') deep purple flowers.

'Sikkim Form': a rather unsatisfactory form with pale leaves and rather small purplish-blue flowers. It has one advantage in being early in flower.

Meconopsis henrici Bur. & Franch.   [Pl. 129]

This is a very charming and striking monocarpic species recently brought back into cultivation and now of limited availability. Seed had been introduced by Ernest Henry Wilson in 1904 from Sichuan, but, although plants flowered two years later, the plant was soon lost to cultivation. A later Kingdon-Ward introduction of 1921 also failed to establish in cultivation.

Plants form a stout taproot that supports a lax basal tuft (scarcely a rosette) of oblong to spatular-shaped, bristly leaves that gradually taper to a narrow stalk. The leaves generally have an untoothed margin, although forms with a sinuate or distantly toothed margin are known. Both leaves and stems are covered in reddish-brown bristles. The flowers, 7.5–10 cm (3–4 in) across, are borne singly on thick erect basal scapes up to 20 cm (8 in) long, though generally less, and face sideways, the deep violet-purple petals spreading widely apart to reveal a mass of yellow or orange anthers. A diagnostic feature of the stamens is the filaments which are characteristically dilated in the basal half. The fruit capsule is oblong-elliptical in outline and sparsely bristly at maturity, splitting by 4–6 short valves at the apex.

M. henrici is distributed from south-eastern Qinghai and south-western Gansu south through much of western Sichuan, where it inhabits rocky alpine meadows and slopes at 3350–4570 m (11,000–15,000 ft), where it flowers normally in June and July.

The species was first discovered by Bonvalot and Prince Henri d'Orleans (in whose honour the species is named) near Tatsien-lu (now Kangding) in western Sichuan in the late nineteenth century. Two varieties are usually recognised. In the typical plant, **var. *henrici*** (Syn. var. *genuina* G. Taylor) plants produce up to 11 flowers in succession from the basal leaf tufts. On occasions the flowers are borne on scapes from a simple non-bracted central stem, but this condition is rare. This is the plant found throughout western Sichuan.

var. *psilonomma* (Farrer) G. Taylor (Syn. *Meconopsis psilonomma* Farrer) plants produce a single scape and one extra large flower. This is the typical form found to the north of the species range in south-eastern Qinghai, south-western Gansu and the neighbouring regions of northern Sichuan, at rather similar altitudes.

This variety is a striking feature of the high sloping meadows above Huang-long-si in northern Sichuan, where I saw it in 1993. With its large, solitary flowers, it is one of the most imposing high-altitude alpines of the area, growing in association with other highly garden-worthy plants such as *Incarvillea compacta*, *Astragalus yunnanense* and *Androsace tapete*. On the same slopes the Yellow Poppywort, *Meconopsis integrifolia* and *M. quintuplinervia*, were also in bloom, while *M. horridula* was still in young bud. Not more than two kilometres away, large colonies of the extraordinary *M. punicea,* with its pendent scarlet flowers, were seen.

Seed was introduced by E.H. Wilson in 1906 and later by both Reginald Farrer and Frank Kingdon-Ward. However, although flowering plants resulted, the species failed to persist in cultivation. Reginald Farrer introduced seed of var. *psiolonomma* that had been collected in the Min Shan by his Chinese servants. However, it was later reported that it had 'failed miserably in cultivation'. *Meconopsis henrici* has been re-introduced into cultivation on several occasions in recent years and a number of plants have reached flowering. However, it seems a poor shadow of its wild glory in cultivation and seems unwilling to persist for long. This is a pity, for it is a super little plant. Perhaps the best chance of growing it is in a pot in the confines of a well-ventilated alpine house or in a trough in the garden, where it can be safely guarded against marauding slugs and the worst of winter wet. The more recent collections perhaps hold out greater hope, provided that growers are able to persuade plants to set seed regularly.

Meconopsis horridula Hook. F. & Th.   **[Pl. 130–131]**
(Syn. *M. horridula* var. *typica* Prain, *M. racemosa* var. *horridula* sensu Farrer)
PRICKLY BLUE POPPY

This is undoubtedly one of the true gems of the genus. It is a constant surprise to me that a plant which is so prickly in leaf and stem can be so exquisite in flower. The cupped flowers bear semi-transparent petals of pale to deepest blue, sometimes flushed with lilac or red, like the finest stained glass, but a transient beauty to cherish and to admire. I have seen *M. horridula* on many occasions in the Nepalese Himalaya, where it is widespread and relatively common at high altitudes, well above the tree line and in those uncertain bleak regions of rock and snow where the summers are short and the winters intensely cold. In its finest forms the flowers are a clear blue and nod or half-nod like little umbrellas to shield the centre of the flower from the rain, for this is a plant of the monsoon summers.

I have been struck by the differences which are clearly observable in the Nepalese plant and those seen in various parts of western China during recent years. It is difficult to equate the tall spikes of the meconopsis seen around Zhongdian (in north-western Yunnan), at relatively low altitudes, with those squat high-altitude plants of the Nepal Himal. Even the high altitude forms of *M. horridula* seen in parts of western China look different and cannot be easily equated with those found much further to the west.

In his 1934 monograph George Taylor discusses at length the polymorphic character of *M. horridula* and concludes that these differences cannot be separated out: 'It is in the disposition of the flowers that the most evident variation is displayed. These can be borne on basal scapes or on a central flowering axis which is bracteate towards the base and ebracteate towards the apex, but all transitions are found between these extremes . . . Marked differences are also shown in the number and colour of the petals, in the texture of the leaves and colour of their spines, and also in the shape, pubescence, and dehiscence of the capsule.'

However, plants do not 'act' in the same way in the wild. Besides the fact that some are clearly low-altitude plants, differences can be found in the general habit and morphology of plants from one region to another. This is, to some extent, borne out by plants in cultivation. The typical plant from the high Himalaya has proved fiendishly difficult to grow and maintain in cultivation, even with the aid of a protective alpine house. In contrast, the far taller, more leafy, lower altitude plants from south-western China are very easy in cultivation and will succeed readily in the open garden without any protection whatsoever, even seeding themselves around profusely in

Fruit capsules of *Meconopsis horridula*

favoured gardens. This has led me to suspect that several distinct taxa are involved here and their characteristics can be summarised briefly here:

1. *M. horridula.* Dwarf plant with rather narrow densely bristly, usually deep green, leaves, the bristles arising from small dot-like purple bases. Flowers nodding to half-nodding, scapose, mostly basal from the leaf rosette, sometimes several of the central scapes partly fused together to form a short central stem, but without leaflike bracts. Flowerbuds and capsules densely bristled. Anthers yellow to orange. Var. *racemosa* is essentially similar, except that the flowers are borne raceme-like on a well-developed stem with the lowest flowers often with leaflike bracts, but usually without scapose flowers; anthers cream to white.

2. *M. prattii.* A tall plant with rather narrow, moderately to rather sparsely bristled, bright fresh-green leaves, the bristle without a purple base. Flowers short-stalked, sideways directed, borne on a very well-developed central stem which is very leafy in the lower half, with at least the lower flowers having leaflike bracts at the base of the pedicels. Flowerbuds and capsules moderately to sparsely bristled. Anthers white to cream.

3. *M. rudis.* A dwarf plant with rather broad, undulate-margined blue-green leaves, with sparse bristles arising from a large purple base. Flowers short-stalked, sideways directed to semi-erect, borne on a short central stem which is leafy towards the base, the lower flowers with small leaflike bracts usually. Flowerbuds and capsule densely bristly. Anthers cream or white.

The plant long-cultivated as *M. horridula* in gardens equates with *M. prattii.* It is not surprising that this plant has proved so much more amenable in cultivation than its brethren, as it is a plant of considerably lower altitudes in the wild. Seed was gathered on quite a few occasions from south-western China early in the century, most notably through the collections of George Forrest, Frank Kingdon-Ward and Ernest Henry Wilson.

The following description applies to *M. horridula* in the strict sense:
A monocarpic plant with a narrow, somewhat fleshy, taproot, generally not more than 25 cm (10 in) tall in flower, often only a third to a half that height. Leaves deep green, all basal, borne in an untidy rosette, elliptical to narrow-oblong, up to 25 cm (10 in) long, narrowed below into the petiole, the margin untoothed, flat to somewhat undulate, the whole surface beset with sharp yellowish or purplish spinelike bristles, which arise from a prominent purple, wartlike base. Flowers solitary and scapose, without bracts, occasionally the central flowers (the first to open) have their scapes partly fused together, especially in the lower half; scapes sparsely to moderately bristly, 7.5–25 cm (3–10 in) long. Flowers pale to deep blue, sometimes suffused with lilac or purple, semi-transparent, 5–7.5 cm (2–3 in) across, nodding to half-nodding; petals oval to rounded, 4–8, overlapping one another to form a broad cup shape. Stamens with filaments the same colour as the petals and with yellow to golden anthers. The narrow-oblong fruit capsules have a long apical style and are covered in prominent spreading, usually straw-coloured, spines.

M. horridula is distributed from central Nepal eastwards through the Himalayas as far as western Bhutan and northwards into the neighbouring regions of Tibet, generally at altitudes between 4100–5945 m (13,450–19,500 ft); it is also present as far north as north-western Sichuan and southern Qinghai, although the latter requires further more detailed investigation. It is a plant of high alpine rocky meadows and screes, as well as old moraines, often in very exposed positions. On occasions it grows amongst dwarf rhododendrons and other small shrubs such as cassiopes and willows, on high mountain moorlands, or in rock crevices.

The 1921 Mt Everest Expedition collected *M. horridula* at 5790 m (19,000 ft); at such altitudes, plants are reduced and very dwarf, as little as 10 cm (4 in) tall in full flower.

The species was first described from material collected in the Sikkim Himalayas in 1855 by Hooker and Thomson. The plants which they saw in Sikkim had separate basal scapes or the central scapes agglutinated to form a central stem. This is a plant of the utmost beauty; it is one of those plants that I would walk a thousand miles to see, for it has few rivals amongst all the races of poppies.

Seed of the true *M. horridula* has been introduced on numerous occasions, especially during the past thirty years and mostly from Nepal. Despite this, plants have proved tricky to grow and it is difficult to keep them in cultivation. Like other members of this association, *M. horridula* forms a leaf-rosette for two or three years before it flowers, residing through winter as a small bud nestling at the soil surface. Plants are readily raised from seed, and the seedlings should be pricked out as soon as they have formed their first or second true leaf. Thereafter, unfortunately, problems start and numerous losses are generally to be expected, especially if seedlings do not gain enough size before the onset of their first winter (an early spring sowing, rather than a summer one is therefore advisable). The greatest success has been found growing plants in a gritty, well-drained mixture in pots in a very well-ventilated alpine house. Plants do not set too much seed in cultivation, which is another reason why it has proved difficult to maintain. The best seed set is to be expected when several flowering plants are placed side by side, for bees will transfer pollen from one to another, even in the alpine house.

var. *racemosa* (Maxim.)Prain (Syn. *M. racemosa* Maxim.) **[Pl. 132]** is similar in the details of the leaves and flowers; however, the flowers are aggregated into distinct racemes up to 40 cm (16 in) tall, although often less, with the uppermost flowers opening first. The flowers tend to face sideways and are borne on short pedicels, although occasionally several scapose flowers are borne directly from the leaf-rosette and separate from the raceme. The anthers are normally cream or pale yellow.

This variety has a very wide distribution that encompasses much of the eastern Himalayas, central and east Tibet and western China, northwards as far as Qinghai and Gansu, much of western Sichuan and north-western Yunnan. It occupies similar habitats, but at the lower altitudinal range for the species, rarely exceeding 5000 m (16,400 ft).

The relationship of var. *racemosa* to the typical plant, var. *horridula*, is not properly understood and requires further more detailed investigation. Var. *racemosa* is the normal form seen in cultivation, although it has been badly muddled in gardens, as well as in literature, with *M. prattii*, so that it is difficult to evaluate this variety in cultivation with any confidence. Unfortunately, many plants in this complex have been grown under the name *M. racemosa* for years; indeed, the name is probably still better known to gardeners than *M. horridula*. Suffice it to say that var. *racemosa* is far easier to grow than var. *horridula*, especially plants grown from seed gathered at the lower altitudinal range for the variety. As with any in the group, it pays to rogue out poor flower forms and colours, concentrating on those with beautiful formed and symmetrical blooms and those with the best blue colour.

A golden-yellow form was found by Ludlow, Sherriff and Taylor in south-eastern Tibet in 1938, at altitudes of 4570–4880 m (1500–16,000 ft) and named by them as var. *lutea*. From the photographs and dried material of this plant that I have been able to observe, this plant would be better placed under *M. prattii*, which is found further to the east in north-western Yunnan.

Meconopsis impedita Prain

(Syn. *M. impedita* var. *morsheadii* Prain, *M. i.* var. *rubra* Kingdon-Ward, *M. morsheadii* (Prain) Farrer, *M. rubra* Kingdon-Ward)

This attractive little species was described in 1915 from specimens collected in north-western Yunnan by Monbeig, Forrest, Maire and others. It has been cultivated for a few years from early collections, but has never become established. Recent collections, under the name have generally proved to be the related and equally desirable *M. lancifolia,* although the allegiance of *M. impedita* is more to *M. venusta* and *M. pseudovenusta.*

Yet another species related to *M. horridula*, it is distinguished by its sparsely bristly leaves and narrower fruit-capsules. The flowers are all borne on basal scapes. The striking flowers have four to ten petals and are dark, being described as 'reddish-purple or dark-violet to almost black' and the anthers 'cream, orange, golden, or yellow'.

M. impedita has a range from Upper Burma (Myanmar) northwards to north-western Yunnan and south-eastern Tibet (Xizang) where it is a plant of alpine meadows, screes and rocky slopes at an altitude of 2850–4575 m (9350–15,000 ft).

This desirable little species has been introduced a number of times, but has never persisted in cultivation for long. Forrest, Kingdon-Ward and Rock all collected seed early in the century, but to no avail and we must await new introductions. Like others of this *M. horridula* persuasion, seedlings appear to be difficult to overwinter and bring successfully to maturity. Most are plants of rather drier mountains, but with most of the rainfall in the summer and with a protective layer of snow during the winter months. The leaves die down to a resting bud during the winter.

Meconopsis integrifolia (Maxim.)Franch.   **[Pl. 133–134]**
(Syn. *Cathcartia integrifolia* Maxim.; *Meconopsis integrifolia* var. *souliei* Fedde;
M. souliei (Fedde) Farrer)
YELLOW POPPYWORT, FARRER'S LAMPSHADE POPPY

A rather variable monocarpic species that has been cultivated in gardens for
many years now, certainly since early in the twentieth century with the
introductions of Ernest Henry Wilson, Reginald Farrer, William Purdom,
George Forrest and others. Since the first edition of this book, I have been
able to re-evaluate *M. integrifolia* in light of further field observations by
myself and others (notably Peter Cox) and the re-introduction of seed from
the wild from a number of different locations. As a result, *M. integrifolia* can
be divided into two distinct, yet closely allied species *(M. integrifolia* and *M.
pseudointegrifolia)* based on their gross morphology and various details of leaf
and flower. In both species the leaf-rosette dies back to a large overwintering
bud that nestles at the soil surface. The emerging buds in spring can be
extremely attractive, often being flushed with orange or pink.

  M. integrifolia has a solitary leaf-rosette, which eventually gives rise to a
simple unbranched stem 20–100 cm (8–40 in) tall, and covered for the most
part, like the leaves, in rather soft golden-yellow or rufous hairs, although old
stems and leaves may have lost most of their hairs. The leaves are mostly
aggregated into a basal rosette and are elliptical to oblanceolate, up to 37 cm
(15 in) long and 5 cm (2 in) wide, narrowed below into a long tapered stalk,
while the margin is untoothed. The stem leaves are similar to the basal ones
(except they are short-stalked) and are scattered, although the uppermost are
aggregated into a whorl beneath the flowers, as in *M. grandis.* A distinctive
feature of the leaves are the three primary veins which run parallel from the
base close to the apex. The upper whorl of leaves supports 3–5, but occasionally up to 10, flowers. In stout specimens one or two superfluous flowers may
be borne below the leaf-whorl, from the axils of the uppermost alternate
leaves, but this is never a consistent feature. The flowers are erect or sometimes sideways directed, but never nodding, and range from mid to deep
yellow and are up to 22 cm (9 in) across. They range in shape from goblets
with incurved petals to a more open bowl-shape and bear 6–8 broad and
overlapping petals. The boss of numerous stamens have yellow filaments and
yellow, orange or blackish anthers, depending on their maturity. The ovary
bears a sessile to very short-styled stigma with 4–7 rays that does not protrude
beyond the boss of stamens. The densely hairy fruit capsule, borne on stalks
up to 47 cm (19 in) long, splits with as many valves as there are rays to the
stigma, these running down for about one-third the length of the capsule
from the top.

  This is rather an extended description, needed in order to make a proper
comparison with *M. pseudointegrifolia.*

  M. integrifolia was first discovered by Przewalski in Gansu (Kansu) in 1872
and has subsequently been collected on numerous occasions. Its known
distribution extends from north-eastern Tibet (Xizang) to southern Qinghai,
western and southern Gansu, western Sichuan and north-western Yunnan,

as well as much of the neighbouring part of eastern Tibet, although the precise distribution is a little unclear because of past confusion with *M. pseudointegrifolia*. In these remote regions it inhabits moist grassy meadows and screes, often on steep slopes, as well as open scrub of rhododendrons and willows. The altitudinal range is quite marked, from 2800 to 5300 m (9200–17,400 ft), those from the higher elevations generally being small and rather squat plants.

This and *M. pseudointegrifolia* are the largest-flowered species of *Meconopsis*. The species in question is, in its best forms, a very beautiful plant. However, it is variable in stature and flower shape in the wild and this is reflected in cultivated material.

I have seen this species on a number of occasions in the wild. The first time was on a high steep meadow on the eastern flanks of the Yulong Shan (Lijiang Snow Range, or the Jade Dragon Mountains of Yunnan), in the heart of George Forrest country, where it grew in scattered colonies. The plants were moderately tall, up to 60 cm (24 in), with rather small, globular, pale yellow flowers which were erect or semi-erect. Later I also saw it further to the north-west on the high rocky meadows of the Big Snow Mountain (Da-xue-shan) on the Yunnanese frontier with Sichuan, where the plants were very similar. These colonies are located south of the main distribution of the species and bear several distinctive features; for this reason, they have been afforded subspecific rank (see below). On another journey I was able to see *M. integrifolia* in large numbers in the border region of north-west Sichuan and neighbouring Gansu, particularly around Jui-zhai-gou and Huang-long-si. Here the plants were often far more robust, with large, goblet-shaped flowers, very similar to plants that have been cultivated in Britain for many years and sourced through introductions of seed earlier in the twentieth century. However, there have been a number of subsequent introductions, particularly in the 1980s and 1990s, which have introduced a greater range of forms into our gardens.

Reginald Farrer (1921, 'Rainbow Bridge') considered the lampshade poppy to be a rather ungainly species referring to its 'plethoric profusion and its usual gollopshiousness of stature', when observed in the wilds of Gansu, where the species is especially abundant.

This is the largest flowered species of *Meconopsis* which, in its best forms, is a very beautiful plant. It is very variable in stature, flower shape and size in the wild. Early authors attempted to split off a number of variants as separate species or varieties, but none proved particularly satisfactory. George Taylor in his monograph of 1934 acknowledges this variability, but includes all of them under a single species – others have tended to accept this view.

subsp. *lijiangensis* Grey-Wilson (Syn. *M. integrifolia* var. *brevistyla* Hort. ex Prain, *M. i.* var. *microstigma* Prain ex Kingdon-Ward) **[Pl. 135]** grows 45–75 cm (18–30 in) tall, with a well-defined stem which is generally leafless except for the whorl of leaves below the flowers. The flowers are pale to mid-lemon yellow, cup-shaped, the petals not markedly incurved as they generally are in the typical plant, subsp. *integrifolia*. The ovary is narrowobconical, rather than barrel-shaped and densely hairy, bearing a short style, 2–4 mm (½₂–⅙ in) long, with a 4–7-rayed stigma not more than 7 mm (¼ in) in diameter. In contrast, the stigma of subsp. *integrifolia* is without a style and 10–12 mm (⅖–½ in) in diameter. Subsp. *lijiangensis* is distributed from south-western Sichuan (Muli southwards) to north-western Yunnan (particularly in the Lijiang, Haba Shan and Da-xue-shan areas), flowering in the wild in May, June and early July.

This subspecies is in cultivation from a number of recent expeditions, particularly the 1994 Alpine Garden Society Expedition (ACE).

M. integrifolia is not particularly difficult in cultivation and generally sets copious seed, which is easy to germinate. Indeed, it has been known to self-sow in favoured gardens. It responds to a rich diet and a deep, humusy soil, but will succumb to summer drought if not carefully attended. The symmetrical rosettes have a charm of their own and in the second year appear as an expanding tuft flushed with pink and yellow or bluish-grey. Plants generally bloom in their second season, but may linger on to the following year. The form most widely available is of moderate size with globular, erect, good yellow flowers, which may open fairly close to the ground, but in the best specimens up to ten are borne on a plant 40–60 cm (16–24 in) tall.

Seedlings grow on fast and, if well fed, will be large enough to plant out by midsummer, allowing them to become well established before winter.

White-flowered forms have been reported from the wild, but these are not in cultivation.

M. × *beamishii* (*M. integrifolia* × *M. grandis*) **[Pl. 136]** is a hybrid similar to *M.* × *sarsonii* (p. 166), but with leaves like *M. grandis* tapered below into the stalk. The large, rather elegant flowers are cream, sometimes flushed or streaked with purple in the centre – these make it an easy plant to identify in the garden. The hybrid is fertile and resultant seedlings may be perennial or monocarpic. Good forms of the former can be increased by vegetative division of the parent plant. This is a hybrid which well deserves a large following in gardens – the colour and size of the flowers make it an interesting addition to any collection.

M. × *finlayorum* (*M. integrifolia* × *M. quintuplinervia*) is a rather improbable cross that has produced a plant of great charm, with neat fresh-green leaf-rosettes and nodding bell-shaped flowers of ivory, sometimes with a greenish-yellow tinge towards the base. This was a deliberate hybrid raised by Mike and Polly Stone of Fort Augustus and given the name 'Askival Ivory'. The finest forms are dwarf and fully perennial.

Meconopsis lancifolia (Franch.) Franch. ex Prain.   **[Pl. 137–138]**

An extremely variable species, again of the *M. horridula* type, which, despite a number of seed introductions earlier in the century (primarily by George Forrest), has never succeeded in cultivation. In the best forms, this is a plant with deep rich purple flowers. The flowers can be scapose or borne in a distinct raceme in which the flowers are bractless or the lower have leaflike bracts (in *M. horridula* the lower flowers are borne in the axils of leaves or minute, scale-like bracts). In some forms of *M. lancifolia* the leaves may be pinnately lobed, although most have entire or undulate leaves.

M. lancifolia has a wide range from Upper Burma (Myanmar) to Yunnan, south-eastern Tibet (Xizang) and south-western Gansu. It is a plant primarily of limestone formations, inhabiting screes and rocky meadows and cliffs, often in rather shady places and at an altitude of 3350–4880 m (11,000–16,000 ft).

George Taylor in *An Account of the Genus Meconopsis* (1934) discusses the variability of this interesting little species, stressing the fact that although some elements have one distinguishing feature or other, they are joined together by such a network or variability that separation into distinct species is practically impossible. Such minutiae need not concern us here. Suffice it to say that among the best forms of this species there are some highly desirable little alpine poppies.

This is altogether a delightful little species. I have seen it in flower on several occasions on the Big Snow Mountain (Da-xue-shan) in north-western Yunnan, close to the Sichuanese border, growing on rocky alpine moorland together with several other exciting alpines such as *Corydalis pachycentra*, *Primula minor* and *P. russeola*. In all the plants observed the flowers were an attractive deep violet-blue. On another occasion plants were found further to the west, close to the Mekong River on the high elevations of the Beima-shan; here the flowers were more substantial and decidedly more pink than blue.

In recent years seed has been introduced by a number of expeditions, most particularly the Alpine Garden Society's China Expedition (ACE) of 1994. It was misidentified in the field as *M. impedita* and under that name the seed was introduced, until later corrected. Some of these have produced nice little flowering plants in the hands of a number of different growers and it is to be hoped that it will persist in cultivation rather longer than did the earlier introductions whose failings in cultivation, like that of many 'tricky' plants, was more to do with the disruption caused by the Second World War than the growers' ability.

Despite this, *M. lancifolia* is generally divided into two more or less distinct varieties. In the typical plant, **var. *lancifolia*** (syn. *M. eximia* Prain, *M. lancifolia* var. *limprichtii* Fedde ex Limpr., *M. solitariiflora* Fedde, *M. lepida* Prain), the leaves are generally undivided, or occasionally slightly lobed, and the 4–8-petalled flowers are borne, up to 12, on a bractless stem (up to 42.5 cm or 17 in tall), but sometimes accompanied by solitary flowers on basal scapes. This variety is widely distributed from south-western Gansu to south-eastern Tibet and Upper Burma (Myanmar), including north-western Yunnan.

var. *concinna* (Prain) G. Taylor is a smaller plant distinguished by having very variable leaves ranging from oblong to elliptic, linear or spatular-shaped, but with at least some on each plant deeply pinnately lobed. In addition, the 4-petalled flowers are borne single on basal scapes. This variety, which is sometimes treated as a distinct species – see 'Flora of Bhutan' 1,2 (1984) – has a disjunct distribution with several localities known in central Bhutan, and the others much farther to the east in south-western Sichuan and north-western Yunnan. In China, at least, it appears to be far the least common of the two.

Meconopsis latifolia (Prain) Prain
(Syn. *M. sinuata* var. *latifolia* Prain)

This species is regarded by some as the most beautiful in the group characterised by *M. horridula* and *M. aculeata*. It is perhaps most closely allied to the latter, being distinguished by having less cut leaves and softer spines on the leaves and stems. Flowering plants may reach 1 m (3 ft) or slightly more in height, being leafy in the lower half, but with a pyramidal raceme of flowers above. The leaves, up to 20 cm (8 in) long, are oblong in outline with regular rounded teeth along the margin, or pinnately lobed, sparsely covered on both surfaces by rather soft, straw-coloured spines; the lower leaves are stalked, the upper ones unstalked. The flowers, which are often described as being duck-egg to mid-blue, are 4.5–6 cm (1⅘–2⅖ in) across and cup-shaped, with orange-yellow anthers and a purple stigma. There are four, almost rounded petals, which have a satiny appearance, being slightly wavy along the margin. The oblong fruit-capsule is covered with dense spreading spines and splits by the four to seven valves close to the styled apex.

M. latifolia is endemic to northern Kashmir in the western Himalayas, where it reportedly inhabits rock crevices and screes at altitudes of 3125–4060 m (10,500–13,300 ft).

It is perhaps surprising that this species is not more common in gardens. The exquisite flowers, which are longer lasting than its brethren, would excite any gardener. Plants are quite easy to raise from seed and provided they are not allowed to dry out during summer or winter, kept free from waterlogging in winter and given the usual rich, humusy, moisture-retentive soil in sun or partial shade, there should be no real problem. Plants normally flower in their second season, emerging after the winter as an expanding silvery rosette, flushed with pink. At this time they may be prone to both severe frost and marauding slugs, so some protection may be required. It is certainly wise to put some form of slug bait down before growth begins as plants can be ruined before any damage is noticed.

M. latifolia has been in cultivation since 1908, having been introduced by Appleton from Kashmir. Appleton stated that it 'is always found growing in the crevices of rocks or among loose piles of stone debris on stone slides and below cliffs. It likes the full sun, and springs to full growth after the snow melts off, while the ground is still damp!' White-flowered forms have been seen in the wild, but are not in cultivation.

A beautiful poppy well deserving a greater audience and worth every bit of attention that can be lavished on it.

Putative hybrids with *M. aculeata* [Pl. 35] have been reported from gardens. These are often fine plants distinguished by the greater degree of dissection of the leaves and in the stigmas that may often be green or whitish, rather than purple. Another reported hybrid is *M. grandis* × *M. latifolia* (Farrer,

The English Rock Garden) which seems rather improbable and cannot be proved as the plant in question is no longer in cultivation.

Meconopsis longipetiolata G. Taylor & Hay

A close and little known relative of *M. paniculata*, but a generally smaller and more graceful plant, with lower leaves that bear unusually long petioles, as the specific name implies. The plant bears large panicles of rather small, 5–6 cm (2–2⅖ in) diameter, pale yellow flowers. The leaves are deeply incised and bear a mixture of stiff bristles and finer hairs, which are densely borne on both surfaces. In *M. paniculata*, by contrast, the very dense indumentum is composed of much-branched hairs, as well as substellate ones.

M. *longipetiolata* is confined to the Nepalese Himalayas, where it apparently occupies rather similar habitats and altitudes to *M. paniculata*. However, it is a much rarer and more localised species; indeed, its precise distribution and habitat are unknown. The name does appear in gardening literature from time to time, but it is extremely doubtful whether the plants referred to are the real thing and not one of the manifestations of *M. paniculata*. In fact, the species has been in cultivation, for the original description was based on plant grown from seed sent from Nepal and which flowered in Britain in 1932. Unfortunately, the type material, which was deposited at the British Museum (Natural History) was subsequently lost. This interesting species was recently re-discovered in the wild in the Upper Langtang Valley of Central Nepal. Plants flowered at the Royal Botanic Gardens, Kew, in July 2000.

Meconopsis lyrata (Cummins & Prain) Fedde

(Syn. *Cathcartia lyrata* Cummins, *C. polygonoides* Prain; *Meconopsis compta* Prain, *M. polygonoides* (Prain) Prain)

This is an interesting, though little known, monocarpic species, generally of rather weak constitution, with thin glabrous or almost glabrous stems up to 50 cm (20 in) tall, although as little as a quarter that height on occasions. The basal leaves have generally withered by flowering time, but the blade varies enormously in shape from oval to spatular-shaped, with a rounded or heart-shaped base and a sheathing petiole, the margin untoothed to deeply incised or lobed, but not more than 4 cm (1⅗ in) long, hairless or slightly hairy overall. The stem leaves are similar, but somewhat larger and usually deeply lobed. 1–5 flowers are borne in the axils of the upper stem leaves (more rarely on leafy basal scapes); these are half-nodding, small, up to 3.75 cm (1½ in) across, and vary in colour from pale blue to pink, rose or white, with contrasting golden anthers; petals 4–6. The narrow-oblong fruit capsule is smooth and splits with only 3–4 valves close to the apex.

M. *lyrata* has a wide distribution from central Nepal eastwards through Sikkim to north-western Yunnan, where it inhabits rocky alpine meadows and screes at 3050–4880 m (10,000–16,000 ft).

This species was described from material collected in Sikkim at the beginning of the nineteenth century. It is poorly represented in herbarium collections and its precise distribution is unclear. However, plants at the eastern end of the known range (in north-western Yunnan) appear to show far more leaf variation than those to the west and this requires further investigation. It comes closest to *M. lancifolia* (especially var. *concinna*) which differs in its dark purple flowers borne usually on simple leafless basal scapes.

M. lyrata is not in cultivation at the present time. It is rather a small, weakly species and likely to appeal only to the 'must have' brigades, who are keen to grow as many species as possible.

One very interesting feature of some dried specimens in the west of the range of the species is the presence of bulbils (vegetative buds) at the stem leaf-axils. These presumably allow the plant to reproduce vegetatively, especially if the bulbiled stems were to lie on the ground. This feature is highly unusual in the poppy family. *M. lyrata* is the only monocarpic species to have such a method of propagation, but it is not common to all specimens. The only other species known to have bulbils is the widely grown perennial *M. chelidonifolia*. In the case of the latter, these bulbils can be detached and grown on; if *M. lyrata* were to come into cultivation, the bulbils presumably afford a ready means of increase.

Meconopsis napaulensis DC   [Pl. 139–140]
(Syn. *Papaver paniculatum* D. Don, in part; *Stylophorum nepalense* (DC.) Spreng., in part)
SATIN POPPY

One of the most robust species, which is widely grown in gardens. Plants are monocarpic, forming a large leaf-rosette 60 cm (24 in) across, sometimes larger, in the first two or three years. The solitary, stiff, erect, leafy stem rises to 2.5 m (8 ft) in vigorous specimens and is covered, like the leaves, in dense rather bristly hairs. The leaves may be as much as 50 cm (20 in) long, oval to elliptical and pinnately lobed, less deeply so in the upper half, and below tapering into the petiole. The bowl-shaped flowers are pendent or semi-pendent, red or purple, occasionally white, 6–8 cm (2⅖–3 in) across, borne in a narrow panicle with the lower branches having several (up to 17) flowers, the upper often with a solitary flower. The broad-oval, almost

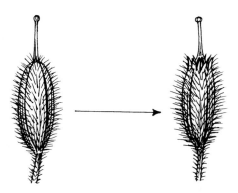

Fruit capsule of *Meconopsis napaulensis*, before and after dehiscence

rounded petals are usually four in number. The stamens bear orange or yellowish anthers. Stigma greenish. The oblong capsules are covered in dense appressed or slightly spreading bristles and dehisce by five to eight short valves close to the apex.

M. napaulensis is distributed from the central Nepalese Himalaya eastwards into south-eastern Tibet and western China, north as far as western Sichuan, where it inhabits woodland margins, scrub, stream banks and alpine meadows at altitudes of between 2800 and 5300 m (9200–17,400 ft).

Although plants are widely available under this name, few can be said to be the pure species. The very ease of cultivating *M. napaulensis* and its close cousins *M. paniculata* and *M. regia* has rather led to their downfall, for they hybridise readily with one another. The result is a hybrid mixture, often of uncertain parentage. Admittedly, many of these plants are very handsome and exciting to look at and indeed are fine and easy garden plants well worth growing. To find the species proper, one must look to recent introductions, particularly from Nepal. To keep these 'pure' in the garden, they must be isolated from their promiscuous cousins.

M. regia can be distinguished by its unlobed, finely toothed leaves and yellow flowers with their noticeable purplish-black stigma. *M. paniculata* also bears yellow flowers, which have a 'giveaway' soft-purple (not greenish) stigma amongst the boss of yellow anthers. The leaves are similar to those of *M. napaulensis*, but have a rather hoary appearance, rather than the more rusty hairs characteristic of the latter.

The winter rosettes of these three species are quite magnificent and when interplanted can produce a most striking effect. Those of *M. napaulensis* often take on a golden hue during the winter, as do the larger, silkier leaf-rosettes of *M. regia*. Those of *M. paniculata* are, on the other hand, greyer or greener. These rosettes can be so striking when well grown that it can be a disappointment to loose them to flowers in due course. Only then do the rosette leaves begin to die away.

Producing robust plants requires a moist, well-manured place and regular feeds during the growing season. In flower, poor forms should be ruthlessly discarded; select only the best coloured and most floriferous. In any event, it is more than likely that plants will not be pure species, but hybrids between those already referred to, and will produce a range of flower colours from yellow through to orange, apricot and various shades of pink and red, some even being bicoloured. A few of the red and yellow forms appear to breed true to form, but most do not. Many are first-rate garden plants to arrest the sight and astound the neighbours. Evidence of parental genes often reveal themselves over several generations. Thus large yellow flowers and undissected leaves reveal *M. regia*; hoary dissected leaves and smaller yellow flower, *M. paniculata*; and pink and red flowers and dissected, rusty-haired leaves, *M. napaulensis*. Purists will, however, want to seek out the genuine *M. napaulensis*. Unfortunately for them, hybrids are fully fertile and set copious seed and, in favoured gardens, will sow themselves around.

Whether true *M. napaulensis* or hybrid, the evergreen rosettes may take as many as six years to reach flowering size – three to four is a good average.

As with *M. paniculata*, *M. regia* and their allies, some winter protection – cloches or frame-lights placed overhead – will prevent crown-rot in some plants, but care must be taken that the rosettes do not desiccate beneath their protective cover, especially during dry but windy winter weather.

Readers will have perhaps noticed a complete lack of any mention of blue-flowers in relation to *M. napaulensis*. Such colour turns up in *M. wallichii* (p. 212). George Taylor lumped this plant into *M. napaulensis* in his monograph, but there is no doubt in my mind that it is a distinct species native to central and east Nepal and Sikkim, where I have been lucky enough to observe it on a number of occasions.

Besides the hybrid complex between *M. napaulensis*, *M. paniculata* and *M. regia*, *M. napaulensis*, or what often purports to be that species, also hybridises with *M. dhwojii*, but the offspring are disappointing in most respects, and fortunately sterile.

Meconopsis neglecta G. Taylor

This species is very little known, being restricted to Chitral, in northern Pakistan, in the western Himalayas. It was collected by Toppin in Kafiristan (now Chitral in part) before 1934 but, unfortunately, details of date, flowering time and altitude were not given.

M. neglecta is closely related to the western Himalayan *M. aculeata*, differing primarily in bearing all its flowers on basal scapes instead of in a well-developed bracteate, racemose inflorescence. Plants bear up to 12 rather small (presumably bluish-purple) flowers, each about 4 cm across, on scapes up to 15 cm long. The leaves are all basal and not more than 10 cm long, deeply pinnately lobed and adorned with stiff bristles on both surfaces.

George Taylor, who described the species in 1934, has suggested that this may represent no more than a depauperate form of *M. aculeata*, but the scapose state of the plant is unusual. In this respect it matches the scapose manifestation of *M. horridula* (i.e. var. *horridula*) found further east in the Himalayas. There is no doubt that this would make an exciting little introduction into cultivation. It is perhaps surprising that it has not come to light during more recent botanical explorations of the region.

Meconopsis oliverana Franch. & Prain

This species finds its closest ally in western Chinese *M. chelidonifolia*, differing mainly in its glabrous fruit capsules that are 4–5-valved, narrow-oblong, almost cylindrical in shape, whereas those of *M. chelidonifolia* are more elliptical in outline and sparsely bristly, 5–6-valved.

The species was based on collections made in the latter part of the nineteenth century in Sichuan by Abbé Farges and in Hubei by Augustine Henry. In fact, its known distribution is restricted to eastern Sichuan and western Hubei. The altitude was not recorded and it is assumed that it inhabits rather similar places to *M. chelidonifolia* (i.e. damp shrubberies and stream-side thickets).

M. oliverana is not in cultivation and is unlikely to have great appeal because of its very close resemblance to *M. chelidonifolia.*

Meconopsis paniculata (D. Don) Prain   [Pl. 141–144]
(Syn. *Papaver paniculatum* D. Don, in part; *Meconopsis himalayansis* Hort. ex Hay)

This robust monocarpic species is generally likened to a yellow-flowered *M. napaulensis* and, indeed, the two species have much in common. In cultivation much confusion as to the true identity of these species and *M. regia* has resulted from their habit of freely hybridising with one another (p. 191). To gardeners, what matters most is not species purity but a good growable and attractive plant – the hybrids certainly conform to these criteria well. Most plants sold as *M. paniculata* are in fact of hybrid origin. These are likely to have yellow flowers and dissected leaves, but not necessarily so.

True *M. paniculata* is common in the eastern Himalayas, from eastern Nepal through to Assam, inhabiting open pine and fir forest, shrub, stream banks and, at higher altitudes, sloping grassy meadows, often below ridge tops. The altitudinal range is 3125–4500 m (11,900–14,800 ft).

In leaf, plants form handsome spreading rosettes, the individual leaves oval to elliptical, pinnately lobed in the lower half, less so above, the surface covered in dense hoary hairs giving them a somewhat greyish appearance. The stems rise to 2 m (7 ft), more in particularly strong specimens. The yellow flowers, 5–7 cm (2–3 in) across, are similarly shaped to both *M. napaulensis* and *M. regia*, but rather smaller, the petals always rather pale yellow and, if anything, more spreading. The anthers are yellow or orange-yellow and the stigma is characteristically pale purple – an extremely useful diagnostic character lost in yellow-flowered hybrids with *M. napaulensis.*

Much has been made of the differences in the hairs of *M. napaulensis* and *M. paniculata*, those of the latter being apparently more branched, especially near the leaf-surface. However, this character is difficult to observe and in all probability quite variable. For most purposes, it is better to concentrate on better visual characters such as dissected leaves, smaller yellow flowers and purple stigma.

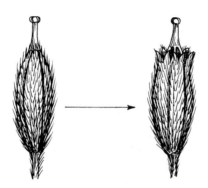

Fruit capsule of *Meconopsis paniculata*, before and after dehiscence

M. paniculata, like *M. napaulensis* and their hybrids, is easy to raise from seed and worth growing as much for its winter rosettes as for its towering inflorescences. A sheltered site is advisable, as a strong wind at peak flowering can bruise plants or, worse still, knock them over. Gaps in shrubs borders or a woodland setting are ideal. A slope or hollow where one can look down upon them, or view them from below, can be most effective.

Meconopsis pinnatifolia

A recently described species of the *M. discigera* persuasion, differing primarily in its pinnately-lobed leaves. Similar leaved plants were described by Ludlow and Sherriff during their forays in Bhutan and Tibet, and these were assigned to *M. discigera*. However, their localities are not too distant from Jilong on the Tibet/Nepal border, the type locality of *M. pinnatifolia*. Knowing the great variation in leaf shape found in some species of *Meconopsis,* one must view this new species with some scepticism. However, this clearly requires further close scrutiny before any real judgement can be made. Interestingly, the only photograph of *M. discigera* in the *Bulletin of the Alpine Garden Society* (Vol. 22, p. 316) shows a plant with markedly pinnately-lobed leaves that clearly belongs to *M. pinnatifolia*, whatever its eventual status is declared to be.

Meconopsis prattii (Prain) Prain   [Pl. 145–146]
(syn. *M. prainiana* Kingdon-Ward, *M. sinuata* Prain var. *prattii* Prain; also possibly *M. calciphila* Kingdon-Ward)

For a general discussion see under *M. horridula*, p. 181.

This interesting species is common in the Zhongdian (Chungtien) region of north-western Yunnan, where it grows in open shrubberies or on rocky slopes below the tree line at modest altitudes. This fact alone serves to distinguish the plant from its high-altitude cousins, particularly *M. horridula* and *M. rudis*. It is rather surprising that it has been so consistently confused with *M. horridula*. Indeed, most plants grown under the latter name invariably, in my experience, turn out to be *M. prattii*. The species is tall and elegant, producing long racemes of flowers. It is quite a feature of the Zhongdian area in June, especially around Napa-hai and Beta-hai, where it often colonises steep-sloping, rocky, roadside embankments.

M. prattii is a monocarpic plant forming a medium-sized bristly rosette in the first one or two years, before it flowers, when the plants can reach 1.2 m (48 in) tall, although two-thirds of that height is normal; stem often suffused with purple. The leaves are inclined to erect and a bright fresh green, narrow-elliptical to oblanceolate, covered all over with rather pale straw-coloured bristle (like the stems), without a purple base, the margin entire but somewhat undulate; lower half of the stem leafy, with the leaves gradually decreasing in size upwards and merging into bracts, which are located only at the lowermost flowers. Flowers blue to violet-blue, generally directed sideways on short pedicels, similar in size to *M. horridula*, but the petals usually spreading widely apart to form a rather flat flower. Stamens with filaments similar in colour to the petals and with white to cream stamens. Fruit capsule moderately bristly, with spreading straw-coloured bristles.

This plant is very distinctive in its very well-developed racemose inflorescences, which generally bear 15 flowers or more, in the narrow and erect, unspotted foliage and in its cream or more often white anthers. *M. prattii* is found in an arc from north-western Yunnan (particularly the Zhongdian area) westwards into south-eastern Tibet (certainly as far as the Temo La) and probably also including Upper Burma (Myanmar) and north in China into south-western and western Sichuan, north as far as Kangding.

The plant was described by David Prain as *M. sinuata* var. *prattii* from specimens collected near Tatsien-lu (now Kangding) in western Sichuan towards the end of the nineteenth century, but was raised to specific level in 1906 by the same author.

It is widely cultivated, being easy to cultivate and, in many favoured gardens, it has been known to seed around with profusion. Indeed, so dense are the young seedlings at times that rigorous thinning of the seedlings is necessary. In flower it is all-together a charming and elegant plant, but is apt to blow over in all but the most sheltered spot. It has been suggested by George Taylor and others that decapitating the plant when it begins to throw an inflorescence forces the plants to produce several lesser inflorescences and a less lanky appearance as a result.

Meconopsis primulina Prain

An attractive little Himalayan alpine species described by Prain in 1896, based on material gathered by native collectors on the Bhutan-Tibet border. This is a small monocarpic species overwintering as a bud just below the soil surface. The basal leaves are elliptical to oblanceolate, with an entire margin, bristly overall or more or less glabrous, up to 7.5 cm (3 in) long, including a 2–3 cm (⅘–1⅕ in) long petiole; basal leaves generally withered by flowering time and represented by a tuft of persistent fibrous leaf-bases. Stem leaves few and located near the base of the stem, similar to the basal leaves, but usually present at flowering time. One to three blue flowers, each 3–4 cm (1⅕–1⅗ in) across, are borne on long bristly, scapelike pedicels; petals 4–8, overlapping and spreading widely apart. The 4-valved fruit capsule is cylindrical, 3–4 cm (1⅕–1⅗ in) long and it generally bears a few scattered bristles.

The species is endemic to western Bhutan and the neighbouring Chumbi valley, where it is a denizen of alpine slopes, particularly amongst dwarf rhododendrons, but also on screes and moraines, at 3190–4600 m (10,450–15,100 ft); flowering in the wild from late May until July.

Unfortunately, this charming little species is not in cultivation and never has been. It finds its closest ally in the far more widespread *M. lyrata*, differing from that species in the presence of the densely tufted persistent leaf-bases, in the actual leaf shape, and in the somewhat bristly rather than glabrous ovary and fruit.

Meconopsis pseudointegrifolia Prain   **[Pl. 147–148]**
(Syn. *M. integrifolia* var. *uniflora* C.Y. Wu & H. Chuang)

This extremely handsome species is superficially similar to *M. integrifolia*, a species with which it has long been confused. However, there are a number of prime areas of distinction. First, the leaves are pinnately veined and do not have three prime parallel veins as in *M. integrifolia*. Second, the flowers are nodding or half-nodding and have widely spreading petals; they are overall more saucer- than bowl-shaped. Third, the ovary always bears a distinct style, 3–11 mm (⅛–½ in) long, that pushes the narrow 7–10-rayed stigma beyond the boss of surrounding stamens. These differences are easy to observe in cultivated specimens.

Even so, *M. pseudointegrifolia* is quite a variable plant in the wild, with a distribution rather to the west and south of that of *M. integrifolia*, although the species do probably overlap in distribution in eastern Tibet and the neighbouring parts of north-western Yunnan and south-western Sichuan. However, I have no evidence that the two grow together in the wild. In fact, evidence to date suggests that they occupy rather different habitats; *M. integrifolia* prefers the open mountain moorland slopes, whereas *M. pseudointegrifolia* is more partial to shrubberies and rather more shaded and sheltered spots, although this requires further investigation.

subsp. *pseudointegrifolia*
Plants are seldom more than 50 cm (20 in) tall with scarcely a well-developed stem, the whorl of stem leaves held amongst or close to the basal leaf-rosette. The flowers tend to be scapose, being borne on very long stalks (pedicels), and are an attractive sulphur-yellow, generally 12–17 cm (5–7 in) across. The ovary bears a style 3–6 mm (⅛–¼ in) long and both the style and the stigmatic rays bear short bristles. The fruit capsule is densely hairy. This subspecies has a rather limited distribution in north-western Yunnan, particularly in the region of the Salween/Mekong/Yangtse watersheds, as well as the neighbouring region of Tibet, west as far as the Temo La.

Prominent collections of this species (mostly collected as *M. integrifolia*) were made by Abbé Farges and George Forrest early in the twentieth century and in recent times by the SBLE (Sino-British Lijiang Expedition), CLD (Chungtien, Lijiang and Dali Expedition) and ACE (Alpine Garden Society China Expedition), so that there is a fair amount of material in cultivation at the present time.

subsp. *robusta* Grey-Wilson
This is by far the more widespread and better known manifestation of the species. Plants are generally large, up to 1.2 m (4 ft) tall, although not always so. However, they always have a well-developed stem, bearing scattered leaves which often bear superfluous flowers in the upper axils, below the whorl of leaflike bracts. The flowers range from pale lemon-yellow to sulphur-yellow, nodding or half-nodding and ranging in size from 14–22 cm (6–9 in), the petals spreading widely apart. The ovary tends to be rather sparsely hairy compared with subsp. *pseudointegrifolia* and bears a glabrous

style 7–11 mm (¼–½ in) long. The fruit capsule is glabrous or subglabrous. This subspecies has a wide distribution in north-western Yunnan (Salween/ Mekong/Yangtse divide region, but not to the east of the Mekong/Yangste watershed), and in south and east Tibet from north of Bhutan eastwards and Upper Burma (Myanmar). It is also possibly found in south-western Sichuan.

I first came across this very striking subspecies in the company of Tony Schilling and Ron McBeath in 1987, when we ventured into north-western Yunnan on to high marshy meadows on the Mekong/Yangtse divide close to Li-ti-ping. Beneath a colony of rather spindly willows grew a simply breathtaking stand of what in the event has turned out to be subsp. *robusta*. These formed large plants, the tallest a full metre (3 ft) in height, and bearing huge, deep lemon-yellow flowers, exquisite in their nodding poise and their spreading oval petals. This was a plant to cherish and one of those moments 'in the field' that lingers on long in the memory.

On a previous occasion Frank Kingdon-Ward discovered an interesting form of *M. pseudointegrifolia* in the mountains of Upper Burma (Myanmar) in 1926, at 3960 m (13,000 ft). These plants (there are several sheets at the herbarium at the Royal Botanic Garden, Edinburgh) were the first to be found outside China and Tibet. The Burmese plants were described by Kingdon-Ward as var. *gracilis*, because the plants are noticeably more slender and bear small, nodding flowers. The plant in question is not in cultivation and until it can be further investigated, no further pronouncement on its status can be made. Unfortunately, this remote and forbidden region on the Tibet/Burmese border is wholly inaccessible at the present time.

subsp. *daliensis* Grey-Wilson

An interesting and rather isolated subspecies known from only a few collections (none, apparently, in the modern era). The plants are dwarf, not more than 25 cm (10 in) tall, and are covered in dense silky hairs on both stems and leaves. The stem is reduced and not more than 10 cm (4 in) tall so that the whorl of bractlike leaves are mixed with the basal leaves of the rosette or held just above it. The flowers are erect rather than nodding and about 9 cm (3⅗ in) across. The ovary is also densely silky and the style short but distinct, 2–5 mm (¹⁄₁₂–⅕ in) long. The fruit is barrel-shaped and densely hairy. Subspecies *daliensis* is restricted, as its name suggests, to the Dali region of north-western Yunnan, being confined to the high slopes at the northern end of the Dali Range (Cangshan Mountains).

This subspecies is based on a George Forrest collection (no. 29125) made early in the twentieth century. This subspecies is unfortunately not in cultivation, but it would be well worth introduction. It is remarkable for the dense silky indumentum of the leaves and stems, which is especially prominent on the emerging leaf-rosettes in the spring and on the flower stalks. Interestingly, the individual hairs measure 6–9 mm (¼–⅜ in) in length, whereas those of the other subspecies and *M. integrifolia* are no more than 4 mm (¹⁄₁₆ in) long. This fact, together with the erect nature of the flowers, gives the plant a distinctive appearance and, when more is known about it in the wild, it may well warrant raising the plant to specific status.

The poise of the flowers in *M. pseudointegrifolia* has been questioned. The buds and newly opened flowers are fully nodding, but as the flowers age and pollination is effected they gradually assume a half-nodding to semi-erect position. This is wholly consistent with the fruit capsule, which is erect. In *M. integrifolia* the buds are erect from the start, so that the flowers open in an upright poise.

Meconopsis pseudovenusta G. Taylor

A highly desirable alpine species that would make a great addition to the garden, but unfortunately this little gem is not in cultivation, although seed has possibly been introduced from Yunnan in the past few years. These small Chinese species (including *M. impedita*, *M. lancifolia* and *M. venusta*) appear to be rather tricky in cultivation, and are certainly awkward to maintain for any length of time. Seed viability may be a problem, especially if the seed has been collected in the wild and poorly stored. These species inhabit regions which have a warm dry spring and a very wet, often cooler summer, when the monsoon dominates the climate. They therefore require impeccable drainage and a dryish winter rest, when they retreat to dormant buds at or close to the ground surface. They then need to be coaxed back into growth as the spring arrives, supplying enough water for the bud and leaf development, but avoiding excess water that might cause them to rot.

M. pseudovenusta is very closely related to *M. venusta*, differing in the broader more egg-shaped fruit-capsules (not more than four times as long as wide) and in the flowers which nearly always have more than 4 and up to 10 petals. In *M. venusta* the fruit capsules are long and thin, more or less cylindrical and up to ten times as long as wide. Another difference is seen in the scapes, which in *M. pseudovenusta* are generally partly agglutinosed into a bractless inflorescence, while in *M. venusta* the flowers are always borne on separate basal scapes. Both species form small low tufts not more than 20 cm (8 in) tall in flower and often less, with the fibrous leaf-base remains forming a collar around the new leaves. The leaves themselves are glabrous, more or less elliptical in outline, but nearly always deeply lobed towards the base. The nodding flowers are shaped rather like those of *M. delavayi* and are a rich purple with a large central boss of orange-yellow stamens.

M. pseudovenusta is restricted to the high mountains of north-western Yunnan and the neighbouring regions of Sichuan and Tibet, where it is a plant of stony alpine meadows and old moraines at 3660–4270 m (12,000–14,000 ft); flowering in June and July in the wild.

This is undoubtedly an exquisite little species, which in a strong specimen can produce as many as 15 flowers that open in succession. It has not been seen very much during recent botanical forays in the high remote regions of north-western Yunnan. However, there is a fine photograph of it in the *Highland Flowers of Yunnan* produced by the Kunming Institute of Botany and published by the Yunnan Science and Technology Press.

Meconopsis punicea Maxim.   **[Pl. 149–150]**
(Syn. *Cathcartia punicea* Maxim.)
RED POPPYWORT

One of the more astonishing species in the genus. It is a perennial, occasionally monocarpic, with a solitary taproot crowded by one or several leaf tufts. The leaves, up to 35 cm (14 in) long, are loosely tufted, oval to elliptical and untoothed, tapering below into the petiole and clothed all over in long, rather soft hairs that give the tufts an overall greyish or somewhat ginger coloration. The solitary nodding flowers arise on slender elegant scapes up to 60 cm (24 in) long, sometimes longer, and are a vivid crimson and shaped like a flared skirt. The satiny petals, generally four (five to six in cultivated plants), are large, up to 10 cm (4 in) long, and elliptical in outline. There are numerous stamens hidden within the 'skirt' which bear dull purplish-brown pollen. The fruits are held on erect stalks, the oblong capsules bristly, although sometimes almost smooth.

M. *punicea* is unique in the brilliant red of its flowers and its streamer-like petals. Reginald Farrer in *The English Rock Garden* (1918) raves about it: '*M. punicea* is well known by now with its thick tufts of loose long oval-pointed hairy green leaves, and its abundant uprising single stems, at the top of each of which comes a single large flower of a royal crimson, so floppy and tired in texture that each blossom hangs on its stem like a blood-stained flag hoisted to its pole on a windless dull day in late autumn.'

Farrer gives the impression that this breathtaking species is easy and common in cultivation. However, this has never been so and early introductions all died out. In 1986 the species was reintroduced by Peter Cox and Peter Hutchinson from Sichuan in China, but unfortunately, despite growing and flowering well since, it gives every impression of eventually going the same way as the earlier introductions, especially as little seed is set if the weather is too warm or dry.

M. *punicea* first came into cultivation as the result of a six-week journey undertaken in 1903 by Ernest Henry Wilson (Chinese Wilson) in north-western Sichuan (Szechwan) especially to gather seed. Although plants successfully flowered the following year in Britain, the plant soon died out. It was reintroduced subsequently by Joseph Rock from south-western Gansu (then Kansu) and others and remained in cultivation until the 1960s. The most recent Cox and Hutchinson collections have been more widely distributed.

The species was discovered by Przewalski in north-eastern Tibet in 1884. Since then its known distribution has extended to cover north-western Sichuan and southern Gansu, where it inhabits damp grassy meadows and slopes and bushy places often dominated by rhododendrons, generally in partial shade and at altitudes of 2960–4500 m (9700–14,800 ft).

There is no doubt that this is a sensational species, worth every effort to maintain in cultivation. Like the best of the blue poppies, it is a real 'eye-catcher' in the garden. A strong plant will carry a close cluster of leaf-tufts up to 30 cm (12 in) across and as many as 20 flowers at a time. The leaves wither away in the late autumn and unfortunately the crowded shoots borne on the

Meconopsis punicea

end of a solitary taproot make it an impossible plant to divide, even if one had the courage to do so. If the taproot dies, then the whole plant perishes.

M. punicea is not particularly difficult to grow. Its decline in cultivation is due more to the apparent low fertility of plants and to the fact that home-produced seed is often difficult to germinate. However, like many a fine but 'difficult' plant there are always those who will succeed wonderfully well with it and their dedication is to our benefit.

James Cobb (*Meconopsis*, 1989) states that it is essential to sow fresh seed of this species in the autumn. It will overwinter to germinate the following spring. Spring-sown seed will skip a year to germinate a year after sowing. Seedlings grown on and fed regularly will soon form plants that will mostly flower the following year – a few may even flower in their first season.

Plants are fully hardy and will thrive equally well in the usual moist rich loamy soils that meconopsis appear to demand, whether it be in sun or partial shade. I have not tried it in my own dry garden, but at the Royal Botanic Gardens, Kew, which is scarcely less dry, it thrived recently for two or three years in a semi-woodland setting. However, even there, plants were hardly as vigorous and impressive as those shown off to perfection in more northerly gardens.

Plants come into flower in late June and will often continue to produce a flower or two well into the autumn. Some plants will behave mono-carpically, others will hopefully survive for several years, though it is doubtful whether plants are ever very long-lived, at least in cultivation. A group grown close together should ensure some seed set, unless the summer is exceptionally dry. Although hardy, during very severe winter weather a protective covering of straw or bracken may be advisable.

One glance of the red petals bursting from the flower buds makes this species worth every effort. It can be guaranteed to create the deepest envy amongst gardening friends.

Recent reports from friends suggest that this glorious species can be found in the wild in a rare white-flowered form, but such a plant has never cropped up in cultivation.

Meconopsis quintuplinervia Regel   [Pl. 151]
(Syn. *M. punicea* var. *limprichtii* Fedde)
HAREBELL POPPY

Reginald Farrer (*The English Rock Garden*) held this very pretty little plant in high esteem: '. . . it is certain that despite its place in the group, *M. quintuplinervia* is going to prove the sounder perennial of the family; and so beautiful that the senses ache at the multitudinous loveliness of its myriad dancing lavender butterflies over the rolling Alps of the Da-Tung chain (Northern Gansu – Tibet). In fact, in well-bred exquisiteness of charm, it stands, in my eyes, supreme over its race.'

M. quintuplinervia is a hardy deciduous perennial that forms a slow-creeping low mat by means of a fibrous root-system and branching underground stems. The lax leaf-rosettes, like exotic plantains, appear in the spring from below-ground resting buds. The simple leaves are up to 25 cm (10 in) in length, oval to lanceolate with an untoothed margin and covered above and beneath with straw- or rust-coloured bristles. The slender flower scapes, which are also bristly, rise to 60 cm (24 in) tall, but are as little as 15–20 cm (6–8 in) in some forms, and carry a solitary nodding bell. The flowers are a delicate shade of pale lavender, each four-petalled, occasionally five or six, and slightly more than 3 cm (1⅕ in) long in the finest forms. The stamens have pale lavender or whitish filaments and usually pale yellow anthers. The fruit-capsule is more or less elliptical in outline, bristly and splitting by three to six valves towards the top.

M. quintuplinervia was first discovered by Przewalski in Gansu, China, in 1880 and described from cultivated plants (sent as seed by him) at St. Petersburg. Introduction to British gardens came through seed sent home in

1914 and 1915 by Reginald Farrer. Since then it has proved to be a fine and rather amenable garden plant, particularly in cooler and damper regions. The perennial creeping habit makes it an easy plant to propagate and most plants are reproduced by division. In fact, seed is rarely produced in any quantity and, even then, it is not very easy to germinate.

M. quintuplinervia thrives in any good garden soil, provided it is moist and a generous helping of compost or leaf-mould has been added. Since it is perennial, an annual dressing of fresh compost, applied before growth commences, should suffice to keep plants vigorous. Even then, it pays to remove clumps and split them up every three or four years, taking the opportunity at the same time to reinvigorate the soil in the bed. It is a super plant for the peat bed or rock garden, given a sheltered site and a sunny or semi-shaded (but not too shaded) aspect. Plants commence flowering in May and will continue on and off all summer provided that dead flowers are removed.

Of the forms in cultivation, the more compact one, known as 'Kaye's Compact Form', is the finest and easiest. It forms compact, close, leaf-rosettes and is not too tall in flower. There is now a fertile seed form of *M. quintuplinervia* that closely matches 'Kaye's Compact Form'. Pink forms of the species appear from time to time, but they scarcely have the charm of the normal pale lavender ones.

Although generally hardy, some protection during the winter may be necessary, if only to keep cats, birds and squirrels from disturbing the bed and uncovering vulnerable resting buds.

In the wild, *M. quintuplinervia* is found from north-eastern Tibet (Xizang) to southern Gansu, north-western Sichuan, eastwards to Shensi, at an altitudinal range of 2340–4375 m (7700–14,350 ft). It is primarily a plant of alpine meadows and open rhododendron scrub. According to Farrer it is abundant in some areas and forms a 'shimmering surf'.

Despite being considered an easy species to cultivate, this charming little species can prove temperamental in some gardens. In my experience it dislikes too much disturbance and being 'bullied' by coarser more robust plants in the border. This is a species well worth nurturing and its dainty harebell flowers will delight all who see it.

M. quintuplinervia finds its closest ally in the red-flowered *M. punicea*, which, apart from flower colour and size, can be distinguished by its monocarpic non-spreading habit.

The species hybridises with *M. punicea* (*M.* × *cookei*), a rare plant of little merit, with muddy purple flowers borne on lanky scapes.

The hybrid with *M. integrifolia* (*M.* × *finlay-orum*) is described on p. 186. Hybrids with *M. cambrica* and *M. betonicifolia* have also been recorded.

M. quintuplinervia is clearly of great potential in breeding programmes – especially in helping to establish a great range of fully perennial forms for gardens. The charm of the species, though, would be difficult to match. Indeed, it would be sad to see the species swamped by coarser and easier hybrids as has happened in so many other genera in cultivation.

Meconopsis regia G. Taylor

This grand species is one of the most handsome and stately in the genus. Its bold leaf-rosettes and towering panicles of yellow-flowers are as eye-catching as any. *M. regia* comes in that close group of similar species exemplified by *M. napaulensis*, *M. paniculata* and *M. wallichii*. It can be distinguished from these species at once by its unlobed, finely toothed, leaf-margins.

M. regia, like its allies, is a monocarpic species. The leaf-rosettes, which may last for up to four years before flowering, are extremely attractive and can (in vigorous specimens) reach more than 1 m (3 ft) across, the whole being covered in soft gold hairs. The leaves, up to 60 cm (24 in) in length, are elliptical, narrowed at the base into a short broad petiole, the margin finely and evenly serrated; the upper stem leaves are similar, but smaller and unstalked. The stout flowering stem often reaches 2 m (6½ ft) in height, the upper flowers solitary on long stalks, the lower several (up to 10 in a good specimen) on a common stalk from the upper leaf-axils. The flowers are a soft pure yellow, deeply cupped, 9–13 cm (3⅗–5⅕ in) across, and with four (occasionally six) overlapping petals. The boss of stamens is yellow with orange-yellow anthers and the style and stigma are a characteristic purple-black. The fruit-capsule is more or less oblong in outline and very densely covered by closely packed, non-spreading, bristles. The fruit-capsule is split by 7–12 valves close to the apex.

This exciting species is confined to the central Nepalese Himalayas at an altitude of 3750–4680 m (12,300–15,400 ft), where it is a plant of open scrub, meadows and stream banks.

M. regia was described by George Taylor in 1929 and first flowered in cultivation in 1931. Since then it has been reintroduced as seed on a number of occasions. The collections of Stainton, Sykes and Williams from Nepal in the 1950s introduced red-flowered forms that possessed the leaf-characters and dark style colour of the type. There were said to be two forms of the yellow type in cultivation at that time that differed in vigour and rosette colouration. In the more vigorous, the leaf-rosettes were golden with hairs; in the less vigorous form, the hairs gave the rosettes a silkier more silvery appearance.

It is a shame that *M. regia* is so rare today in our gardens. Indeed, the true species may not be with us any longer. The problem is not to do with difficulty in cultivation, but rather the reverse, for it hybridises all too readily with its brethren, particularly *M. napaulensis* and *M. paniculata* – the result is a hybrid swarm in which the parental characteristics have been swamped by their hybrid offspring. Many of these hybrids are very attractive and set abundant fertile seed, so they thrive in cultivation. Genuine *M. regia* must be sought anew – its presence in gardens, if it still exists untainted, would be revealed by the uncut leaves and the relatively large flowers with a purple-black stigma.

There is some evidence that *M. regia* and *M. napaulensis* hybridise in the wild where the two species grow in close proximity to one another, but such revelations need careful analysis in the field.

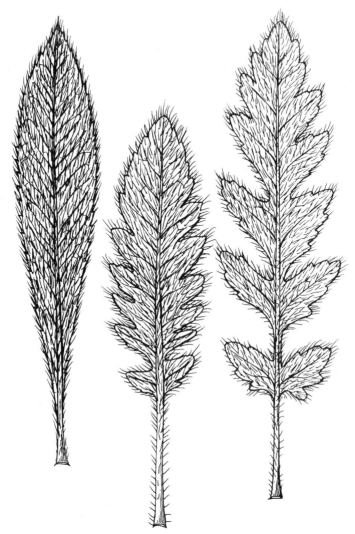

Leaves of *Meconopsis regia* **(left),** *M. paniculata* **(centre) and** *M. napaulensis*
(right)

In the meantime, we must enjoy the multitude of hybrids and await fresh
introductions of seed from the wild.

Like other large-rosetted and monocarpic *Meconopsis* species, *M. regia*
requires a rich humusy soil, plenty of moisture during the growing season
and regular feeding. These are all greedy and require every encouragement
to produce their large handsome rosettes and bold flowering panicles. Where
plants have flourished for a number of years in the garden, they often greatly
impoverish the soil and it is then wise to move new plants on to a fresh site.
These are plants for a sheltered site in sun or partial shade; a woodland setting
is admirable, though so too is a wide space amongst tall shrubs.

Meconopsis robusta Hook. F. & Th.

This is a poorer cousin of *M. paniculata*, but scarcely has the grace and grandeur of that species. Recently brought into cultivation, it is likely to be primarily of botanical interest to those who want to grow as many of the species as possible. Plants generally behave (at least in cultivation) as a biennial and the rosette of deeply dissected leaves can reach 50 cm (20 in) across at the most and are only sparsely hairy (there is an absence of the sub-stellate indumentum observable in the foliage *of M. paniculata*). The rather narrow inflorescences reach as much as 1.5 m (5 ft), with the lower flowers borne two to three from the axils of the leaflike bracts, while the upper flowers are always produced singly. The 4-petalled flowers are pale yellow, and cupped, about 5 cm (2 in) across. The bristly fruit-capsule splits by 6–9 valves close to the apex and just below the persistent style.

In all the available herbarium specimens examined, all the flowers are borne singly from the inflorescence, but in cultivated examples the lower flowers of the inflorescence are often borne 2–3 on a common stalk.

M. robusta, which was described as long ago as 1855, is restricted in the wild to northern India, Kumaon District, at relatively low altitudes, 2400–3050 m (7900–10,000 ft), being essentially a plant of open woodland and shrubberies, especially on slopes and in ravines.

Meconopsis rudis (**Prain**) Prain [Pl. 152–153]
(syn. *M. horridula* var. *rudis* Prain)

For a general discussion see under *M. horridula*, p. 181.

Another plant frequently confused with *M. horridula*, but one that has a very distinctive look. In general stature the two species are very similar, but the leaves of *M. rudis* are a blue-green, broadly elliptical, with a pointed apex and a broad petiole, rather thick and leathery; the margin is rather undulate and often bears several uneven shallow lobes on each side, while the otherwise smooth surface bears a few prominent spinelike bristles, each with a large purple black basal spot. The stem is thick and ridged and the flowers are borne in a distinct but short, rather condensed raceme, seldom more than 25 cm (10 in) tall; they are blue or lilac-blue, sideways directed to semi-erect, and bear whitish or cream anthers.

M. rudis appears to be confined to a rather small region in north-western Yunnan centred on the Yulong Shan (Lijiang Snow Range), at altitudes of about 3940–4880 m (13,000–16,000 ft), where it flowers from late June until August. There are also unconfirmed reports of its presence on Haba Shan, also close to the Yangtse river, further to the north-west. I have been able to observe this interesting plant on a number of occasions in the Lijiang mountains, most notably in the upper Gang-ho-ba on the eastern flanks. Here it grows in very rough rocky places, particularly old limestone screes and moraines, well above the tree line and in association with other interesting alpine plants such as *Saxifraga calcicola* and *Parrya forrestii*. The plant was described from a gathering made by Abbé Delavay in the Lijiang region in the latter part of the nineteenth century.

Seed has been introduced on several occasions in recent years and plants have been raised to flowering. However, it is by no means common in cultivation, although those who have grown it, state that it is rather easier than its cousin *M. horridula*.

Meconopsis sherriffii G. Taylor

This rare and little-known species was discovered by Frank Ludlow and George Sherriff in Bhutan in 1936. It is generally likened to a pink-flowered *M. integrifolia* and the two species are undoubtedly very closely related.

Plants differ often in that they may become properly perennial and multi-crowned, but the single taproot makes it very difficult to divide and, as little seed is ever produced, this has remained a rare species in cultivation and is rarely offered in catalogues or seed lists.

Seedlings need to be handled with great care, but are scarcely as robust as those of *M. integrifolia*. Plants are best protected by a cloche or similar during the winter, and may flower in their second season. Flowers are solitary, borne on a long stem that is leafy in the lower half.

This charming species is very rare in cultivation today. Plants are reluctant to set much seed and there is evidence that the flowers produce very little pollen. This is probably due to the fact that years of inbreeding have had a severe effect on fertility, as it is known to do with quite a few other plants. It is hoped that further seed can be introduced from the wild in the not too distant future.

Young shoots and buds are susceptible to frost damage and care must be made to protect them as growth commences in the spring. Mature leaf-rosettes generally have a collar of persistent leaf-bases below the live leaves.

The discovery of this species is related by Harold Fletcher in *A Quest of Flowers* (1975): '. . . on this pass he [Ludlow] discovered a new poppy which Ludlow thought was the gem of the whole 1936 collection – "rose pink like the first flush of dawn on the snows". Sherriff was rather more restrained in his enthusiasm; "came across a nice meconopsis which I do not know, and cannot make out from Taylor's book. The flowers are a pretty pinkish wine-red, one on a scape and I don't think more than two to a plant. Leaves basal and cauline, all very thickly covered with bristle". Dr George Taylor [later Sir George] appropriately named this beautiful poppy which grows no more than 8 inches high and carried 4 inch flowers with up to 8 petals.'

In the wild, *M. sherriffii* inhabits screes and cliffs as well as alpine scrub, especially of dwarf rhododendrons, at altitudes of 4200–4600 m (13,800–15,100 ft) in northern Bhutan and the neighbouring part of Tibet. It flowers during June and July.

Meconopsis simplicifolia (D. Don) Walp.

(Syn. *Papaver simplicifolium* D. Don; *P.s.* var. *baileyi* Kingdon-Ward; *M. uniflora* Gumbleton; *Stylophorum simplicifolium* (D. Don) Spreng.)

Farrer (*The English Rock Garden*, 1928) regards this species as 'quite the most gorgeous of the single-bloomed Meconopsids, with big flowers of dazzling hue'. Certainly, in its best forms, this is a blue poppy that is a must in any collection.

M. simplicifolia finds its closest ally in *M. grandis*. The most obvious difference is in the scapose flowers of *M. simplicifolia*, where all the leaves are confined to a basal tuft. However, there are other differences: the flowers have five to eight petals, instead of the usual four in most *M. grandis*, and the filaments are the same blue as the petals and not whitish.

M. simplicifolia is perennial, although sometimes monocarpic, and forms a rather dense rosette of leaves or, indeed, a number of close rosettes on top of the slender taproot. The leaves, which vary a great deal in size from plant to plant, are simple and undivided, lanceolate, up to 30 cm (12 in) in length, covered on both surfaces with golden or rather rusty-coloured bristly hairs; the leaf-stalk can be as long as the leaf-blade, the one tapering into the other. The solitary flowers, 6–10 cm (2⅖–4 in) across, arise on bristly scapes up to 60 cm (24 in) tall, though 30–45 cm (12–18 in) is more normal; they are semi-pendulous and vary in colour from pure pale blue to deep blue or purple. The five to eight petals are broadly oval. The fruit-capsule is narrow-oblong, smooth or with reflexed bristles, and splits by four to nine valves in the upper third.

This highly desirable species is found in the wild from central Nepal to south-eastern Tibet (Xizang) at high altitudes of 3450–5450 m (11,300–17,900 ft). In these regions it inhabits alpine meadows, rhododendron scrub, rocky places and screes.

In its best forms, this is a highly desirable species. That it is not as common in cultivation as it should be is perhaps a result of the facts that it sets little seed, that what is produced germinates poorly and that the best forms tend towards being monocarpic. It is a point of irritation to gardeners that the easier perennial forms of this species are usually those with the poorest flowers, especially as regards shape and colour. The best forms are very fine, with flowers of clear sky blue. However, there are others almost as desirable, with good deeper blue or purple flowers – though be warned, some of the purple forms are very poor and a nasty muddy purple that even the compost heap might object to.

Seed should be treated in the same way as for *M. punicea*. Plants require a rich soil, full sun or half-sun, and are fine plants for the rock garden or scree, or alternatively a peat border, provided it is not too moist during the winter months. Winter protection (a cloche or frame light) is necessary; unless one is particularly lucky, some plants will rot off during the winter months.

Until recently there have been two forms in cultivation: a vigorous form with deep purplish-blue flowers that is properly perennial, and a finer form with sky blue flowers that is, unfortunately, usually monocarpic. The latter form was introduced from south-eastern Tibet in 1913 by Col. Bailey and is generally referred to as 'Bailey's Form' (not to be confused with Bailey's Blue Poppy, *M. baileyi*, see *M. betonicifolia*, p. 161). However, the species in the more usual perennial, purple-flowered form, was introduced considerably earlier, having been collected in 1848 in Sikkim during Joseph Dalton Hooker's famous journey in that region and written up so methodically in his *Himalayan Journals* of 1869. More recent collections of seed, especially from Sikkim and Bhutan, have introduced other good forms into our gardens:

M. simplicifolia has been crossed with several other species:

M. × hybrida (*M. simplicifolia* × *M. grandis*) – perennial with flowers on basal scapes. First raised by F.C. Puddle at Bodnant in North Wales.

M. × harleyana (*M. simplicifolia* × *M. integrifolia* (syn. *M. simplicifolia* var. *eburnea*)) – a striking perennial hybrid with basal scapes and large cream-coloured flowers. It occurred by chance in the garden of Andrew Harley in Devonhall, Scotland but is probably no longer in cultivation. It was given the cultivar name 'Ivory Poppy'.

M. sherriffii × *M. simplicifolia* – a spontaneous hybrid between two fairly closely related species. The hybrid, which is perennial and certainly less temperamental than its parents, produces rather small flowers best described as muddy-pink. As it is a fertile hybrid, it may have value in a breeding programme.

Meconopsis sinuata Prain

A poor relation of *M. latifolia*, with few, rather small, blue to purple or violet flowers that reportedly open only one at a time. The leaves grow up to 17.5 cm (7 in) long and are oblong in outline, with an irregularly lobed margin and adorned by sparse bristly spines on both sides. The distinctive fruit pod is slender-oblong, with three or four valves in the top third.

   M. sinuata has been in cultivation, but is no longer so. In gardens it appears to have no particular merits, being inferior in most respects to its brethren. However, new material and better forms may eventually be introduced to prove these statements wrong.

   It is a native of the Himalaya, from central Nepal to eastern Bhutan, where it is stated to be a plant of alpine meadows at 3750–4400 m (12,300–14,400 ft).

Meconopsis speciosa Prain
Meconopsis cawdoriana Kingdon-Ward; *M. ouvrardiana* Hand.-Mazz.

This very striking species falls within Series Aculeatae, which is also occupied by more familiar species, *M. horridula, M. aculeata* and *M. latifolia*. It has been much confused with the latter two in the past, in cultivation. However, *M. speciosa* is not in cultivation today to my knowledge.

   Frank Kingdon-Ward, who collected in the wild, commented that a specimen he gathered 'was 20 inches in height, crowned with twenty-nine flowers and fourteen ripening capsules, with five buds visible below – forty-eight flowers in all', and 'each flower is between 3 and 4 inches in diameter, coloured brilliant azure blue, with the texture of Japanese silk, massed with old gold in the centre'.

Like *M. aculeata*, this is a monocarpic plant with a stout taproot. The pinnately-lobed leaves have oblong to rounded lobes and are beset on both surfaces with reddish-brown bristles, the lower stem leaves and the basal ones stalked, while the upper leaves are rather smaller and unstalked. The fragrant flowers are usually numerous, being borne in a cone-shaped inflorescence with the lowest flowers arising from the axils of the stem leaves while the uppermost arise from small bracts or are bractless. In some instances, the flower stalks are primarily basal and partly fused to each other into a pseudostem. Stems and stalks are covered with reddish-brown bristles. The flowers range from azure-blue to ruddy-purple, 7.5–8.5 cm (3–3⅖ in) across, each with 4–8 rounded, partly overlapping petals. The stamens bear deep blue filaments and orange-yellow anthers. The fruit capsule is elliptical in outline, with persistent, usually purple, spines, splitting by 4–8 valves close to the top, where there is quite a stout style up to 10 mm (⅖ in) long.

M. speciosa is restricted to south-eastern Tibet and the neighbouring regions of north-western Yunnan, at 3660–5180 m (12,000–17,000 ft). It is a denizen of high rocky meadows and stabilised screes on both granitic as well as limestone rocks.

From *M. aculeata* this species differs primarily in its stouter styles and reddish-brown bristles that adorn the ovary and developing fruit. The two are widely separated geographically. *M. latifolia* differs in its shallow-lobed or more generally coarsely toothed foliage and pale blue flowers.

This is undoubtedly a very beautiful species and one that would be a great addition to the garden. Several seed collections have been made in north-western Yunnan in recent years and the results are awaited with great anticipation. It was spotted on two occasions during ACE (Alpine Garden Society's China Expedition) in 1994, but the plants were never in flower. The rosettes of deeply lobed leaves are very distinctive.

The species was first discovered by George Forrest in Yunnan in 1905.

Meconopsis superba King ex Prain

This is another beautiful monocarpic species often likened to a white-flowered *M. regia*. In fact, the two species are particularly closely related. The handsome leaf-rosettes may reach up to 90 cm (36 in) across in time and the leaves, like those of *M. regia*, are unlobed, but with a toothed margin. The evergreen rosettes have a silky and silvery appearance due to the presence of numerous closely appressed hairs. The leafy flowering stems rise to 2 m (7 ft) tall in the strongest specimens, with the upper flowers solitary, but the lower with three or five flowers on short lateral branches, the whole forming a large panicle. The individual flowers are cup-shaped and nodding, 7–9 cm (2⅘–3⅗ in) across, pure white; petals four, occasionally six, rounded; stamens with white filaments and yellow anthers; stigma purple-black and very distinctive. The fruit-capsule is 4–6 cm (1⅗–2⅖ in) long, oblong in outline and covered in appressed hairs, opening eventually by 7–11 short valves close to the apex.

M. superba is restricted in the wild to western Bhutan, where it inhabits screes and dwarf scrub at altitudes of 4100–4250 m (13,450–13,900 ft), flowering from June to August.

Although originally recorded from the Chumbi Region of Tibet, Grierson and Long (*Flora of Bhutan* 1(2), 1984) point out that *M. superba* appears to be endemic to western Bhutan and that the original locality was almost certainly in Bhutan and not Tibet.

In the wild, plants appear to have simple racemose inflorescences, but in cultivation, they are decidedly more paniculate.

The original plants first flowered in cultivation in Britain in 1927, although the origin of the introduction remains a mystery. Ludlow and Sherriff introduced further seed in 1933. *M. superba* can be cultivated in much the same way as *M. regia*. Plants usually take three to five years to come to maturity, although some may flower in their second season. Leaf-rosettes are prone to rotting in the winter and some losses must be expected, so it may be wise to cover them with large frame lights or cloches. Beware, however, that the protected plants do not become too dry during the winter; otherwise, they may well perish. Seedlings are very prone to damping off (like those of *M. betonicifolia*) and thin sowing and the use of fungicides may help prevent the loss of too many at this vulnerable stage in their life. Seeds are slow to germinate and young plants may not be large enough to plant out during their first season and may have to wait until the following year. Like the other evergreen rosette species, plants require ample moisture and generous mulches throughout the growing season. In addition, the inflorescences, when they finally appear, emerge early and may be frosted unless they are protected in some way. This may be one reason why this extremely handsome species is not seen more often in our gardens. This is a pity, for it is a very fine species and worth every effort that can be lavished upon it. There is no doubt that it responds best to cooler, more northerly gardens where the spring arrives late and there is at least some chance of a protective layer of snow during the winter months.

Meconopsis taylori L.H.J. Williams

An interesting plant that can be likened to a pink-flowered *M. regia*, but also differing in difficult-to-observe details such as leaf pubescence and, worse still, chromosome characteristics. This need not concern the reader and in any case, this plant is no longer in cultivation, having made a brief appearance shortly after its discovery. *M. taylori*, which is named in honour of Sir George Taylor, was found in the Nepalese Himalayas (Annapurna Himal) in 1954 by the prolific Stainton, Sykes and Williams expedition of that year, being collected under the numbers SSW 8506, 8507 and 8611. It was found on open grassy slopes at about 3900 m (13,000 ft).

The relationship of this species with *M. regia* has been called into question.

Some dismiss it as no more than a pink-flowered form of *M. regia*. However, there are enough characteristic to distinguish the two, not the least being the flower colour, and the fruit capsule size (nearly twice the size at 6 cm or 2⅖ in), the different pollen morphology and the somewhat barbed nature of the leaf and stem hairs. If that were not sufficient, then a ready means of identification of living plants can be seen in the dark brown rather than purple stigma. This all goes to show that however I try to steer around taxonomic detail, it has a way of revealing itself, for which the reader I hope will forgive me.

The members of the *M. regia* complex (which includes *M. regia* itself, *M. napaulensis*, *M. paniculata*, *M. superba*, *M. taylorii and M. wallichii*) are amongst the most striking members of the genus, grown as much for their very handsome evergreen leaf-rosettes as for the towering panicles of flowers. In cultivation, certainly far less so in the wild, they have a gross tendency to hybridise, so that it is difficult to maintain the pure species in the garden environment, unless they are well isolated from one another.

Meconopsis torquata Prain.
(See also *M. discigera*, p. 171)

A species of the Tibetan High Plateau in an area to the south of Lhasa. Seed was introduced from the region by Ludlow and Sherriff, but the plant failed to stay in cultivation for long. It is certainly never likely to linger long in our gardens and like many similar Himalayan/Tibetan species, their survival in cultivation depends on the skills of a few dedicated growers. Monocarpic species add a further degree of difficulty, for a dry period or frost whilst they are in flower may prevent any seed set – with obvious results.

M. torquata differs from *M. discigera* in several respects. The ovary is without a style (it is distinct and up to 6 mm or ¼ in long in *M. discigera*), while the extraordinary stylar disk is 8-angled rather than fringed. In addition, the flowers are borne in a more congested raceme and petals of *M. torquata* are sparsely bristly on the outside (glabrous in *M. discigera*), this being a unique feature in the whole of *Meconopsis* as far as I am aware.

The species was discovered by Walton in Tibet in 1904, but little is known of its frequency and distribution. It is not in cultivation at the present time, and those that were reared earlier in the twentieth century paid but a fleeting visit to our gardens.

Meconopsis violacea Kingdon-Ward

This is a very attractive species, formerly quite common in cultivation, especially in the cooler, moister, more northern, gardens of Britain, but now apparently lost to us; introduced into cultivation in 1926, it first flowered in 1929. With its narrow, almost zig-zagged leaves and nodding rich bluish-violet to purplish flowers, it must have been exciting to see it in the garden. In the wild it is restricted to Upper Burma (Myanmar) and the neighbouring regions of south-eastern Tibet at 3050–3960 m (10,000–13,000 ft) .

Another close relation of *M. napaulensis* and *M. wallichii*, distinguished primarily by its neat, finely dissected foliage and simple racemose, rather than paniculate inflorescence. In cultivation the lower flowers may sometimes be borne two or three together on short lateral branches. The pendulous flowers, 4–5 cm (1⅗–2 in) across, are a silky bluish-violet and the plant may reach up to 1.5 m (5 ft) in flower.

M. violacea was first discovered in the Burmese Himalayas in 1926 by Frank Kingdon-Ward, who stated that 'in its first year it produces an enormous crown of pale sea-green leaves encased in golden hairs of silken texture'. It was subsequently found close by in adjacent Tibet. It is unlikely to return to cultivation until those remote regions become more accessible and safe to travel in. Coming from the wetter eastern end of the Himalayas, this is undoubtedly a plant for cool, moist gardens and a humid atmosphere, but it must be shielded from too much winter wetness.

Meconopsis wallichii Hook.   [Pl. 155–156]
(formerly included under *M. napaulensis*)

This is an evergreen, monocarpic species of the *M. napaulensis* persuasion. It differs primarily in its narrower, more dissected, yellowish-green leaves with remoter lobes, which are generally more bristly, by having rather smaller pale blue or purplish-blue flowers, and by the small fruit-capsules that are adorned with spreading stiff bristles.

M. wallichii is a splendid plant. In cultivation and in the wild it flowers several weeks later than *M. napaulensis*, *M. paniculata* or *M. regia*. Indeed, I have seen it still in flower in eastern Nepal as late as early September. In cultivation this is to its advantage as only the first (uppermost) flowers are likely to open whilst those of the other species (referred to above) are still in bloom and little hybridisation is likely to result. This can be circumvented easily by ignoring the upper fruits and collecting seed from the fruits of the later flowers, located on the lower lateral branches of the plant. Any hybrids generally produce unsatisfactory muddy blue and purples and are frequently sterile according to James Cobb (*Meconopsis*, 1989). The true species is a charmer and needs every encouragement.

In cultivation it is generally sold under the name *M. napaulensis* blue form or simply 'Wallich's Form'. The blueness of its sky blue flowers is not affected by soil alkalinity.

M. wallichii has a wide distribution in the wild from eastern Nepal to Bhutan, upper Burma (Myanmar), south-eastern Tibet and the neighbouring regions of north-western Yunnan and western Sichuan at altitudes of 2850–3800 m (9350–12,500 ft), flowering in the wild normally from July to September. I have seen it on several occasions on the high forested ridges overlooking the Tamur Valley in eastern Nepal. It has always struck me as a very elegant species with its arching stems, often fully 2 m (6½ ft) tall, and in the purity of its transparent blue flowers and charming bristly fruit capsules. It grows in lush dank places where leeches abound during the monsoon, but is always a total delight to come upon on those distant misty ridges.

Meconopsis wumungensis K. M. Feng

A fairly recently described species discovered on Mt Wumung near Kunming in Yunnan Province. It is fairly closely related to *M. lyrata*, but is said to be annual (this would be highly unusual in a genus that contains no other known annuals). It inhabits damp mountain rocks at about 4000 m (13,000 ft).

Meconopsis zangnanensis L. H. Zhou

Another recently described Chinese species said to resemble a small version *of M. simplicifolia* and with sky-blue flowers. It was discovered on high alpine meadows in the Tibetan border zone east of Bhutan at 4000 m (13,000 ft). It is clearly a little gem and one eagerly anticipates its introduction into cultivation.

The Prickly Poppies
Argemone

No other genus in the poppy family has created over the years quite so much confusion amongst botanists and gardeners. A plethora of names exists and many species and subordinate taxa have been described to confuse and to tantalise.

As it is known today, *Argemone* can be said to contain some 28 species, which are restricted to North and South America and the Hawaiian Islands, the greatest number being concentrated in the south-western USA and Central America.

The majority of species are annual or perennial herbs, although one is a shrub. They are readily distinguished from other poppies by their stiff stems, prickly leaves and prickly fruit-capsules, although these features are very variable between the different species of *Argemone*. When cut, the stems generally ooze a white, yellow or orange sap. The leaves are alternate along the stems and usually noticeably pinnately-lobed; besides the prickly margins, the leaves may also bear further prickles along the veins on one or both surfaces. The flowers are erect in bud and are 4–15 cm (1⅗–6 in) across, and showy, generally solitary; sepals usually three, occasionally two or four to six, smooth bristly or prickly, each sepal terminating in a spine-tipped horn; petals four to six, white, cream, yellow, or occasionally lavender or purple; stamens generally numerous, but sometimes as few as 20, with linear anthers. The fruit-capsule is erect and is composed of three to seven fused carpels, rounded to oblong or egg-shaped, sparsely to densely spiny, sometimes smooth, parting at the top into a number of short valves when ripe; valve number equal to the number of carpels, hence three to seven; style short or absent.

As in *Papaver*, the capsule details are of critical importance in separating the species. Other useful characters are the presence or absence of prickles on the stems and the surface of the leaves, as well as the size and shape of the sepal-horns.

Argemone is a very homogenous group and there is a pronounced morphological similarity between the species. This means that it is not possible to divide the genus into different sections or other types of division. This is in contrast to genera such as *Papaver* and *Meconopsis*, which show a great range of morphological characters. This would indicate to the botanist that *Argemone* is of rather recent origin, evolutionarily speaking.

Their large showy flowers and the ease of cultivation of most of the species would, one might suppose, mean that they are widely grown in gardens. However, this is not so and at the present time only a few species are available, although others can be found within the confines of botanic gardens and private collections. Many of the species are handsome and bold plants. There is something incongruous about plants that are so robustly defensive in their stiff stems and prickly nature and yet produce such large and seemingly delicate flowers with their thin-textured and satiny petals. Yet it is this combination that is so attractive, just like the many cacti and other defensive plants which are able to produce from amongst their spiny masses wonderful blooms of delicate and transient beauty.

The Mexican Poppy *A. mexicana* is by far the best-known species and it has been cultivated for many centuries, primarily as a medicinal plant. The name *Argemone* comes from the Greek for cataract of the eye, *argema*, for it was supposed that the juice of the plant was capable of curing such afflictions. *A. mexicana* was well known to Gerard as *Papaver spinosum* or the prickly poppy. Of it, Miller states: 'Argemone – because it purges away the mistiness of the eyes. It is called the Infernal Fig, because the Capsule pretty much resembles a fig; and Infernal, from its Asperity.'

Miller clearly did not think much of *A. mexicana* as a garden plant, for he says: 'This is an annual plant, which is very common in most parts of the West Indies, and is by the Spaniards call'd Fico de Inferno, or the Devil's Fig; there is no great beauty or use of this plant amongst us, that I know of . . . I have been informed that Gum bouge [Gamboge] is made from the Juice of this Plant.'

To show that these make good garden plants, I can hardly do better than quote Graham Rice (*Garden Flowers from Seed* by Christopher Lloyd and Graham Rice): 'The prickly poppies fall among the unsung heroes of the huge poppy family. Hardly anyone grows them, but their long succession of flowers makes them one of the most desirable of plants for well-drained, sunny but not inhospitable borders.'

Plants are best treated as half-hardy annuals, although the perennial types will overwinter if the weather has been kind. Seed can be sown in April in pots rather than seed trays, as the seedlings get away better if they are not disturbed unduly; cellular trays will of course do just as well. Sow two to three seeds to a pot and thin these to the strongest in due course. Alternatively, seed can be sown where the plants are to flower, especially in mild districts where late frosts are uncommon.

The prickly poppies thrive best in a light, well-drained soil in a sunny sheltered position and are especially showy during hot dry periods in the summer. Seed is set in quantity, but beware, the fruit-capsules are extremely prickly and vicious when ripe, so wear a pair of gloves when collecting seed. *A. mexicana* will often seed around in gardens, but the more handsome white-flowered *A. platyceras* and *A. albiflora* seldom do so in my experience. Scan the seed lists for these last two species and for *A. grandiflora*, *A. squarrosa* and *A. sanguinea*, for they are all worth seeking out to add to the hosts of delightful poppies grown in our gardens.

The most comprehensive revision of the genus was undertaken by Gerald Ownbey at the Department of Botany, University of Minnesota, Minneapolis and published in two parts. Firstly, a 'Monograph of the Genus Argemone for North America' (*Memoirs of the Torrey Botanical Club* 21(1), 1958) and secondly, 'The Genus Argemone in South America and Hawaii' (*Brittonia* 13, 1961).

Although a number of species clearly have great horticultural appeal, others (perhaps a half of the total) are rather less desirable or distinctly 'weedy' – only the more appealing are included here.

A. mexicana was undoubtedly the first species to be cultivated in Europe. Its date of introduction is said to be 1592. However, its first reference in literature is that of Bauhin in *Phytopinax*, 1596, followed closely by Gerard in 1597. Gerard had received seed of it from St Johns Island in the West Indies.

The next species brought to Europe was *A. albiflora*, which Lamarck (1793) distinguished as a white-flowered variety of *A. mexicana*. It was certainly cultivated in Denmark by 1812 and in England by 1820, where it enjoyed great popularity for a number of years. Other species followed: *A. ochroleuca*, *A. grandiflora* and in 1877 Joseph Dalton Hooker introduced *A. polyanthemos* from Colorado (under the name *A. hispida*, it was featured in *Curtis's Botanical Magazine* t. 6402, 1878).

Argemones appear to have been popular in Europe in the period 1827–40, but declined thereafter for some reason or other. In their native countries, particularly in North America, they have never met with great enthusiasm in gardens.

In the Americas the various species of *Argemone* have been traditionally used for their medicinal properties. In Latin America, in particular, the juice extracted from stems and seeds has been employed for a wide variety of different ailments. It is recorded that in Puerto Rico seeds of *A. mexicana* are used as a purgative and the juice of the plants is said to be beneficial in treating various eye conditions. *Argemone* contains a cocktail of different alkaloids. Surprisingly, these have never been thoroughly investigated, despite the modern trends towards 'natural medicines'.

Key to Species

1. Flowers yellow, occasionally golden or bronze 2
   Flowers white, pink or lavender 6

2. Plant shrubby; leaves close, small and holly-like: *A. fruticosa*
   Plants annual or herbaceous perennials; leaves not as above 3

3. Flowers relatively small, 3–6 cm (1⅕–2⅖ in) across; stamens not
   more than 75 4
   Flowers larger, 7–10 cm (3–4 in) across; stamens at least 150 5

4. Flowers pale lemon-yellow, oblong in bud; fruit-capsule always
   prickly;   *A. ochroleuca*
   Flowers bright yellow, rounded in bud; fruit-capsule smooth or
   prickly: *A. mexicana*

5. Petals yellow to gold or bronze; filaments red to purplish: *A. aenea*
   Petals always bright yellow; filaments lemon-yellow: *A. superba*

6. Petals pink or lavender 7
   Petals white 9

7. Lower leaves lobed for less than two-thirds the distance to the
   midrib; upper leaves clasping the stem: *A. polyanthemos*
   Lower leaves lobed almost to the midrib; upper leaves not clasping
   the stem 8

8. Stamens about 80; stem and leaf surfaces prickly, as well as finely
   hairy: *A. rosea*
   Stamens 150 or more; stem and leaf surface sparsely prickly, not
   hairy: *A. sanguinea*

9. Leaves with shallow rounded lobes, not long-spine-pointed;
   flowers often separated from the nearest leaf by a short stalk: *A. munita*
   Leaves shallowly to deeply lobed, the lobes angular, often acute and
   with a long spine-tip; flowers often immediately subtended by one
   or several leaves 10

10. Sepal-horns flattened or angular in cross-section 11
    Sepal-horns rounded in cross-section 12

11. Leaf-surface prickly on the main veins, as well as minutely bristly
    between the veins; fruit-capsule spines compound (with smaller
    spines on the base of the main ones):   *A squarrosa*
    Leaf-surface sparsely prickly along the main veins, otherwise
    smooth; fruit-capsule with simple spines: *A. platyceras*

12. Prickles of flower buds at right-angles to the surface; leaves lobed
    almost to the midrib: *A. sanguinea*
    Prickles of flower buds ascending; leaves generally not lobed
    more than two-thirds the way to the midrib 13

13. Sepal-horns 3–6 mm (⅛–¼ in) long   *A. albiflora*
    Sepal-horns 6–15 mm (¼–⅗ in) long .14

14. Flower buds smooth or with very few spines; upper leaves not
    clasping the stem; fruit-capsules sparsely spiny: *A. grandiflora*

Flower buds always prickly; upper leaves clasping the stem;
fruit-capsules generally rather densely spiny 15

15. Flower buds 18–28 mm (¾–1⅛ in) long; flowers 10–12.5 cm
(4–5 in) across; stamens about 100:   ***A. hunnemannii***
Flower buds 15–22 mm (⅗–⅞ in) long; flowers 7–10 cm
(2¾–4 in) across; stamens 150 or more: ***A. polyanthemos***

Argemone aenea G.B. Ownb.

An annual or short-lived perennial with bright yellow latex when cut, the
stems solitary or few, 30–80 cm (12–32 in) tall, prickly. The grey-green
leaves have bluish veins and are pinnately-lobed, the upper less markedly so
than the lower; lobes with prickle-tipped teeth, generally prickly on the main
veins beneath, less so or smooth above. The buds are moderately prickly,
oblong in outline; sepal-horns, 7–12 mm (¼–½ in) long, round in cross-
section, smooth or with a few prickles at the base. The flowers are deep
yellow or gold, sometimes almost bronze, 7–10 cm (3–4 in) across, each
usually subtended by two small leaflike bracts; petals rounded; stamens about
150, with purplish or red filaments and yellow flushed purple anthers; stigma
purple. The elliptical to oblong fruit-capsule is armed with stout spines.

   A. aenea has a scattered distribution in southern and western Texas and the
neighbouring part of northern Mexico. In these regions it inhabits dry, often
sandy habitats on plains and hills, but also in fields and along roadsides from
sea level to an altitude of about 1450 m (4800 ft), flowering from February
to May.

   This interesting and attractive species is not in cultivation. It finds its closest
ally in *A. superba*, which differs primarily in its smaller, rounder flowerbuds
and pale yellow filaments. In addition, the petals are pure yellow, never
golden or bronzed.

Argemone albiflora Hornem.
(syn. *A. alba* of cultivation)

An attractive annual or biennial up to 1 m (3 ft) tall, though often less; stems
much-branched and usually moderately prickly, oozing a yellow latex when
cut. The leaves can be greyish-green or plain green and are pinnately-lobed,
the lower cut almost to the midrib, the uppermost more shallowly-lobed and
clasping the stem with broad bases; margins spine-toothed, with the
undersurface of the leaf prickly on the main veins, but the upper surface
generally quite smooth. The elliptical or rounded flowerbuds are prickly;
sepal-horns rather short, 3–6 mm (⅛–¼ in) long, rounded in cross-section,
smooth. The flowers vary in size from 5–10 cm (2–4 in) and are pure white,
generally with one or two leaflike bracts close beneath; stamens 150 or more,
with yellowish filaments and yellow anthers; stigma purple. The fruit-capsule
is elliptical to oblong and stoutly spiny.

This species is found over a wide area in the USA, from Mississippi to North Carolina, southwards to Florida and Texas, but it has become naturalised in surrounding areas, generally as an escape from cultivation. It inhabits a variety of soils from sand dunes and beaches to fields, field boundaries, wasteland and roadsides, generally at low altitudes and flowering from about late March to June, sometimes later.

A. albiflora has been cultivated in Europe for almost 200 years, being found in literature of the time as *A. alba*, an invalid name. This is undoubtedly a very fine and attractive species, certainly one of the best of the white-flowered 'group', and can generally be distinguished by the combination of smooth upper leaf-surface, clasping upper leaves and short-horned flowerbuds.

In cultivation, flowers with more than the usual complement of five petals are often seen. These often have eight petals.

The Texan population, which can be distinguished by its fruit-capsules that bear a mixture of stout spines and smaller prickles, is distinguished as subsp. *texana* G.B. Ownb.

Unfortunately, many plants grown under this name (*A. albiflora*) generally prove to be *A. platyceras* – at least in Britain.

Argemone fruticosa Thurber ex Gray
(syn. *A. fruticosa* Mueller)
SHRUBBY PRICKLY POPPY

This species is not in cultivation, but it is so distinctive and unusual amongst the prickly poppies that some mention of it must be made.

The plant is a shrub up to 2 m (7 ft) tall with rigid woody stems becoming bare of foliage below; young stems glaucous, somewhat prickly but densely covered in leaves. The holly-like leaves are leathery, markedly glaucous, oblong, not more than 3.5 cm (1⅖ in) long and armed along the margin with rigid spines. The flowers, 5–10 cm (2–4 in) across, are yellow, often rather pale and immediately subtended by several leaves. The fruit-capsule is broad, egg-shaped and densely armed with stout spines.

A rare and little-known species restricted to the Coahuila region of Mexico, where it inhabits rocky mountain slopes and canyons at 1700–1900 m (5600–6200 ft), flowering from May to August.

This is undoubtedly a very interesting species and it would be well worth bringing it into cultivation. However, it is very unlikely to prove hardy in frost-affected regions.

Argemone grandiflora Sweet

This is another of the white-flowered prickly poppies, but in its typical form it is quite distinct, with its smooth, glaucous, often red-tinged stems, smooth leaves (apart from the prickly margins), entirely smooth flower buds and fruit-capsule with just a few scattered spines. The leaves are more or less glaucous, but are delightfully highlighted by pale, almost white, veins. The six-petalled flowers are large, 6–10 cm (2⅖–4 in) across, white and satiny, with contrasting bright yellow anthers and purple stigma.

This is certainly a very fine plant that surely deserves a greater audience in our gardens. It is a lovely foil for other, more delicate annuals such as the flaxes, viscaria or phacelias; or for those who opt for grey and white, try growing it with *Omphalodes linifolia*. Although the individual flowers do not last very long, as with most of the other prickly poppies, they are produced in succession over a long season. The cultivar 'White Lustre' is a particularly fine form well worth seeking out.

A. grandiflora has been cultivated since the 1820s, being first described from a cultivated plant. In his original description Sweet★ states: 'For the opportunity afforded us of giving a figure of this grand plant, we are obliged to the kindness of Robert Barclay Esq. of Bury Hill, in whose superb collection it was raised this spring, from seed received from Mexico.'

In the wild, *A. grandiflora* occupies a variety of habitats from disturbed soils, roadsides and wastelands, to the hills and mountains, though not above an altitude of 1850 m (6100 ft). Its distribution is confined to east-central Mexico from Hidalgo to Tamaulipas, where it flowers practically throughout the year.

Farther to the north in Mexico, forms with somewhat prickly stems, and leaves with prickles beneath, are distinguished as subsp. *armata* G.B. Ownb.

Argemone hunnemannii Otto & Dietr.
(syn. *A. platyceras* var. *chilensis* Prain; *A. p.* var. *hunnemannii* (Otto & Dietr.) Fedde)
CHILEAN PRICKLY POPPY

This species, which surprisingly is not in cultivation, is unusual in being the only South American prickly poppy with white flowers. It is confined to Chile at rather low altitudes – at least it has not been recorded much above 600 m (2000 ft).

A. hunnemannii clearly comes close to *A. polyanthemos* in general appearance and differs primarily in its larger buds (18–28 mm or ¾–1⅛ in long as opposed to 15–22 mm or ⅗–⅞ in) and flowers that are often 10–12 cm (4–5 in) across. The armature of the fruit-capsule is clearly different; in *A. hunnemannii* the spines are spreading to erect and rather slender, whereas in *A. polyanthemos* they are stouter, spreading or often somewhat recurved.

Argemone mexicana L.   [Pl. 159]
(syn. *Papaver spinosum* Bauhin; *A. spinosa* Moench; *A versicolor* Salisb.; *A. mucronata* Dum.; *A. mexicana* var. *typica* Prain; *A. m.* var. *ochroleuca* Britton; *Ectrus mexicanus* Nieuwland)
MEXICAN POPPY

This is undoubtedly the best-known and most widespread species of *Argemone*. In the wild it is native to Central America and the West Indies, but

---

★ Described and figured in Sweet's *British Flower Garden* 3, t. 266 (1829).

it has had a long association in cultivation and today it has become a widespread weed in tropical and subtropical regions of the world. It is especially prevalent around seaports and has no doubt been transported from port to port over many years. The seeds have a long viability and are able to endure many years before germinating. Its spread is perhaps not so surprising as it, unlike most of its brethren, is very much a coastal or island species.

Gerard (1597) remarked of this species that it was 'so full of sharpe and venemous prickles, that whosoever had one of them in his throte, doubtless it would send him packing to heaven or to hell'.

A. mexicana has attracted a host of common names of which the following are probably only a sample: Bird-in-the-bush, Donkey Thistle, Bermuda Thistle, Flowering Thistle, Gamboge Thistle, Gold Thistle of Peru, Infernal Fig, Jamaican Thistle, Mexican Thistle, Mexican Prickly Poppy, Mexican Thorn Poppy, Queen Thistle and Stinking Thistle.

The species is a variable annual up to 1 m (3 ft) tall, though often less, the stout stem generally branched close to the base, smooth to sparsely prickly. The leaves are grey-green with whitish blotches (bloom) over the conspicuous veins, the lower leaves deeply pinnately-lobed, the upper less so and clasping the stem with rather narrow bases; lobes with slender spine-teeth, the upper and lower surfaces smooth or somewhat prickly on the main veins. The buds are oblong, smooth or with a few prickles; sepal-horns 5–10 mm (⅕–⅖ in) long, round in cross-section, spine-tipped, otherwise smooth. The flowers are bright yellow, very occasionally pale yellow, 4–6 cm (1⅗–2⅖ in) across, closely subtended by one or two leaflike bracts; petals six, obovate usually; stamens few, 30–50, with pale yellow filaments and deeper anthers; stigma purple. The fruit-capsule is oblong to elliptical, to 20 mm (⅘ in) long, smooth or spiny.

The Mexican poppy is native to Central America and the West Indies, south to Guatemala and Nicaragua and northwards to Texas and Florida, but it is widely naturalised outside this region. It is found most often on cultivated, waste and disturbed land, field boundaries, roadsides and seashores, up to an altitude of about 1600 m (5250 ft). *A. mexicana* is a prolific seeder and, in the wild, can be found in flower almost throughout the year.

This familiar species can be readily recognised by its bright yellow flowers and relatively few stamens. Forms with wholly smooth leaves, stems, buds and fruits are assigned to forma *leiocarpa* (Greene) G.B. Ownb. (syn. *A. leiocarpa* Greene; *A mexicana* var. *leiocarpa* Prain; *A. alba* var. *leiocarpa* Fedde). The smooth character of var. *leiocarpa* are maintained in cultivation even when it is grown in association with the more usual prickly form. It is believed that it first originated on the island of Key West, but has since been introduced to other islands and Florida, as well as areas of South America and West Africa.

The fact that this rather charming poppy is so often dismissed as a troublesome weed in some parts of the world should not put one off growing it in the garden, for it is a handsome, floriferous plant that repays by producing flowers over a long season.

The closely related *A. ochroleuca* can be readily distinguished by its pale lemon flowers, consistently spiny fruit-capsules and oblong, rather than almost rounded, flowerbuds. In addition, differences can be observed in the stigmatic lobes, which are spreading in *A. ochroleuca*, but closely appressed to the style at anthesis in *A. mexicana*.

There are undoubtedly a number of forms of *A. mexicana* in cultivation, some with well-marked leaves that recall *Silybum marianum*, a widely grown decorative thistle with handsome leaf-rosettes. Other forms have deep, yellow or tangerine flowers. The only named cultivar is 'Yellow Lustre', which produces luscious bowl-shaped flowers of polished chrome yellow; it is undoubtedly the best form for the garden.

Argemone munita Dur. & Hilg.   [Pl. 160–161]

This is an extremely variable, white-flowered, prickly poppy from the south-western United States and neighbouring Baja California (Mexico).

A. munita is an annual or perennial herb up to 1 m (3 ft) tall, though often very much shorter; stems moderately to densely branched, often purplish, sparsely to densely prickly. The leaves, especially the lower, are pinnately-lobed, the lobes reaching only halfway to the midrib, rounded, prickly along the margin, sparsely to densely prickly on both the upper and lower surfaces; lower leaves stalked, but the upper broader and shorter and clasping the stem with broad bases. The flowerbuds are oblong to elliptic-oblong with prickles at right-angles to the surface; sepal-horns 6–8 mm (¼–⅓ in) long, usually round in cross-section, smooth to prickly. The flowers, 5–10 cm (2–4 in) across, but sometimes larger, are white and with a distinct, though short, stem between the flower and the nearest leaf; petals six, obovate; stamens numerous, at least 150, with pale yellow filaments and yellow anthers; stigma purple. The fruit-capsule is elliptical to lanceolate in outline, 9–15 mm (⅜–⅗ in) long and armed with simple spines or a dense mixture of spines and lesser prickles.

A. munita is native to California and Baja California, Arizona, Nevada and Utah, where it commonly grows on sandy, gravelly or rocky soils, especially in semi-desert regions, to 2600 m (8500 ft) altitude. It flowers in the wild from April until September.

This species is readily recognised by its shallow and blunt leaf-lobes and by the fact that the flowers are separated from the uppermost leaf by a short interval of at least 3–4 mm (⅛ in). Even so, this is an extremely variable species. In his monograph of the North American species (1958), Gerald Ownbey gives three subspecies as well as intermediate forms. Of these, the most widespread is subsp. *rotundata* (Rydb.) G.B. Ownb. (syn. *A. rotundata* Rydb.; *A hispida* Torrey; *A. mexicana* var. *hispida* Wats.; *A. platyceras* var. *hispida* Prain). This subspecies, which is the usual one seen in cultivation, has densely prickly stems, leaves and flowerbuds and the stems are noticeably glaucous with an attractive purple flush. Subspecies *rotundata* covers most of the range of the species, except for the coastal and subcoastal regions of California and Baja California, which is occupied by subsp. *munita*, a far less prickly species in all its main features.

Ownbey points out that an interesting relationship exists between *A. munita* and fire. Areas recently burnt often produce a flush of plants as seed that has lain dormant in the soil is clearly triggered into germination by the heat; the increased germination of many western American plants by exposure to heat is well documented.

Argemone ochroleuca Sweet   [Pl. 162]

(syn. *A. mexicana* var. *ochroleuca* Lindl.; *A. ochroleuca* var. *barclayana* Prain; *A. sulphurea* Sweet ex London)

PALE MEXICAN POPPY

This handsome prickly poppy is very closely related to *A. mexicana* and differs primarily in its pale lemon-yellow flowers and more elongated flowerbuds. In addition, the capsules are more lanceolate and always spiny (never smooth) and the stigmatic lobes are clearly spreading when the flower opens (in *A. mexicana* they are pressed close to the surface of the style).

A. ochroleuca has a distinctly more inland distribution than *A. mexicana*, being found primarily in central and western Mexico and Baja California, where it is a weed of hills, cultivated and waste land, plains and roadsides, flowering almost throughout the year in places. Unlike *A. mexicana*, it has not become a widespread tropical and subtropical weed around the world, although it is naturalised in Australia. Reports of it from South America refer to *A. subfusiformis*, which is found in Argentina, Bolivia, Chile, Ecuador and Peru. This latter species is not, as far as I am aware, in cultivation.

A. ochroleuca is an attractive species in the garden. The subtle combination of greyish leaves and pale yellow flowers, often produced in profusion, give the plant a distinctive character. In gardens both *A. ochroleuca* and *A. mexicana* are highly self-compatible and crosses appear to be rare; in fact most cultivated forms of *A. mexicana* have 2n = 56 chromosomes, where those of *A. ochroleuca* are 2n = 28.

Narrow-petalled forms of *A. ochroleuca* are afforded the rank of subsp. *stenopetala* (Prain) G.B. Ownb. (syn. *A. intermedia* var. *stenopetala* Prain). Both subspecies can be found together in the wild and are distinguishable only in bud and flower. The buds are not more than 12 mm (½ in) long and the flowers smaller, only 3–5 cm (1⅕–2 cm) across, with narrow-elliptical rather than rounded petals.

Argemone platyceras Link & Otto   [Pl. 163–164]

CHICALOTE OR CRESTED POPPY

This is perhaps the finest of the white prickly poppies in cultivation and the one most often seen in gardens. It has been cultivated in European gardens since the 1820s and it was from plants that flowered in Berlin in 1829 and 1830 that the original description and drawing were prepared.

Taxonomically, this species has been much muddled with other white-flowered species from Mexico and the south-western United States, but such things need not concern us unduly here. *A. platyceras* is in fact distinctive in its sparsely and weakly prickly leaves (except for the margin) and stems, flattened sepal horns and densely prickly fruit-capsules. The leaves generally have a few scattered prickles on the upper and lower surface, although they can be wholly smooth. The large white flowers, 10–14 cm (4–5⅖ in) across are pure satiny white, but often open with a faint lemony flush. The stamens vary from pale yellow to lavender, both in the filaments and anthers; the stigma is generally purplish. The fruit-capsule is completely covered by slender spines, so densely as to almost conceal the surface of the capsule.

This is a handsome plant, more robust than *A. mexicana* and, in gardens at least, often attaining 90 cm (36 in) in height. The foliage is deeply and sharply lobed, grey-green but often with an overtone of blue. The flowers, although smaller, are reminiscent of those of its Californian and Mexican cousin *Romneya*.

Although perennial, *A. platyceras* is best grown as an annual, for it is unlikely to overwinter satisfactorily in any but the mildest of districts. In any event, seed is easily raised and plants flower in early summer from an early spring sowing under glass. Purple-flowered forms, sometimes seen in horticultural literature, more correctly, I believe, refer to *A. polyanthemos*, although the colour is decidedly more lavender than purple.

A. platyceras inhabits hills and mountain slopes, often on rocky or volcanic soils, cultivated and fallow fields and wasteland at quite high elevations, 1850–3200 m (6100–10,500 ft). It is widespread in Mexico from Vera Cruz to southern Hidalgo, Oaxaca and Michoacan, as well as the state of Mexico itself.

A hispida Gray (syn. *A. platyceras* var. *hispida* Prain) is a distinct species which A. Gray stated was 'the greatest ornament of the vegetation of Colorado, where it occurs in open grassy or stony places in great profusion, flowering for three months of the year'. It is readily distinguished by its more densely prickly stems, by the leaf-surfaces which, besides being prickly, are covered all over in tiny crisped hairs. The flowers are rather smaller, generally 7–10 cm (2⅘–4 in) across. *A. hispida* does not overlap in distribution in the wild with *A. platyceras*, being confined to the USA from Colorado to Wyoming and New Mexico.

Argemone polyanthemos (Fedde) G.B. Ownb.   **[Pl. 165]**
(syn. *A. intermedia* var. *polyanthemos* Fedde, *A. intermedia* Eastwood)
PLAINS PRICKLY POPPY

This is another of the large white-flowered persuasion closely related to both *A. albiflora* and *A. grandiflora*.

The species was introduced into cultivation in England in 1877 from seed collected by Joseph Dalton Hooker in Colorado. A plant grown at Kew was figured in *Curtis's Botanical Magazine* in 1878 (as *A. hispida* Gray).

In the wild, *A. polyanthemos* is restricted to the Great Plains from the eastern flanks of the Rockies from south-west Dakota to Wyoming, New Mexico and Texas. It is a plant of sandy and gravelly soils, inhabiting fields, roadsides and waste ground as well as the foothills, generally at rather low elevations, but to over 2200 m (7200 ft) in Colorado and New Mexico; flowering from April to August depending on location.

Plants are annual or biennial, often only 40 cm (16 in) tall, but sometimes attaining 80 cm (32 in). The leaves are markedly glaucous and succulent, the lower more deeply lobed than the upper, which clasp the stem, somewhat prickly on the veins beneath, but completely smooth above. The flowerbuds are oblong and moderately prickly, the sepal-horns 6–10 mm (¼–⅖ in) long, round in cross-section. The flowers, 6–10 cm (2⅖–4 in) across, are generally white, but occasionally lavender, with yellow stamens and purple stigma.

This species differs from *A. albiflora* in its longer sepal-horns (only 3–6 mm or ⅛–¼ in long in the latter) and narrower and longer fruit-capsules. Undoubtedly, the two are very closely related and some authorities would surely merge the two, albeit as subspecies or varieties of the same species. The two overlap in part of their ranges in the wild.

The dwarfer habit of *A. polyanthemos* would make it a fine garden plant, especially in its rarer lavender-flowered form. Yet this species does not appear to be at all common in cultivation at the present time; indeed, I do not know of authenticated material in cultivation. This is sad because this and several other fine *Argemone* species are very accessible and could surely be brought into cultivation without too much difficulty. Sometimes our efforts to bring in ever rare and more unusual plants into cultivation makes us, I believe, overlook the simple beauty of some of these easy-to-grow plants. Perhaps a rekindled vogue for annual borders in the garden might propel such species back to our attention.

Argemone rosea Hook.

(syn. *A. mexicana* var. *rosea* (Hook.) Reiche; *A. platyceras* var. *chilensis* Prain; *A. platyceras* var. *hispido-rosea* Fedde)
ROSE PRICKLY POPPY

Although not in cultivation, *A. rosea* merits a mention. It is restricted to a relatively small area in Coquimto Province, Chile.

The species is an annual with stems, leaves and flower buds densely covered with prickly bristles. The leaves are deeply and narrowly pinnately-lobed and sharply spine-toothed; upper leaves much reduced, but not clasping the stem. The flowerbuds have small horns, only 2–4 mm (1/12–⅙ in) long, and finely pointed. The flowers are 6–10 cm (2⅖–4 in) across and lavender (reports of white-flowered forms have not, to my knowledge, been substantiated); stamens about 80 and stigma purple.

Argemone sanguinea Greene

(syn. *A. mexicana* var. *rosea* Coulter ex Greene; *A. platyceras* var. *rosea* Coulter; *A. purpurea* Rose ex Pringle)

This is yet another species unaccountably not in cultivation at the present time. It is, in many ways, similar to *A. albiflora* and certainly in its lavender-coloured forms is distinctive enough. However, it often occurs with white flowers and these are more difficult to separate. In *A. sanguinea* the sepal-horns are clearly larger, 5–10 mm (⅕–⅖ in) long (not 3–6 mm or ⅛–¼ in) and generally with a few prickles in the lower part. The fruit-capsules of *A. sanguinea* are usually three- to five-parted (carpellate), whilst those of *A. albiflora* are four- to seven-parted; the capsular spines are stouter and often recurved in *A. sanguinea*.

A. *sanguinea* comes from southern Texas and the neighbouring regions of northern Mexico. It is a plant of the chaparral, of fields and field-margins, wasteland and disturbed ground and along roadways from sea level to an altitude of about 1600 m (5250 ft), flowering primarily from February to June.

Argemone squarrosa Greene

This species is very similar in general appearance to *A. platyceras*, but it is a far more prickly plant overall. Both stem and leaves are generally moderately prickly, the leaf-prickles confined to the main veins, but the areas in between covered in tiny bristles. The pure white flowers are 10–12 cm (4–5 in) across usually and bear yellow stamens and a purple stigma. The fruit-capsules are densely spiny and are unusual in that the main spines are compound with lesser spines borne on their basal half; this is in contrast to the simple spines of the fruit-capsules of *A. platyceras*. In addition, the stamens of *A. platyceras* are often reddish-lavender or lavender and this can provide a quick means of distinction.

A. *squarrosa* is primarily a prairie species, being found there and in the surrounding foothills (often sandy soils) from Kansas and Oklahoma to south-eastern Colorado and New Mexico, generally at altitudes of between 1000–1850 m (3300–6100 ft). It can be found in flower between May and September.

In cultivation it is generally present as subsp. *glabrata* G.B. Ownb., which differs only in having little or no fine bristles between the main leaf-veins, or indeed on the flowerbuds or fruit-capsules. This subspecies is confined to western Texas and south-eastern New Mexico.

In cultivation, subsp. *glabrata* is often, and perhaps not surprisingly, confused with *A. platyceras*. If the stamens are pink or purplish rather than yellow, then the plant will certainly prove to be the latter. However, the fruit-capsule characters are perhaps more convincing. In subsp. *glabrata* the main spines will certainly be compound (as described above) and 8–15 mm (⅓–⅗ in) long; in *A. platyceras* they are simple and no more than 10 mm (⅖ in) in length.

Argemone superba G.B. Ownb.

This bright and cheerful species was described in 1958 from material collected west of Ciudad del Maiz in Mexico by Gerald Ownbey and F. Ownbey. The species comes very close to *A. aenea* in leaf characters and in the character of the flower buds and fruit-capsules. The prime differences lie in the plain bright yellow flowers of *A. superba*, with no hint of gold or bronze, in the yellow rather than red or purple stamen filaments and in the narrower stigma – only 2.5–3 mm (⅛ in) wide. These differences seem rather slight in many respects and further investigations may well show that the two elements could be easily encompassed within a single species, perhaps at subspecific or varietal level.

In fact, the two do not overlap in distribution in the wild, that of *A. aenea* being to the north and east of *A. superba* and separated in Mexico by the Sierra Madre Oriental.

This fine species would be a splendid introduction to our gardens. Both it and *A. aenea* are unlikely to be confused with the other yellow-flowered species in cultivation (namely *A. mexicana* and *A. ochroleuca*) on account of their larger flowers and far more numerous stamens.

The Desert Poppies
Arctomecon

A small genus of three species restricted to the south-western USA, where they inhabit extremely dry sandy and stony habitats. All three are both fascinating and delightful, yet little known in cultivation. In addition all three have extremely attractive greyish- or bluish-white leaf rosettes covered in long soft hairs, this being most marked and beautiful in the exquisite rosettes of *A. merriamii*, which is worth growing for its foliage alone. The flowers are typical poppies and bear generally 2, occasionally 3, smooth sepals and 4–6 petals, and a boss of numerous stamens. Although the plants are relatively small (*A. humilis* is one of the smallest members of the Papaveraceae, but the Californian *Canbya candida* wins the tiniest award), the flowers are proportionately large and showy. The flowers are nodding in bud, but open in an erect position. The 4–6 valved fruit capsule is also erect and is capped by a small, rather narrow 4–6 lobed persistent stigma. The hairiness of the plants alone is enough to distinguish this genus from the other Papaveraceae in the region. However, their perennial habit is also a noteworthy feature.

Arctomecon californica Torr. & Frém.   [Pl. 166–167]

This is the largest of the three species. Plants form low tufts of greyish-white spatular- or spoon-shaped leaves that are lobed and toothed at the apex and adorned with soft whitish hairs that give the foliage a rather fuzzy appearance. The flowers are borne on relatively stout erect stems (bearing up to 20 flowers) that are branched from quite low down, with leaflike bracts only at the lower joints. The flowers, 5–7.5 cm (2–3 in) diameter, bear 3 sepals usually and 5–6 broadly overlapping acid-yellow petals. There is a dense boss of yellow stamens surrounding a dark reddish-black ovary that makes a neat small eye in the centre of each bloom.

A. californica is distributed from the Mojave Desert in California to southern Nevada and south-western Arizona centred upon the Lake Mead National Recreation Area, inhabiting very dry hot terrain, on harsh alkaline soils, generally at altitudes of 500–800 m (1640–2625 ft) and flowering in April and May. Associated plants include two annual poppies, *Eschscholzia glyptosperma* and *E. minutiflora*.

This is an elegant species that certainly deserves to be known in cultivation, although in temperate regions it would definitely require the protection of an alpine house or similar to ward off the worst of the winter wetness.

Arctomecon humile Colville   [Pl. 168]
SMALL DESERT POPPY

Plants form small rather dense tufts of grey-green leaves. These are roughly spatular-shaped, with a lobed, often 3-lobed, apex and narrowed gradually below into a slender petiole. The foliage is rather sparsely hairy and without the fuzzy appearance of the other two species. The small white flowers, 2.5–5 cm (1–2 in) diameter are borne on branched stems just clear of the foliage, with the lower branches bracted. There is a rather small boss of

Arctomecon californica

yellow stamens in the centre of the flower, surrounding the greenish-yellow ovary.

One of the rarest poppies in the world that is restricted to a single site in Utah close to both the Nevada and Arizona state lines. Unfortunately, the only known site is within the boundaries of the rapidly developing site of St George and although the site is offered some protection, the species may ultimately succumb to town planners and the need for further industrialisation. Local conservationists might be well advised to try and establish another colony from seed in a safer locality. Signs along the roadside margin of the site proclaim the fact that it is the only known place in the world where this little gem grows and plead for no damage or off-the-road vehicle activity. The site is roughly 1.6 × 3.2 km (1 × 2 miles) in extent and is a generally barren gypsum-based soil dominated by Creosote Bush (*Larrea*) at an elevation of about 800 m (2625 ft*). A. humilis* makes little multi-bloomed posies on the ground.

Arctomecon merriamii Cov.   [Pl. 169–170]
DESERT POPPY, BEAR POPPY

A. merriamii is native to southern California (primarily in Inyo County). Some seventeen sites are known, stretching roughly from the northern end of the Death Valley National Monument, southwards along the Californian border to State Line Park in the eastern Mojave Desert, the locality near Ubehebe Crater being the most southerly. This makes it the most widespread of the three species of *Arctomecon*. *A. merriamii*, like its cousins, inhabits hot desert regions, where it is found growing in rocky and sandy places in the hills, often in Creosote Bush Scrub, on red serpentine soils that get baked hard in the summer heat, generally between 850 and 1400 m (2800–4600 ft), flowering in April and May.

This species is readily recognised by its scapose white flowers that are held well above the leaf rosettes. In the other white-flowered species, *A. humile*, the plants are very much smaller and the flowers are held just clear of the foliage. Both it and the yellow-flowered *A. californica* bear flowers in lax-branched, bracted inflorescences.

A perennial herb up to 30 cm (12 in) tall, occasionally taller, with a stout taproot; stem often somewhat branched close to the base. The leaves are mostly basal, grey- or blue-green, 2.5–7.5 cm (1–3 in) long, wedge-shaped and with a coarsely toothed apex, and covered in long brownish hairs, giving the leaf-tufts a distinctly silky appearance. The solitary white flowers, 4.5–7 cm (1⅘–2⅘ in) across, are nodding in bud and borne on long, slender, hairy scapelike stalks (peduncles); sepals three, shaggily-hairy; petals six, obcordate and somewhat overlapping one another, drying and persisting around the developing capsule; stamens numerous. The fruit-capsule is three- to six-valved, 2.5–3.5 cm (1–1⅖ in) long, and contains shiny black seeds.

This highly attractive species is said to be rare in the wild and it clearly inhabits extremely harsh conditions – it grows, for instance, in the Death Valley region. I can find no record of it having been in cultivation, but its hairiness and perennial nature would almost certainly make it a difficult plant to overwinter in the open garden, except for those who garden in hot, dry conditions. However, its tufted nature and attractive flowers would make it a fine subject for the alpine house, where conditions might perhaps be controlled to its liking. Such plants make an interesting challenge for those dedicated enthusiasts who like to grow the 'rare and tricky'.

The Pygmy Poppies
Canbya

If *Romneya* has claim to have the largest flowers in the poppy family, then the members of the little American genus *Canbya* certainly have the smallest. There are only two species, both desert ephemeral annuals of little interest to the gardener, but of more than passing interest to the botanist.

The genus is named in honour of the American amateur botanist William Marriott Canby, who was born in 1813.

Apart from their small size (neither species is more than 5 cm or 2 in tall) the genus is characterised by its thick, tufted leaves, three sepals, persistent corolla of six petals and by having relatively few stamens (not usually more than 15). The dried and shrivelled petals cling on around the base of the developing fruit, a feature little seen in the poppy family as a whole.

Canbya aurea S. Wats.
YELLOW PYGMY POPPY

A tufted annual 2.5–5 cm (1–2 in) tall, forming discreet little cushions of leaves. The leaves are linear to narrow-elliptical, not more than 12 mm (½ in) long. The tiny flowers have six golden petals, scarcely 3 mm (⅛ in) long, and 3–15 stamens.

C. aurea inhabits sandy and stony places, often in sagebrush, in eastern Oregon and north-western Nevada, as well as northern Mexico, where it can be found in flower during May and June.

Canbya candida Parry ex A. Gray
WHITE PYGMY POPPY

This species is even more diminutive than its cousin *C. aurea*, being rarely more than 2.5 cm (1 in) tall, with narrow, rather thick leaves up to 6 mm (¼ in) in length; both leaves and stems are borne in small tufts. The solitary flowers are borne on threadlike stalks and have six white petals, about 3 mm (⅛ in) long, and only six to nine stamens.

C. candida inhabits sandy dry places in the western Mojave Desert in California, flowering during April and May, occasionally earlier.

The Wind Poppy
Stylomecon

The genus *Stylomecon* contains a single species, *S. heterophylla*, from western North America. Originally described as a species of *Meconopsis* (*M. heterophylla*) by George Bentham, it was subsequently transferred to its own genus by George Taylor in 1930, although the plant has been cultivated since 1826. As in *Meconopsis*, the fruit-capsule has a distinct, though short style, but its annual habit and dimorphic leaves serve to distinguish it clearly from *Meconopsis*.

Stylomecon heterophylla (Benth.) G. Taylor   **[Pl. 171]**
(Syn. *Meconopsis heterophylla* Benth.)
WIND POPPY

A slender-stemmed, somewhat bristly, annual up to 60 cm (24 in) tall, though often less; stem unbranched or few-branched, with a yellow sap when cut. Leaves rather few, grey-green, the lower pinnately-lobed, with oval to elliptical, often toothed segments, long-stalked; upper leaves linear, generally unlobed, toothed or not, more or less sessile. The solitary bright orange-red or coppery-orange flowers, 3–3.5 cm (1⅕–1⅖ in) across, have a distinct dark purple centre and are pendent in bud, but become erect; sepals two, bristly at the apex, soon shed as the flowers open; petals usually four, broad and somewhat overlapping one another, with a slightly frilled margin; stamens numerous, with purplish filaments and golden anthers; style short, capped by a rather flaired, whitish stigma. The small, erect fruit-capsule is club-shaped with an undulate, turban-like disk at the apex, crowned by the short style, many-seeded.

This delightful and colourful annual is a plant of grassy and bushy habitats in California, especially on the north coast ranges, the foothills of the Sierra Nevada and the offshore Channel Islands; it also extends southwards into Baja California, flowering in these places during April and May.

The flowers, although rather delicate looking, are surprisingly long-lived and have a pleasing fragrance reminiscent of that of Lily-of-the-Valley (*Convallaria majalis*). One interesting feature of the flowers is the way in which most of the stamens are crowded above the ovary – the flowers generally face sideways.

S. heterophylla is surprisingly rare in our gardens. This is a great shame, for it is a very cheerful little annual and quite hardy. Seed can be sown in the spring where the plants are required to flower. A light, well-drained soil is preferable and a sunny sheltered site. They will generally come into flower in late June or early July and bloom through until September.

Alternatively, seed can be sown earlier in pots under glass, pricking the young seedlings out into deep pans for flowering indoors in the later spring and early summer; 5–7.5 cm (2–3 in) between plants should be sufficient, keeping them in a light airy position to avoid the plants becoming too drawn.

Although the usual colour is a rich deep orange, pale orange or reddish orange forms also occur in the wild. A splendid pure white cultivar, which is grown in California in particular, has the cultivar name 'White Satin' [Pl. 172].

The Wind Poppy is unlikely to be mistaken for any other member of the poppy family except perhaps for one or two *Papaver* species. The short style and leaf characters are sufficiently distinct to enable accurate identification.

Stylomecon heterophylla

The Californian Tree Poppies
Romneya

The genus *Romneya* was named in honour of the Reverend T. Romney Robinson, astronomer of Armagh, Ireland (1792–1882). The type species was discovered by Dr Thomas Coulter, an Irish botanist and friend of the Rev. Robinson, in California in 1833; the type species commemorates both friends in *Romneya coulteri*. Seed was not introduced into cultivation until 1875, the first plant flowering at the Glasnevin Botanic Garden in Dublin the following year.

Romneya is without doubt one of the most spectacular members of the poppy family, with its striking grey leaves and flamboyant white flowers set off by a huge boss of yellow stamens. It has become deservedly popular in gardens. Many gardeners think that this splendid plant is too tender for their own gardens, coming as it does from the sun-drenched regions of California, but this is not so. *Romneyas* are suckering subshrubs with the stems becoming woody towards the base; even when they survive unscathed, these stems are never long-lived. Instead, shoots spring from the base of the stems or from underground suckers; these will often flower during the same season. A vigorous mature plant will produce countless flowers over a long season from July to September.

Both the known species require similar conditions in cultivation. A warm sunny site is ideal, especially if backed by a south- or west-facing wall, but sheltered corners in the open garden will often prove satisfactory, although in more exposed, cooler positions plants cannot be expected to grow so tall. The soil should be light and well-drained, preferably deep and well prepared, with well-rotted compost or manure added; plants are equally happy on neutral or calcareous soils.

Young vigorous pot-grown plants should be purchased and planted out in the spring once the worst danger of frost has passed by. *Romneyas* hate disturbance once established and no attempt should be made to move them. Their suckering habit can prove annoying, although excess suckers can be removed with a sharp spade – in fact, suckers can arise at a considerable distance from the parent plant.

Pruning consists of tipping back shoots in the spring or removing old or dead growth to ground level. Some gardeners regularly prune the entire plant to ground level without adverse effect.

Propagation is often rather tricky. Cuttings of firm young stem sections can be attempted, though the success rate is often very poor. Suckers removed and replanted rarely succeed, although young suckers carefully removed with some roots attached, potted up and placed in a propagating frame can produce good results, but the resultant plants should preferably not be planted out until the following year. The best means of propagation, however, is by root cuttings. Thick, healthy pieces of roots should be unearthed, taking care not to damage the parent plant unnecessarily. These can then be sliced up into 5 cm (2 in) portions and laid flat in trays of sharp sand and peat (60:40) and covered to a depth of 2.5–5 cm (1–2 in). Placed in a propagating frame or over a heated bench in the glasshouse, these will, with luck, sprout in due course.

Against a sheltered wall, plants can be most spectacular and certainly more floriferous than those in the open garden, the stems reaching as much as 3 m (10 ft) in height in a good hot summer. In Britain these highly desirable plants can be grown in all but the very coldest regions, providing some shelter is possible. In my own garden in East Anglia, *R. coulteri* has survived in an open position for several years, despite severe winter frosts and biting east winds that have devastated other plants from less favourable parts of the world. *Romneya* would appear to come close to *Dendromecon*, another Californian genus, which, however, is readily separated on account of its entire leaves and smaller, yellow flowers. However, the two genera are widely separated in the family (belonging to separate subfamilies) and have markedly different fruits.

Romneya coulteri Harvey
CALIFORNIAN TREE POPPY

A subshrubby, suckering plant with rather fleshy erect, sometimes branched stems up to 3 m (10 ft) tall, though often only half that height. Leaves rather leathery, grey-green, variable in size according to vigour, but generally 7–12 cm (3–5 in) long, ovate to lanceolate, the lower with five to seven narrowly triangular lobes, the upper with fewer lobes, or coarsely toothed or occasionally entire, glabrous save for a few bristles on the short stalk and midrib. The large white flowers are solitary or paired and mostly terminate short twigs near the top of the stems, each 10–13 cm (4–5 in) across and with a large central, rounded boss of numerous golden-yellow stamens; there are five or six overlapping satiny petals; the three leathery, smooth sepals quickly fall once the flowers begin to open. The fruit-capsule is egg-shaped, covered with stiff, golden, spreading bristles and is many seeded.

This glorious plant, with its showy, rather floppy flowers, which carry a sweet fragrance on a warm sunny day, comes from a limited area of southern California, but is especially abundant in the mountains to the south-east of Los Angeles where it inhabits sunbaked rocks and gullies.

R. coulteri is a larger plant than its close cousin *R. trichocalyx*, but is less invasive with its suckers and for that reason it is perhaps the better one to choose for the smaller garden. It would make a spectacular plant for a mass planting in large gardens or parks in a sheltered site, though few have attempted such an effect.

Romneya trichocalyx Eastw.   [Pl. 173–174]

This species is superficially very similar to *R. coulteri*; indeed, for many years they were considered to be one and the same species. However, in 1898 Alice Eastwood separated it, having studied plants closely in the Golden Gate Park in San Francisco.

Romneya trichocalyx

R. trichocalyx differs primarily in its slender stems, more finely cut and less leathery foliage and more clustered flowers. In addition, the flowerbuds are adorned with appressed bristles close to the apex (they are not beaked as in *R. coulteri*) and the fruit capsules also bear appressed, rather than spreading, bristles. Because of early confusion with *R. coulteri*, the date of introduction of *R. trichocalyx* into cultivation is uncertain, though it was probably around the turn of the twentieth century.

This species hails from California (primarily to the south of *R. coulteri* in San Diego and Ventura counties) and extending southwards into the Mexican state of Baja California.

Hybrids with *R. coulteri* have been called *R. × hybrida* Hort. (syn. *R. × vandedenii* Correvon *nom. nud.*). This interesting hybrid is almost intermediate in its principal characteristics between its parent species; this is especially noticeable in the beaked flowerbuds, which bear a few bristles close to the top. The plant generally seen in cultivation of this cross has a bushier habit than *R. trichocalyx*, but the flowers bear the fragrance of *R. coulteri*.

'White Cloud' [**Pl. 175**] is an especially fine cultivar of the hybrid raised in the USA. It has exceptionally large and fragrant flowers contrasting with attractive blue-grey foliage.

IV
Subfamily
Platystemonoideae

Cream Cups
Platystemon

This charming little genus comes from California and adjacent regions. Most modern authorities recognise a single species, *Platystemon californicus*, but it is extremely variable from one population to another. It is therefore not surprising that various other species and subordinate categories have been proposed in the past. In fact, almost 60 different names exist; fortunately most of these have been sunk into synonymy. However, some of the variants are worth recognising at varietal level.

The genus gets its name from its relatively broad stamens (from the Greek *platus*, broad and *stemon*, stamen); the stamens have expanded, almost petal or staminode-like, filaments. *Platystemon* is very distinctive in fruit; there are between six and 20 carpels, which are united in a ring at first, but at maturity they become monilliform (beadlike) and separate, breaking off transversely into single-seeded units. No other genus has this type of fruit in the Papaveraceae. Despite this, *Platystemon* finds its closest ally in another primarily Californian genus, *Meconella*. In this latter genus the fruit consists of a three-valved capsule which splits to release the seeds. Both genera usually have six-petalled flowers, rather than the more usual four.

Platystemon californicus Benth.   [Pl. 176–179]
CREAM CUPS

A small, rather slender, softly-hairy annual up to 30 cm (12 in) tall, occasionally more, with stems branched below, spreading to erect; juice colourless. The leaves vary from alternate at the base to opposite or whorled above, but are generally crowded into the basal half of the plant; they are linear-lanceolate to almost linear, up to 8 cm (3⅕ in) long, though often not

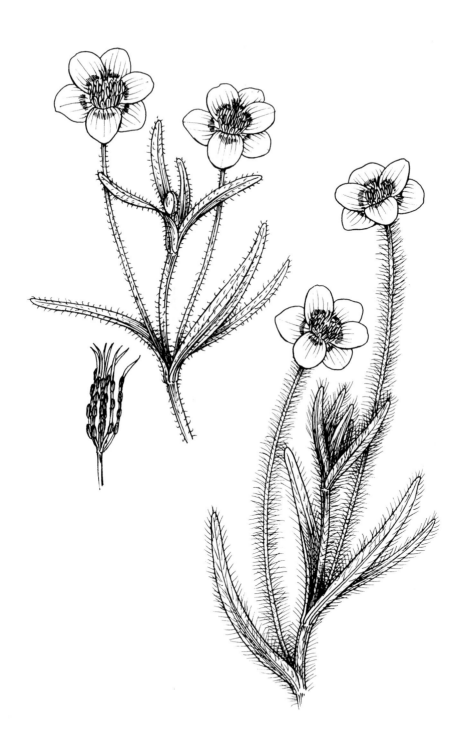

Platystemon californicus **var.** *californicus* **(left) and var.** *crinitus* **(left)**

more than 5 cm (2 in), with an untoothed margin. The cream to yellow flowers, which are nodding in bud, are borne on long, slender, hairy stems, which may be as much as 15–20 cm (6–8 in) in length, each flower 18–25 mm (¾–1 in) across; sepals three, softly-hairy; petals six, in two series, elliptical to oval; stamens numerous cream or yellowish, with distinctly dilated filaments. The cylindrical fruit consists of three or more carpels fused around a hollow core, 10–16 mm (⅖–⅔ in) long, each carpel topped by a persistent filiform style and becoming beaded on maturity.

The species has a distribution from southern Oregon to western Colorado, Utah, Arizona, California and Baja California at altitudes rarely exceeding 1500 m (4900 ft). It inhabits open grassy, sandy or clayey soils, scrub or desert fringes, sometimes sowing profusely in areas that have been burnt over; flowering in the wild from February to early June, depending on locality.

Of the various variations in this polymorphic species, the following can be recognised here:

Var. *californicus* (including *P. leiocarpus* Fisch. & Mey.) has cream, cup-shaped flowers; plants moderately hairy. Oregon, Utah, Arizona, California and Baja California, generally on grassy slopes and coastal hills.

Var. *ciliatus* Dunkle is very like the previous variety, but the plants adorned with short hairs. California in Santa Barbara county.

Var. *crinitus* Greene is similar, but the whole plant more shaggily hairy and flowers yellow. Western Colorado to California and Baja California, growing on the desert and mountain slopes primarily.

Var. *horridus* (Greene) Jepson is similar to var. *californicus*, but with the petals spreading widely to form a flat flower and the fruit-carpels covered in stiff white hairs at first; in var. *californicus* they are glabrous or softly-hairy. Western foothills of the Sierra Nevada, especially in the south.

Var. *nutans* Bdg. This variety has distinctive nodding fruits, otherwise it is rather like var. *californicus*. California from Western San Diego county to Santa Cruz and Santa Rosa.

Var. *ornithopus* (Greene) Munz is very like var. *californicus*, but it is a small hairless plant not more than 10 cm (4 in) tall and with the fruits scarcely beaded. California from San Miguel and San Nicolas to Santa Rosa.

Of these varieties, only the widespread var. *californicus* is seen in cultivation, while of the others, the most attractive is the deep yellow-flowered var. *crinitus*.

P. californicus is a cheerful and hardy little annual for the front of a flower border. It will also succeed in the cracks in paving, terraces or on the scree garden. Seed can be sown in the autumn in mild warm areas; however, a safer bet is to sow it along with other annuals in the early spring. It prefers a warm, sandy or loamy, well-drained and sunny position, although plants will wither in the very hot weather of midsummer. The pale airy flowers, produced in quantity, are a charming foil to other small summer annuals such as *Linum grandiflorum, Nemophila menziesii, Omphalodes linifolia* or *Phacelia tanacetifolia.* In favoured gardens it may self-sow, although it cannot be relied upon to do so; therefore, it is wise to collect some seed each year.

Platystigmas
Platystigma

Another western North American genus consisting of eight to nine annual herbs related to *Platystemon*, but differing in having a three-valved capsule, rather than a fruit consisting of six or more carpels, which are free at maturity. The genus is also closely related to *Meconella*, but can be quickly separated by having basal leaf tufts and scapose flowers. Two species are cultivated, but are rarely seen in our gardens today.

Platystigma lineare Benth.
(syn. *Meconella linearis* (Benth.) Jepson; *Hesperomecon lineare* Benth.)

A slender annual to about 20 cm (8 in) tall, occasionally more. The leaves are crowded into a dense basal tuft and are linear to linear-elliptical, entire to 6.5 cm (2⅗ in) long. The small pale yellow flowers, 16–22 mm (⅔–⅞ in) across, are borne on slender, unbranched, bristly scapes; sepals three, brownish, soon falling; petals six, oval to elliptical or obovate, stamens 12–15, sometimes more, with linear filaments. The fruit-capsule is elliptical to narrow pear-shaped in outline, up to 18 mm (¾ in) long, not twisted.

This is a little Californian poppy, found along the coast ranges, but extending northwards into Oregon and southwards to the foothills of the Sierra Nevada and the Tahachapi Mountains. It grows primarily in sandy and gravelly soils and flowers during March and April.

This little annual can be treated as a hardy annual, sowing the seed in the early spring where the plants are required to flower. It has been cultivated since 1833 (originally as *Hesperomecon lineare*), although seed is rarely available today.

Platystigma pulchellum Greece
(syn. *Meconella linearis* var. *pulchellum* Jepson)

Rather similar to *P. lineare*, but a somewhat hairier plant with flowers 22–28 mm (⅞–1⅛ in) across, with the outer petals yellow, the inner narrower and white; stamens numerous with filaments winged in the lower half.

A rather rare plant in the wild, being a Californian endemic found along the coast from San Francisco to Sonoma County, where it inhabits sandy and stony ground.

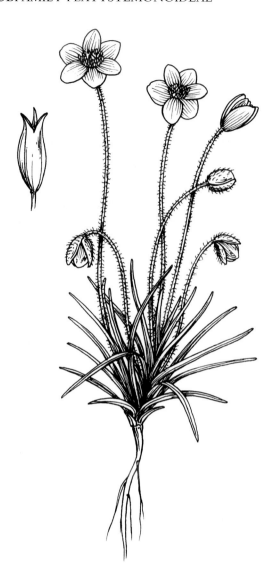

Platystigma lineare

   This pretty little poppy first came into cultivation round about 1836, but is rarely seen in gardens today. It is sometimes recorded in cultivation as *P. lineare*, but is very distinctive with diverse petals and winged stamens. Treat as for *P. lineare*.

Meconellas
Meconella

This is another small, western North American genus, little known in cultivation, but certainly worthy of attention. The name *Meconella* perhaps conjures up a dainty *Meconopsis* – the name from the Greek literally means tiny or diminutive poppy (*mekon*, poppy, and *ella*, tiny). However, the genus finds its closest ally not in Old World genera but in the Cream Cups, *Platystemon*. It differs in two major characteristics: first, the flowers have few stamens, generally only 6–12; second, the fruit consist of three fused carpels, which eventually dehisces to form a three-valved capsule. As in *Platystemon*, the plants are slender annuals, with long flower-stalks (pedicels), and they bear six-petalled flowers with two or three sepals.

The species look superficially very similar to *Platystemon*, but can be clearly differentiated by their smaller flowers and distinctive slender, twisted, fruit-capsules. They differ from *Platystigma* in their leafy, branched stems and twisted fruit-capsules; in *Platystigma* the leaves are apparently all basal, their scapes unbranched and the fruit-capsule is untwisted, although a similarly three-valved capsule.

Meconella californica Torr. [Pl. 180]

A slender glabrous annual up to 15 cm (6 in) tall, with most of the leaves basal, elliptical to almost spathulate, entire, up to 4 cm (1⅗ in) long, though usually less, generally narrowing into a short petiole at the base; stems slender and erect, branched, bearing several pairs of opposite leaves, rarely in threes. Flowers solitary, white, or cream or yellow with a white centre, 17–20 mm (⅔–¾ in) across, borne on slender stalks, erect or half-nodding in bud; sepals often reddish, soon falling; petals six (rarely eight), ovate to elliptical; stamens 8–12. Fruit-capsule linear, twisted, up to 3 cm (1⅕ in) long, borne on erect or deflexed stalks.

M. californica is native to California from San Francisco Bay Region southwards along the Sierra Nevada foothills, where it grows on rocky slopes, flowering there during March and April. This delightful little species, like some of the other Californian annual 'poppies', is sometimes found in large numbers, particularly after a wet winter.

Not in cultivation, but it would make a dainty little annual for the front of the flower border.

Meconella oregana Nutt. ex Torr. & Gray
(syn. *M. denticulata* (Jepson) Greene; *M. californica* var. *denticulata* Jepson; *M. oregana* var. *denticulata* Jepson)

Rather similar to *M. californica*, but often taller, up to 30 cm (12 in), and glabrous. The leaves vary from oval to spathulate or linear, the basal ones being the broadest, entire and stalked, the upper being sessile and sometimes finely toothed. The small white flowers are only 10–18 mm (⅖–¾ in) across; sepals soon falling; petals six, rarely four, oval; stamens six. The fruit-capsule is linear and twisted, up to 3 cm (1⅕ in) long at maturity.

M. oregana is found in California from the foothills of the Sierra Nevada and the coastal regions, southwards into Baja California, as well as on Santa Cruz Island. It is a plant of rocky and sandy places, often on grassy hillslopes or openings in chaparral or sagebrush, as well as in shaded canyons, generally below 1000 m (3300 ft); flowering from March to May. Plants are often frequent, but are rather inconspicuous.

Not in cultivation.

Allied Genera

(formerly subfamily Hypecooideae)

(Two genera sometimes included in the Papaveraceae, see p. 29).

The Little Poppies
Hypecoum

A small genus of charming little annuals wholly neglected in gardens, but pretty and effective *en masse*. There are about 15 species scattered primarily in the Mediterranean region and western Asia, but with one or two species found as far east as northern China and Mongolia.

Plants are rather delicate, often glabrous and glaucous, herbs with watery latex and finely cut foliage, reminiscent of some of the smaller species of Californian Poppies, *Eschscholzia*. The small yellow flowers are borne in a cymose inflorescence; sepals two, minute, quickly falling as the flowers begin to open; petals four, in two rows, the outer two unlobed to three-lobed, the inner, deeply three-lobed, with the outer lobes narrow and the middle one often fringed with hairs; stamens four only, with winged filaments. Fruit-capsule long and narrow, jointed and splitting transversely into numerous one-seeded portions, or splitting longitudinally into two valves, usually many-seeded.

In *Hypecoum* an interesting pollination device can be observed. The middle lobes of the inner two petals are somewhat stalked and with an expanded, sometimes somewhat hooded, apex. These apices wrap around the stamens before the stigma is receptive and form a chamber that collects the pollen shed from the anthers. When visited by an insect (nectar is secreted at the base of the filaments) these lobes spring apart, dusting the insect with pollen, which it then transports to the next flowers it visits. The stigma of the first flower then becomes receptive and can receive pollen from another insect.

They are hardy annuals and prefer an open sunny position in the garden and a well-drained soil. As they are low-growing, they require the front of the flower border, though to my mind they look best in a gravel area, seeded along the edge of a path or driveway, where they are not likely to be trampled on. If you can acquire seed, these friendly and cheerful little plants are worth encouraging. Direct sowing where the plants are to flower is recommended, as they dislike being moved and will sulk or die as a result. From a spring sowing they will provide a display of little blooms from June until late summer.

Key to Species

1. Flowers yellow and violet or pale whitish-violet 2
    Flowers yellow or orange, not bicoloured, but inner petals
    sometimes violet-spotted 3

2. Flowers pale whitish-violet; fruit-capsules scarcely lined or
    thickened at the margins: *H. leptocarpum*
    Flowers yellow and violet; fruit-capsules lined and thickened
    at the margins: *H. aegyptiacum*

3. Stems smooth; outer petals almost twice as long as wide, unlobed . . . 4
    Stems lined; outer petals almost as wide as long, three-lobed 5

4. Fruit-capsule pendent on recurved stalks, not jointed; middle
    lobe of inner petals rounded and stalked: *H. pendulum*
    Fruit-capsule erect, weakly jointed; middle lobe of inner
    petals linear: *H. ponticum*

5. Bracts leaflike with many divisions; petals pale yellow usually,
    the outer with a large middle lobe: *H. procumbens*
    Bracts linear, not leaflike, entire or with few divisions; petals orange
    usually, the outer with more or less equal lobes or the middle one
    somewhat smaller 6

6. Fruit-capsules erect to ascending, jointed and readily breaking into
    segments: *H. imberbe*
    Fruit-capsules pendulous and with thick walls, breaking with
    difficulty: *H. trilobum*

Hypecoum aegyptiacum (Forsk.) Aschers. et Schweinf.
EGYPTIAN HYPECOUM

A rather distinctive little species with bicoloured flowers. It is a spreading to ascending annual, not more than 25 cm (10 in) tall, though often less, with finely cut leaves, the segments acutely pointed. The flowers are about the same size and shape as *H. imberbe*, with large bright yellow, three-lobed outer petals; however, the smaller inner petals are yellow with a contrasting purple-brown or violet base or blotch. The erect fruit-capsules are lined and somewhat thickened at the margins.

   H. aegyptiacum can be found in cultivated and waste lands, stony and sandy habitats, in the extreme eastern Mediterranean region – Palestine, Egypt and the surrounding regions in particular. Unfortunately, this is yet another charming little poppy rarely seen in cultivation.

Hypecoum imberbe Sibth. & Smith   **[Pl. 182]**
(Syn. *H. grandiflorum* Benth.)
ORANGE HYPECOUM

Very similar to *H. procumbens*, but it can be readily distinguished by its more finely cut foliage, small linear bracts (not leaflike) and more pronouncedly branched inflorescence. In addition, the flowers are generally orange-yellow, 10–20 mm (⅖–⅘ in) across, with the outer petals evenly lobed or with the central lobe somewhat smaller than the lateral lobes; the inner petals are often spotted with violet. The fruit-capsule is scarcely jointed.

    H. imberbe has a similar distribution to *H. procumbens*, although its range extends eastwards to Iraq and Iran. However, it is not a coastal species, being generally found inland on cultivated, fallow and waste ground, both lowland and in the hills and low mountains and flowering from January to June.

    Formerly cultivated in gardens, but now seldom seen, which is a pity for it is a true little delight and very floriferous.

Hypecoum leptocarpum Hook. f. & Th.

A biennial species that forms a small rosette of greyish leaves in the first season, but, in the second, spreading stems produce a series of small pale whitish-lilac flowers. The outer petals are oblong and unlobed and only 5–6 mm (⅜ in) long. The linear fruit-capsules, up to 3 cm (1⅕ in) long, are borne on erect stalks and are jointed, readily breaking into segments.

    This species, which is not in cultivation, is a plant of dry rocky ground,

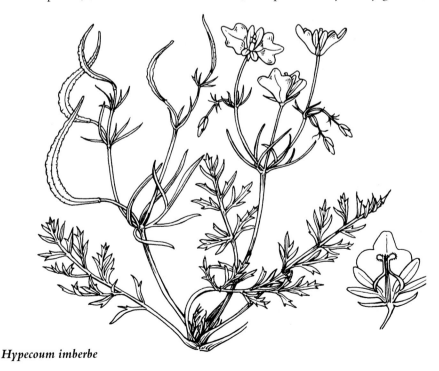

Hypecoum imberbe

riverbeds and stony slopes from the Pamir Mountains to the western Himalaya, Xizang (Tibet) and Mongolia.

Hypecoum pendulum L.
PENDENT HYPECOUM

A small annual with erect or ascending, smooth stems up to 20 cm (8 in) tall, often less. The fennel-like leaves are two- or three-pinnately lobed, with greyish green linear lobes; bracts threadlike. The pale yellow flowers are borne in small cymes, 8–15 mm (⅓–⅗ in) across; outer petals unlobed, oval to diamond-shaped, but the inner deeply lobed, with the lateral lobes lanceolate whilst the middle lobe is stalked, rounded and with a hairy margin. The fruit-capsule is clearly pendent, 4–6 cm (1⅗–2⅖ in) long, with four distinct angles, but not jointed, tapered at both ends.

Like the previous species, *H. pendulum* is a plant of cultivated fallow and waste land, sometimes being found along roadsides, often in large colonies and sometimes mixed with *H. imberbe*. It has a wide distribution, including the Mediterranean Basin, North Africa, east to the Caucasus.

H. pendulum is a dainty and floriferous annual and I look forward to the day when seed is more freely available.

Hypecoum ponticum Velen.
PONTIC HYPECOUM

A lesser-known species allied to *H. pendulum*, but with the middle lobe of the inner two petals linear, rather than rounded, and fruit erect. The sepals are also sharply pointed rather than blunt, but soon fall off, so that they are often difficult to observe.

H. ponticum inhabits coastal sands of the Black Sea region, primarily in Bulgaria and Turkey. It is not in cultivation.

Hypecoum procumbens L.
PROCUMBENT HYPECOUM

A small procumbent to spreading annual not more than 25 cm (10 in) tall, often as little as 5 cm (2 in); stems lined, often more or less erect at first, but becoming gradually procumbent as the fruits mature. The leaves are in a basal tuft, two-pinnately lobed, with grey- or bluish-green, slender, linear divisions, generally pointed. The flowers are borne in one- to five-flowered cymes and are pale to bright yellow, 8–16 mm (⅓–⅔ in) across; outer petals broadly rhombic and three-lobed, the middle lobe somewhat longer than the others; inner petals are deeply three-lobed, the outer (lateral) lobes oblong and hairless, the middle lobe spatular-shaped and with a hairy margin. The fruit-capsule is erect to ascending, straight or curved, 4–8 cm (1⅗–3⅕ in) long, with prominent transverse joints.

H. procumbens is a plant of sandy habitats, especially close to the sea, although it can occasionally be found growing inland. It occurs throughout the Mediterranean Basin, as well as coastal Portugal and the region of the Black Sea, where it can be found in flower from February to early June.

This delightful little species has been cultivated in gardens since 1596. However, it is seldom seen in gardens today; indeed, seed is not easy to obtain, except from the wild.

Hypecoum trilobum Trautv.   **[Pl. 181]**

This Asian species is similar in flower to *H. imberbe*, being seldom more than 15 cm (6 in) tall and differing primarily in having pendulous rather than erect fruit-capsules. In addition, the fruits of *H. trilobum* have thickened walls and do not break readily at the joints. The flowers are somewhat larger, bright yellow with the inner petals spotted with violet.

H. trilobum is a plant of fields, arable land and roadsides in the semi-desert steppes of Central Asia, from Iran to the Pamir Mountains and the Tienshan. I have seen it along the roadsides south of Samarkand towards the frontier of Afghanistan, where it grows in abundance, often in association with *Roemeria refracta*, and forming a haze of yellow. Although apparently not in cultivation outside the CIS, this is a cheerful and floriferous little annual well worth seeking out.

The Fern Poppy
Pteridophyllum

Japan has many exciting little woodlanders to offer our gardens. Few are as unusual and charming as *Pteridophyllum racemosum*. Out of flower, this tufted perennial could be all too easily mistaken for a fern in the neat divisions of its frondlike leaves; hence the generic names, which clearly alludes to this deception. Even in flower, the airy little 'racemes' scarcely betray their family affinities. However, look at one of the tiny flowers closely and they do clearly resemble a scaled-down poppy flower, especially in their two sepals and four petals, although there are rather few stamens.

The genus *Pteridophyllum* contains just one species, native to the mountains of central Japan, where it was discovered in the province of Sinano by Siebold in the middle of the nineteenth century (it was described in 1843).

It is difficult to ascertain the affinities of this little gem and it appears to hold a rather isolated position within the family. The fruit, a two-valved siliqua, clearly puts it close to subfamily Chelidonioideae together with *Chelidonium*, *Dicranostigma*, *Stylophorum* and several other genera (p. 29). Some authors have suggested that it makes an obvious link with *Hypecoum* and hence the Fumariaceae, which contains the fumitories (*Fumaria*) and *Corydalis*, but this is by no means certain and, besides, this aspect needs further careful research. The Fumariaceae was, of course once part of the poppy family, but is now generally regarded as being distinct.

Pteridophyllum racemosum Sieb & Zucc.
FERN POPPY

This is a small tufted perennial, not more than 25 cm (10 in) tall in flower, often less; the shoots arise from a short branched rhizome, all the leaves being basal. The short-stalked leaves, up to 15 cm (6 in) long, are oblanceolate to elliptical in outline, but divided into many small, oval to almost linear, leaflets; these leaflets are largest in the middle of the leaf, decreasing in size at both ends and touching or slightly overlapping one another, being held at right angles to the midrib (rachis); the leaflets are sometimes slightly notched at the apex and are glabrous except for a few bristles beneath. The scapes' inflorescence is erect and appears to be racemose, but is actually a narrow cymose panicle. The flowers are white with pale yellow stamens, being borne on slender stalks; sepals two, rounded, quickly falling once the buds start to open; petals four, half-spreading, oval, 5–6 mm (⅕–¼ in) long, soon falling; stamens few. The fruit-capsule is a two-valved siliqua.

The species is native to Japan's Honshu Island, where it inhabits montane coniferous woodland.

This plant was introduced into cultivation in 1914 and there is a fine picture of it in *Curtis's Botanical Magazine* (tab. 8743). It has never found great favour in gardens and today it is listed by only one or two nurseries. In *The English Rock Garden* Reginald Farrer says of it that 'In the midst (of the tuft of leaves) rises in July a stem six inches or a foot (or more), unfolding a spike, most airy and graceful, of tiny white flowers, which, though poppies, look much more like the loose spire of some small-flowered white crucifer.' However, for those who, like me, are excited by these cool little woodlanders, this is certainly a gem not to be overlooked.

P. racemosum is quite hardy in the open garden, though it needs a cool, shady place; in the woodland or a peat bank, where there is moist leafy or peaty soil. Its pleasing ferny appearance also makes it suitable for a nook in the rock garden; it greatly dislikes summer drought. In favoured mild gardens plants remain more or less evergreen. However, elsewhere the leaves tend to die away during the winter. Grown like a choice petiolarid primula, it will also make a first-rate pan plant for the shaded frame or alpine house; a compost of fibrous loam, leaf-mould and grit will suit it admirably.

In my experience the young leaves are very prone to attack from marauding slugs and snails and these little horrors must be kept at bay; otherwise, the plant will quickly succumb. Vine weevils can also prove bothersome.

Propagation is by seed, when available, or by division of the parent plant in the early spring before growth commences, although this is not always easy. Plants flower from May to July. Despite the fact that the flowers are all too fleeting in appearance, the attractive leaf tufts add interest at other times of the year.

Major References

Cobb, J.L.S. (1989). *Meconopsis*, Christopher Helm (Batsford), London/ Timber Press, Portland, Oregon.

Cullen, J. (1965). Papaveraceae in Davis, P.H., *Flora of Turkey*, volume I.

—(1966). Papaveraceae in Rechinger, K.H., *Flora Iranica* 34/16.

Debnath, H.S. and Nayar, M.P. (1986). *The Poppies of the Indian Region*. Botanical Survey of India.

Ernst, W.R. (1962). *Comparative Morphology of the Papaveraceae*.

Farrer, R. (1928). *The English Rock-Garden*.

Fletcher, H.R. (1975). *A Quest for Flowers*.

Gerard, J. (1597). *The Herball or Generall Historie of Plantes*, London.

Grey-Wilson, C. (1993). *Poppies*, first ed., Batsford.

Hussain, A. and Sharma, J.R. (1983). *The Opium Poppy*. Central Institute of Medicinal and Aromatic Plants, Luchnow, India.

Huxley, A. (Ed.) (1992). *The New Royal Horticultural Dictionary of Gardening* – in 4 volumes.

Lloyd, C. and Rice, G. (1991). *Garden Flowers from Seed*.

Meikle, R.D. (1977). *Flora of Cyprus*. Bentham-Moxon Trust, Royal Botanic Gardens, Kew.

Miller, P. (1768). *The Gardener's Dictionary*, 8th ed, London.

Munz, (1974). *A Flora of Southern California*.

Ownbey, G.R. (1958). Monograph of the Genus *Argemone* for North America and the West Indies in *Memoirs of the Torrey Botanical Club* 21(1).

—(1961). The Genus *Argemone* in South America and Hawaii in *Brittonia* 13.

Popov, (1937). Papaveraceae in Flora *USSR*, volume 7.

Rice, G. (1999). *Discovering Annuals*. Frances Lincoln.

Taylor, G. (1934). *An Account of the Genus Meconopsis*. Reprinted in 1985 by Waterstone, London.

Tutin, T.G. *et al* (1964). *Flora Europaea*, volume 1. Cambridge University Press.

Glossary

Amplexicaule – clasping; generally refers to leaves that have heart-shaped bases which clasp the stem.

Anther – the male organ of the flower, which contains the pollen.

Anthesis – flowering time, when the flower bud opens (more accurately when the pollen is shed).

Appressed – lying flat against another organ – as hairs on a stem.

Capsule – a dry, many-seeded, fruit that dehisces (splits) in various ways (according to the species) when ripe to expel the seeds.

Carpel – the basic female unit of the flower, which contains the ovules and makes up the ovary; an ovary may consist of one or several separate or united carpels.

Cultivar – a plant, species or form (often with a name, e.g. 'Goliath'), maintained by cultivation.

Decumbent – spreading to prostrate stems that bend upwards in the upper part.

Dimorphic – in two forms.

Elliptic – a flat shape broadest in the middle and pointed at each end.

Entire – not toothed or lobed – leaf-margin usually.

Ephemeral – an annual that completes its life-cycle in just a few weeks.

Filament – the stalk that joins the anther to the receptacle or corolla.

Filiform – threadlike.

Glabrous – hairless.

Glaucous – bluish-green or bluish-grey in general colour – usually applies to leaves.

Globose – shaped like a globe – spherical.

Inflorescence – flowers aggregated into formal arrangements (branched or not) together with their accompanying bracts and pedicels (i.e. the whole structure).

Lanceolate – an ellipse that is broadest just below the middle; same as narrow-ovate.

Latex – milky juice; can be white, yellow or orange in poppies.

Leaf-axil – the angle between the leaf and the stem.

Monilliform – beadlike.

Obcordate – reversed heart-shape.

Oval – a flat shape broadest in the middle and with rounded ends.

Ovary – the female organ of the flower, which contains the ovules that, upon fertilisation, develop into seeds.

Ovate – egg-shaped.

Petiole – leaf-stalk.

Pinnate – a compound leaf in which the leaflets are placed in pairs along a common axis (rachis); 2-pinnate where the prime divisions of the leaf are themselves pinnate.

Procumbent – trailing along the ground.

Prostrate – growing flat on the ground.

Rachis – the axis of a compound leaf or an inflorescence to which the leaflets or flowers are attached – not the stalk.

Scape – a leafless flowering stem on plants which have entirely basal leaves.

Scapose – with scapes.

Sessile – stalkless; leaves, without a petiole.

Siliqua – a two-valved, podlike fruit which is at least three times longer than broad.

Stamen – the male organ of the flower; consists of the filament and the anther that bears the pollen.

Stigma – the receptive tip of the style that receives the pollen.

Style – the stalklike appendage on top of the ovary that bears the stigma(s).

Torus – a semicircular disklike ridge.

Trifoliate – a leaf composed of three leaflets.

Zygomorphic – asymmetrical flowers, which have bilateral (one plane of) symmetry.

Index

Synonyms in *italics*;* indicates a line drawing; Pl. refers to a colour plate